PATERNOSTER THEOLOGICAL MONOGRAPHS

Being Human, Being Church

PATERNOSTER THEOLOGICAL MONOGRAPHS

Being Human, Being Church

The Significance of Theological Anthropology for Ecclesiology

Patrick S. Franklin

Foreword by James C. Peterson

Copyright © Patrick S. Franklin 2016

First published 2016 by Paternoster

Paternoster is an imprint of Authentic Media
PO Box 6326, Bletchley, Milton Keynes, MK1 9GG

authenticmedia.co.uk

The right of Patrick S. Franklin to be identified as the Author of this Work
has been asserted by him in accordance with the Copyright, Designs
and Patents Act 1988.

All rights reserved. No part of this publication may be reproduced, stored in a retrieval system, or transmitted, in any form or by any means, electronic, mechanical, photocopying, recording or otherwise, without the prior permission of the publisher or a licence permitting restricted copying. In the UK such licences are issued by the Copyright Licensing Agency, Saffron House, 6-10 Kirby Street, London, EC1N 8TS.

British Library Cataloguing in Publication Data
A catalogue record for this book is available from the British Library
ISBN 978-1-84227-842-0
978-1-78078-071-9 (e-book)

Printed and bound in Great Britain for Paternoster
by Lightning Source, Milton Keynes

Elena, Josiah, Samuel, and Eliana
You continually help me to understand and live out what it means to be more genuinely human

PATERNOSTER THEOLOGICAL MONOGRAPHS

Series Preface

In the West the churches may be declining, but theology, serious, academic (mostly doctoral level) and mainstream orthodox in evaluative commitment shows no sign of withering on the vine. This series of Paternoster Theological Monographs extends the expertise of the Press especially to first-time authors whose work stands broadly within the parameters created by fidelity to Scripture and has satisfied the critical scrutiny of respected assessors in the academy.

Such theology may come in several distinct intellectual disciplines historical, dogmatic, pastoral, apologetic, missional, aesthetic and no doubt others also. The series will be particularly hospitable to promising constructive theology within the evangelical frame, for it is of this that the church's need seems to be greatest.

Quality writing will be published across the confessions Anabaptist, Episcopalian, Reformed, Arminian and Orthodox across the ages patristic, medieval, reformation, modern and counter-modern and across the continents. The aim of the series is theology written in the twofold conviction that the church needs theology and theology needs the church which in reality means theology done for the glory of God.

Series Editors

Trevor A. Hart, Head of School and Principal of St Mary's College, School of Divinity, University of St Andrews, Scotland, UK

Anthony N.S. Lane, Professor of Historical Theology and Director of Research, London School of Theology, UK

Anthony C. Thiselton, Emeritus Professor of Christian Theology, University of Nottingham; Research Professor in Christian Theology, University College Chester; and, Canon Theologian of Leicester Cathedral and Southwell Minster, UK

Kevin J. Vanhoozer, Research Professor of Systematic Theology, Trinity Evangelical Divinity School, Deerfield, Illinois, USA

Nicholas Ansell, Assistant Professor of Theology, Institute for Christian Studies, Toronto, Canada

Contents

Acknowledgements	xv
Foreword by James C. Peterson	xvii
Introduction	1
Situating the Argument in the Scholarly Discussion	5
Previous Research that is Relevant to the Topic	5
Contribution of the Present Project	6
Methods, Models, and Frameworks	7
Historical-Philosophical Narrative	8
Typology	8
Application of Hermeneutical-Doctrinal Lens	9
A Trinitarian Framework for Theological Anthropology	
and Ecclesiology	10
Theological Commitments	11
Primary Conversation Partners	12
Dietrich Bonhoeffer	13
Miroslav Volf	13
Stanley Grenz	14

PART I: THE CHALLENGE

Chapter 1

Current Problems with Defining the Human Person	15
Lack of Precision About the Human Person in Contemporary Culture	15
Lack of precision about what constitutes a human person	15
The problem of the fragmented self	16
The world-mastering, self-mastering, rational self	17
The self-focused, self expressive self	22
The fragmentation of the self	23
Abandonment of teleology	25
The problem of scientific reductionism	30
Loss of a theological narrative	34
Implications for Community and Society	38
Dissolution of human community	38
Dichotomization and disintegration of personal	
and social ethics	41
Collapse of social and global justice	44
Concluding Summary	49

Chapter 2
Rival Accounts of Being Human and Being in Community in Contemporary Culture   51
Introduction   51
Rival Accounts of Being Human and Being in Community   52
   The rational being of the Enlightenment   52
      Type 1: A social contract between consenting individuals   52
      Type 2: A moral association of cause and duty   56
   The self-defining individual of Existentialism   60
      Type 3: Erotic communities of desire and self-assertion   61
      Type 4: Phileic communities of common interest and Expression   63
      Evaluation of existentialist notions of human community   65
   The self-preserving animal of sociobiology   68
      Type 5: An instrumental good for its members   70
   Being human as caring-for others   73
      Type 6: Concentric circles of care   74
Impact of Contemporary Views of Personhood on the Church   77
   Social contract and the attractional church   78
   Self-defining existentialism and the emerging church   78
   Self-perpetuation and the church growth movement   80
   Church as a community of care   82
Concluding Summary: Two Problems to Address   82

PART II: THEOLOGICAL ANTHROPOLOGY IN TRINITARIAN PERSPECTIVE

Chapter 3
The Human Person as a Relational Creature   84
Introduction   84
Trinitarian Love is God's Essential Nature   85
   One God, three persons   85
   God's redemptive mission is grounded in God's nature as love   88
Trinitarian Love is Constitutive of the Human Person   89
   The imago Dei and being in relationship   89
   Historical roots of the relational view   90
   Imago Dei *and the Trinity*   96
   Openness to the world, exocentricity, and relationality   98
Love and the Relational Ethical Dimension   100
   God's reconciling love opens the human heart for reconciliation with God and others   101
   God's transforming love and abundant communion with God and others   107
   General implications for Christian ethics   108

Chapter 4
The Human Person as a Rational Creature — 111
Introduction — 111
   Creation as intelligible trinitarian conversation — 111
Rational and Ethical as Mutually Defining — 112
   Imago Dei, *morality, and rationality* — 112
   Breakdown of the conversation and the limits of human
      access to the moral law — 116
   Redemption from captivity of the mind — 118
      Incarnation and the realignment of rationality — 118
      Pentecost and the Spirit's renewal of our minds — 121
      The Christian life of wisdom — 122
Faith and the Rational Ethical Dimension — 123
   Building trust, growing in love and wisdom — 123
   Command, character, and Christian ethics in a
      Trinitarian framework — 124
   Theology as knowing God and cultivating biblical
      Wisdom — 125
      Theology and the knowledge of God
   Reading Scripture as a theological-ethical practice — 134
      Interpretation is an inherently ethical activity — 134
      Virtues and biblical interpretation — 138
      Practical reasoning (phronesis) and biblical
         interpretation — 140
Concluding Summary — 142

Chapter 5
The Human Person as an Eschatological Creature — 144
Introduction — 144
Called by the Father for a Purpose and Mission — 144
   Creation, imago Dei, *and calling* — 144
      Created to advance and develop over time — 144
      Imago Dei *as commission and task* — 148
   Usurpation and the distortion of the commission — 154
Saved From a Purposeless and Self-Destructive Destiny — 158
   Recreated in the image of Christ — 158
   Reoriented and realigned to serve Christ our Lord and King
      as his steward-priests — 160
   Transformation by the Spirit into the likeness of the Son — 161
Hope and the Eschatological Ethical Dimension — 164
   New Creation — 164
   Serving the kingdom of God in the power of the Spirit — 169
   An eschatological qualification of teleological ethics — 170
   New Creation and the call to sustain, restore, and

improve as steward-priests	172
Concluding Summary	175

PART III: THE CHURCH AS COMMUNITIES OF THE NEW HUMANITY

Chapter 6
The Church as Relational Communities of Love — 176

Introduction	176
The church as communities of the new humanity	176
The church as relational communities of love	178
Inner Community Life of the Church	178
The theological basis of Christian community	178
Union with each other in Christ by the Spirit	178
Participating in the Trinity	182
The church as the Body of Christ	186
Relational ministries of the church	190
Constitutive and formative relational practices	192
The Church Engaging the World	197
The church participating in Christ's priestly ministry	198
As ambassadors of reconciliation	198
As the church for others	199
Theology of the cross as a model for cultural critique and the proclamation of justice	201
Means of engagement	204
Conclusion: Living out of Love in an Egocentric World	206

Chapter 7
The Church as Rational Communities of Faith — 207

Introduction	207
Inner Community Life of the Church	208
The church as the People of God	208
Communities of faith that cultivate wisdom	210
Wisdom comes from God	211
Worldly wisdom versus godly wisdom	212
Ministries of the church that cultivate godly wisdom	214
Wisdom cultivation through theological formation	216
Wisdom cultivation through constitutive and formative practices that shape the mind	221
Wisdom cultivation through wise leadership	226
The Church Engaging the World	226
Participating in Christ's prophetic ministry	226
As witnesses and servants of the truth	226
Incarnation as a model for demonstrating truth in the church's engagement with the world	229

Incarnational means of engagement	232
Conclusion: Living by Faith in a World of Distrust and Scepticism	234

Chapter 8
The Church as Eschatological Communities of Hope — 236

Introduction	236
Inner Community Life of the Church	237
The church as the Temple of the Holy Spirit	237
The church as a kingdom community	241
Called to a task and a destiny	241
The church and the kingdom	242
Communities of kingdom character formation	244
Ministries of kingdom orientation and training	249
Word and sacramental ordinances	250
Formative practices	252
The Church Engaging the World	256
Participating in Christ's reign	256
As heralds and representatives of the kingdom	256
As a missional church	257
Resurrection as a model for moving in God's power into new possibilities	259
Means of engaging the world with eschatological hope and resurrection power	260
Conclusion: Living with Hope in a World of Fear and Despair	263

Conclusion:
Church for the Twenty-First Century — 265

Introduction	265
Inner Community Life of the Church as the New Humanity	266
A community in union with Christ in the Spirit	266
An ethical community	270
A formative community of kingdom disciples oriented to the new creation	272
The Church Engaging the World as the New Humanity	273
Participating by the Spirit in Christ's mission	273
Social-ecclesial ethics of love, faith, and hope	274
Christ and Culture: Which posture best suits the Church as the new humanity	275
A Trinitarian revision of missional ecclesiology	277
The Church in the Service of Human Flourishing: Some Preliminary Implications	281

Appendix
Anthropology and Ecclesiology: A Typology	285

Bibliography 286

Indexes 308
Author Index 308
Scripture Index 314
Subject Index 320

Acknowledgements

There are many whom I want to acknowledge and thank. In particular, I am deeply grateful:

To Jim Peterson, for your graciousness, wise guidance, faithful encouragement, and conceptual clear-headedness. You are a God-given mentor, teacher, and friend. I could not have asked for a better supervisor.

To Steve Studebaker, for your critical precision in reading the manuscript and your encouragement throughout my PhD studies.

To Jens Zimmermann, for your comments, criticisms, and suggestions concerning the manuscript. Gently yet incisively, you encouraged and pressed me toward further depth and clarity.

To Dennis Ngien, for your ongoing mentoring, encouragement, and gentle prodding to study, reflect, and publish for the betterment of both church and academy. It was you who first exhorted me to pursue advanced theological studies, for which I am deeply grateful.

To Charles Ringma, for awakening my interest in Bonhoeffer, Christian community, and philosophical and theological hermeneutics. You exhorted that this study would change me. Your gentle mentoring and support has called me ever deeper into greater embrace of who I am and of who God is.

To Mark Boda, for your contagious passion for integrating biblical study with theological wisdom. You have inspired me to do theology *biblically* and to read the Bible *theologically*.

To Roy Matheson, the first to model for me the integration of disciplined, rigorous study of God's Word with building and edifying the church.

To Russell and Shannon Doerksen, for ably and meticulously compiling and organizing the author, Scripture, and subject indices (and for noticing a few typos and grammatical mistakes as well).

To Allen and Elaine Smith (and Mark and Sue Davis / Vernon-Smith) for generously providing me with the use of your cottage and the surrounding beauty while writing.

To the people of Chartwell Baptist Church and Kings Community Church, for your enduring friendship, faithful prayers, and generous financial support. The writing of this book would not have been possible without you. This has indeed been a joint journey. A special thank you to my small group at Kings, my 'little church' – Ruth and Steve Malinowski, Sharon Wong, Phil and Elena Haskell, and Joel and Ashleigh Wagner. You nurtured and encouraged me more than I can say! Thanks

Acknowledgements

also to my good friends the Barringtons, the Bowerings, the Broadus's, the Dycks, the Harveys, and the Pecks.

To my parents, my mother and father in law, my siblings and sisters-in-law, and my extended family and friends for your ongoing love and support.

To friends that have impacted my thinking about church, culture, and social justice through conversation, companionship, and modelling: Trevor Brisbin, Wayne Cheng, Rob Harvey, Jack Kiervin, Garry Koop, Ross Macdonald, David Peck, Kevin Ramessar, Peter Roebbelen, Lyness Wark, and the leadership teams of King's Community Church and Chartwell Baptist Church.

I dedicate this work, this labour of love, to Elena, Josiah, Samuel, and Eliana. You continually help me to understand and live out what it means to be more genuinely human. I simply would not be the same person without you. Thank you for your patience, encouragement, and support. This has been a marathon for all of us! Thank you, Elena, also for the many conversations we've had about church and for offering your suggestions on my final manuscript.

Finally, to God be all glory, honour, and praise. "Praise the Lord! Give thanks to the Lord, for he is good! His faithful love endures forever" (Ps 106:1).

Patrick S. Franklin

FOREWORD

My favorite chapter is number 2. Granted, I can understand why one might favor the first chapter. It clearly lays out the confusion and challenges evident in our culture about what human beings are and can be. Here and throughout the book, Franklin is in dialogue with research on the human person not just in theology, but also in the sciences and the social sciences. His first degree was in psychology, and later studies have continued on through his PhD in theology. His insights into humanity and the human situation come also from his guiding the latest developments as the editor of the theological journal *Didaskalia*, and as the lead book review editor for the influential journal, *Perspectives on Science and Christian Faith*.

Of course, one could just as well recommend chapters 3, 4, and 5 in Part II. They describe what a human being is and should be, from a theological perspective. Human beings are designed and intended to be in right relationship with God and one another. We are to be transformed to that end through the renewal of our minds, to look forward to and be guided by God's plan for our future. All of this takes place through our participation in Christ by the Spirit. There is theological depth, thorough analysis, and rich bibliography in these chapters as all through the book.

Chapters 6, 7, and 8 are likely to be particularly appreciated because they outline how the church can be used by God to develop God's people into the new humanity described in the previous chapters. The church is a gift that can shape us from who we are, to who we are meant to be and, by God's grace, will be. It is insightful and motivating to see what the plan is, and to be encouraged to join in. Franklin clearly knows and loves the church not only as a scholar who has prepared pastors at McMaster Divinity College, Tyndale Seminary, and now Providence Theological Seminary, but also as an experienced pastor, himself.

But chapter 2 remains the one that most intrigues and empowers me. Franklin discerns six dominant accounts of what it is to be a human that have been widely assumed in our culture. Each one is described succinctly, including strengths and weaknesses. He then marks out how each rival perspective has shaped a particular way of doing church that is currently popular. Attractional, emergent, church growth, and community of care are all here. Each of these approaches so builds upon just one of these pictures of humanity that the resulting churches are hobbled

Foreword

by their particular partial truth. Granted, half-truths are half true. They contribute, but also fall far short when the resulting churches miss essentials in the whole counsel of God for his people. What is needed is a more comprehensive understanding and practice that more than resolves the otherwise embedded false dichotomies. The church is a place of choice *and* deep commitment, creative exploration *and* grounded tradition, evangelism *and* discipleship, personal *and* social ethics. Franklin explores how these can work together to better both.

In the conclusion, Franklin brings together a Trinitarian model of incarnation, cross, and resurrection, exemplifying and enabling the creative, redemptive, and transformative presence of God the Father, Son, and Spirit. The resulting church is becoming humanity as God intended it to be, practicing in communities of love, faith, and hope. Franklin brings this framework together with insights and implications for the life, in its fullest sense, of God's people.

It is rare to find a work that can be so thoroughly, deeply, informed, while also envisioning a breath-taking panorama. Here you have a sense-making and inspiring view of what the church is and can be, developed with subtle and fine understanding. Every line rewards attention.

But chapter two is still my favorite.

JAMES C. PETERSON
Editor-in-Chief, *Perspectives on Science and Christian Faith*
Schumann Professor of Christian Ethics
Director of the Benne Center for Religion and Society
Roanoke College, Salem, Virginia

Introduction

As human beings we are each of us members of particular communities. Our views and expectations about the purpose and functioning of community are intimately linked with our understanding of what it means to be human.[1] Within contemporary western culture various conceptions of the human person exist, leading to differing ways of understanding and practicing community.[2] This link between what it means to be a human person and what it means to be in community impacts Christian ecclesial communities as well. How one conceives of the nature, purpose, and outworking of Christian community is grounded in and informed by a theology of the human person, whether or not this theology is explicit, well understood, clearly articulated, and coherently worked out in particular Christian traditions.

In the contemporary setting, an inadequate theological understanding of the meaning and *telos* or purpose of the human person often distorts the church's understanding of its own nature (its inner integrity, the nature of its sociality) as well as its understanding of its mission in the world and the intrinsic relation of that mission to personal, social, and global ethics. A deficient theological anthropology leads the church to emphasize and attend to certain aspects of being human while simultaneously neglecting others. What should be viewed as an integrated whole (a holistically redemptive community of human beings) becomes disintegrated and fragmented. As a result, dualisms and false dichotomies begin to plague the inner life of the church, such as inner-outer purity or righteousness, justification-sanctification, individualism-collectivism, personal-communal piety, spirituality-ethics, and discipleship-evangelism. Similar dualisms and false dichotomies distort the relationship between the church and the world, some of which include secular-sacred, syncretism-withdrawal, triumphalism-powerlessness, justice as extrinsic/secondary versus justice as all-

---

[1] Charles Taylor, *Sources of the Self: The Making of the Modern Identity* (Cambridge, MA: Harvard University Press, 1989), 105–106.
[2] Linda Woodhead, "Theology and the Fragmentation of the Self," *International Journal of Systematic Theology* 1 (March, 1999): 59–66. Woodhead, in dialogue with S. Tipton, identifies and explicates four strands of modern identity: the authoritative strand (the bestowed self), the liberal humanistic strand (the rational self), the expressive strand (the boundless self), and the utilitarian strand (the effective self).

encompassing, and mission as soul-saving versus mission as social transformation.

Thus, despite the importance of the church in Scripture and tradition, many present-day western Christians feel significant tension with regards to the church. We hear that a person can worship God anywhere and serve Jesus anywhere; both statements are true, of course, but in common parlance they tend to downplay the significance of the church. Many today express interest in Jesus and even in spiritual formation, but struggle to connect either of these explicitly with church. A recent book on Christian spirituality written by a well known Christian author emphasizes the importance of spiritual awakening and transformation for human becoming; and though it recognizes the role of community in Christian spirituality its portrayal of the church is often negative and the intrinsic connection between spirituality and ecclesiology is left unexplored. The Christian spiritual journey appears primarily to be the individual's quest for self-actualization.[3] Others, inspired by the ethical vision of Jesus, are passionate about social justice and caring for the poor and marginalized, but they are disappointed with the institutional church and thus seek to serve the kingdom of God in the world beyond the confines of the church. Their approach certainly resonates with much that is at the heart of Christ's character and teachings, yet it lacks the emphasis that Jesus himself placed on the centrality of the church as the community in which the kingdom of God becomes manifest (e.g., Matt 16:17–19).[4]

The lack of precision and agreement in much of contemporary thought about what it means to be human has led to some destructive consequences for both church and society, with potentially even more devastating implications. Specifically, vagueness about what it means to be human and about the human *telos* renders problematic: (a) the basic intrinsic worth of the human being, on which conceptions of human dignity are usually based; (b) the grounds and purpose of human community; and (c) clear and coherent grounds for personal, social, and global ethics. A significant step forward in overcoming these problems is to recapture the intrinsic connection of ecclesiology to theological anthropology. This will allow us to address two interrelated questions. First, what grounds and characterizes the church's inner sociality (i.e., its inner community life)? Stated differently, what kind of human community is the church and what sort of life sustains it? Second, what grounds and characterizes the church's public mission (i.e., its outward engagement with the world)? In what follows, we will explore these issues in depth and develop implications for the sociality

---

[3] David G. Benner, *Spirituality and the Awakening Self: The Sacred Journey of Transformation* (Grand Rapids: Brazos, 2012). I find much of Benner's work to be quite helpful. I am simply pointing out an ecclesiological deficiency in this particular book.

[4] On the intrinsic connection between kingdom and church (and kingdom work and church work), see Scot McKnight, *Kingdom Conspiracy: Returning to the Radical Mission of the Local Church* (Grand Rapids: Brazos, 2014).

Introduction

of the church, the church's engagement with the world (including personal, social, and global ethics), and the intrinsic connection between the two.

My approach to theological anthropology is framed within a trinitarian theology of personhood. The latter is trinitarian in two primary respects. First, it views human personhood as being in some respects analogous to divine personhood, even while preserving a qualitative difference between God and human beings. Second, what it views as being unique about human beings is not something that can be attributed comprehensively to their own biological nature as such (some static quality or capacity they possess), rather it arises as a result of God's uniquely triune personal way of relating to them.[5] Specifically, I am setting forth a theological anthropology that depicts the human person as (1) a relational creature (via relational ontology, in which humans are created to be in other-oriented relationships with God and other human beings), (2) a rational creature (combining *rational* with *ethical* to form *wisdom*), and (3) an eschatological creature (created for a purpose and destiny yet to be fulfilled), to whom God relates as Reconciler, Creator, and Perfecter. An ethical dimension to being human both pervades and proceeds from each of the three aforementioned aspects of theological anthropology. Thus, *human being is intrinsically ethical being*. In light of this, we will explore the ethics of being human in each of the anthropology chapters, under the rubric of: *love* and the relational ethical dimension (chapter 3), *faith* and the rational ethical dimension (chapter 4), and *hope* and the eschatological ethical dimension (chapter five).

Correspondingly, the church as the *new humanity* exists concretely as relational, rational, and eschatological communities (chapters 4–6).[6] As such, churches are communities in which redeemed persons are formed to become more genuinely human, being remade gradually into the image of Christ. This means that being in the church is intrinsically related to the believer's salvation, not because the church is an institutional dispenser of salvation but because it is the concrete community in which reconciliation is embodied and transformation takes place. It is the communal context in which redeemed human persons practice and live out concretely their restored relationships with God and others. Since the church is such a transformative community, it is also intrinsically an *ethical* community—a place of personal and social ethical orientation and formation. Moreover, its particular way of being an ethical community leads to the implication that the church exists not *merely* for its own sake but

---

[5] However, as James Peterson points out, human beings do possess an *emergent capacity* that makes a relationship with God possible. James C. Peterson, "*Homo Sapiens* as *Homo Dei*: Paleoanthropology, Human Uniqueness, and the Image of God," *Toronto Journal of Theology* 27, no. 1 (2011): 17.

[6] In employing the words "community" or "communities" I am trying to avoid overly institutional connotations presently associated with the word "church". To draw a parallel with Luther, I refer to community in a way similar to Luther's preference for Gemeinde over Kirche.

also for the sake of the world, in the proleptic, eschatological form of foretaste, catalyst, or leaven of the present-yet-coming kingdom of God.

The threefold ethical dimension of the church as the new humanity forms the basis of its engagement with the world. The church lives out of its ethical dimension and engages the world not merely by its own strength, vision, and resources, but by participating by the Spirit in Christ's ministry and mission in the world. Thus, it engages the world relationally by participating in Christ's *priestly* ministry, as ambassadors of reconciliation. It engages the world rationally (in wisdom) by participating in Christ's *prophetic* ministry, as witnesses and servants of the truth. It engages the world eschatologically by participating in Christ's *reign*, as heralds and representatives of the kingdom and as steward-priests of the new creation.

Understanding ecclesiology in light of a trinitarian theological anthropology helps us to clarify the missional nature of the church by specifying and integrating the *grounds, character, and goal* of the church's mission *as the new humanity*. A trinitarian ecclesiological framework entails a *participatory* model of mission, in which the mission of God flows from the ecstatic, overflowing love of God. As an expression of God's love for the world, the Father elects the church to participate by the Spirit in Christ's mission in and for the world. This approach prevents missional ecclesiology from degenerating into mere functionalism, pragmatism, and/or activism, because it grounds the church's mission holistically in the church's nature as a redeemed and redeeming human community of love.

The trinitarian model of cultural engagement that I propose leads to some preliminary implications for the church's God-given mandate to serve general human flourishing.[7] While I cannot address these issues in anything like a comprehensive manner (a task that I intend to pursue in future books), in the final chapter I posit some basic guidelines regarding how one might proceed in light of the conclusions reached in this book.

---

[7] "Human flourishing" is standard nomenclature for natural law approaches to ethics. While I want to affirm some aspects of natural law ethics (for example, the existence of something like a moral law with corresponding natural consequences for obedience and disobedience), my understanding of human flourishing is somewhat different. For example, a theological understanding of genuine human flourishing considers both natural and supernatural aspects and/or orientations (e.g., body and soul; time and eternity) and requires both natural knowledge (derived from reason) and revelatory knowledge (received as God's own self-communication to us) of what it means to be a human person. Non-theological accounts of human beings as social, rational, and future-oriented beings are certainly possible and may very well resonate with theological approaches. However, my theological description of human persons as relational, wise, and eschatological beings before God, while not contrary to reason, is also dependent upon revelation and thus not self-evident on the basis of reason alone (whether in its rational or empirical forms).

Introduction

Situating the Argument in the Scholarly Discussion

Previous Research that is Relevant to the Topic

There are three strands of research that are directly relevant to the topic. The first strand, which includes authors such as Colin Gunton, John Macmurray, Alistair McFadyen, John Zizioulas, Catherine Mowry LaCugna, and Stanley Grenz, is theological work done on the relationship between the Trinity and the human person.[8] The primary insights gained here concern the intrinsic relationality of both God and human beings. This is often opposed to the Aristotelian view that *relation* belongs to the category of accident rather than substance, and is therefore something extrinsic to substance, essence, or being. According to trinitarian critics, such a view leads to individualistic and static notions of God (i.e., Aristotle's Unmoved Mover) and the human person in which relationships are not essential but peripheral to being and personhood. This research advances a relational understanding of the human person, but does not develop the full implications of this for ecclesiology, ethics, and mission.

A second strand of research focuses on communitarian ecclesiology. This strand explicitly links (and develops to some extent) a trinitarian conception of personhood with a trinitarian ecclesiology. It tends to proceed in one of two directions. The first (e.g., Stanley Grenz, Emil Brunner) focuses on the church as a community of persons in relationship.[9] It provides a helpful critique of institutional views of the church and is faithful to the predominantly relational portrayals of the church in the New Testament. However, it is not sufficiently missional or ethical (oriented to justice) in its characterization of the church. The second direction theologians take (e.g., John Zizoulas, Miroslav Volf) is to apply insights gained about the relational approach to theological anthropology and church to the problem of church unity.[10] Such work is very helpful when considering and weighing the tensions involved in genuine church unity, but it tends to lack a sufficient missional quality. Both of these approaches run the

---

[8] Colin E. Gunton, *The One, the Three, and the Many: God, Creation, and the Culture of Modernity* (New York: Cambridge University Press, 1993); John Macmurray, *Persons in Relation* (Atlantic Highlands: Humanities Press, 1991); Alistair I. McFadyen, *The Call to Personhood: A Christian Theory of the Individual in Social Relationships* (Cambridge: Cambridge University Press, 1990); John D. Zizioulas, *Being as Communion: Studies in Personhood and the Church* (Crestwood, NY: St. Vladimir's Seminary Press, 2002); Catherine Mowry LaCugna, *God For Us: The Trinity and Christian Life* (New York: HarperSanFrancisco, 1993); and Stanley J. Grenz, *The Social God and the Relational Self: A Trinitarian Theology of the Imago Dei* (Louisville: Westminster John Knox, 2001).

[9] Stanley J. Grenz, *Theology for the Community of God* (Grand Rapids: Eerdmans, 1994); Emil Brunner, *Man in Revolt: A Christian Anthropology*, trans. Oliver Wyon (London: Lutterworth, 1939). See also Avery Dulles, *Models of the Church* (New York: Doubleday, 1987), chapter 3.

[10] E.g., Miroslav Volf, *After Our Likeness: The Church as the Image of the Trinity* (Grand Rapids: Eerdmans), 1998 and Zizioulas, *Being as Communion*.

risk of degenerating into sentimental communitarianism if they are not qualified and developed in certain ways.[11]

A third strand of research invokes the Trinity as the basis for constructing a social program for mission or justice. One approach, characteristic of some liberation and feminist theologians (e.g., Leonardo Boff, Juan Segundo, Anne Carr, Cynthia Campbell), is to employ the Trinity as a model for just societal relations or structures of social and/or gender equality.[12] A second approach, characteristic of missional ecclesiology (e.g., Darrell Guder) is to employ the Trinity as a model for mission. The missional view argues that mission is not just a sub-category of ecclesiology, but is part of the essence of what it means to be the church. The church does not "do" mission; rather, the church "is" mission. The church does not "have" a mission; rather, God has created a sent-church, a missional church.[13] Both of these approaches are quite helpful in emphasizing that justice and mission are intrinsic to the very essence of the church. However, when separated from a sufficiently relational anthropology and from communitarian conceptions of the church, they run the risk of degenerating into pragmatism and/or functionalism.

Contribution of the Present Project

As discussed above, many trinitarian conceptions of the church focus on the relational character of the human person and the church in order to deal with questions of unity and diversity. Others place a communitarian focus on the church but fail to account sufficiently for the church's missional nature. Still others focus on mission and/or justice without a sufficiently robust theological anthropology and communitarian ecclesiology. Most of these approaches lack sustained reflection on the ethical nature of the church, derived from God's

---

[11] I cite Volf as an example of applying trinitarian ecclesiology primarily to the problem of church unity, not as one lacking in ethical concern (Volf's writings usually have both implicit and explicit ethical implications).

[12] Leonardo Boff, *Ecclesiogenesis: The Base Communities Reinvent the Church*, trans. Robert R. Barr (Maryknoll: Orbis, 1986) and *Trinity and Society*, trans. Paul Burns (Maryknoll: Orbis, 1988); Juan Segundo, *Our Idea of God* (Maryknoll: Orbis, 1974); Anne Carr, *Transforming Grace: Christian Tradition and Women's Experience* (San Francisco: Harper and Row, 1988); Cynthia Campbell, "The Triune God: A Model for Inclusion," *Austin Seminary Bulletin* 97 (1981): 13–20 and "Imago Trinitatis: the Being of God as a Model for Inclusion," *Austin Seminary Bulletin* 102 (1987): 5–15. See also Jürgen Moltmann, *Trinity and the Kingdom: The Doctrine of God*, trans. Margaret Kohl (San Francisco: Harper and Row, 1981); Leonard Hodgson, *The Doctrine of the Trinity* (New York: Charles Scribners Sons, 1944); Miroslav Volf, "'The Trinity as our Social Program': The Doctrine of the Trinity and the Shape of Social Engagement," *Modern Theology* 14, no. 3 (July 1998): 403–23; and John L. Gresham, Jr., "The Social Model of the Trinity and its Critics," *Scottish Journal of Theology* 46, no. 3 (1993): 325–43.

[13] Darrell L. Guder, "Missional Theology for a Missionary Church," *Journal for Preachers* 22, no. 1 (1998): 5, and Guder, ed., *Missional Church: A Vision for the Sending of the Church in North America* (Grand Rapids: Eerdmans, 1998).

Introduction

purposes for redeemed human persons that constitute the new humanity. The present book provides an approach that employs theological anthropology in the service of ecclesiology, in order to articulate a theology of church that sufficiently integrates being human, being in community, and being missional, making explicit the intrinsic connection of each of these to spirituality and ethics. It offers a trinitarian revision of missional theo-logic and an anthropological and ethical revision of ecclesiology. My primary goal is to construct a theology of the church as the new humanity, existing concretely in relational, rational, and eschatological communities of love, faith, and hope.

In addition to this primary goal, I suggest that this project makes a modest, but important, threefold contribution to contemporary ecclesiology. First, it offers a way of resolving or transcending dualisms and false dichotomies that plague both the inner life of the church and its outer engagement with the surrounding culture. In place of these dualisms and false dichotomies, it promotes a holistic or integrated view of personhood and community and a corresponding approach to cultural engagement based upon a threefold model of cross, incarnation, and resurrection. Second, by constructing ecclesiology in light of a trinitarian theological anthropology, it suggests an anthropological modification of social trinitarianism. I do not propose a literal parallel between Trinity and the church, rather I envision redeemed human persons as exocentric (other-centered) beings bound together in Christ by the indwelling Spirit, thus mirroring the Trinity analogously.[14] Finally, it offers a novel typology that compares and contrasts rival contemporary conceptions of the human person and their corresponding views of human community and church. In so doing, it exposes and analyzes potentially unexamined philosophical and theological assumptions that implicitly influence our understanding and practice of church.

Methods, Models, and Frameworks

This book represents a constructive project in systematic theology, more specifically ecclesiology. As such, the primary question it poses is systematic and thematic in nature, rather than biblical or historical. Consequently, its methodology is oriented primarily toward addressing broad, systematic (and often philosophical), cross-textual issues, rather than focusing on biblical-exegetical or historical details. Thus, it engages biblical and historical scholarship only when such scholarship is relevant to the question(s) at hand.[15] A broad, synthetic approach is fitting because human personhood and community are broad and synthetic subjects involving several intersecting disciplines. The strength of this

---

[14] As an *analogy* (something that participates in what it depicts), this version of social trinitarianism avoids both literalism and mere symbolism. In this sense, the church is a sacrament of the Trinity.

[15] Stephen Fowl sets forth the rationale for this approach to biblical scholarship in his book *Engaging Scripture: A Model for Theological Interpretation* (Oxford: Blackwell, 1998), 179–90.

approach is that it allows an author to relate and discuss interconnected themes in an integrated way and to demonstrate the far reaching significance of their scope and implications. A potential weakness is that it is unable to treat every subtopic in comprehensive detail (especially the intricate, intra-disciplinary debates of particular specializations). The methods employed thus serve the purpose of developing major themes while inviting further conversation, debate, criticism, and elaboration from other scholars in the joint pursuit of knowledge (scholarship *can be* a human and humanizing conversation!). In the course of answering my primary and secondary questions, I employ several methods and/or frameworks.

Historical-Philosophical Narrative

The first chapter makes use of a historical-philosophical narrative (e.g., MacIntyre, Rorty, Taylor), in order to describe the context which gave rise to the problems that I seek to address. Specifically, it narrates the abandonment of a theological and teleological approach to anthropology, the resulting lack of precision in attempts to define human personhood, and the corresponding problems this poses for our understanding and practice of human community and society. This chapter does not set forth the thesis of the book, but sets the stage for that argument. It employs this method in a descriptive rather than a constructive manner, thus its historical-philosophical narrative uses primary and interpretive literature. In particular, it engages the work of Stanley Grenz, Alasdair MacIntyre, Charles Taylor, and, to a lesser extent, Stanley Hauerwas and F. LeRon Shults.[16]

Typology

In chapter two, I employ a typological method to compare and contrast typical rival views of what it means to be human and their corresponding conceptions of community in modern and postmodern culture. This method has its theological precedents in writers such as H. Richard Niebuhr and Avery Dulles.[17] Crucial to understanding the typological method and employing it fruitfully is the

---

[16] Alasdair MacIntyre, *After Virtue: A Study in Moral Theology* (Notre Dame: University of Notre Dame Press, 1984) and *Whose Justice? Which Rationality?* (Notre Dame: University of Notre Dame Press, 1988); Stanley J. Grenz, *Rediscovering the Triune God: The Trinity in Contemporary Theology* (Minneapolis: Fortress, 2004) and *The Social God and the Relational Self*; F. LeRon Shults, *Reforming Theological Anthropology: After the Philosophical Turn to Relationality* (Grand Rapids: Eerdmans, 2003); Taylor, *Sources of the Self*; Stanley Hauerwas, *A Community of Character: Toward a Constructive Christian Social Ethic* (Notre Dame: University of Notre Dame Press, 1981), *Character and the Christian Life: A Study in Theological Ethics* (San Antonio: Trinity University Press, 1975), *In Good Company: The Church as Polis* (Notre Dame: University of Notre Dame Press, 1995), and *The Peaceable Kingdom: A Primer in Christian Ethics* (Notre Dame: University of Notre Dame Press, 1983).

[17] H. Richard Niebuhr, *Christ and Culture* (New York: HarperSanFrancisco, 2001) and Dulles, *Models of the Church*.

Introduction

recognition that it is a heuristic device that posits constructs of general motifs and ideas. I do not intend a taxonomy, which is a system of classification according to observations of empirical differences, generally used in the biological sciences to describe individuals. Rather, a typology classifies according to conceptual differences and is generally used for broad affinity classes.[18] As Niebuhr explains,

> A type is always something of a construct, even when it has not been constructed prior to long study of many historical individuals and movements. When one returns from the hypothetical scheme to the rich complexity of individual events, it is evident at once that no person or group ever conforms completely to a type.[19]

Thus, typology is a method befitting *conceptual clarification* as opposed to strictly historical or empirical investigation. As such, "The method of typology, though historically inadequate, has the advantage of calling to attention the continuity and significance of the great motifs that appear and reappear in the long wrestling of Christians with their enduring problem."[20] This approach fits my purpose in chapter two, which is to compare and contrast the conceptual differences between rival conceptions of the human person and their implications for understanding the character and goal of community.

Application of a Hermeneutical-Doctrinal Lens

My primary argument regarding the significance of theological anthropology for ecclesiology brings together two related doctrines and interprets one in light of the other. It therefore relies on the application of a hermeneutical lens (theological anthropology) through which it explores its primary subject matter (ecclesiology). Two relevant theological precedents for this include the ecclesiology of Vatican II, which conceives of the church through the lens of sacramental theology, and missional ecclesiology, which conceives of the church through the lens of missiology.[21] It should be noted that I do not apply this hermeneutical lens in a strictly linear fashion. While the primary aim is to rethink ecclesiology in light of theological anthropology, I recognize that the latter also receives clarification from trinitarian theology and ecclesiology. In other words, what it means to be human and what it means to be the church are dialogically related and mediated by trinitarian theology. This leads to the application of a trinitarian framework for theological anthropology and ecclesiology.

---

[18] Kenneth D. Bailey, *Typologies and Taxonomies: An Introduction to Classification Techniques* (Thousand Oaks: Sage, 1994), 6.

[19] Niebuhr, *Christ and Culture*, 43–44.

[20] Niebuhr, *Christ and Culture*, 44.

[21] Regarding sacramental ecclesiology, see the Vatican II document *Lumen Gentium* 9, 48 (cited by Dulles, *Models of the Church*, 56); see also Veli-Matti Kärkkäinen, *An Introduction to Ecclesiology: Ecumenical, Historical and Global Perspectives* (Dowers Grove: InterVarsity Press, 2002), 28–29. Regarding missional ecclesiology, see Guder, ed., *Missional Church*.

A Trinitarian Framework for Theological Anthropology and Ecclesiology
I employ a trinitarian framework in two different ways. First, I use it to stimulate reflection on human persons as being, in some ways, analogous to divine persons (chapter 3). Similarly, I employ it to describe Christian social relations in the church as being, in some ways, analogous to the trinitarian relations of divine persons (in the ecclesiology section). This approach has its roots in social models of the Trinity, from Augustine (his mutual love model, appropriated by Jonathan Edwards) to Richard of St. Victor, to the trinitarian personalism of Bonhoeffer, Barth, and Brunner, through to modern social trinitarians such as Colin Gunton, John Zizioulas, Catherine LaCugna, Stanley Grenz and Miroslav Volf.[22] My approach takes its initial cue from two sources, namely the Augustinian mutual love model of the Trinity (qualified and developed in dialogue with T.F. Torrance) and Bonhoeffer's relational interpretation of the *imago Dei* (qualified and developed in dialogue with Pannenberg, Grenz, and Volf).[23]

---

[22] Augustine, *The Trinity*, vol. 5 of *The Works of St. Augustine: A Translation for the 21st Century*, ed. John E. Rotelle, trans. Edmund Hill (New York: New City, 1991); Steven M. Studebaker, *Jonathan Edwards' Social Augustinian Trinitarianism in Historical and Contemporary Perspectives* (Piscataway, NJ: Gorgias, 2008) and "Jonathan Edwards's Social *Augustinian* Trinitarianism: an Alternative to a Recent Trend," *Scottish Journal of Theology* 56, no. 3 (2003): 268–85; Richard of St. Victor, "Book Three of the Trinity," in *Richard of St. Victor: The Twelve Patriarchs, The Mystical Ark, and Book Three of the Trinity*, trans. Grover A. Zinn (New York: Paulist, 1979); Dietrich Bonhoeffer, *Creation and Fall: A Theological Exposition of Genesis 1–3*, vol. 3 of *Dietrich Bonhoeffer Works*, ed. John W. de Gruchy, trans. Douglas Stephen Bax (Minneapolis: Fortress, 1997); Karl Barth, *The Doctrine of Creation: Church Dogmatics III*/1 (London: T & T Clark, 2009); Emil Brunner, *The Christian Doctrine of Creation and Redemption*, trans. Oliver Wyon (Philadelphia: Westminster, 1953) and *Man in Revolt*; Colin E. Gunton, *The One, the Three, and the Many* and *The Promise of Trinitarian Theology* (Edinburgh: T & T Clark, 1991); Zizioulas, *Being as Communion* and *Communion & Otherness*, ed. Paul McPartlan (London: T & T Clark, 2006); LaCugna, *God For Us*, Grenz, *The Social God and the Relational Self* and *Theology*; Volf, *After Our Likeness*. See also: Macmurray, *Persons in Relation*; McFadyen, *The Call to Personhood*; and Boff, *Trinity and Society*.

[23] Dietrich Bonhoeffer (*Creation and Fall*, 65ff.) proposed that a relational analogy (*analogia relationis*) maintains between divine and human personhood. In contrast to an analogy of being (*analogia entis*), which posits a correspondence between God's being (essence) and the human being as a substance (intrinsic qualities such as rationality or consciousness), an analogy of relationship posits a correspondence between divine and human personhood on the level of relationship. Human personhood is analogous to divine personhood because it is inherently relational. To be a human person is to be a being-in-relationship with God (who first relates to humans and thereby constitutes their personhood) and with other human beings. For Bonhoeffer, this *analogia relationis* is not something that humans possess in and of themselves, apart from God. It consists only in the fact that humanity points to or illustrates the divine, and it extends only as far as human beings fulfil this purpose in relationship to God and others. Karl Barth appropriated Bonhoeffer's *analogia relationis* in his 1942 *Doctrine of Creation* ("The Work of Creation," *Church Dogmatics* III/1).

Introduction

Second, I employ a trinitarian framework to describe God's threefold way of relating to humans beings and thereby constituting their genuine humanity.[24] Thus, each chapter on theological anthropology (3–5) employs a trinitarian framework to discuss a particular aspect of being human. With regard to the relational aspect of being human: The *Son* reconciles us to the Father by the Holy Spirit, who unites us to Christ and draws us into fellowship with God and one another. With regard to the rational aspect of being human: we are opened and led to discern the *Father's* creational design, through the Son's wisdom, in and by the Spirit's illumination and empowerment. With regard to the eschatological aspect of being human: the *Holy Spirit* transforms us into the likeness of the Son and orients us toward the Father. In this trinitarian framework the three persons of the Trinity always work inseparably (I therefore reject modalist or tritheistic paradigms), yet within this unity each trinitarian person takes a primary role in making us genuinely human.[25] As Grenz rightly observes, "A theological construction that is truly trinitarian does not simply involve organizing beliefs around the three persons of the Trinity. More importantly, it entails viewing all aspects of Christian doctrine in a trinitarian light."[26]

Theological Commitments

I write self-consciously from a broad, evangelical perspective, in continuity with the apostolic, Nicene, and Chalcedonian tradition of historic Christianity.[27] Such a perspective prioritizes the authority of Scripture, even while maintaining the importance of religious experience, tradition, and reason.[28] With regards to ecclesial tradition, my own interpretation of Scripture, in ongoing dialogue with

---

[24] That God's relating to human beings constitutes their personhood is a point made throughout David Kelsey's *Eccentric Existence: A Theological Anthropology*, 2 vols. (Louisville: Westminster John Knox, 2009).

[25] With this statement I am appealing to two important trinitarian doctrines, namely the unity of divine operations and the doctrine of appropriation.

[26] Grenz, *The Social God and the Relational Self*, x. Theologians such as Karl Barth and Wolfhart Pannenberg are exemplary in this regard. See Barth, *Church Dogmatics*; Wolfhart Pannenberg, *Systematic Theology*, 3 vols., trans. Geoffrey W. Bromiley (Grand Rapids: Eerdmans, 1991–98).

[27] On locating evangelicalism more precisely and historically, see David W. Bebbington, *Evangelicalism in Modern Britain: A History from the 1730s to the 1980s* (London: Routledge, 2005) and Timothy Larsen, "Defining and Locating Evangelicalism," in *The Cambridge Companion to Evangelical Theology*, ed. Timothy Larsen and Daniel J. Treier (Cambridge: Cambridge University Press, 2007), 1–14.

[28] As Stephen Fowl writes, "[G]iven the ends towards which Christians interpret their scripture, Christian interpretation of scripture needs to involve a complex interaction in which Christian convictions, practices, and concerns are brought to bear on scriptural interpretation in ways that both shape that interpretation and are shaped by it" (*Engaging Scripture*, 8). See also Daniel J. Treier, "Scripture and Hermeneutics," in *The Cambridge Companion to Evangelical Theology* (Cambridge: Cambridge University Press, 2007), 35–49.

tradition, reason, and the guidance of the Holy Spirit, leads me to endorse a version of the Free Church tradition—namely the Baptist tradition—though not without reservation or qualification. Two major aspects of the Baptist tradition resonate with me. First, I believe the notion of the believer's church represents a faithful and fitting interpretation of the New Testament data. Second, its congregational structure resonates with me, as I find it to be in keeping with the New Testament's portrayal of the flexibility of church to adapt its structures to pursue its mission effectively in concrete and changing cultural contexts (I prefer Luther over Calvin on this point). My perspective is that the New Testament does not present us with one single model for church governance, but rather several or perhaps even limitless possibilities (within the bounds of faithfulness to Christ as head), especially if we find underlying principles rather than specific and rigid commands.[29] The congregational model accentuates the New Testament's portrayal of diversity in the early Christian communities and, accordingly, promotes freedom to structure the church in a way that best fits a congregation's present context. Furthermore, the flexible and non-hierarchical (yet deeply covenantal) nature of the congregational model holds promise for being and doing church within the fluid and changing context of postmodern culture.

On the other hand, a congregationalist approach must be careful to maintain a fuller kingdom perspective, which acknowledges that God wants to use many churches to reach cities and nations. Otherwise, a congregationalist vision can too easily become myopic and self-centered. It can begin to assume that its own corner of the kingdom is all that exists.[30] It has to remember that it is a servant and witness of the kingdom, not the kingdom itself. Just as the diverse members of a local congregation make up one community, so the local congregation is itself a uniquely contributing part of Christ's Body, one that needs the other members for its own health and effectiveness.

Primary Conversation Partners

While the book engages the work of many theologians through the course of its argument, my primary conversation partners are Dietrich Bonhoeffer, Miroslav Volf, and Stanley Grenz. This is most evident in the theological anthropology section (chapters 3–5). Chapters six through eight, which explore the significance of theological anthropology for ecclesiology, depend on these three theologians for their basic orientation but are also constructive in nature. There are several reasons for consulting these particular theologians, reasons which relate

---

[29] Charles Ringma, *Catch the Wind: The Shape of the Church to Come—And Our Place in It* (Vancouver: Regent College, 1994), 105.

[30] Perhaps it can learn to appreciate the importance of the oneness of the universal church from the Roman Catholic tradition. This does not mean accepting the need for an Episcopal structure headed by bishops, but it does mean taking the unity of the universal church seriously and making an intentional effort to build relationships with other churches.

Introduction

both to my purposes and to my prior theological assumptions and commitments. First, all three stand in the Protestant tradition and affirm the primacy of Scripture for theology, while appreciating the interpretive and formative role of church tradition, reason, and experience of the Holy Spirit. Second, all three explicitly relate theological anthropology to ecclesiology in ways that I wish to affirm (though not uncritically). Third, all three theologians have interests in theological anthropology, community, and ethics (personal or social justice). However, fourth, all three make proposals that are suggestive but require development, refinement, and/or corrective. Finally, the selection of three theologians from different ecclesial traditions (Lutheran, Pentecostal/Croatian evangelical, and Baptist) allows for a degree of breadth and cross-fertilization which, hopefully, makes the present project accessible and interesting for a broad evangelical audience.

In selecting these three primary conversation partners I wish to affirm at the same time the importance of the entire historic Christian tradition, including the early patristic period (e.g., Athanasius, Irenaeus, the Cappadocians, Augustine), the theologians of the medieval period who continued and developed the patristic tradition (e.g., Anselm, Aquinas, Richard of St. Victor), and the theologians of the Reformation and Great Awakening (e.g., Luther, Calvin, Wesley, Edwards). Though I interact with many of these theologians during the course of the argument (in both the body and the footnotes), I cannot engage them comprehensively given the nature and scope of the present project. Moreover, Bonhoeffer, Volf, and Grenz are themselves deeply rooted in the historic Christian tradition, hence I engage them consciously as partners in an ongoing theological conversation that both precedes and follows them.

Dietrich Bonhoeffer

As attested by the recent publication of the authoritative English addition of *Dietrich Bonhoeffer's Works* (16 vols.) by Fortress Press, Bonhoeffer continues to intrigue the theological community. Some of his ideas that I intend to develop further (and sometimes modify) include the *imago Dei* understood relationally as *being-for-others* (including freedom *for* others), his corresponding conception of the church as the *church-for-others* and as the *new humanity*, and his understanding of the church as an *ethical and formative community*. The unique contribution that Bonhoeffer brings to the present topic (relative to Volf and Grenz) is his creative and compelling, yet underdeveloped, integration of theological anthropology, ecclesiology, and ethics/justice. Moreover, Bonhoeffer contributes a deeply holistic spirituality to the discussion, one that restores the biblical spirituality of the prophets, being oriented to the reality of God and thus attentive to the intrinsic connection between genuine spirituality and social justice.

Miroslav Volf

Miroslav Volf has long been interested in understanding what it means to be human, especially with regard to issues of identity and otherness and their relation to ethics and church. He explores these issues initially in his award-winning book *Exclusion and Embrace*. In *After Our Likeness* he broadens and develops his insights further to apply them to the problem of the church's unity and diversity. *After Our Likeness* is particularly relevant to the present book because it constructs a trinitarian ecclesiology for the Free Church tradition (and is ground breaking in this respect). Other pertinent aspects of Volf's theology include his writings on ethics and justice, his theology of work and vocation (directly relevant to chapter six), and his theological stress on hope.[31] The unique contribution that Volf makes to the present topic is his trinitarian ecclesiology, which he develops through ecumenical discussion with Ratzinger and Zizioulas and articulates within a Free Church framework.[32] Volf's trinitarianism is more developed than Bonhoeffer's and is different from Grenz's in its emphasis on church unity. In addition, as a theologian who is very intentionally involved in ongoing conversation with others who hold diverse (and differing) ideas and represent diverse traditions and cultures, Volf brings a welcome dimension of theological, ecumenical, and geographical breadth to the discussion.[33]

Stanley Grenz

Before his untimely death in 2005, Stanley Grenz was widely regarded as a leading evangelical theologian. His many books address a wide variety of issues, some of which include theological method, the doctrine of the Trinity, ethics, church, culture (and postmodernity), Baptist ecclesiology, and historical theology.[34] Of particular relevance are his writings on Trinity and the human person, his development of a Baptist ecclesiology, and his theological stress on eschatology (learned from his mentor, Wolfhart Pannenberg). Grenz's unique contribution to the topic includes his emphasis on the *imago Dei*, and his construction of a Baptist, trinitarian-communitarian ecclesiology.[35]

---

[31] See Volf, *The End of Memory: Remembering Rightly in a Violent World* (Grand Rapids: Eerdmans, 2006), *Free of Charge: Giving and Forgiving in a Culture Stripped of Grace* (Grand Rapids: Zondervan, 2005), and *Work in the Spirit: Toward a Theology of Work* (Eugene, OR: Wipf and Stock, 2001).

[32] Volf, a Croatian evangelical and Pentecostal, currently attends an Anglican church.

[33] See Mark Oppenheimer, "Miroslav Volf Spans Conflicting Worlds," *The Christian Century* (January 11, 2003): 18–23.

[34] Stanley J. Grenz, *Rediscovering the Triune God*; *Theology*; *A Primer on Postmodernism* (Grand Rapids: Eerdmans, 1996); *The Moral Quest: Foundation of Christian Ethics* (Downers Grove: InterVarsity Press, 2000); *The Baptist Congregation: A Guide to Baptist Belief and Practice* (Vancouver: Regent College, 1996); and *Reason for Hope: The Systematic Theology of Wolfhart Pannenberg* (Oxford: Oxford University Press, 1990). See also Stanley J. Grenz and John Franke, *Beyond Foundationalism: Shaping Theology in a Postmodern Context* (Louisville: Westminster John Knox, 2000).

[35] Grenz, *The Social God and the Relational Self*; *Theology*; and *The Baptist Congregation*.

Part I: The Challenge

CHAPTER 1

Problems with Defining the Human Person

Lack of Precision About the Human Person in Contemporary Culture

Lack of precision about what constitutes a human person

It seems to be immediately evident that the concept of the human person, or the human being, is of utmost importance to the most basic values, beliefs, and commitments of contemporary Western societies. Generally speaking, we attribute great worth and dignity to humans, hence to treat someone *as a human being* is to treat them with the utmost respect. To protect and advocate on behalf of those who are vulnerable, such as minorities, the poor, children, and those who are oppressed or suffering unnecessarily, we appeal to *human rights*, which we usually regard as inalienable and grounded in the inherent worth of human persons.[1] We use words such as *humane* or *humanizing* to describe the kind of caring or empathetic action befitting of human beings in their treatment of other human or non-human creatures. When we speak of *human community* we usually mean something more than mere association or even the cooperation of individuals; we envision human community as something inter-*personal*, involving a higher degree of intimacy, mutual care, and responsibility to and for one another.

Despite this apparent dependence on the concept of the human, there is surprisingly little consensus around and precision about what it actually *means* to be human. In fact, there is growing uncertainty (even cynicism) that a definition is possible or even desirable.[2] Yet without it, such notions as human rights, the

---

[1] United Nations, *Universal Declaration of Human Rights*, in *Human Rights Documents: Compilation of Documents Pertaining to Human Rights* (Washington: Committee on Foreign Affairs, 1983), 63 (Preamble); Michael J. Perry, *The Idea of Human Rights* (New York: Oxford University Press, 1998), 5; Nicholas Wolterstorff, *Justice: Rights and Wrongs* (Princeton: Princeton University Press, 2008), 312.

[2] Marc Cortez, *Theological Anthropology: A Guide for the Perplexed* (New York: T & T Clark, 2010), 2; Joel B. Green, *Body, Soul, and Human Life: The Nature of Humanity in the Bible* (Grand Rapids: Baker Academic, 2008), 1; Jean Bethke Elshtain, "The Dignity of the Human Person and the Idea of Human Rights: Four Inquiries," *Journal of Law and Religion* 14, no. 1 (1999–2000), 56; Niels Henrik Gregersen, "Varieties of Personhood: Mapping the Issues," In *The Human Person in Science and Theology* (Grand Rapids: Eerdmans, 2000), 2; James C. Peterson, *Changing Human Nature: Ecology, Ethics, Genes, and God* (Grand Rapids: Eerdmans, 2010), 217–19;

humane treatment of others, and human community remain inescapably vague and perhaps even groundless, despite the rhetorical power they presently possess. Several factors have contributed to our culture's current anthropological agnosticism, the most significant of which include the problem of the fragmented self, an abandonment of *teleology* with respect to understanding human persons (i.e., what is their purpose and destiny?), the problem of scientific reductionism, and the loss of a theological account situating human persons before God. Exploring these factors will yield a better understanding of the present predicament and its implications for our understanding of and engagement in community and society.

The problem of the fragmented self

According to Stanley Grenz, "no concept has been more important for the understanding of the human person in Western intellectual history than the 'self.'"[3] He notes that contemporary people tend to conceive of the self in terms of inwardness or interiority (i.e., the real self within) and continuity (a sense of personal identity as a unified being).[4] This conception of the self is distinctly modern, and thus relatively recent, but has a long intellectual history dating back at least to Augustine.[5] Augustine noticed that his life lacked a unifying center; like a small boat in a tumultuous sea, Augustine felt himself tossed about by inner moral conflict, competing desires preying on his impoverished will, and the expectations of other people. To overcome this fragmentation Augustine turned inward, to God, to find his authentic identity. In prayerful contemplation he wrote, "Man, this part of your creation, wishes to praise you. You arouse him to take joy in praising you, for you have made us for yourself, and our heart is restless until it rests in you."[6] Augustine's reflections, both in con-

---

Charles Taylor, *Sources of the Self: The Making of the Modern Identity* (Cambridge, MA: Harvard University Press, 1989), 12, 60. Many, following thinkers such as Michel Foucault, fear that all attempts to define a human person (whether according to nature, purpose/function, or a transcendent vantage point) lead inevitably to some form of oppression. There are historical precedents that justify this concern, for example Nazi eugenics, however abandoning the effort to understand and articulate what it means to be human is not a satisfying solution. I argue this point in more detail later in this chapter (section B.3).

[3] Stanley J. Grenz, "The Social God and the Relational Self: Toward a Theology of the Imago Dei in the Postmodern Context," *Horizons in Biblical Theology* 24, no. 1 (2002): 34.

[4] Stanley J. Grenz, *The Social God and the Relational Self: A Trinitarian Theology of the Imago Dei* (Louisville: Westminster John Knox, 2001), 60.

[5] Grenz, "The Social God," 35.

[6] Augustine, *The Confessions of St. Augustine*, trans. John K. Ryan (New York: Doubleday, 1960), 44. As another poignant example of someone turning to God as the source and center of one's true identity in the midst of inner conflict and chaotic life circumstances, see Dietrich Bonhoeffer's poem "Who am I?" Written from his prison cell (Bonhoeffer was imprisoned for his role in the resistance movement against the Nazis), the last line of the poem reads, "Who am I? They mock me, these lonely

tent and method (introspective autobiography), profoundly influenced the trajectory of Western theological anthropology. For example, drawing on Augustine over a millennium later, Calvin argued that genuine knowledge of God and genuine knowledge of oneself arise together.[7] Conversely, to the degree that they are separated, both God-knowledge and self-knowledge become impoverished and corrupted. The impact of Augustine's inward turn reached beyond theology, to philosophy and psychology, eventually leading "to the concept of the self as the stable, abiding reality that constitutes the individual human being."[8] Grenz charts two trajectories in the development of the modern self leading to two competing conceptualizations of selfhood in modernity.[9] He calls the first conception the "world-mastering, self-mastering rational self" (or the "therapeutic self") and the second the "self-focused, self-expressive self".[10]

The world-mastering, self-mastering rational self
Grenz's first conception of the self, which he identifies as predominant in modernity, focuses on mastery of self and world. This view envisions individual persons as particular instances of the ideal, universal, rational man. It combines Augustine's turn toward inwardness with an emphasis on the individual rational subject. Grenz traces this latter emphasis back to Boethius, who famously defined the person as "the individual substance of a rational nature".[11] Boethius's

---

questions of mine. Whoever I am, Thou knowest, O God, I am Thine!" Dietrich Bonhoeffer, *Letters and Papers from Prison*, vol. 8 of *Dietrich Bonhoeffer Works*, ed. John W. de Gruchy, trans. Isabel Best, Lisa E. Dahill, Reinhard Krauss, and Nancy Lukens (Minneapolis: Fortress, 2010), 459–60.

[7] John Calvin, *Institutes of the Christian Religion*, trans. Henry Beveridge (Grand Rapids: Eerdmans, 1989), I.I.1–3 (pp. 37–39).

[8] Grenz, "The Social God," 35.

[9] Linda Woodhead cautions against oversimplifying the modern notion of self by depicting it as something stable and homogeneous. Instead, she offers four conflicting conceptions of the modern self, including the bestowed self, the rational self, the boundless self, and the effective self. See Linda Woodhead, "Theology and the Fragmentation of the Self," *International Journal of Systematic Theology* 1 (March 1999): 53–57. Though Grenz offers just two trajectories, his portrayal of the modern self is sufficiently nuanced to avoid this criticism (and actually touches on each of Woodhead's themes though with different terminology). On the other hand, his hard distinction between the modern 'stable' or 'centered' self and the postmodern 'fluid' or 'decentered' self should be qualified. While his distinction accurately describes conceptual differences, it does not account for the complexity of modernity or postmodernity from a historical perspective (i.e., granted conceptual philosophical differences, actual people living within those cultural phases are not ideal types).

[10] Grenz, *The Social God and the Relational Self*, 96–97, and "The Social God," 35–38. These correspond to Charles Taylor's two versions of human agency: the self engaged in free, disengaged subjectivity and the self engaged in expressivist self-understanding (*Sources of the Self*, 106).

[11] Quoted in Grenz, *The Social God and the Relational Self*, 65. See also F. LeRon Shults, *Reforming Theological Anthropology: After the Philosophical Turn to Relationality* (Grand Rapids: Eerdmans, 2003), 31, 168, 225.

definition was dependent upon Aristotle's distinction between substances and accidents, with the implication that *person* belongs to the realm of unchanging substance or essence rather than the realm of changeable characteristics.[12] Boethius put forth an essentialist view of personhood in which the inner *essence* of a person is stable and remains unchanged by *accidental* factors, such as time (or historical development), the body, or relationships.[13]

Later, Enlightenment thinkers built upon this individualist conception of the rational self. Descartes, representing the rationalist stream of Enlightenment thought, conceived of the human person as a thinking substance. For Descartes, a person is an autonomous subject that exercises rationality to gain knowledge through contemplating the universal truths of reason (mathematics being a preeminent discipline).[14] Rather than turning to inwardness as a way of finding oneself in God (as with Augustine), the Cartesian self turns within in order to discover the autonomous power of reason to order the world. Hence Descartes's notorious declaration, "I think therefore I am." Locke, representing the empiricist stream of Enlightenment thought, envisioned the human person as a disengaged self-conscious being that gains knowledge not by contemplating universal rational truths but by objectively employing proper methods to analyze and manipulate empirical data. For Locke, the key property of personhood is self-awareness or self-consciousness, which elevates a person above the level of animal instinct to be a "disengaged subject of rational control".[15] Charles Taylor calls Locke's view of personhood the "punctual" or "neutral" self, since "the self is defined in abstraction from any constitutive concerns", its only constitutive property being self-awareness.[16] Kant's philosophy added the element of universality to the emerging modern picture of the individual, rational, autonomous, disengaged self. In contrast with empiricism, which held that the mind begins as a blank slate and is passive in the knowing process (the senses are central and formational for the mind), Kant argued for the centrality of the mind as the agent that actively organizes and systematizes raw data provided by

---

[12] Grenz, *The Social God and the Relational Self*, 66.

[13] Bonhoeffer calls this conception of personhood 'atomistic', though in Bonhoeffer's context this theory arose from Kant's distinction between the *noumenal* and *phenomenal* realms (one's personal center is a *thing-in-itself* and remains unaffected by social relationships). See Dietrich Bonhoeffer, *Sanctorum Communio: A Theological Study of the Sociology of the Church*, vol. 1 of *Dietrich Bonhoeffer Works*, ed. Clifford J. Green, trans. Reinhard Krauss and Nancy Lukens (Minneapolis: Fortress, 1998), 38–40, 252–57.

[14] Grenz, *The Social God and the Relational Self*, 70.

[15] Taylor, *Sources of the Self*, 49.

[16] Taylor notes that "Locke recognizes that we are not indifferent to ourselves; but he has no inkling of the self as a being which essentially is constituted by a certain mode of self concern—in contrast to the concern we cannot but have about the quality of our experiences as pleasurable or painful" (*Sources of the Self*, 49). See also Gregersen, "Varieties of Personhood," 2.

the senses.[17] It achieves this through an *a priori* synthesis, a process called transcendental apperception, in which perceived reality is filtered through universal categories of reason already present in the mind, such as space and time. In so doing the mind takes an active role in constructing reality as it is perceived by the knower through rational, universal categories of reason. In light of this, Kant recognized that there must be a distinction between reality itself, which he termed the *noumenal* realm, and reality as we perceive it to be, which he termed the *phenomenal* realm. The implication of this is that the individual knowing subject becomes the center of reality, through which all of reality is mediated and interpreted. This did not imply radical subjectivism (much less relativism) for Kant, because it was the subject's grasp of *universal and objective reason* that Kant emphasized. This leads to radical subjectivism only when a belief in the universality and objectivity of reason is rejected, as in postmodern subjectivism. Moreover, since it operates by using universal categories of reason, which are accessible to all, the individual thinking subject attains universal knowledge of self and world. As Grenz puts it, the self, in knowing itself, thereby knows all selves as well as the structure of any and every possible self.[18]

According to Grenz, the Enlightenment's emphasis upon subjectivity and empiricism affected the later development of the Puritan and Pietist movements, as well as the evangelical awakenings of the eighteenth century. For example, the Puritans debated empirical evidences for the assurance of their election.[19] The Pietists emphasized a religion of the heart, which "shifted the locus of true Christianity from baptism to personal conversion, from the objective to the subjective, from the external to the internal, from the rites of the faith community to the divine work within the individual soul."[20] However, this emphasis on interiority did not lead to passivity and quietism.[21] To the contrary,

---

[17] Hence Kant's understanding of the human person as a pure rational agent (Taylor, *Sources of the Self*, 12; Gregersen, "Varieties of Personhood," 3).

[18] Grenz, *The Social God and the Relational Self*, 77.

[19] See also Carter Lindberg, "Introduction," in *The Pietist Theologians*, ed. Carter Lindberg (Malden, MA: Blackwell, 2005), 11. Lindberg traces the roots of this development to the Reformed Pietist William Perkins.

[20] Grenz, *The Social God and the Relational Self*, 81. For the significance of empiricism for John Wesley and the early developing Wesleyan movement, see Henry D. Rack, *Reasonable Enthusiast: John Wesley and the Rise of Methodism* (London: Epworth, 2002), 32–33, 167–69, 383–88. Rack refers to Wesley as a "reasonable enthusiast," being "rational in form but enthusiast in substance." See also F. Dreyer, "Faith and Experience in the Thought of John Wesley," *American Historical Review* 88 (1983): 12–30.

[21] Lindberg, "Introduction," 7. Johannes Wallmann provides a helpful summary statement: "Pietism pressed for the individualization and interiorization of the religious life, developed new forms of personal piety and communal life, led to sweeping reforms in theology and the church, and left profound marks on the social and cultural life of the countries grasped by it." Wallman, *Der Pietismus*, vol. 4/01 of *Die Kirche*

early Pietists such as Philipp Jakob Spener emphasized holistic transformation of individuals and society.[22] Evangelicals, who inherited aspects from both Puritanism and Pietism, focused on the centrality of a personal conversion experience, through which believers gained assurance of their salvation.[23] As Grenz puts it, "the believing soul not only gains mastery over self but thereby also tests and knows with certainty the status of being the recipient of God's salvation."[24] In parallel with the new scientific method's focus on experimentation, eighteenth century evangelicals often referred to their own approach as "experimental religion", meaning religious faith tested and proved by experience.[25] This approach, combined with a stress on growing in holiness (or perfection) fit with the Enlightenment impulse toward self mastery or improvement and opened the door to what Grenz calls the "self-sufficient, self-constructing, therapeutic self" of modern psychology.[26] Grenz does not consider whether the

---

in ihrer Geschichte (Göttttingen: Vandenhoeck and Ruprecht, 1990), 7. Quoted in Lindberg, "Introduction," 4.

[22] Spener's most famous book, *Pia Desideria* (published in 1675) envisioned the reformation of society through the ongoing reformation of the church. In this work, Spener offered six concrete reform proposals: (1) a more comprehensive use of Scripture by clergy and laity; (2) the establishment and exercise of a lay spiritual priesthood; (3) a stress upon righteous Christian living; (4) better participant conduct in religious controversies; (5) a pious reform of theological education; and (6) the preaching of sermons that would produce faith and its fruits. K. James Stein, "Philipp Jakob Spener (1635–1705)," in *The Pietist Theologians*, ed. Carter Lindberg (Malden, MA: Blackwell, 2005), 84–85.

[23] See Timothy Larsen, "Defining and Locating Evangelicalism," in *The Cambridge Companion to Evangelical Theology* (Cambridge: Cambridge University Press, 2007), 10–12.

[24] Grenz, *The Social God and the Relational Self*, 85. A classic example is the account of John Wesley's conversion. In 1738, at a meeting in Aldersgate, Wesley experienced a deep, personal encounter with God and suddenly understood the significance of the doctrine of justification by faith for his own life. In his words, "I felt my heart strangely warmed. I felt I did trust Christ, Christ alone for salvation; and an assurance was given to me that had had taken away *my* sins, even *mine*, and saved *me* from the law of sin and death." John Wesley, *The Works of John Wesley*, vol. 1 (Grand Rapids: Zondervan, 1958), 103.

[25] Speaking of John Wesley, David Hempton writes, "His teaching on experience and assurance, really a complex mixture of Lockean empiricism and the witness of the Spirit, was designed to show that the Christian believer can 'know' that s/he is saved because 'the Spirit witnesses with his spirit that he is a child of God.'" Hempton, "John Wesley (1703–1791)," in *The Pietist Theologians*, ed. Carter Lindberg (Malden, MA: Blackwell, 2005), 258. This is part of what is meant by the term 'experimental religion' in the Wesleyan movement (257).

[26] Grenz, *The Social God and the Relational Self*, 84, 86. The relationship between Pietism and the Enlightenment is complex and not strictly linear in either direction. Carter Lindberg refers to Pietism and Enlightenment as "sibling movements," but stresses that the latter cannot account for the complexity, influence, and spiritual depth of the former. For example, the post-millennial eschatology in Spener's Pie-

Enlightenment impulse toward self-mastery had deeper roots in the historic Christian tradition. While the Enlightenment ideal proposed *autonomous* self-mastery, the notion of *self-development in relationship with God* actually has deep Christian roots, evident, for example, in the patristic notion of *theosis*.[27]

Grenz attributes the emergence of the therapeutic self to theorists such as William James, Eric Fromm, and especially Abraham Maslow.[28] James abandoned transcendental views of the mind, including its relation to the soul, and instead promoted a functional or utilitarian understanding that associates mental activity strictly with the selection of means to attain ends. For James, only actions that show a deliberate choice of means to accomplish specific goals can properly be called expressions of the mind. Eric Fromm also stressed a teleological approach to mental activity (connecting means to ends), but believed that psychologists were mistaken to abandon concepts such as the soul or human nature. Fromm believed that mental health should help individuals achieve aims that are not only deliberate, but, more importantly and specifically, serve the fulfilment of human nature as defined by qualities such as independence, integrity, and the ability to love. Maslow also believed that psychology should assist people in realizing the full potential of their inherent human nature. He proposed a hierarchy of needs that moved from basic or survival needs (e.g., food, shelter, sex) to more abstract, advanced stages of self-actualization.[29] Essentially, Maslow combined an instrumental approach to rationality with an essentialist conception of human nature to propose his theory of self-actualization aided by the therapeutic practice of the psychologist. Significantly, his conception of essential human nature deliberately rested on biological observations rather than theological or philosophical assumptions. He envi-

---

tism preceded the Enlightenment's concern for self-improvement. See Lindberg, "Introduction," 12.

[27] Athanasius articulates the basic meaning of *theosis* as follows: "For he was made man that we might be made God" (meaning not that we literally become God but that we are drawn to share in the divine life, because Christ shared in our humanity). See *On the Incarnation of the Word* 54.3, in *NPNF2–04: Athanasius: Select Works and Letters*, ed. Philip Schaff (New York: Christian Literature, 1892), 65. In chapter five, I develop this theme in terms of the basic, created "eschatological openness" of human beings toward God, others, and the future.

[28] Grenz, *The Social God and the Relational Self*, 88–96.

[29] Maslow's proposal of "self-actualization" or "full-humanness" rested on three assumptions. First, man has an essential nature with biological needs befitting that nature (and these needs are good or neutral, not evil). Second, full health and normal development require the actualization of this nature, but many people encounter obstacles to this or pursue a misconstrued nature. Third, psychology is necessary to uncover and correct the misunderstanding or denial of this essential nature. See Abraham Maslow, *Motivation and Personality* (New York: Harper and Row, 1954), 340.

sioned the quest for meaning and self-fulfillment as a secular rather than a religious enterprise.[30]

The self-focused, self-expressive self
The second major conception of the self that emerged in modernity is what Grenz calls the "self-focused, self-expressive self". This conception also has roots in Augustine's turn inward, but focuses on individual self-expression rather than self-mastery. It posits a self that is unique and particular, rather than ideal and universal, a "self-focused rather than an essence-focused self."[31] Early representative thinkers, such as Montaigne and Rousseau, were not satisfied with previous attempts to found the self by means of a purported universal human nature. They proposed that human nature is person-specific, thus true self knowledge is attained not by means of a detached scientific method but by contemplating one's thoughts and feelings through introspection and autobiography. According to Rousseau, the foundational orientation of the human person is toward self-preservation. The passions (including love) arise out of and function to preserve the self. Since Rousseau regards the inner nature of the person as essentially good, the purpose of introspection is not to master the self in accordance with an external standard but to discover the goodness already present within and bring it to explicit expression. The goal is increasingly to be oneself.[32]

The Romantic Movement built upon the legacy of Rousseau's emphases on introspection and the uniqueness of the individual, but also aimed for universality through the individual person's intuition of being connected with the wholeness of reality. Romanticism involved a quasi-religious awareness of an energy, presence, or cosmic self animating the world and every creature within it. For example, Emerson conceived of God as a dynamic mover of the cosmos, an "Over-Soul" present within the human mind as all-embracing, transcendent Reason. Correspondingly, he viewed other people as lenses though which a person reads her own mind. In light of this, he saw the self not as a static reality but a continuing goal to be attained.[33] Similar ideas were expressed within an explicitly theistic framework, as for example with Schleiermacher's stress on "feeling", described as God-consciousness, absolute dependence, a "sense and taste for the infinite," and an intuition of "the unity of all things".[34] The Romantic Movement thus retained the Enlightenment's ideal of a centered self, but

---

[30] By *secular*, I am referring here to the modern notion of a distinct sphere autonomous from the *sacred*. However, to anticipate what I will argue later in chapters four and seven, from a Christian perspective the secular has renewed significance and integrity in light of the Incarnation of Jesus Christ.
[31] Grenz, *The Social God and the Relational Self*, 100.
[32] Grenz, *The Social God and the Relational Self*, 103–109.
[33] Grenz, *The Social God and the Relational Self*, 114.
[34] Friedrich Schleiermacher, *On Religion: Speeches to Its Cultured Despisers*, trans. John Oman (Westminster: John Knox, 1994), 7, 36, 39, 45, 77, 141, 237.

construed it as a self-expressing rather than a self-mastering centered self.[35] This self had its basis in the Romantic idea of the infinite within the finite, which gave it both a sense of continuity and a capacity to transcend its own particularity to achieve new possibilities.

The fragmentation of the self
The Romantic idea of the infinite within the finite was too unstable a center to sustain the self-expressing self.[36] It took for granted the Kantian distinction between *noumena* and *phenomena* and was vulnerable to the criticisms of philosophers such as Fichte and Schopenhauer. Fichte rejected Kant's *noumenal* realm of universal categories that structure the mind and focused instead on the thinking *I* as the ground of its own consciousness and knowledge. Accordingly, Fichte defined the *I* as the self that apprehends and thereby posits itself. Curtis Bowman explains that Fichte's self "is not a static thing with fixed properties, but rather a self-producing process", which implies that "it must be free, since in some as yet unspecified fashion it owes its existence to nothing but itself."[37] As a free act, this self-positing requires the deliberate exercise of the will.[38] Thus, while Kant attributes the perceiving and organizing of reality to the structures of the unconscious mind (beyond experience), Fichte attributes this process to the will. Schopenhauer accepted Fichte's emphasis on the will but made the innovative claim that the will is nonrational, arational, or irrational (whereas both Fichte and Kant viewed the will as rational). The will is the source of insatiable desire.[39] This move infused a degree of arbitrariness or meaninglessness into reality (because it is reconstructed by an irrational will). Nietzsche took Schopenhauer's claim a step further and argued that since all human claims to knowledge, truth, and moral values are meaningless and groundless, they are really just veiled assertions of the will to power. As Nietzsche put it, "A living thing seeks above all to *discharge* its strength—life itself is *Will to Power*."[40] In light of this, Nietzsche celebrated ambitious self-assertion and deplored the Judeo-Christian tradition's emphasis on humility and its ethic of empathy and responsibility for the weak, the poor, and the destitute.[41]

---

[35] Taylor, *Sources of the Self*, 12.
[36] Grenz, *The Social God and the Relational Self*, 118.
[37] Curtis Bowman, "Johann Gottlieb Fichte (1762–1814)," *Internet Encyclopedia of Philosophy*, D, para. 1, online: http://www.iep.utm.edu/fichtejg/
[38] Grenz, *The Social God and the Relational Self*, 118–22.
[39] Elaborating on Schopenhauer's thought, Taylor writes, "The will strives only to perpetuate itself and its objectifications, and what we think are our desires are in a sense only its unconscious strategies to achieve this end." (Taylor, *Sources of the Self*, 442.)
[40] Friedrich Nietzsche, *Beyond Good and Evil: Prelude to a Philosophy of the Future* (Mineolo: Dover, 1997), 10 (emphasis original).
[41] Nietzsche writes, "To demand of strength that it *not* express itself as strength, that it *not* be a desire to overwhelm, a desire to cast down, a desire to become lord, a thirst for enemies and resistances and triumphs, is just as nonsensical as to demand of

The final stage of the fragmentation of the self progresses through the structuralist, post-structuralist, and postmodern movements.[42] Saussure's structuralism maintained that a universal cultural system structures human mental processes and is evident in language and social institutions. It regarded modern ideas of selfhood as social constructs that influence and form the self, which has no control over the process. Grenz explains, "Similar to the unit of language, the individual (of whose mind language is the highest expression) is essentially a structure of intersecting relations. Like a linguistic expression, the self finds identity only through its place in the larger system."[43] This reflects Saussure's linguistic insight that meaning must be understood by analyzing not just individual words but the underlying structure of the whole language. The implication of the stucturalist perspective is that personal identity and selfhood can be understood only by analyzing the underlying societal structures in which the person is situated. Poststructuralists, in turn, agreed that human persons are the products of underlying social structures, but denied that these structures were inherent to a universal human condition. Michel Foucault, for instance, worried that his predecessors elevated universality and homogeneity while suppressing difference or otherness. Following Nietzsche, Foucault abandoned all pretence to objectivity and devoted his attention to the particular and different rather than the general and universal. One of the most significant universals that Foucault sought to undermine was the concept of human nature, which he claimed was nothing other than the projection of social norms and influences that had been unconsciously internalized. In so doing, he was able to posit the death of the self as dissolved into the structures of society, an extension of Nietzsche's analogy of the death of God.[44] Following Foucault, the postmodern ethos celebrates this demise of the self, believing that the modernist search for the true self, along with its emphasis on unity and self-mastery, was at best illusory and at worst oppressive. No longer seen as an agent of subjectivity overagainst real objects, the postmodern self is a self-referential system. This self is highly de-centered and fluid, finding its identity in its various relationships and interests. Lacking stability and continuity, one could potentially have as many selves as the number of social groups to which one belongs (professional, recreational, religious, virtual, etc.). In short, the self of postmodernity is an arbitrary bundle of fluctuating relationships, preferences, and expressions, with no

---

weakness that it express itself as strength." Nietzsche then goes on to exalt the Romans as most noble and strong and to castigate the Jews as being a weak "priestly people of *ressentiment* par excellence" (emphasis original). *On the Genealogy of Morals*, quoted from Robert C. Solomon, *Existentialism* (New York: Oxford University Press, 2005), 82–83. See also Taylor, *Sources of the Self*, 13.

[42] Grenz, *The Social God and the Relational Self*, 129–36.

[43] Grenz, *The Social God and the Relational Self*, 129. Similarly, Lévi-Strauss's structural anthropology envisioned the human person as the product of genetics, language, and culture-bound education.

[44] Grenz, "The Social God," 40.

transcendent reference point beyond the cultural web to anchor ultimate meaning.[45]

Abandonment of teleology

In order for human beings to make sense of their world, to orient themselves and make meaningful life decisions within it, they inevitably rely on what Charles Taylor calls "frameworks".[46] A framework is "that in virtue of which we make sense of our lives spiritually. Not to have a framework is to fall into a life which is spiritually senseless."[47] Much like the concept of a worldview, a framework provides a "background picture" or "ontological account" of one's basic intuitions and assumptions about the world and the meaning of life.[48] As such, it is the source of a person's ultimate values and commitments.[49] Frameworks often operate implicitly in our reasoning and decision making, even if we remain unaware of their existence or are unable to articulate them explicitly. Crucial to any framework is a set of what Taylor calls "qualitative distinctions", which are basic value distinctions enabling moral and practical judgment. Taylor explains, "To think, feel, judge within such a framework is to function with the sense that some action, or mode of life, or mode of feeling is incomparably higher than others which are more readily available to us."[50] The precise nature of the value distinctions vary; one might perceive a decision or course of action as being fuller, or purer, or deeper, or more admirable, or truer than alternatives. The point is that these basic value distinctions exist and structure our ways of seeing and judging. Taylor argues that such basic values are "incomparably higher" because they stand independent of our own desires and preferences as standards by which these are evaluated. They are "incomparable" in the sense that they cannot be measured quantitatively on the same scale as other ends and goods; they are qualitatively and definitively superior.

Frameworks are essential to human personhood for at least three reasons. First, as mentioned above, they provide the background assumptions (explicit or implicit) that enable our moral judgments and intuitions. As Taylor explains it,

---

[45] Taylor observes that a sense of meaninglessness defines the present age (*Sources of the Self*, 18).
[46] Taylor, *Sources of the Self*, 3–24.
[47] Taylor, *Sources of the Self*, 18.
[48] Taylor prefers to speak of what he calls "social imaginaries" rather than worldviews. His point is that the term 'worldview' tends to prioritize intellect and theory whereas "social imaginary" emphasizes that our vision of the world is itself embodied within traditions, rituals, symbols, and narratives. Thus, for Taylor, the social imaginary is a more holistic, integrative notion than worldview.
[49] Examples of frameworks that Taylor provides include the honour ethic (ancient warrior or citizen-soldier), self-mastery through reason (rationalism), vision and expressive power (Romanticism), and naturalist reductionism (*Sources of the Self*, 20–22).
[50] Taylor, *Sources of the Self*, 19.

To articulate a framework is to explicate what makes sense of our moral responses. That is, when we try to spell out what it is that we presuppose when we judge that a certain form of life is truly worthwhile, or place our dignity in a certain achievement or status, or define our moral obligations in a certain manner, we find ourselves articulating inter alia what I have been calling here 'frameworks.'[51]

Second, frameworks are constitutive of human identity and agency.[52] The question "who am I?" cannot be answered adequately simply by stating one's name and genealogy. A meaningful answer requires knowledge of one's deepest commitments and identifications (Taylor's "qualitative distinctions", which he also speaks of as "defining orientations"). Frameworks are formative for personal identity because they provide the stable background structures through which one can determine where one stands concerning what is good, valuable, worthwhile, or admirable and from which one can make sensible decisions.[53] Accordingly, the disruption of one's framework leads to a crisis of identity, a sense of losing oneself resulting from confusion over or inability to define what is ultimately significant and meaningful. Third, frameworks are necessary because human beings cannot function without some orientation toward the good. As Taylor puts it, "we are only selves insofar as we move in a certain space of questions, as we seek and find an orientation to the good."[54] Religious frameworks define the good in relation to God or some other notion of transcendent, ultimate reality, while secular frameworks offer definitions according to strictly historical (and typically modern) principles, such as the struggle between good and evil, or progress and reaction, or socialism and exploitation.[55] In any case, one's orientation to the good requires both a framework that defines it and a commitment on the part of the agent to move toward it. For example, if one's framework is defined by a modern narrative of progress, one might envision the good as overcoming the limits of nature or the social boundaries of particular traditions to achieve the goal of self mastery and independence, accountable only to universal reason. One might then reject religious commitments, which are perceived as arising within particular communities and having a tendency to venerate the past.

The notion of being orientated toward the good corresponds with a teleological view of the human person, in which human beings are seen to possess a specific nature with certain aims and goals that move them toward a specific

---

[51] Taylor, *Sources of the Self*, 26.
[52] Taylor, *Sources of the Self*, 27.
[53] Taylor writes, "[I]t belongs to human agency to exist in a space of questions about strongly valued goods, prior to all choice or adventitious cultural change" (*Sources of the Self*, 31).
[54] Taylor, *Sources of the Self*, 34; see also 41–45.
[55] Taylor, *Sources of the Self*, 45.

telos.[56] The end or *telos* need not be defined too narrowly, as if the purpose and destiny of human beings could be reduced to a single rational principle (e.g., freedom) or calculated as the best outcome for the greatest number of people (as in consequentialism). To avoid such reductionism, a teleological approach must offer a *thick description* of human life, which takes into account the role of frameworks or worldviews, as well as the social, cultural, and linguistic situatedness of human existence.[57] Moreover, it must avoid defining the human *telos* in essentialist terms, depicting human nature as something static or fully predetermined, genetically, socially, metaphysically, or otherwise.[58] Positively, it has to account for the historical quality of human existence, as human beings find their identity and make meaningful choices in the present, having been formed in the past and in anticipation of the future.[59] Human persons discover their identity and purpose through an ongoing process of being and becoming.[60] As Alasdair MacIntyre puts it, to be oriented toward the human *telos* is "to find oneself placed at a certain point on a journey with set goals; to move through life is to make progress – or to fail to make progress – toward a given end."[61] Thus, a human life directed toward the human *telos* is characterized by both continuity and development, which are held together in what MacIntyre calls "the unity of a narrative quest".[62]

Despite the importance of frameworks and narrative for meaningfully human existence, contemporary culture largely rejects the idea that human persons have a specific *telos*. This rejection has roots in the Enlightenment and developed in two trajectories. The first trajectory goes back to the seventeenth and eighteenth centuries, when several thinkers in England and France transferred the scientific conceptual framework of physics to their understanding of human nature and behaviour, including the overarching view that all of reality is gov-

---

[56] Alasdair MacIntyre, *After Virtue: A Study in Moral Theology* (Notre Dame: University of Notre Dame Press, 1984), 148.
[57] The term *thick description* comes from Clifford Geertz, *The Interpretation of Cultures* (New York: Basic, 1973), 3–30.
[58] Christian Smith, *What is a Person? Rethinking Humanity, Social Life, and the Moral Good from the Person Up* (Chicago: University of Chicago Press, 2010), 10; James C. Peterson, *Genetic Turning Points: The Ethics of Human Genetic Intervention* (Grand Rapids, Eerdmans, 2001), 283–84.
[59] "To be historic means that I must be capable of making a succession of 'events' a narrative – not just any narrative, but a narrative that is sufficient to give me a sense of self, one which looks not only to my past but points to the future, thereby giving my life a telos and direction." Stanley Hauerwas, *The Peaceable Kingdom: A Primer in Christian Ethics* (Notre Dame: University of Notre Dame Press, 1983), 36.
[60] As James Peterson writes, "The telos is not a set image of what human beings already are or should be, but rather one to be discovered, one that changes and develops as human beings change and develop" (Peterson, *Changing Human Nature*, 88).
[61] MacIntyre, *After Virtue*, 34.
[62] MacIntyre, *After Virtue*, 219.

erned by natural physical laws.[63] To achieve scientific credibility, such thinkers purged the human sciences of all speculative references to human intentions, purposes, and reasons for actions, because such references presupposed the centrality of the beliefs of the human agents—and beliefs were not properly the subject matter of scientific inquiry.[64] This led eventually to a reductionist understanding of the human person in the social sciences, which claimed the ability to explain and predict human behaviour on the basis of pseudo-scientific, law-like generalizations.[65] We will return to the problem of reductionism shortly (see below). The second trajectory is rooted in the philosophical struggle to free the human person from the confines of essentialism and Idealism, a struggle exemplified by existentialist thinkers such as Jean Paul Sartre. Existentialists sought to refute the tendency of traditional philosophy, from Plato through to Hegel, to give precedence to essence over existence.[66] In contrast, Sartre, taking an explicitly atheistic viewpoint, argued that if God or Ultimate Being or The Good does not exist, then human nature, identity, and purpose cannot be determined by metaphysical or theological concepts. They must be derived solely from human existence as human self-creation.[67] Actually, for Sartre, strictly speaking there is no such thing as human nature, since there is no God to conceive it. Human beings are free to determine their own identities, purposes, values, and goals.[68] As Sartre puts it, "Man is nothing else but what he

---

[63] MacIntyre, *After Virtue*, 83.

[64] MacIntyre, *After Virtue*, 80–83. MacIntyre writes, "The notion of 'fact' with respect to human beings is thus transformed in the transition from the Aristotelian to the mechanist view. On the former view human action, because it is to be explained teleologically, not only can, but must be, characterized with reference to the hierarchy of goods which provide the ends of human action. On the latter view human action not only can, but must be, characterized without any reference to such goods. On the former view the facts about human action included the facts about what is valuable to human beings (and *not* just the facts about what they think to be valuable); on the latter view there are no facts about what is valuable." (84)

[65] For MacIntyre's narration and critique of this development in the social sciences, see *After Virtue*, 88–107. See also Christian Smith's arguments for the importance of ontology for the social sciences and the need for social scientists to engage ontological questions via critical realist philosophy (Smith, *What is a Person?*, esp. 90–98 but argued throughout the book).

[66] See, for example: Simone De Beauvoir, *The Ethics of Ambiguity*, trans. Bernard Frechtman (New York: Citidel Press; Kensington Publishing, 1948), 44–51, 128–30; Christine Daigle, ed., *Existentialist Thinkers and Ethics* (Montreal; Kingston: McGill-Queens University Press, 2006), 6–8; Nino Langiulli, "Two Cheers for Existentialism," *Logos: A Journal of Catholic Thought and Culture* 7, no. 4 (2004): 95–96; Nietzsche, *Beyond Good and Evil*, x, 10, 55–70; Shults, *Reforming Theological Anthropology*, chapters 2–3.

[67] Sartre, *Existentialism*, 15.

[68] Sartre writes, "If existence really does precede essence, there is no explaining things away by reference to a fixed and given human nature. In other words, there is no determinism, man is free, man is freedom" (*Existentialism*, 21–22).

makes of himself."⁶⁹ Without recourse to a normative human *telos*, human beings are free to create their own values.

Corresponding to this rejection of teleological approaches to human personhood is the rejection of the frameworks or over-arching narratives that define the good and our relation to it. Premodern societies generally viewed individual human persons within a broader context of social groups and corresponding roles. A religious worldview, sustained by the stories, rituals, and traditions of particular communities, undergirded these groups and roles by integrating the structure of the cosmos and the place of humans within it. Enlightenment thinkers attempted to redefine human nature according to strictly rational and objective foundations (pure reason or empirical observation) without reference to religion or tradition. Post-Enlightenment thinkers, in turn, uncovered the hidden assumptions and values implicit within these purportedly rational and objective foundations, which their predecessors took for granted. While they largely accepted the Enlightenment critique of premodern worldviews as being superstitious, mythical, and unscientific, post-Enlightenment critics exposed their forebears' own dependence on modern but equally mythical (because not based on pure reason or empirical data) underlying assumptions, beliefs, and grand narratives about the nature and purpose of the world and of human beings. Rather than attempting to replace these with even more objective and universal foundations, postmodern perspectives embrace the demise of all foundations and grand narratives, emphasizing instead the particular, contextual, heterogeneous, and interpretive quality of all human knowledge, experience, and conceptions of meaning and purpose.⁷⁰ The ensuing postmodern ethos is radically individualistic, rejecting not only the holistic or integrated worldviews of traditional societies but also the qualified individualism of modernity.⁷¹ Lacking a common *telos*, each individual must invent her own story about the meaning of life as well as her own purpose and destiny within it. When one considers the religious and cultural pluralism, moral relativism, and unrestrained consumerism of contemporary liberal democracies, this individualism becomes even more pronounced. Consequently, as Stanley Hauerwas argues, the only common story we share in contemporary liberal culture is that *we have no story* except that

---

⁶⁹ Sartre, *Existentialism*, 15.

⁷⁰ Hence Lyotard's famous depiction of the postmodern condition as "incredulity toward metanarratives." Jean-François Lyotard, *The Postmodern Condition: A Report on Knowledge*, trans. Geoff Bennington and Brian Massumi (Minneapolis: University of Minnesota Press, 1984), xxiv.

⁷¹ While some strands of modernity prioritized the individual (e.g., Western, democratic societies), others emphasised the collective (e.g., North-eastern communist countries). Moreover, even those that emphasized the individual aspired to universality and often envisioned the human race as being united by a common metanarrative, such as a collective journey toward freedom, or scientific and technological progress, or the recognition of universal human rights, or the vision of world peace and a united human family. In contrast, radical postmodernism emphasizes the individual while rejecting all such metanarratives.

which we choose for ourselves. The situation is deeply ironic and disturbingly self-deceptive, because the untold story *that we have no story* subversively impacts our values, judgments, and aspirations, lending credence (in a manner that is existentially powerful but rationally incoherent) to contemporary ideals such as tolerance, pluralism, and personal autonomy.[72] As Hauerwas observes, "The story that liberalism teaches us is that we have no story, and as a result we fail to notice how deeply that story determines our lives."[73]

The problem of scientific reductionism

In the seventeenth and eighteenth centuries the human sciences began to discuss human existence by borrowing from the conceptual framework of the physical sciences. In so doing, they purged their inquiries of all considerations of human beliefs, intentions, and purposes, which were not considered to be the proper domain of the hard sciences.[74] This began a trend that led gradually to various reductionist conceptions of human personhood and existence.[75] For example, in psychology Freud conceptualized "a kind of natural science of the mind", which focused not on questions of agency but on the mechanism underlying personality formation (which he termed "identification").[76] B.F. Skinner's behaviourism, indebted to empiricist epistemology, viewed the person as a blank slate whose personality and behaviour are shaped through operant conditioning. Skinner appealed to the mechanism of operant conditioning as a "technology of behaviour" to explain and offer solutions to a wide range of human experiences and problems, including language acquisition, education, politics, and culture.[77] In the 1970s, the sociobiology movement sought to account for human social behaviour purely on the basis of biology. As it developed, its scope expanded toward explaining all of human behaviour according to biological natural selection.[78] In extreme cases it reduced complex human subjects to

---

[72] James Logan, "Liberalism, Race, and Stanley Hauerwas," *Cross Currents* 55 (Winter 2006): 523.

[73] Stanley Hauerwas, *A Community of Character: Toward a Constructive Christian Social Ethic* (Notre Dame: University of Notre Dame Press, 1981), 84.

[74] MacIntyre, *After Virtue*, 80–83.

[75] While such reductionism has particularly devastating implications for the humanities, it also has a detrimental effect on higher education as a whole. Originally, universities were founded to serve the betterment of society by cultivating exemplary human beings, who were good citizens of character, wisdom, and discernment. In contrast, the contemporary university lacks a deep sense purpose and holism (evidenced by disciplinary fragmentation). Devoid of any underlying shared foundation, universities are increasingly adopting a consumerist approach to education. See Norman Klassen and Jens Zimmermann, *The Passionate Intellect: Incarnational Humanism and the Future of University Education* (Grand Rapids: Baker Academic, 2008), 14–15.

[76] Taylor, *Sources of the Self*, 446–47; See also Grenz, *The Social God and the Relational Self*, 125–26.

[77] Louis M. Smith, "B.F. Skinner," *Prospects* XXIV, no. 3/4 (1994), accessed online: http://www.ibe.unesco.org/publications/ThinkersPdf/skinnere.PDF, pp. 3–7.

[78] Richard Joyce, *The Evolution of Morality* (Cambridge, MA: MIT, 2006), 4–5.

simplistic evolutionary mechanisms, for example Michael Ruse's depiction of morality as "a collective illusion foisted upon us by our genes".[79] Reductionism also had an impact on the study of religion, as university religious studies departments sought to objectify religion by discussing it purely in descriptive, historical terms, as opposed to making constructive theological proposals or evaluating religious truth claims.[80] A similar trend is observable in the field of biblical studies, as scholars focused on scientific approaches to biblical interpretation (e.g., the historical critical method) and began to prioritize method and historical detail over theological output.[81] These scholars emphasized the (purported) objectivity and detachment of the interpretive task, which the interpreter conducted by employing objective analytical methods of grammatical, textual, and historical analysis.[82] Such interpreters tended to distrust or even disown the role of faith, doctrine, and tradition, which they considered to be too subjective and more likely to distort the text than to clarify it.[83]

---

[79] Michael Ruse, *Taking Darwin Seriously: A Naturalistic Approach to Philosophy* (Oxford: Blackwell, 1986), 253.

[80] George M. Marsden, *The Outrageous Idea of Christian Scholarship* (New York: Oxford University Press, 1997), 22.

[81] As N.T. Wright quips, "many systematic theologians . . . have become impatient with waiting for the mountains of historical footnotes to give birth to the mouse of theological insight." N.T. Wright, "The Letter to the Galatians: Exegesis and Theology," in *Between Two Horizons: Spanning New Testament Studies and Systematic Theology*, (Grand Rapids: Eerdmans, 2000), 206.

[82] R.R. Reno, "Series Preface," in *Brazos Theological Commentary on the Bible: Matthew* (Grand Rapids: Brazos, 2006), 12–14. See also Stanley E. Porter, "The Future of Theology and Religious Studies from a Confessional Standpoint," *McMaster Journal of Theology and Ministry* 11 (2009–10): 123–29.

[83] This trend in biblical theology can be traced back to J.P. Gabler, who in his inaugural lecture at the University of Altdorf in 1787 distinguished between biblical and systematic theology as co-existing yet separate disciplines. (See Johann P. Gabler, "An Oration on the Proper Distinction Between Biblical and Dogmatic Theology and the Specific Objectives of Each," in *Old Testament Theology: Flowering and Future* [Winona Lake: Eisenbrauns, 2004], 501–506). For Gabler, biblical theology is a descriptive, historical undertaking. It seeks to uncover the thought of the biblical authors, by isolating and abstracting the trans-historical truths contained in their writings from their historically conditioned expression. Once this is accomplished, the ideas of particular authors can be analyzed and compared with those of other authors, and then the themes of various eras (i.e., Old and New Testaments) are analyzed and compared. In contrast, systematic theology is a didactic, prescriptive enterprise. Its task is to articulate for the present age the timeless, normative truths discovered by biblical theology. To accomplish this, a theologian "philosophises rationally about divine things, according to the measure of his ability or of the times, age, place, sect, school, and other similar factors" (Gabler, "Oration," 501). For more on this development, see: Gerhard F. Hasel, "The Relationship Between Biblical Theology and Systematic Theology," *Trinity Journal* 5 NS (1984): 113–27; B.C. Ollenburger, "Biblical Theology: Situating the Discipline," in *Understanding the Word: Essays in Honour of Bernard W. Andersen* (Sheffield: JSOT Press, 1985), 37–62; and Kevin J.

A common problematic feature of scientific reductionist perspectives is that they deny altogether the necessity of frameworks, as well as the importance of narrative contextualization or "thick description" to account for the wholeness of reality.[84] Instead, they attempt to explain reality on the basis of a single principle, method, or discipline. Donald MacKay refers to such reductionism as "nothing buttery", since a phenomenon is described as "nothing but" a manifestation of some elemental part (e.g., human love is nothing but chemical reactions in the brain).[85] However, reality is complex, multi-layered, and thus irreducible to some elemental part. Of course, scientific explanations themselves are not problematic; they only become so when they claim to explain human existence *comprehensively*. Human life simply cannot be described comprehensively from one point of view.

James Peterson provides an insightful analogy to stress this point.[86] A physicist identifies an instance of a molecule movement, but then a chemist observes that this movement can be explained further as glucose converting to lactic acid to generate ATP. A biochemist then describes the event as being part of the contraction and release of a particular muscle. Next, a physiologist adds another layer by noticing that the muscle is increasing the tension within a human vocal chord. Then, a neurologist clarifies that a deliberate attempt is being made to produce sound, namely a musical note. A musician recognizes the sound as singing and that the person is performing a piece from an oratorio called *The Messiah*. An economist points out that the singer is a professional musician being paid to perform. But then a sociologist suggests that something larger is taking place, because the singer is performing with a choir and derives meaning and fulfilment from her relationships with other people in the choir. Finally, a theologian observes that the performance features sacred music and that the

---

Vanhoozer, "Exegesis and Hermeneutics," in *New Dictionary of Biblical Theology* (Leicester/Downers Grove: InterVarsity Press, 2000), 52–64. By contrast, R.R. Reno (the series editor of the *Brazos Theological Commentary on the Bible*) argues that "doctrine provides structure and cogency to scriptural interpretation" ("Series Preface," 12).

[84] Taylor, *Sources of the Self*, 30–31, 59–60. Worse than being reductionist, such accounts can even lead to a pathological view of the human person. In response to the hypothetical possibility of a person operating without frameworks, Taylor asserts: "Such a person wouldn't know where he stood on issues of fundamental importance, would have no orientation in these issues whatever, wouldn't be able to answer for himself on them. If one wants to add to the portrait by saying that the person doesn't suffer this absence of frameworks as a lack, isn't in other words in a crisis at all, then one rather has a picture of frightening dissociation. In practice, we would see such a person as deeply disturbed." (31)

[85] Donald M. MacKay, *Human Science and Human Dignity* (Downers Grove: InterVarsity Press, 1979), 27, 48.

[86] I have borrowed and paraphrased the following analogy from Peterson, *Genetic Turning Points*, 32.

whole exercise is deeply spiritual, as an expression of the singer's personal faith in God.

The illustration demonstrates both the power and limits of scientific explanation. While reductionist accounts should be rejected because they distort our picture of the interconnected wholeness of reality, non-reductive scientific insights and perspectives are helpful and welcome as we seek to understand human nature and personhood in breathtaking detail and complexity. In the latter approach both nature and nurture are crucial to the formation and development of personhood, hence the human person "emerges as a result of the *interference* between the biological roots of human personhood and the cultural nexus of which any human person is part."[87] Unfortunately, many traditional ontological accounts (theological or otherwise) do not sufficiently accommodate the valid contributions of recent scientific discoveries.[88] For example, conceptions of human personhood that qualitatively distinguish humans from animals on the basis of their possession of some innate capacity (e.g., reasoning, emotion, etc.) are increasingly proving to be untenable.[89] As another example, conceptions of personhood that are based on simplistic metaphysical dualisms are giving way to more integrative theories (e.g., mind–body holism and non-reductive physicalism).[90] According to D. Gareth Jones, "The old distinctions between brain, mind, and soul appear, at best, quaint and, at worst, a hindrance to understanding the human condition."[91] More recent theories identifying complex neural processes and integrating mechanisms, such as supervenience, emergence, and top-down causation, are helping scientists to transcend the now obsolete dichotomous choice between dualist and reductive materialist views of human nature.[92] A third example is that scientific advancements in our understanding

---

[87] Gregersen, "Varieties of Personhood," 6–7; cf. Seybold, Kevin S. Seybold, "Biology of Spirituality," *Perspectives on Science and Christian Faith* 62 (June 2010): 90–94.

[88] Gregerson also faults personalist and existentialist philosophies of the human person for bypassing insights from the natural sciences ("Varieties of Personhood," 7).

[89] Green, *Body, Soul, and Human Life*, 46, 65; Peterson, *Changing Human Nature*, 20. Many contemporary theological proposals distinguish humans from animals not on the basis of unique innate capacities but on the basis of a unique relationship with the Creator leading to a unique vocation or calling.

[90] See my article, "The Human Person in Contemporary Science and Theology," *Perspectives on Science and Christian Faith* 64, no. 2 (June 2012): 120–29. See also: Paul N. Markham, *Rewired: Exploring Religious Conversion* (Eugene: Pickwick, 2007), 103–104; Paul Moes, "Minding Emotions: The Embodied Nature of Emotional Self-Regulation," *Perspectives on Science and Christian Faith* 62 (June 2010): 75, 84–85; Shults, *Reforming Theological Anthropology*, 175–88.

[91] D. Gareth Jones, "Peering into People's Brains: Neuroscience's Intrusion into Our Inner Sanctum," *Perspectives on Science and Christian Faith* 62 (June 2010): 123.

[92] Niels Henrik Gregersen, "God's Public Traffic: Holist Versus Physicalist Supervenience," in *The Human Person in Science and Theology* (Grand Rapids: Eerdmans, 2000), 153–57; Philip Hefner, "Imago Dei: The Possibility and Necessity of the Human Person," In *The Human Person in Science and Theology* (Grand Rapids: Eerd-

of human evolution and genetic mutation have undermined essentialist views of the human person, which conceive of human nature as something static or fixed (e.g., Idealistic views rejected by existentialist thinkers such as Sartre and De Beauvoir).[93] In contrast, human nature is dynamic and changing.[94] Paradoxically, developing and improving one's nature *is part of human nature*. As James Peterson puts it, "human nature is constantly changing and, consciously or not, we play a role in what we become."[95]

In sum, advancements in neurology, physiology, biology, and other relevant sciences should inform our understanding of human personhood. Both the natural and human sciences are relevant to the discussion. Ignoring one in favour of the other inevitably leads to a distorted picture of human personhood resting on false dichotomies and polarizing arguments.

Loss of a theological narrative

However one assesses the merits of religion or its place in contemporary public life, it is difficult to deny that, at least in Western democratic countries, the Christian religion has provided a sense of stability to the concept of human personhood. Its doctrine of humanity made in the image of God played a crucial role in grounding the uniqueness and intrinsic value of human beings before God.[96] The doctrines of incarnation and resurrection strongly affirmed bodily existence and material reality as inherently good (though fallen and then redeemed).[97] The doctrine of the Trinity contributed a relational and dynamic

---

mans, 2000), 75–76; Markham, *Rewired*, 109–21; Peterson, *Changing Human Nature*, 22, 172 n.4.

[93] Peterson explains, "If we are convinced that evolution has adapted humanity so far, then the very nature of humanity is to continue to change and adapt to an environment quite different from that in the past" (*Changing Human Nature*, 119). See also Francis S. Collins, *The Language of God: A Scientist Presents Evidence for Belief* (New York: Free Press/Simon & Schuster, 2006) and Denis O. Lamoureux, *Evolutionary Creation: A Christian Approach to Evolution* (Eugene: Wipf and Stock, 2008).

[94] Peterson, *Changing Human Nature*, 81–82, 88–89, 101, 119, 127.

[95] Peterson, *Changing Human Nature*, 101. See also 10, 32, 54.

[96] The best recent treatment of this theme is David P. Gushee, *The Sacredness of Human Life: Why an Ancient Biblical Vision Is Key to the World's Future* (Grand Rapids: Eerdmans, 2013). See also: Agnes Cunningham, Donald Miller, and James E. Will, "Toward an Ecumenical Theology for Grounding Human Rights," *Soundings* 67 (Summer 1984): 213–14; Elshtain, "The Dignity of the Human Person," 63; Jürgen Moltmann, *On Human Dignity: Political Theology and Ethics* (Minneapolis: Fortress, 1984), 10, 23, 25; Wolterstorff, *Justice*, 94–95, 341–52 (Wolterstorff argues that the doctrine of *imago Dei* contributes to the grounding human rights, though by itself it is not fully adequate to do so).

[97] Peterson, *Changing Human Nature*, 47–48, 65–66; N.T. Wright, *Surprised by Hope: Rethinking Heaven, the Resurrection, and the Mission of the Church* (New York: HarperOne, 2008), 149, 210, 221. Wright elsewhere states "The early Christians saw Jesus' resurrection as the action of the creator god to reaffirm the essential goodness of creation and, in an initial and representative act of new creation . . . through which

view of human personhood and community.[98] The bookending doctrines of creation and eschatology promoted a non-reductive, non-essentialist, teleological, historical framework that provided a sense of purpose, vocation, and destiny to human existence.[99] In sum, variations of the Christian vision have profoundly, though often subtly or even unconsciously, shaped the basic values and beliefs of Western civilizations.[100] Even Richard Rorty, a critic of Christianity, acknowledged the formational contribution that the Christian view of personhood bestowed to Western culture, a contribution which grounded notions of human dignity and respect as well as the formulation of human rights. Despite this observation, however, Rorty believed that since such values and rights are already firmly established in our present culture, we presently can and should dispense with our outmoded Christian heritage, particularly its doctrines and traditions.[101] Many others have expressed similar sentiments concerning other contributions of the Christian heritage, such as the emergence of science, democracy, capitalism, the abolishment of slavery, and the struggle for social and global justice.[102] The reigning contemporary posture seems to be: Granted, Christianity played an important role in establishing and promoting modern views of personhood along with corresponding societal values, but in our present pluralistic context it is in our collective best interest to retain the ethical kernel (human personhood, freedom, worth, autonomy, etc.) but dispense with the religious shell. Contemporary people want to hold on to a remnant of traditional moral values, but without accepting any transcendent basis for those values.[103]

---

the whole new creation could now come to birth." See N.T. Wright, *The Resurrection of the Son of God* (Minneapolis: Fortress, 2003), 729–30.

[98] Michael Novak, "The Judeo-Christian Foundation of Human Dignity, Personal Liberty, and the Concept of the Person," *Journal of Markets and Morality* 1 (October 1998): 114–15; T.F. Torrance, *The Christian Doctrine of God: One Being Three Persons* (New York: T & T Clark, 1996), 102, 160; John D. Zizioulas, *Being as Communion: Studies in Personhood and the Church* (Crestwood, NY: St. Vladimir's Seminary Press, 2002), 34–40.

[99] Cunningham et al., "Toward an Ecumenical Theology," 221–22; Shults, *Reforming Theological Anthropology*, 236–42.

[100] In section two I explicate these themes in much greater detail.

[101] See Wolterstorff, *Justice*, 320–21, 391.

[102] For the formative role Christianity played in these, see for example: Rodney Stark, *The Victory of Reason: How Christianity Led to Freedom, Capitalism, and Western Success* (New York: Random House, 2005) and *For the Glory of God: How Monotheism Led to Reformations, Science, Witch-hunts, and the End of Slavery* (Princeton: Princeton University Press, 2003); Novak, "The Judeo-Christian Foundation of Human Dignity," 107.

[103] Mark A. Noll, "What Happened to Christian Canada?" *Church History* 75 (June 2006): 261. Commenting on the Canadian context, Noll observes, "The social cohesion that the churches once provided is now offered by political and economic loyalties or by ideologies of toleration, personal growth, and multiculturalism." Noll comments that in the case of the United Church (the largest Canadian denomination),

The societal transformation of religious convictions and doctrines into secular sentiments and ideologies has its theological and epistemological roots in a process that began with Kant and culminated with Feuerbach (with implications developed by thinkers such as Freud and Marx). According to Kant, concepts such as God, freedom, and human personhood lie outside the bounds of reason; they exist only in the unknowable noumenal realm beyond the phenomenal realm of human sense perception. Despite this separation of noumena and phenomena, Kant preserved one access point into the noumenal world, namely morality. The universal experience of morality points to the existence of a universal moral law, which implies a Lawgiver. Kant writes, "Morality thus leads ineluctably to religion, through which it extends itself to the idea of a powerful moral Lawgiver, outside of mankind, for Whose will that is the final end (of creation) which at the same time can and ought to be man's final end."[104] By this move, Kant reversed the traditional theological method of founding morality upon the existence of God and God's character, purposes, and revealed will. For Kant, God is not the epistemological foundation of ethics but the logically necessarily *postulate* of ethics.[105] Knowledge of God does not determine knowledge of ethics; rather, knowledge of ethics determines (and limits) our knowledge of God.[106]

Schleiermacher subsequently rejected Kant's restriction of religious knowledge to morality as being lifeless and dull: "It is as if a religion had no pulse, no vasculary [sic] system, no circulation, and so had no heat, no assimilative power."[107] Furthermore, such a view of religion does not sufficiently account for human experience, because it does not consider all areas of life. For example, artwork does not really fall under the category of moral or immoral and yet art can be good and praiseworthy. Even so, Schleiermacher accepted Kant's epistemological inversion and took it a step further by locating knowledge and awareness of God directly within the religious experience of the individual (the Romantic notion of *feeling*). For Schleiermacher, God is the infinite Whole and true religion is the individual's sense and taste of that infinite Whole, her intuitive perception of the unity of all things.

In Hegel, God is identified with human beings even more. Hegel sought to resolve the Kantian divide by means of a synthesis, in which the phenomenal world is gradually absorbed into the noumenal. This occurs through a process

---

a modernized social gospel resonated with its members but left the denomination with little to offer by way of specific Christian content. This, when combined with the government's increasing activity in providing social services and welfare, left the United Church without a unique mission.

[104] Immanuel Kant, *Religion Within the Limits of Reason Alone*, trans. Theodore M. Greene and Hoyt H. Hudson (New York: Harper & Row, 1960), 5–6.

[105] Immanuel Kant, *Critique of Practical Reason*, trans. Werner S. Pluhar (Indianapolis: Hackett, 2002), 157–67.

[106] Kant, *Religion Within the Bounds of Reason*, 4–6, 129–31.

[107] Schleiermacher, *On Religion*, 231.

of historical necessity, in which the Infinite, Universal, and Eternal (God) temporarily becomes finite, particular, and historical, only to be subsequently reabsorbed in the gradual process of Absolute Spirit becoming self-conscious.[108] Through human beings' awareness of the unity of finite and infinite, God comes to a new self-awareness (Hegel calls this *Reconciliation*). Thus, for Hegel, the goal of essence is to eclipse existence, the goal of the future is to abolish the present, and the goal of the universal or collective is to overcome individuality and distinctiveness. In Hegel's Idealism, individual human beings are all but absorbed into God, as "the individual is only an abstract moment in the History of absolute Mind."[109]

This process reached its pinnacle with the publication of Feuerbach's *The Essence of Christianity*. Following Hegel, Feuerbach maintained a dialectical synthesis but rejected Hegel's Idealism and located the synthesis entirely within human consciousness. He aimed to demonstrate that "the antithesis of divine and human is altogether illusory, that it is nothing else than the antithesis between the human nature in general and the human individual; that, consequently, the object and contents of the Christian religion are altogether human."[110] In contrast to Hegel, it is not that God actualizes Godself in humanity; rather, humanity actualizes itself by projecting and objectifying its highest ideals in the form of what we call *God* and subsequently working toward their realization. For Feuerbach then, religion is nothing other than man's subjective ideals made to seem objective and separate from himself. Feuerbach went on to reinterpret traditional Christian doctrines according to his projection thesis. For example, God as a perfectly moral being is merely the moral law personified. The Incarnation is merely a personification of love for the benefit of humanity. Israel's God is merely the ego of Israel, "the personified selfishness of the Israelitish people, to the exclusion of all other nations,—absolute intolerance, the secret essence of monotheism."[111] It is not difficult to see the impact of Feuerbach's thesis on some of the most influential atheistic thinkers of the twentieth century, such as Freud (religion is a coping mechanism that projects a god to satisfy unmet needs) and Marx (religion is opium for the people, a projection to help them cope with and accept their oppression).

---

[108] Georg Wilhelm Friedrich Hegel, *The Philosophy of History*, trans. J. Sibree (New York: Dover; Toronto: General Publishing Company, 1956).

[109] De Beauvoir, *Ethics of Ambiguity*, 104. For a different interpretation of Hegel's conception of the relationship between infinite and finite, God and the world, see Martin J. De Nys, *Hegel and Theology* (New York: T & T Clark, 2009), 82–107.

[110] Ludwig Feuerbach, *The Essence of Christianity*, trans. George Eliot (Amherst: Prometheus, 1989), 13–14.

[111] Feuerbach, *Essence of Christianity*, 114.

Implications for Community and Society

Dissolution of human community

Questions about the possibility, meaning, and character of human community emerge from the foregoing analysis, three of which I will raise presently. First, what options for grounding human community remain once ontological and teleological accounts of personhood are abandoned? Six ways of grounding society are most influential, though none are satisfying from the perspective of theological anthropology as developed in section two of this book. One option is to envision community as a social contract based serving the mutual benefit of its members (Hobbes). A second is to depict community as a kingdom of ends or a rational association of cause (Kant). A third is to see community as defined by competing desires and self-assertions (Nietzsche, postmodernism). A fourth possibility is community as an embodiment of collective self-interest and expression (Sartre, existentialism). A fifth conception is community as an instrumental good for its members (sociobiology). A sixth alternative is community as concentric circles of care (Noddings). We will explore each of these possibilities in chapter two, evaluating their strengths and weaknesses.

Second, what is the meaning of human community in a postmodern context in which personal identity is fluid, constantly shifting according to changing preferences and relationships? In premodern societies people received their sense of identity, belonging, orientation to the good from within their *given* communities, as contributing members of those communities. Conversely, in postmodern societies individual choice is the starting point. Lacking stable grounding in a formative community that is united in a vision of the good, the postmodern individual defines herself in the residual void of consumerist individualism. One chooses whom to be, where to belong, and what is ultimately good and meaningful. Or else, one chooses to remain undecided or uncommitted about all of these and then searches for social connections that accommodate or allow for the exploration of such preferences.[112] In light of this, one suspects that the very notion of a *postmodern community* is inherently incoherent.[113] It would seem so, if we mean *community* in the Christian sense of a group of people profoundly bound together spiritually, committed to sharing

---

[112] MacIntyre argues that the determinative question becomes: what kind of social contract with others is it reasonable for me to enter into? (*After Virtue*, 251) By contrast, Christian community "joins us with others to further the growth of a tradition whose manifold storylines are meant to help individuals of a tradition identify and navigate the path to the good. The self is subordinate to the community rather than vice versa, for we discover the self through a community's narrated tradition" (Hauerwas, *Peaceable Kingdom*, 28).

[113] Unless one is free continually to redefine the meaning of community, in which case the concept becomes too vague to be useful. It might be helpful to distinguish between *postmodern community*, which being founded upon postmodern assumptions seems internally incoherent, and a *community that operates within and engages postmodern culture*.

life together, pursuing a common vision of what is good and true, toward which end children are raised and instructed and newcomers are initiated and integrated. Granted, a postmodern individualist could choose to band together with others of like mind and commit to a chosen lifestyle or mission, but without a deeper spiritual bond or shared ultimate convictions mere choice is an unstable and potentially misleading foundation (i.e., which lifestyle, which mission?). Moreover, as we will see in chapter three, genuine Christian community cannot be constituted or sustained on the basis of mere personal choice. Genuine Christian community is something that God establishes between believers as the Holy Spirit unites them spiritually to Christ and one another. In addition, Christian community is not homogeneous but brings together and reconciles people of diverse backgrounds, interests, and passions.

Third, how can we hope to preserve stable and abiding communities when we deny the existence of a common story that tells us who we are, where we have come from, and where we are going? Competing rationalities, embodied in different traditions and narratives, lead to rival conceptions of what is good and just.[114] A community united in pursuing a vision of the good requires a unifying narrative. As Hauerwas argues, "Good and just societies require a narrative, . . . which helps them know the truth about existence and fight the constant temptation to self-deception."[115] Unfortunately the only narrative that modern liberal society accepts and teaches is that *we have no such narrative.*[116] This implies that we have no common (coherent) rationality with which to

---

[114] Alasdair MacIntyre, *Whose Justice? Which Rationality?* (Notre Dame: University of Notre Dame Press, 1988), 1, 391, 396.

[115] Hauerwas, *Community of Character*, 18. Recall also Taylor's argument that frameworks provide the necessary background for moral judgment and are required for human agency (*Sources of the Self*, 26–32).

[116] Hauerwas, *Community of Character*, 84. I am taking Hauerwas to be referring to the failure of the Enlightenment project in its attempt to ground morality solely on abstract principles of pure reason. Ironically, though liberalism claims to be free of all tradition, it has become its own tradition with its own conception of a just order and of the human good (MacIntyre, *Whose Justice? Which Rationality?*, 344–45). Moreover, many influential philosophers and ethicists have discerned a common story impacting Western values (even if others deny or repress that story). For example, John Rawls argues that beneficence/nonmaleficence, autonomy, and fairness are characteristic of Western ethics (Rawls, *A Theory of Justice* [Cambridge, MA: Harvard University Press, 1999]). Beauchamp and Childress argue that the principles of nonmaleficence, beneficence, autonomy, and justice, permeate and inform bioethics. They claim to have abstracted these principles from common Western morality. See Tom L. Beauchamp and James F. Childress, *Principles of Biomedical Ethics* (New York: Oxford University Press, 2001). Granted, as James Peterson points out, we must not think of these values as merely abstract rational principles without any grounding in history and tradition. As mere abstract principles, they are partially helpful but not specific enough to guide concrete action. They need to be interpreted and applied within a broader context of a 'thick' descriptive framework. See Peterson, *Changing Human Nature*, 164–65.

evaluate and adjudicate between the competing values, beliefs, and preferences of individuals.[117] Consequently, what holds modern society together is not a communal sense of purpose but a shared context of conflict and struggle.[118] This struggle characterizes modern politics, which at its best takes the form of negotiation and at its worst degenerates into sheer sophistry and empty rhetoric.[119] MacIntyre thus portrays modern liberal society as "a collection of citizens of nowhere who have banded together for their common protection" and as a "shipwrecked collection of strangers".[120] While I agree with Hauerwas and MacIntyre that (post)modern liberalism is not the ideal form of human sociality and cannot serve as a sufficient basis for *Christian community*, I believe that a version of liberalism is still the best practical option we have for our contemporary pluralistic and democratic *society*.[121] Moreover, I do not see this as a compromise or watering-down of Christianity, but rather a valid and potentially fruitful expression of it.[122]

To summarize then: Our culture's current anthropological agnosticism has led to an erosion of the grounds, the meaning, and the stability of human community.[123]

---

[117] MacIntyre says that "in the practical reasoning of liberal modernity it is the individual *qua* individual who reasons" (*Whose Justice? Which Rationality?*, 339).

[118] MacIntyre, *After Virtue*, 253; Kathryn Tanner, *Theories of Culture: A New Agenda for Theology* (Minneapolis: Fortress, 1997), 45–48.

[119] MacIntyre, *Whose Justice? Which Rationality?*, 336–43.

[120] MacIntyre, *After Virtue*, 156, 250.

[121] Logan, "Liberalism," 527–31; Todd Whitmore, "Beyond Liberalism and Communitarianism in Christian Ethics: A Critique of Stanley Hauerwas," *Annual of the Society of Christian Ethics* (1989): 207–209. In a very interesting article M. Cathleen Kaveny demonstrates that contract law can be conceived as a MacInyrean tradition offering productive insights about truth and justice that avoid both sceptical relativism and naive foundationalism (673–87). Moreover, she argues a common law approach leaves room in society both for a common morality (interpreted by public law) and for movements and traditions that influence and shape that common morality, which common law then takes into account (693–94). See M. Cathleen Kaveny, "Between Example and Doctrine: Contract Law and Common Morality," *Journal of Religious Ethics* 44, no. 4 (2005): 669–95.

[122] Novack, "Human Dignity and the Social Contract," 54–55, 58; Nicholas Wolterstorff, "Jeffrey Stout on Democracy and its Contemporary Critics," *Journal of Religious Ethics* 33, no. 4 (2005): 633, 643–47.

[123] By questioning tradition, modern society has made important contributions to freedom and the quality of human life, (e.g., issues such as slavery, racism, and the status of women in society). At the same time, it is important to acknowledge that such advancements were typically based in a modern metanarrative (e.g., freedom, reason, etc.) or on a traditional view of the human person (e.g., as possessing intrinsic worth). Whether such values can continue to be sustained without appealing to a metanarrative or a definitive view of human personhood is debated.

Problems with Defining the Human Person

Dichotomization and disintegration of personal and social ethics

A clear grasp of what it means to be human is crucial for Christian ethics, not only for addressing particular ethical questions and quandaries but even more fundamentally for creating and sustaining an integrative vision of what constitutes a good and significant human life in its wholeness. As Ellen Wondra puts it,

> How theologians speak of persons is crucial to Christian ethics and the Christian life. How persons understand themselves deeply shapes how they approach others, how they cherish and judge their relationships, and how they go about being faithful to the truth of the gospel proclamation that God's work of creation, providence, and salvation is carried out in part through human life with its various structures, groupings, and modes of reflection and expression.[124]

Not only Christian ethics but all ethical systems maintain and depend upon assumptions about human persons. Correspondingly, no description of human persons is purely neutral; every conception of what it means to be human has ethical implications for how human beings ought to conduct their lives. "A description of human nature always both presumes and entails a prescription for human living. The *what/who* questions and the *how* question are inseparable."[125] Consequently, any worldview that remains naive, vague, or elusive in its understanding of human personhood (intentionally or non-intentionally) lacks the ability to articulate and practice a coherent and consistent human ethic. Ethical confusion or chaos ensues. Worse, a fallacious view of what it means to be human leads to a misguided, reductionist, or sometimes even destructive ethical system, in which case oppressive dehumanizing policies can ensue.

In his influential book *After Virtue* Alasdair MacIntyre argues that the contemporary modern world is in a state of grave moral disorder resulting from a history of moral deterioration. We currently possess only fragments of a once-unified moral scheme, but have lost the contexts that previously gave them significance and cohesion. We use bits and pieces of traditional moral language, but have rejected key aspects of the worldview that made such language meaningful. Consequently, in the modern world, we make ethical claims that have the appearance of being rational and objective but are actually based upon arbitrary choices. We cloak these arbitrary assertions in quasi-rational and mythical notions, such as "utility", "rights", and "therapeutic" and "bureaucratic" expertise.[126] Moreover, the disappearance of a common and cohesive moral scheme has led to a situation in which opponents in moral debate frequently argue from

---

[124] Ellen K. Wondra, "Participating Persons: Reciprocity and Asymmetry," *Anglican Theological Review* 86 (Winter 2004): 58–59.

[125] Cortez, *Theological Anthropology*, 3.

[126] MacIntyre, *After Virtue*, 79–86.

incommensurable premises and therefore have no recourse to a rational resolution of issues. This state of affairs stems from the Enlightenment's rejection of the Aristotelian ethical tradition, and particularly the latter's teleological orientation. In its place we are left with either Stoic rule-following (the Enlightenment tendency) or sheer Emotivism (Nietzsche's alternative), both of which are prevalent in contemporary culture and exist as two sides of the same teleologically deprived coin.[127]

The notion of an ultimate human *telos* is crucial for the Aristotelian ethical tradition that MacIntyre wishes to defend and endorse. This is because one can make factual evaluative judgments about something only if one understands its *telos*, its purpose or goal. For example, one can make the evaluative judgment "this is a good watch" or "this is a bad watch" only if one understands that the purpose of a watch is to tell time. Thus, a conception of *telos* is a necessary link between factual statements and evaluative judgments. Without recourse to *telos*, facts and values become separated and moral judgement degenerates into personal tastes and preferences. Moreover, this separation of facts and values, leading to the relegation of morality to the beliefs and preferences of individuals, would create a bifurcation between personal and social ethics. While personal ethics continues to be guided by private beliefs, social ethics gets reduced to the lowest common denominator of public consensus about so-called facts. Personal beliefs and convictions are acceptable only so long as they do not interfere with a person's public roles and responsibilities or intrude upon public discussions of ethical issues. Reflecting on modern Western society, Lesslie Newbigin refers to the abandonment of teleology as "the central citadel of our culture" and describes it as:

> ... the belief that the real world, the reality with which we have to do, is a world that is to be understood in terms of efficient causes and not of final causes, a world that is not governed by an intelligible purpose, and thus a world in which

---

[127] Taylor refers to Enlightenment moral approaches generally as "ethics of obligatory action," since they focus on the principles, injunctions, or standards which guide action while altogether neglecting visions of the good. Their concern is with what one ought to *do*, not with what is intrinsically valuable or what one should admire or love. This one-sided focus on action, to the neglect of being or loving, leads to a procedural or method-driven conception of ethics. For example, neither utilitarianism nor Kantianism defines what is ethical according to a vision of the good; both associate ethics with a form of reasoning—for the latter practical reasoning is the method of universalization while for the former practical reasoning is the method of calculating maximum utility. Similarly, on a larger societal level, the social contract is not defined by a vision of the good but by a particular procedural starting point (democratic consent). If we cannot agree on what we should do, let us agree on who should decide. Like MacIntyre, Taylor points to Nietzsche as one who saw the inherent contradictions in the theories of obligatory action (he saw through their claims to objectivity and exposed their veiled will to power). See Taylor, *Sources of the Self*, 79, 84–90.

the answer to the question of what is good has to be left to the private opinion of each individual and cannot be included in the body of accepted facts that control public life.[128]

At the same time, however, teleological *assumptions* seem to be inevitable, even in our contemporary postmodern culture which generally endorses relativism and rejects appeals to an ultimate human *telos*.[129] Even relativists rely on a limited and tacit understanding of *telos* to make rational evaluative judgments about objects like watches. They can do so consistently only because a watch is the creation of human beings who have intentionally defined its *telos*. This *telos* is not ultimate but contingent upon human intention. The statement "this is a good watch" is true, given the purpose that human beings have ascribed to it, but they could just as easily have ascribed another purpose, which would alter the truth status of the statement. However, without reference to a transcendent human *telos*, relativists cannot make moral judgments that they consider to be ultimately true. Morality is not a matter of discerning transcendent truth; it is about being faithful to the purpose or *telos* that *one creates for oneself*. Conversely, for the Aristotelian tradition moral judgments are grounded in appeals to the ultimate *telos* of human beings, hence they are factual judgments and not mere assertions.

From a Christian perspective, this Aristotelian teleological perspective highlights the important connection between Christian ethics and theological anthropology. In the moral sphere, factual ethical judgments are possible only when the *telos* of human beings is understood. Our understanding of what it means to be human deeply impacts our understanding and practice of ethics. At a societal level, the creation of a just civil order depends upon a shared vision of the good toward which human beings may collectively aspire. Conversely, the trivialization of questions concerning the identity, purpose, and destiny of human beings impairs the ethical enterprise at both the personal and social lev-

---

[128] Lesslie Newbigin, *Foolishness to the Greeks: The Gospel and Western Culture* (Grand Rapids: Eerdmans, 1986), 79, and *The Gospel in a Pluralist Society* (Grand Rapids: Eerdmans, 1989), 7.

[129] One could argue that an understanding of *telos* impacts most, if not all, ethical systems. For example, in Utilitarianism, how could one decide what leads to the greatest utility or happiness for human beings unless one understands something about their purpose for living (i.e., what does it mean to be happy or useful)? Yet this is problematic because utilitarians argue amongst themselves over what is the good to be maximized. Even Existentialism requires the notion of *telos*, though it defines itself in opposition to it. Sartre's position, that there is no such thing as a human nature or a human *telos*, is foundational for his understanding of ethics as the creation of each individual. One of Dostoyevsky's characters is famous for his repeated claim, which has become the personal motto for many existentialists: "If there is no God, everything is permissible." Thus, Nietzsche's critique of modern ethics seems justified (i.e., that they are self-contradictory, masking their own ultimate claims under a facade of neutral objectivity).

els. Furthermore, misguided or flawed anthropologies breed inadequate or even harmful ethical views and political systems.

Collapse of social and global justice

In the modern (and postmodern) Western world, the call for social justice and efforts to attain it usually rest on a belief in the inherent worth of human persons.[130] Such a belief maintains that all human beings are intrinsically valuable and should be respected and protected accordingly. This belief in the basic worth or dignity of human persons grounds most conceptions of and appeals to human rights. For example, the preamble to the United Nations' *Universal Declaration of Human Rights* states that "recognition of the inherent dignity and of the equal and inalienable rights of all members of the human family is the foundation of freedom, justice, and peace in the world."[131] The preamble makes two claims about the basic status of all human persons. The first is that human persons have inherent dignity. This means that they have intrinsic worth (rather than instrumental or conferred worth) that is sufficient to ground their possession of certain natural rights. Second, the natural rights that human beings inherently possess are equal and inalienable. This means that all human beings possess them without measure or discrimination and that such rights cannot be withdrawn, altered, ignored, violated, or trumped in favour of some other human life-good.[132]

Given the traditional and widespread grounding of human rights in the intrinsic worth of human beings, an important question surfaces: *what warrants this belief in the inherent worth of human beings*? Why is a being of this kind inherently worthy of such great respect? How can we justify the claim that such beings have certain rights that *must not be violated*, regardless of the good or utility that might be achieved by doing so? The question is particularly vexing in our contemporary cultural context of anthropological agnosticism. If we cannot even agree on the meaning and purpose of human beings, how can we attribute inherent worth to such beings and what would motivate us to respect their basic rights?

---

[130] See, for example: Elshtain, "The Dignity of the Human Person," 53; Novak, "The Judeo-Christian Foundation of Human Dignity," 100–11, 115–16; Perry, *Idea of Human Rights*, 5; Michael Nai-Chiu Poon, "Show me the Worth of a Human Person: an East Asian Perspective," *Transformation* (January 1998): 13.

[131] *Universal Declaration*, 63 (preamble). Moreover, article 1 makes the link between universal human rights and inherent dignity explicit by stating, "All human beings are born free and equal in dignity and rights" (64). Other official documents also make the link. For example, both the *International Covenant on Economic, Social, and Cultural Rights* (69) and the *International Covenant on Civil and Political Rights* (79) include the words from the Universal Declaration preamble quoted above and additionally state: "*Recognizing* that these rights derive from the inherent dignity of the human person . . ." (69; emphasis original).

[132] Wolterstorff, *Justice*, 291.

Problems with Defining the Human Person

Some have acknowledged the problem and attempted to base human rights on something other than inherent worth or dignity. In his book, *Justice: Rights and Wrongs*, Nicholas Wolterstorff surveys and rejects several such attempts, which he collectively labels "right order" as opposed to "inherent rights" approaches. A basic feature of "right order" proposals is that they envision human rights as being always conferred (often socially) rather than inherently possessed.[133] For example, Wolterstorff summarizes Richard Rorty's position as follows: "There is no human nature for human rights to be grounded in. It is only the social practice of according certain rights to each and every human being that attaches rights to the status of being human."[134] Accordingly, Rorty recommends abandoning notions of inherent human rights based on dignity or worth (what he calls "rights foundationalism") and instead expanding the scope and reach of our current human rights practices beyond our own culture by telling "sad and sentimental stories" to evoke sympathy and compassion.[135] Leaving aside the problem that Rorty's position seems to endorse a kind of arbitrary cultural imperialism (arbitrary because abandoning rational criteria for sheer cultural consensus), Rorty takes for granted that such stories will in fact evoke sympathy without the need for underlying convictions and beliefs about the worth of human persons. Yet dehumanizing the other has a long history, full of examples of people who demonstrate great charity, sympathy, and compassion toward some people while committing horrendous acts against others, usually because they see these others as being of lesser worth or as being less than fully human (for example, the Nazi who is also a loving husband, father, and community leader). Something more than mere sentiment is required to sustain and motivate a strong belief in and commitment to universal and inalienable human rights. As Max Stackhouse powerfully asserts,

> If human rights are the product of scribblers and sophists only, or even of pioneers and pilots, they will not long endure. Sentiments will change, and other construals will be imagined, other paths found, other channels dug. Human rights will be like civil rights—what is promulgated by one ruler or passed by one legislature can be rescinded by the next. The erosion of the gains for human rights could easily occur, at tremendous human cost, if the idea of human rights is based on nothing more than the changing course of historical experience and discourse about it.[136]

---

[133] Wolterstorff, *Justice*, 35.

[134] Wolterstorff, *Justice*, 321. Wolterstorff corrects a misunderstanding that he detects in Rorty's position, namely the misunderstanding that one needs to believe in human 'nature' in order to believe in natural human rights.

[135] Wolterstorff, *Justice*, 320.

[136] Max L. Stackhouse, "Human Rights and Public Theology: The Basic Vindication of Human Rights," in *Religion and Human Rights: Competing Claims?* (Armonk, NY: M.E. Sharpe, 1999), 14.

Perhaps a more promising approach is to ground human rights in prior obligations. However, Wolterstorff raises four objections to such a proposal.[137] First, the totality of one's duties is too narrow to account for all of one's rights; some rights have no corresponding duties (e.g., certain rights to privacy and respect). Second, it erroneously envisions our obligations as fixed or given and our rights as being determined out of these obligations. However, this linear progression from obligations to rights is neither obvious nor consistent; sometimes rights lead to obligations and sometimes the removal of a right removes an obligation (which makes the simple ordering of obligations to rights problematic).[138] Third, some human beings have no duties because they are incapable of forming intentions (babies, patients in a coma, etc.) yet such human beings have rights and can be wronged. Finally, Wolterstorff argues that a comprehensive theory also has to account for God's rights, but God is entitled to certain rights that have no corresponding (much less foundational) obligations (e.g., God has a right to our worship).[139]

If Wolterstorff is correct that social conferral or "right order" approaches are insufficient to sustain human rights (I believe he is) and that the only plausible basis is the inherent worth of human persons, then our initial questions remain: *what warrants a belief in the inherent worth or dignity of human persons and what would motivate us to respect their basic rights*? Moreover, as this is a matter of belief, a second question lies at the heart of the issue, namely: "is the idea of human rights ineliminably religious?"[140] Writers such as Wolterstorff, Michael Perry, and Max Stackhouse answer persuasively in the affirmative; the various secular attempts to ground human rights are either incoherent or insufficient. One proposed option for a secular basis of human rights is to ground the notion of human dignity in some capacity that human beings uniquely possess, such as rationality (this is the approach Kant pursued). However, there are at least three problems with all capacities-based approaches to grounding human dignity: (1) inevitably some human beings do not possess the named capacity and therefore fall outside the circle of human dignity (e.g., infants and the severely mentally disabled lack the capacity for rational agency); (2) some animals do possess the capacity (e.g., emotion, rational agency) and thus it cannot

---

[137] Wolterstorff, *Justice*, 246–48. In particular, Wolterstorff is here responding to Paul Ramsey's proposal in *Christian Ethics and the Sit-In* (New York: Association, 1961), chapter 1.

[138] Wolterstorff provides the following example. Suppose that it is indispensible to the fulfilling of one's obligations to travel to work, in which case one has a right to travel freely to work. But suppose that a terrorist attack has rendered such travel impossible, in which case one no longer has those obligations that could not be fulfilled without travelling to work. Nevertheless, one still has a right to travel to one's office and is wronged in being prevented from doing so.

[139] For Wolterstorff's full criticism of attempts to ground human rights in obligations or duties, see *Justice*, 244–84.

[140] This is the title of the first chapter of Michael J. Perry's *Idea of Human Rights*, 11–41.

qualify as uniquely human;[141] and (3) the possession of an innate capacity is unlikely by itself to impress someone who already abuses human rights.[142]

Another option for a secular basis of human rights is to provide a nonreligious interpretation of the sacredness of human life. For example, Ronald Dworkin argues that sacredness does not reside within human beings themselves but is attributed to them because there is something special about how they came to be. In particular, two characteristics stand out: first, human beings are the highest product of natural creation; second, they are the product of human creativity (creative masterpieces). These two features lead to the breathtaking realization of the sacredness of human life. Dworkin's argument is unconvincing for at least two reasons. First, by identifying a mature property in human beings it becomes vulnerable to the same charge levelled at capacities-based approaches. Specifically, it inevitably excludes some human beings because not every human being measures up to the standard of being a creative masterpiece of natural and self-creation.[143] Second, how does sacredness as Dworkin explains it differ significantly from merely being awe-inspiring, and why are only human beings sufficiently awe-inspiring to be considered sacred? Similarly, Michael Perry asks, "How does the fact that something is a masterpiece of natural and human creation make that something not merely a creative masterpiece but sacred?"[144] Perry suspects that Dworkin is trading in on the greater strength of the objective sense of sacred as it is commonly used (i.e., sacredness as attributed from the outside, from God, not just a subjective experience of awe), thereby smuggling into his secular interpretation connotations of value, mystery, and transcendence that properly belong to the religious concept.

A third possibility for attempting a secular grounding of human rights (though without reference to human dignity) is to employ what Perry calls the self-regarding strategy.[145] Conceptually similar to Hobbesean social contract theory, this approach begins with the need for self-preservation—whether of

---

[141] For evidence that some animals possess the capacity for rational agency, see for example Alasdair MacIntyre, *Dependent Rational Animals: Why Human Beings Need the Virtues* (Chicago: Open Court, 1999). On the other hand, it is important to point out that no animal grasps rationality to the emergent level of basic human beings. See James C. Peterson, "The Religion of Genetics in Epistemology and Ethics," *Theology and Science* 9, no. 2 (2011): 213–21.

[142] See Wolterstorff, *Justice*, 330–33.

[143] Wolterstorff, *Justice*, 334. For example, it is difficult to argue that a person with a severe mental impairment qualifies as the highest product of natural creation a creative masterpiece of self-creation.

[144] Perry, *Idea of Human Rights*, 27. Later he states, "that something is a creative masterpiece and understandably inspires awe in us entails neither that it is sacred nor even that we believe it to be sacred (in the strong sense)." (28)

[145] Perry, *Idea of Human Rights*, 32–35. Wolterstorff discusses and critiques a similar approach endorsed by Alan Girwith (*Justice*, 335–40). He notes that Girwith's is a capacity-based (though not dignity-based) proposal.

individual persons, families, tribes, races, religions, etc.—and posits that certain rights must necessarily be attributed universally to all in order to safeguard the rights of oneself or those of the group to which one belongs. Unfortunately, such an approach cannot provide a solid basis for universal human rights, especially for the kind of rights endorsed by the United Nations.

One problem is that a self-regarding approach is dependent on the existence of fear, but what motivates and sustains an agreement when no fear is present or when existing fear is alleviated?[146] An agreement to respect the rights of others makes sense for those who have relatively little power and influence, but what would motivate powerful individuals, groups, or nations to endorse it? Granted, powerful parties might be interested in entering into a contract with other powerful parties, but what would motivate them to safeguard the rights of the powerless? Another problem stems from its self-orientated or self-motivated nature. An agreement of mutual respect makes sense between two parties who have complementary incentives and resources (trade, security, natural resources, etc.). However, what would motivate a rich and self-sufficient party to respect the rights of a poor and needy one?[147] For example, the human rights scholar Richard Bilder writes, "Despite considerable effort, it has been difficult to construct a wholly convincing 'selfish' rationale for major U.S. national commitments to promote the human rights of foreigners."[148] Given such observations, Bilder considers self-regarding arguments to be difficult to prove and unpersuasive.

In light of the foregoing discussion, I surmise that secular approaches to grounding the inherent worth of human persons are neither fully coherent nor sufficiently satisfying.[149] Moreover, secular approaches tend to lack sufficient

---

[146] Thus, Perry says it amounts to little more than a "mere non-aggression treaty" (Perry, *Idea of Human Rights*, 32). Does a self-regarding approach have to begin with fear? Could it begin with personal advantage instead? Concerning those human rights that are basic human freedoms and protections, it is difficult to see what one would stand to gain in protecting basic freedom unless the possibility of their being violated existed. Some human rights could perhaps be established on the basis of mutual advantage (e.g., the right to education or the right to food and clothing), but whether or not these are genuine *inalienable human rights* is questionable and disputed. Wolterstorff, for example, argues that relatively few positive rights are truly *human* rights (i.e., recognized inherently on the basis of one's humanity). See Wolterstorff, *Justice*, 314.

[147] Alasdair MacIntyre observes that the very notion of a just wage makes no sense within the confines of modern liberalism (devoid of teleology), in which contracts are by definition self-motivated (*Whose Justice? Which Rationality?*, 111).

[148] Quoted in Perry, *Idea of Human Rights*, 34.

[149] As Jens Zimmermann notes, "Any honest genealogy of humanism shows us that the ideals of secular humanism are impossible without their Christian antecedents. When we look not for the actual use of the term humanism but for the basic concepts we associate with this term—a focus on a common humanity marked by human freedom, dignity, and creative ability—when we do this, we find that humanism originates from Judaic and Christian roots." See his essay, "Being Human, Becoming Human: Dietrich Bonhoeffer's Christological Humanism," in *Being Human, Becoming Hu-*

motivational power. Consequently, with Wolterstorff and others, I have serious doubts about whether a human rights culture can be sustained on a secular basis that lacks a strong belief in the intrinsic worth or dignity of the human person.[150] It seems to me that the logical outcome is that with the passing of time and the changing of circumstances there will be an erosion of our culture's affirmation of universal and inalienable human rights, especially if circumstances change from affluence and stability to economic decline and instability (perhaps such erosion has already begun with the willingness of some to compromise basic human rights?).[151] Given our culture's current state of confusion, I suggest that what is needed is a fresh explication of what it means to be human, one which helps us grasp and safeguard the inherent worth of each person as intrinsically valuable before and deeply loved by God. What is needed, in other words, is not merely an anthropology but a robust and compelling *theological* anthropology.

Concluding Summary

My aim in this book is to demonstrate the significance of theological anthropology for ecclesiology. In particular, I want to explore how the former can help us better understand the nature and character of the church's (inner) sociality and its (outward) relation to the world, especially with respect to personal, social, and global ethics. The present chapter provides the background context in which the problems I seek to address have emerged. It began by observing that many of our culture's most treasured values and moral commitments depend on particular beliefs and convictions about human beings, yet in our current cultural context there is much confusion, disagreement, and controversy about the meaning and purpose of being human, leading to a kind of anthropological agnosticism. In our contemporary culture, people often struggle to find a secure sense of identity and purpose. They feel alone in a world that seems meaningless and absurd, and hence they are vulnerable to the powerful and disorienting forces of individualism, relativism, reductionist materialism, and consumerism.

The chapter then discussed four factors that have contributed to or intensified the problem, including the fragmentation of the self, the lack of consensus about the *telos* of the human person, the problem of scientific reductionism, and

---

man: *Dietrich Bonhoeffer and Social Thought*, ed. Jens Zimmermann and Brian Gregor (Eugene, OR: Pickwick, 2010), 26.

[150] Max Stackhouse observes that in recent times explicitly secular governments and regimes have been the most frequent and ruthless violators of human rights. He cites the examples of Papa Doc's Haiti, Pol Pot's Cambodia, Marcos's Philippines, Mao's China, Stalin's Soviet Union, and many petty tyrants in Latin American and Africa, "all of whom rejected theology in favor of 'modern scientific' approaches to social reality" ("Human Rights," 21).

[151] For a brief summary of this position, see Wolterstorff, "Can Human Rights Survive Secularization?" (parts 1 and 2).

the loss of a transcendent reference point situating human persons before God. Three implications of the present predicament were subsequently discussed, namely the dissolution of human community, the dichotomization and disintegration of personal and social ethics, and the collapse of social and global justice. The chapter concluded by identifying the need to formulate a robust and compelling theological anthropology. Such a project could help us to understand and begin to practice a deeper, more holistic and transformative approach to Christian community, with an intrinsic connection to personal, social, and global ethical formation and engagement. However, before proceeding with this task (in chapters three through six), it will be helpful first to identify and evaluate the options for human community that remain given the current context of anthropological agnosticism. We now turn to this discussion in chapter two.

CHAPTER 2

Rival Accounts of Being Human and Being in Community in Contemporary Culture

Introduction

Our understanding of community is intimately linked with our understanding of what it means to be human. Yet as the previous chapter argued, in contemporary Western culture what it means to be human is not sufficiently clear. This chapter will offer an overview of six dominant typological ways of construing community, based on conflicting views of the human person that are implicitly or explicitly operative in contemporary (post-) modern culture.[1] I do not intend a taxonomy, which is a system of classification according to observations of empirical differences and is generally used in the biological sciences to describe individuals. Instead, I offer a typology, which classifies according to conceptual differences and is generally used for broad affinity classes.[2] Each community type I propose corresponds to a particular view of the human person. Types 1 and 2 correspond to the human person as the rational being of the Enlightenment. Types 3 and 4 correspond to the human person as the self-defining individual of existentialism. Type 5 corresponds to the human person as the self-preserving animal of sociobiology. And type 6 corresponds to the human person as one caring-for others (as in the ethics of care). *

After developing the typology, I will suggest ways in which these approaches have shaped contemporary church expressions and/or movements. It is important that churches become aware of their implicit assumptions about being human, because such assumptions have deep implications for understanding and practicing Christian community, mission, and personal and social ethics.

---

[1] Miroslav Volf remarks that contemporary society is neither consistently modern nor consistently postmodern, but represents an uneasy combination of both. It is "caught in an ambiguity . . . that stems above all from the fact that it is precisely modernity that keeps generating the most conspicuous features of the postmodern condition." See his *Exclusion and Embrace: A Theological Exploration of Identity, Otherness, and Reconciliation* (Nashville: Abingdon, 1996), 30.

* Please see p.285 for a quick-reference table outlining the typology.

[2] Kenneth D. Bailey, *Typologies and Taxonomies: An Introduction to Classification Techniques* (Thousand Oaks: Sage, 1994), 6. See also my discussion of this methodology in the Introduction.

Rival Accounts of Being Human and Being in Community

The Rational Being of the Enlightenment

Enlightenment views of the human being typically associate personhood with the capacity for rational thought and reasoning. They place an emphasis on individual subjectivity, agency, and freedom, but tend to downplay or deny the role of tradition and sociality in constituting personhood. Thus, for Descartes the human being is an individual thinking substance, for Locke a disengaged subject of rational control, and for Kant a pure rational agent.[3] From this starting point one can construe at least two accounts of human community: as a social contract and as a rational association of cause and duty.

Type 1: A social contract between consenting individuals

While many different forms of the social contract have been proposed, for our purposes we will focus on the ideas of Thomas Hobbes and John Locke, since both thinkers are seminal to its initial development.[4] For both Hobbes and Locke, the need for human beings to band together formally arises out of what they refer to as humankind's natural condition. In this condition, human beings are without a political society and government; they live in a state of anarchy.[5] Accordingly, they have no recourse to established laws against which to measure and analyze disputes, no access to a non-partial judicial system with the authority to settle them, and no power or means to execute settlements made or

---

[3] Stanley J. Grenz, *The Social God and the Relational Self: A Trinitarian Theology of the Imago Dei* (Louisville: Westminster John Knox, 2001), 69–74; Charles Taylor, *Sources of the Self: The Making of the Modern Identity* (Cambridge, MA: Harvard University Press, 1989), 12, 49. Even Schleiermacher, who recognized the importance of sociality for Christian life, tended to prioritize the individual over the community. For him, the church is the place where free and equal people who are already religious gather to share their religious feelings (i.e., their joint sense of sharing as finite individuals in the Infinite). See Friedrich Schleiermacher, *On Religion: Speeches to Its Cultured Despisers*, trans. John Oman (Westminster: John Knox, 1994).

[4] See also, David Novak, "Human Dignity and the Social Contract," in *Recognizing Religion in a Secular Society: Essays in Pluralism, Religion, and Public Policy*, ed. Douglass Farrow (Montreal; Ithaca: McGill-Queens University Press, 2004), 51–68; John Perry, "John Locke's America: The Character of Liberal Democracy and Jeffrey Stout's Debate with the Christian Traditionalists," *Journal of the Society of Christian Ethics* 27, no. 2 (2007): 227–52; John Rawls, *A Theory of Justice* (Cambridge, MA: Belknap of Harvard University Press, 1999); Jeffrey Stout, *Democracy and Tradition* (Princeton: Princeton University Press, 2004); and Nicholas Wolterstorff, "Jeffrey Stout on Democracy and its Contemporary Christian Critics," *Journal of Religious Ethics* 33, no. 4 (2005): 633–47.

[5] It is not important to the argument whether this natural state precedes the political society historically; what matters is the way Hobbes and Locke develop this conceptually (as if they were telling us to imagine a group of humans living in close proximity without any form of governance).

agreements reached.⁶ Hobbes argues that in this condition nature divides human beings and predisposes them to invade and destroy one another. Competition over scarce resources, the resulting need for self-defence, and the desire for greater glory lead respectively to conflicts to secure gain, safety, and reputation.⁷ Each individual is caught in a struggle for survival against all other human beings (Hobbes calls it a "war") and each is equally vulnerable to misfortune and attack.⁸ Consequently, the life of a human being is "solitary, poor, brutish, and short."⁹

Hobbes discerns two "fundamental laws of nature," which derive rationally from this state of affairs.¹⁰ First, human beings must seek peace, but if they cannot attain it they are entitled to defend themselves (Hobbes takes the absolute natural right to self-preservation and self-defence as a basic assumption). Second, they must be willing to accept limitations on their unrestrained natural freedom for the sake of common peace. This second law leads to the notion of a social contract, by which every individual agrees to surrender a degree of personal freedom in order to attain greater security and productivity as a group.¹¹ Hobbes reasons that such an agreement could be effectively binding—for all parties involved, in both the present and the future—only if a higher authority were established that possessed the resources and coercive power necessary to enforce the contract. Once constituted, this governing authority would regulate the efforts of individuals who are seeking personal gain and self-preservation, in order to promote the common good for all. It would wholly take upon itself the responsibility to protect individual rights and to administer justice when such rights are offended.¹² For Hobbes and Locke, the social contract lies at the foundation of political or civil society.¹³

The social bond uniting a community together in the social contract theory is a contractual arrangement to pursue common mutual benefits. The social contract provides a powerful model of society and governance that deeply and

---

⁶ John Locke, *Two Treatises of Government*, in *Philosophical Works and Selected Correspondence of John Locke* (Charlottesville: InteLex, 1995), 351.
⁷ Thomas Hobbes, *Leviathan*, ed. A.P. Martinich (Peterborough: Broadview, 2005), 94–95. See also Locke, *Two Treatises*, 350.
⁸ Hobbes, *Leviathan*, 93–97; Locke, *Two Treatises*, 351–53.
⁹ Hobbes, *Leviathan*, 96.
¹⁰ Hobbes, *Leviathan*, 99–100.
¹¹ For Locke, the chief purpose of entering by social contract into a commonwealth is to secure the property of individuals (by 'property', Locke means their lives, liberties, and estates). See Locke, *Two Treatises*, 350.
¹² Thus, by entering into contract individuals surrender their natural rights to unrestrained self-preservation (now regulated by government) and to vengeance (now wholly assumed by government). See Locke, *Two Treatises*, 351–52.
¹³ As Locke writes, "Those who are united into one body, and have a common established law and judicature to appeal to, with authority to decide controversies between them, and to punish offenders, are in civil society one with another." Locke, *Two Treatises*, 323.

broadly impacts the way people in contemporary Western democracies think about human sociality. Not only have contractual concepts come to dominate our political theory and practice, they have also shaped our basic values and ideas concerning relationships in general (e.g., our views of marriage and family, student-teacher relationships in education, patient-doctor relationships in medicine, and laity-clergy relationships in religious institutions). Envisaging community as a social contract has both strengths and weaknesses. One strength is that a social contract is a good way to secure broad and basic consent in a pluralist and secular context of competing values, beliefs, and worldviews. A community conceived according to social contract notions could tolerate a high degree of diversity and accommodate a variety of interests and ideas, even while ruling out some basic forms of nonconformity. A second strength is its realism concerning the human propensity toward self-interest and the inevitable conflict that such self-interest fuels. Accordingly, the social contract model recognizes the importance of capable leadership and effective authority structures, with proper checks and balances, to the healthy functioning of community. A third strength is that the social contract model has a good historical record of generally securing peace and personal liberty for its members (especially when compared to other forms of government). Even communities that do not agree with its basic foundations should appreciate and learn from its track record of establishing relatively just and equitable conditions for its members (as long as the bargaining parties are relatively equal in the negotiation).

However the model also has problems. First, it lacks a sufficiently positive motivating vision for human sociality, often basing human social bonds on a foundation of mutual fear and suspicion.[14] Even if one wishes to resist Hobbes's pessimistic portrayal of natural human existence as "solitary, poor, brutish, and short," every version of the social contract model still begins with mutual self-interest, which then needs to be regulated, mitigated, suppressed, or somehow channelled positively for the sake of the common good.[15] It is doubtful that at least some of the values, goods, and practices crucial to the functioning of a healthy community (especially a genuinely Christian community) could be sufficiently and stably grounded and sustained by collective self-interest alone. What is needed is a thicker, redemptive account of humanity's dignity/worth, purpose, and destiny. A second weakness is that the social con-

---

[14] A related criticism is that the social contract depends upon the association of individual wills, in other words it is voluntaristic in nature. This voluntaristic orientation developed in the wake of the breakdown of the sacramental approach to community that characterized classical Christian thought. See Oliver O'Donovan and Joan Lockwood O'Donovan, *Bonds of Imperfection: Christian Politics, Past and Present* (Grand Rapids: Eerdmans, 2004) and Jean Bethke Elsthain, *Sovereignty: God, State, and Self* (New York: Basic, 2008).

[15] On the notion of channelling self-interest into serving the common good, see Michael Novak, *The Spirit of Democratic Capitalism* (New York: Simon and Schuster, 1982). See also Robert Nozick, *Anarchy, State, and Utopia* (New York: Basic, 1974).

tract builds community upon an individualistic foundation, which implicitly assumes that relationships are secondary and perhaps even peripheral to essential personhood. The model seems to envision already mature individuals joining into community with other mature individuals in order to pursue common goals and goods.[16] It fails to account for the constitutive role that relationships and community play in the formation of personal identity and worldview and in the development of practical reasoning.[17] Moreover, a social contract model of community has difficulty accounting for the theological conviction that the ultimate basis for Christian community is the spiritual union of believers with Christ, leading to their joint participation in the life and communion of the triune God.[18] This includes but goes far beyond the pursuit of common ideas, benefits, tasks, and goals. A third weakness of the social contract model as a basis for community is that social consensus alone does not provide a sufficient grounding for morality and justice. Questions of morality and justice concern the discernment of truth, not simply the weighing and tallying of preferences. The morally appropriate course of action might not always be the popular one. Moreover, while social consensus might achieve a high degree of social cohesion, it might also ignore or overrule legitimate minority views within the group.[19] Similarly, common agreement might not be consistent between groups (especially if other such groups are also founded in the collective self-interest of their members), leading to inter-group or inter-community conflict and potentially to wrongs committed against outsiders. Finally, social consensus is insufficient because sometimes entire groups choose to support morally abhorrent ideologies and policies. One thinks immediately of Nazi Germany, South African Apartheid, the status of women and/or children in many cultures, or the widespread acceptance of slavery throughout human history. Such examples demonstrate that social consensus alone does not provide adequate critical controls for truthful and just communal moral discernment and practice. Accordingly, modern society often hopes that if it cannot reach consensus on what is

---

[16] Hobbes employs the social contract as a kind of thought experiment, rather than a descriptor of actual human experience. Even so, the thought experiment is individualistic. This might be sufficient for applying the social contract within the context of a modern pluralistic society but it is an insufficient basis for Christian *community*, which begins with peace and unity in Christ by the Spirit.

[17] See Alasdair MacIntyre, *Whose Justice? Which Rationality?* (Notre Dame: University of Notre Dame Press, 1988).

[18] Dietrich Bonhoeffer, *Life Together*, ed. Geffrey B. Kelly, trans. Daniel W. Bloesch and James H. Burtness, vol. 5 *Dietrich Bonhoeffer Works* (Minneapolis: Fortress, 1996), 31, 35–38; Miroslav Volf, *After Our Likeness: The Church as the Image of the Trinity* (Grand Rapids: Eerdmans, 1998), 129.

[19] This is why the United States could not agree on its constitution until it established the Bill of Rights, which guarantees rights for individuals against the coercive power of the majority. In Canada, the Charter of Rights and Freedoms likewise affects the interpretation of the constitution and protects individual rights.

the right thing to do, it can at least agree on who gets to decide. Agreement is on the process, not the ends.

Type 2: A moral association of cause and duty
In contrast to the social contract model of Hobbes and Locke, which is based on empirical observations concerning human nature, Immanuel Kant develops both his view of the human person and his view of community through *a priori* reasoning in accordance with the universal principles of reason. For Kant, the human being is a rational moral agent born with an innate capacity for practical (moral) reasoning as well as a sense of duty or obligation to obey the moral law. One of the ways that Kant states the basic law of pure practical reason is: "So act that the maxim of your will could always hold at the same time as a principle of universal legislation."[20] We can observe three fundamental and distinctive Kantian emphases in this statement. First, the concept of universality is crucial to all of Kant's thought, including his epistemology, his anthropology, his ethics, and his view of community. Whatever is true is true universally, for all human beings. What is morally binding for one person is binding for everyone. This focus on universality allows Kant to resist various forms of moral relativism, emotivism, and utilitarianism.[21] Second, Kant stresses the importance of free will. One must *choose* to adopt those maxims (personal rules) that could become universal laws. For Kant, morality does not consist in blind conformity to an external law or authority; rather, it has its basis in the practical reasoning and decision making of the free moral agent.[22] This preserves the dignity of the human being as a rational creature and protects moral agents against the control or manipulation of external forces (e.g., authority figures or institutions, religious or moral systems). Third, in close relation to his emphasis on freedom, Kant underscores the importance of personal autonomy. For Kant, true virtue cannot be coerced because morality concerns one's will and motivation, not merely one's actions. As a clear and simple illustration of Kant's point, it would be morally irrational for me to command someone to love me. Such a command cannot have binding moral force because love cannot be coerced but involves personal will and motivation and must be freely given and received. This example is representative of Kant's moral reasoning generally, except that Kant prioritizes duty as the primary ethical motivation. One should act ethically simply because it is the right thing to do, not because

---

[20] Immanuel Kant, *Critique of Practical Reason*, trans. Werner S. Pluhar (Indianapolis: Hackett, 2002), 45.

[21] For example, Kant argues that 'personal happiness' cannot supply dependable moral laws because it is too subjective: what counts as happiness differs with each person according to tastes and preferences (*Critique*, 33–34).

[22] For Kant, the freedom of the will is the source of the moral law. We can say that one *ought* to do something only if the possibility for choosing that course of action exists. Conversely, one is not obligated to do what one cannot possibly do (*Critique*, 48–60).

one stands to gain by such action or because one is being coerced into doing it.[23]

Two other formulations of Kant's basic moral law lead to the envisioning of community. The first is that one should treat every rational being as an end in itself, never as merely a means to an end. This formula universalizes the freedom, autonomy, and dignity belonging to each rational individual. The second is that, having accepted the criterion of universality for all of one's own ethical maxims, one should envision oneself as a member in a universal moral realm or a "kingdom of ends." In this ethical commonwealth, every person devotes herself to obeying the moral law and to treating every other person as an end and not merely as a means to an end. Thus, according to Kant, community serves the constructive purpose of uniting free and responsible moral agents in the common pursuit of obedience to and equality under the moral law.[24] Moreover, in keeping with his basic assumptions of universality, freedom, and autonomy, Kant emphasises the non-coercive nature of an ethical commonwealth.[25] People enter the commonwealth voluntarily and remain together under non-coercive moral laws (by which Kant means laws chosen and followed voluntarily, rather than civil laws enforced publicly). For Kant, the most genuine ethical commonwealth can be realized only in the form of a church, which he depicts as a household or family under a common (though invisible) moral Father.[26] Kant further describes the church as "a voluntary, universal, and enduring union of hearts" and identifies four defining characteristics, including universality, morality, freedom, and stability.[27] Primary among these is universality; for Kant, universality is the token of a true church.[28]

---

[23] Divine laws are different, because they always and universally command obedience for the sake of doing what is right and because God knows the state of one's heart and will (Kant would strongly disagree with the view that God gives arbitrary laws or is content with mere external conformity to them). Human laws can never be equivalent in status or force to divine laws (or the moral law), but if human laws are truly just then obedience to them is required by our obligation to the moral law.

[24] Immanuel Kant, *Religion Within the Limits of Reason Alone*, trans. Theodore M. Greene and Hoyt H. Hudson (New York: Harper & Row, 1960), 85–91.

[25] Kant, *Religion*, 87–91.

[26] Kant, *Religion*, 93.

[27] Universality concerns the unity of the church under pure practical reason without sectarian divisions. Morality concerns the purity of the ecclesial union, as people are motivated to join together for moral reasons rather than superstitious or fanatical ones. Freedom characterizes both the internal relationships of members to one another as well as the external relation of the church to political power. Stability means that the church operates under an unchanging constitution with settled laws, though its administration may be subject to change. See *Religion*, 93.

[28] Kant, *Religion*, 100–105. Accordingly he argues that pure religious faith, which in essence is reverence for God and obedience to the universal moral law, must be the "highest interpreter" of particular, historical, and revealed faith. Conversely, "a church dispenses with the most important mark of truth, namely, a rightful claim to universality, when it bases itself upon a revealed faith" (105).

The bond of community in a Kantian approach is common submission to the moral law. The greatest strength of Kant's approach is that it views community as being inherently ethical in nature. In his view, ethics is not an afterthought to be worked out secondarily as a group pursues more pressing and central goals and objectives; rather, community *in its very essence* is an ethical entity. Consequently, serious and ongoing reflection on pertinent ethical questions, issues, and commitments is vital to the constitution and continuing vitality of genuine community. From a Christian perspective, this fits well with the New Testament's depiction of the church as a community characterized by and devoted to holiness and progressive sanctification.[29] A second strength of Kant's approach is that his ethical theorems are basically sound and helpful. The categorical imperative, bearing some resemblance to Jesus's Golden Rule, is a helpful guide for considering how our potential actions might impact others and is likely to promote justice, fairness, and respect for the dignity of human persons. Additionally, his "kingdom of ends" provides a welcome critique of forms of community that are based in collective self-interest or driven by consumer values and choices. Kant effectively demonstrates that consequentialism or utilitarianism cannot provide a sufficient rational foundation for ethics or community. A third strength is that Kant's emphasis on rationality helpfully guards against forces of mindless conformity, groupthink, fanaticism, and emotionally manipulative forms of leadership. Thus, it helps to defend and prioritize the dignity of individual persons as free and intelligent moral agents. This resonates with a theological description of the church as a rational community of wisdom and discernment (see chapter 7).

One weakness of the Kantian approach is its dependence on the notion of a moral law that is universally accessible to and binding for all. This dependence tends toward a naive conception of ethics as a matter of just being rational (naive because the meaning of rational is largely taken for granted). This is problematic epistemologically, because there are many different cultures with many different conceptions of morality, each depending upon a different form of practical reasoning or rationality, thus prompting the question: *Whose* justice? *Which* rationality?[30] In response to this objection, a Kantian proponent might argue that a demonstrably high degree of consensus existing between cultures on crucial moral issues points to the existence of a universal moral law. This might well be the case, yet three problems remain. First, moral consensus alone does not provide sufficient grounds or warrants for ethics according to the rules of Kantian practical reasoning. From a Kantian perspective, it is not enough that people arrive at the same moral conclusions; rather, they must arrive at them for the same reasons (duty to the moral law). The existence of widespread consensus on major moral issues does not amount to compelling evidence for the universal moral law (conceived according to Kantian *a priori* reasoning) if

---

[29] E.g., Matt 5–7; Rom 12; Eph 4:17–32; Phil 3:17–21; 1 Pet 2:9–12; 1 John 2–3.
[30] Hence the title of MacIntyre's book, *Whose Justice? Which Rationality?*

such consensus does not derive from a common form of practical reasoning and is not inspired by a common motivation. Second, even if we grant the existence of a universal moral law, at a practical level the lowest common denominator of abstract and universally applicable rules might not provide the flexibility or specificity required for concrete and particular moral dilemmas.[31] Third, the universal moral law is deficient from a theological perspective, not so much because of what it says and teaches but because of what it fails to say and teach. General revelation needs to be clarified, augmented, and personalized by special revelation.[32] As I argue in chapter four, God's commands are not abstract but are based upon God's character, which God reveals personally in the economy of salvation history and especially in the person and actions of Jesus Christ. Most importantly, a Kantian generalizing or universalizing approach fails to account for the personal Lordship of Jesus Christ and softens his more radical teachings.[33]

A second weakness of a Kantian approach is that its conception of community is not inherently relational. While it emphasizes that persons are ends in themselves, united together in a kingdom of mutual ends, it still envisions *community itself* as being only a means to an end. This is because relational bonds are secondary to the practical or ethical goal of following the moral law. From a theological perspective, this fails to account fully for the incarnational, embodied, and intrinsically social character of human existence (in its creation, reconciliation, and transformation).[34] Lacking in the Kantian view is a relational ontology that envisions human beings as bound together deeply by the Spirit and drawn into the life and community of the Trinity (see chapter 3).[35] A third weakness of a Kantian model of community is that it lacks a sufficiently practical and biblically faithful strategy for Christian ethical and spiritual formation. Specifically, it does not account adequately for the authority and formative role of Scripture or the importance of ritual and tradition to the vitality of Christian

---

[31] See Dietrich Bonhoeffer, *Ethics*, ed. Clifford J. Green, trans. Reinhard Krauss, Charles C. West, and Douglas W. Stott, vol. 6, *Dietrich Bonhoeffer Works* (Minneapolis: Fortress, 2005), 219–20.

[32] See, for example, Richard J. Mouw, *He Shines In All That's Fair: Culture and Common Grace* (Grand Rapids: Eerdmans, 2001).

[33] For example, Jesus once commanded a rich man to sell all of his possessions (Matt 19:16–30), but the categorical imperative would not allow for such a thing because if everyone acted this way the results would be disastrous. The command is warranted not because of its universality but because of the personal lordship of Jesus Christ and its implications for this particular individual.

[34] Kant prioritizes the individual's relationship to the universal moral law, and downplays the importance of traditions and other institutional means of embodying moral reasoning (see, for example, *Religion*, 97).

[35] This is not surprising, given Kant's views on the Incarnation, the person and work of Jesus Christ, soteriology, and the doctrine of the Trinity. Concerning these doctrines, Kant's assumptions place him closer to Arianism and Pelagianism than to historically orthodox mainstream Christianity.

community (e.g., worship, catechism, sacraments, and spiritual disciplines).[36] In addition, grounding community in duty and devotion to rules, rather than in love and character formation, leaves the Kantian approach vulnerable to legalism. Epistemologically, Kant proceeds from the recognition of ethical imperatives to the positing of spiritual and metaphysical indicatives. This manoeuvre reverses the model clearly endorsed by the New Testament (observable, for example, in all of the Pauline epistles), which is a movement from the indicatives of grace and union with Christ to the imperatives of obedience and ethical living.

The Self-Defining Individual of Existentialism

A second influential way of conceiving what it means to be human is to view the human person as an individual self-creation. This approach begins with subjectivity and particularity, rather than with objectivity and universality, and emphasizes becoming over being and existence over essence. Epitomized in various ways by existentialist thinkers, it focuses on promoting individual freedom and responsibility, authentic existence, and resistance to the system or collective (each conceived in existentialist terms).[37] For our present purposes, we will restrict our focus to two of its seminal thinkers, Friedrich Nietzsche and Jean-Paul Sartre, exploring how each conceives of human existence and the implications these conceptions have for human community.[38]

---

[36] For the importance of these to Christian life and community see, for example: Bonhoeffer, *Life Together*; Richard A. Burridge, *Imitating Jesus: An Inclusive Approach to New Testament Ethics* (Grand Rapids: Eerdmans, 2007); Stephen E. Fowl and Gregory Jones, *Reading in Communion: Scripture and Ethics in Christian Life* (Grand Rapids: Eerdmans, 1991); Stanley Hauerwas, *A Community of Character: Toward a Constructive Christian Social Ethic* (Notre Dame: University of Notre Dame Press, 1981); Reinhard Hütter, *Bound to be Free: Evangelical Catholic Engagements in Ecclesiology, Ethics, and Ecumenism* (Grand Rapids: Eerdmans, 2004); Christine D. Pohl, *Making Room: Recovering Hospitality as a Christian Tradition* (Grand Rapids: Eerdmans, 1999); Dallas Willard, *Renovation of the Heart: Putting on the Character of Christ* (Colorado Springs: NavPress, 2002); N.T. Wright, *After You Believe: Why Christian Character Matters* (New York: HarperOne, 2010).

[37] Alasdair MacIntyre suggests a slightly different scheme of four key existentialist themes, including intentionality, being and absurdity, freedom and choice, and angst and death. See his entry "Existentialism," in *The Encyclopaedia of Philosophy*, vol. 3., ed. Paul Edwards (New York: Macmillan and Free Press, 1967), 147–54. See also Christine Daigle, "The Problem of Ethics for Existentialism," in *Existentialist Thinkers and Ethics* (Montreal; Kingston: McGill-Queens University Press, 2006), 6–12.

[38] I am aware of the controversy concerning which thinkers should properly be categorized as existentialists (Kierkegaard and Nietzsche are two prominent examples). In his sampling of existentialist writers, Solomon includes S. Kierkegaard, I. Turgenev, F. Dostoevsky, F. Nietzsche, H. Hesse, M. Heidegger, R.M. Rilke, M. de Unamuno, K. Jaspers, F. Kafka, G. Marcel, A. Camus, J-P. Sartre, M. Merleau-Ponty, S. de Beauvoir, H.E. Barnes, M. Buber, P. Tillich, K. Nishitani, C. Wilson, V.E. Frankl, G.G. Márquez, S. Beckett, L. Borges, H. Pinter, J. Heller, P. Roth, and A. Miller. See Robert C. Solomon, *Existentialism* (New York: Oxford University Press, 2005). For

Rival Accounts of Being Human and Being in Community

Type 3: Erotic communities of desire and self-assertion

Nietzsche rejects metaphysics as a starting point for philosophy and as a valid source of knowledge for human existence and ethics. He especially rejects all forms of Platonism, which posit and then prioritize the beyond over present existence, the universal over the particular, and the absolute over the concrete (his immediate targets were Enlightenment thinkers such as Kant who attempted to construct philosophical and ethical systems on the basis of *a priori* universal truths).[39] He also rejects Christianity, believing it to be a form of "Platonism for the people."[40] Nietzsche's rejection of Platonic modes of thought follows two lines of critique. First, Platonism lacks epistemological credibility. Nietzsche argues that ever since Plato philosophers have believed that they could attain an objective apprehension of the good, from which they could rationally derive truth about human nature and formulate ethical imperatives. However, according to Nietzsche, this belief is both illusory and deceptive. What is actually going on is that philosophers begin with their own (often unconscious) assumptions and then project them onto reality disguised as universal and self-evident truths. Subsequently, they make truth claims and derive ethical rules and laws from these supposedly self-evident and objective universal truths. As Nietzsche puts it, philosophers "pose as though their real opinions had been discovered and attained through the self-evolving of a cold, pure, divinely indifferent dialectic", whereas in fact, "a prejudiced proposition, idea, or 'suggestion' which is generally their heart's desire abstracted and refined, is defended by them with arguments sought out after the event."[41] According to Nietzsche, what actually lies behind all such systems and claims is a veiled will to power, a desire to dominate, control, and rule.[42] This will to power is the basic existential reality of all animals, including human beings. Nietzsche believes that we should recognize and celebrate our will to power for what it is, not hide it behind appeals to purportedly transcendent values or claims to truth. He writes, "It is nothing more than a moral prejudice that truth is worth more than semblance; it is, in fact, the worst proved supposition in the world . . . Indeed, what is it that forces us in general to the supposition that there is an essential opposition of 'true' and 'false'?"[43] For Nietzsche, there is no connection between this world and the beyond, between the particular and the universal, or

---

my present purposes, it is sufficient that both Sartre and Nietzsche address the 'existential' themes under consideration in the present chapter section.

[39] Friedrich Nietzsche, *Beyond Good and Evil: Prelude to a Philosophy of the Future* (Mineolo: Dover, 1997), 5–8.

[40] Nietzsche, *Beyond Good and Evil*, x.

[41] Nietzsche, *Beyond Good and Evil*, 3.

[42] Nietzsche asserts, "A living thing seeks above all to *discharge* its strength—life itself is *Will to Power*" (*Beyond Good and Evil*, 10).

[43] Nietzsche, *Beyond Good and Evil*, 26.

between the concrete and the absolute. Goodness, truth, and God are myths.[44] All we can talk about is our existence as individuals in the phenomenal world.

Nietzsche's second line of critique is that the Platonic approach is morally reprehensible, because it elevates the universal over the particular and thus leads to a "herd instinct" that fosters a "herding animal morality."[45] Nietzsche argues that, historically, it was the rich, the powerful, or the aristocratic who typically appealed to the beyond or to transcendent values. They did so in order to assert and justify their status and significance over against the masses. Thus, for the aristocratic, the appeal to the beyond was really an expression of the will to power. For the masses, however, belief in the beyond was a means of coping with their lowly state, fostering within them a "herd instinct" (i.e., there is comfort in knowing one's place).[46] Marx expressed a similar idea when he branded religion as opium for the people, because it leads people to be content with poverty and repression by creating a story that rationalizes their current circumstances. In addition, this herd morality is always maintained as a collective value system, in which the dreams and aspirations of individuals are repressed because they threaten the system's equilibrium. What is seen as good is whatever maintains the status quo of the commanding class; what is seen as evil is whatever threatens it. Goodness especially includes passive or acquiescing qualities, while evil includes rigorous, aggressive, and ambitious qualities.[47] In opposition to such a herd morality, Nietzsche envisions a world that is beyond good and evil, one in which the will to power is given free reign. In particular, the Judeo-Christian moral sentiments of surrender, sacrifice for one's neighbour, self-renunciation, and disinterested contemplation must be rejected.[48] Nietzsche asks us to imagine a world in which "nothing else is 'given' as real but our world of desires and passions, that we cannot sink or rise to any other 'reality' but just that of our impulses. . . ."[49] The heroes of this world are the "new philosophers" who possess "minds strong and original enough to initiate

---

[44] Alasdair MacIntyre describes the implications of Nietzsche's moral philosophy as follows: ". . . if there is nothing to morality but expressions of will, my morality can only be what my will creates. There can be no place for such fictions as natural rights, utility, the greatest happiness of the greatest number. I myself must now bring into existence 'new tables of what is good.'" See *After Virtue* (Notre Dame: University of Notre Dame Press, 2003), 114.

[45] Nietzsche, *Beyond Good and Evil*, 68.

[46] Nietzsche, *Beyond Good and Evil*, 65.

[47] Nietzsche writes, "The lofty independent spirituality, the will to stand alone, and even the cogent reason, are felt to be dangers; everything that elevates the individual above the herd, and is a source of fear to the neighbour, is henceforth called *evil*; the tolerant, unassuming, self-adapting, self-equalising disposition, the *mediocrity* of desires, attains to moral distinction and honour" (*Beyond Good and Evil*, 67; emphasis original).

[48] Nietzsche, *Beyond Good and Evil*, 25.

[49] Nietzsche, *Beyond Good and Evil*, 27.

opposite estimates of value, to transvalue and invert 'eternal valuations.'"[50] They exhort individuals to resist the collective, the herd, and instead to assert their will and be the masters of their own destiny.

In a Nietzschean perspective human sociality takes the form of *erotic* communities of desire and self-assertion, in which the bond of unity is the will to mutual subjugation and exploitation. In such communities, one joins together with others in order to assert one's own desires for power and control, self-fulfillment, recognition, and/or honour. From this view, the conversation of Jesus's disciples concerning who among them would be the greatest in the kingdom was exemplary in its honesty, courage, and calculating shrewdness in light of the cold, hard truth of human existence. Put in psychological terms, a Nietzschean perspective cynically views all relationships as being codependent. Notions of equality, democracy, genuine interdependence and other-centeredness are regarded not only as illusions but as a weak and degrading acceptance of mediocrity and powerlessness.[51] Of course, in actual communities this will to power is rarely recognized for what it is; generally, it remains hidden, disguised, or buried in the subconscious minds of its members. The key assumption is that however altruistic, loving, generous, or selfless people might appear to be, they are at base simply seeking community in order to use others to satisfy their own needs and goals. Someone who serves others has a base need to be needed. Someone who empathizes with others has a base need for emotional connection. Someone who teaches and mentors others has a base need for influence and respect the fulfilment of which requires that others be followers.

Type 4: Phileic communities of common interest and expression
Like Nietzsche, Sartre was critical of deterministic or essentialist conceptions of the human person, which he observed in philosophical Idealism and assumed were intrinsic to all theological accounts of personhood. In response, he began from an intentionally and explicitly atheistic starting point.[52] He argued that our understanding of the world, human nature, and ethics cannot be determined by appeals to transcendence or universal Being or God. Conversely, the crucial epistemological commitment is that *existence precedes essence* or, stated dif-

---

[50] Nietzsche, *Beyond Good and Evil*, 69. For example, Nietzsche writes, "severity, violence, slavery, danger in the street and in the heart, secrecy, stoicism, tempter's art and devil or every kind,—that everything wicked, terrible, tyrannical, predatory, and serpentine in man, serves as well for the elevation of the human species as its opposite . . ." (31–32).

[51] Nietzsche, *Beyond Good and Evil*, 16, 31. Nietzsche also argues that the idea of the common good is a contradiction in terms, because what is common is always of low value (30).

[52] Jean-Paul Sartre, *Existentialism and Human Emotions* (New York: Philosophical Library, 1957). He writes, "Existentialism is nothing else than an attempt to draw all the consequences of a coherent atheistic position." (51)

ferently, subjectivity is the starting point.[53] The implication of this is that "human beings create themselves". They first "exist", "turn up", "appear on the scene", and only subsequently define themselves.[54] Sartre writes, "If existence really does precede essence, there is no explaining things away by reference to a fixed and given human nature. In other words, there is no determinism, man is free, man is freedom."[55] Moreover, "There can no longer be an *a priori* Good, since there is no infinite and perfect consciousness to think it."[56] Without recourse to divine purpose or to *a priori* ethical principles based on the good, human beings are alone and must reinvent themselves moment by moment by their choices and actions. For Sartre, this is a terrible and awesome responsibility, leaving human beings in a predicament characterized by anguish, forlornness, and despair. "Condemned to be free", human beings must choose their own meaning and destiny.[57] Yet Sartre remains hopeful that the existentialist approach frees people from deliberation and encourages action, since they are no longer required to be preoccupied with questions of ultimate good and evil or paralyzed by a fixed cosmic order.

Sartre is confident that his perspective is liberating not only for individuals, but for human community and society as a whole. This is because Sartre believes that his philosophy intensifies ethics as taking personal responsibility for how one's choices in the present shape the future. Moreover, he is optimistic that people will realize that their actions have universal implications. He argues, "for every man, everything happens as if all mankind had its eyes fixed on him and were guiding itself by what he does."[58] Simone de Beauvoir elaborates on the meaning and implications of Sartre's position. She states that the freedom of the individual person is "the source of all values" and the "universal, absolute end", yet such freedom assumes and requires the freedom of others.[59] As she puts it, "To will oneself free is to will others free."[60] This is because one's own freedom depends upon an open future, which, in turn, depends upon the willingness and charity of others not to interfere.[61] Individual freedom is maximized when people work collaboratively toward universal freedom for all. In light of such remarks, Beauvoir seems to envision a kind of unofficial

---

[53] Sartre, *Existentialism*, 13.
[54] Sartre, *Existentialism*, 15.
[55] Sartre, *Existentialism*, 21–22.
[56] Sartre, *Existentialism*, 22.
[57] Sartre, *Existentialism*, 23, 32.
[58] Sartre, *Existentialism*, 20. Elsewhere he writes, "The man who involves himself and who realizes that he is not only the person he chooses to be, but also a lawmaker who is, at the same time, choosing all mankind as well as himself, can not help escape the feeling of his total and deep responsibility" (18).
[59] Simone de Beauvoir, *The Ethics of Ambiguity*, trans. Bernard Frechtman (New York: Citidel Press; Kensington Publishing, 1948), 58.
[60] Beauvoir, *Ethics of Ambiguity*, 73.
[61] Beauvoir, *Ethics of Ambiguity*, 82.

social contract to maximize the liberty of all.[62] However, in the existentialist approach the emphasis lies not on the need for community as an authority structure to guard against the weaknesses or selfishness of human nature, as in the Hobbesean social contract model, but on the intrinsic goodness of choice itself and the absolute value of freedom to seek one's own preferences and to express one's own individuality and uniqueness. In this model, individuals come together in community in order to pursue their interests and to express themselves with and amongst other like-minded people. Thus, the bonds of community according to this model are the shared interests and experiences of its members. On a societal level the logical outcome of such an approach is the creation of many homogenous groups of common tastes and preferences. This implication is especially likely in a consumer society, in which choices and products are multiplied to match aggregate consumer demand. I have called this approach to community *phileic* (friendship love) because it is akin to a contemporary understanding of friendship as a relationship based in common interest and expression.[63]

Evaluation of existentialist notions of human community
An existentialist model of human community has at least three strengths. First, its stress on the importance of human freedom protects individual persons from being absorbed into a collective that represses individuality and mistakenly equates unity with uniformity. It helpfully depicts community as something that preserves and celebrates the diversity and differences of its individual members. Christian theology also emphasizes human freedom. In fact, one of the key metaphors that the Bible employs to describe Christ's atoning death as a saving event is redemption or ransom. Thus, a major emphasis in Christian soteriology is that the atoning work of Christ sets people free.[64] This insight has

---

[62] Beauvoir writes, "to be free is not to have the power to do anything you like; it is to be able to surpass the given toward an open future; the existence of others as a freedom defines my situation and is even the condition of my own freedom" (*Ethics of Ambiguity*, 91). For a more detailed discussion of Beauvoir's understanding of freedom, see Daigle, "The Ambiguous Ethics of Beauvoir," *Existentialist Thinkers and Ethics*, 120–41.

[63] This contemporary understanding of friendship differs markedly from both an Aristotelian and a biblical–theological understanding of friendship, both of which view friendship in relation to the pursuit of the good or God.

[64] The New Testament says that Christians are redeemed from the curse of the law (Gal 3:13; 4:4), from all wickedness (Titus 2:13), and from an empty way of life (1 Pet 1:18). They are ransomed by the Son of Man (Jesus Christ) who gave his life on their behalf (Matt 20:28; Mark 10:44; 1 Tim 2:6) to set them free from sins (Heb 9:15). On account of Christ's atoning work, they are freed from their sins (Rom 6:7, 18, 22; Rev 1:5), from the law of sin and death (Rom 8:2) from the rituals of the law (1 Cor 8), from accusation (Col 1:22), and from slavery to the fear of death (Heb 2:15). Moreover, they are set free to love (Gal 5:13), to serve God (1 Pet 2:16), to approach God with confidence (Eph 3:12), and to partake in the freedom of the Spirit (2 Cor 3:17). In addition, the Gospels depict Jesus's ministry as freeing people from suffer-

implications for spiritual and ethical formation in Christian community. For example, Christian formation is not about blind conformity to social regulations or unquestioned obedience to the teachings of leaders; rather, it seeks to foster in each person the renewal of their mind and the cultivation of spiritual discernment, wisdom, and maturity. A second strength of the existentialist model is its emphasis on authenticity and responsibility. It reminds us that while a person's identity is inevitably shaped and influenced by community, it should not be fully determined by the views and expectations of other people. One of the implications this has for Christian community is that we must release others from the confines or boxes in which we see them (perhaps based on past experiences) and from our personal expectations and ideals for their future. Personhood and identity are not static or fixed entities; genuine existence is constantly in the making and requires the determination to accept responsibility and to make wise choices. We must allow each individual the freedom to change and develop into the person that Christ intends him or her to become.[65] A third strength of the existentialist model is its resistance to oppressive systems and structures that claim a special possession of absolute truth and expect unconditioned loyalty from adherents. Such resistance stems from its focus on individuality and particularity, concreteness, and contingency, as opposed to universality, abstractness, and Idealistic immanency. It is no coincidence that Christian theologians who stood against Nazi ideology in Germany during the Second World War, such as Barth and Bonhoeffer, were deeply influenced by the existentialist insights of writers such as Kierkegaard and Buber.[66] Moreover, existentialism's resistance to systemic oppression resonates with the biblical polemic against demonic structures that attempt to take Christ's place in claiming our ultimate allegiance.[67]

---

ing and disease (Mark 5:34; Luke 13:12) and freeing prisoners from their captors (Luke 4:18). Furthermore, Christ's followers are set free by the truth (John 8:32) and by the Son of God himself (John 8:36).

[65] See Bonhoeffer, *Life Together*, 95.

[66] Kierkegaard stressed the contingent character of ultimate truth and divine revelation while Buber articulated the I–Thou personal structure of all genuine relationships.

[67] The oldest atonement theory, the *Christus Victor* theory, depicts the soteriological significance of Christ's death as a victory over cosmic forces of evil. These forces could include Satan, demonic beings, or even evil political forces and structures. Moreover, several biblical passages expose and challenge evil in its structural and political forms. For example, in the Old Testament, one thinks of God's confrontation with Pharaoh in Exodus, God's judgment against Israel for making unholy allegiances with foreign kings in Isaiah, or God's condemnation of structural and political injustice and oppression in prophets like Jeremiah and Amos (taking advantage of the poor, the widows and orphans, exploiting people by charging unfair interest, and using religion to justify their evil). Several New Testament passages also contain a polemic against structural and political evil. Jesus's teachings and ministry often provoke confrontations with religious and political leaders. Many Pauline letters contain polemical elements that challenge oppressive political structures. For example, his

Existentialism arose largely as a criticism of the epistemology and corresponding ethics of Enlightenment and Idealist thinkers. A somewhat reactionary movement, its critiques are often incisive but its constructive proposals are less than satisfying.[68] Consequently, its greatest critical strengths correspond with deficiencies in its proposed solutions. First, while its stress on the uniqueness and difference of each person is a welcome challenge to views of community that tend toward uniformity, its own proposals lead to radical individualism. Thus, the same criticisms of the individualism of Enlightenment models (Hobbes/Locke, Kant) apply here as well, but to an even greater degree. Given the epistemological commitments of existentialism, the social bonds of a community amount to little more than similar personal tastes and preferences. Since tastes and preferences are subject to constant change (especially in a postmodern, consumer culture), the foundation of an existentialist model of community is highly unstable. Moreover, basing a community upon the common desires of its members fails to account for the Christian stress on truth lived out in *agape* love. Insightful and instructive in this regard is Dietrich Bonhoeffer's distinction between genuinely spiritual community and emotional or psychic community. For Bonhoeffer, genuine spiritual community is created, centred, and formed in and by Christ, while false forms of community depend on human agendas, ideals, and emotions. Bonhoeffer writes:

> The bright love of Christian service, *agape*, lives in the spiritual community; the dark love of pious-impious urges, *eros*, burns in the self-centered community. In the former, there is ordered Christian service; in the latter, disordered desire for pleasure. In the former, there is humble submission of Christians to one another; in the latter, humble yet haughty subjection of other Christians to one's own desires. In the spiritual community the Word of God alone rules; in the emotional, self-centered community the individual who is equipped with exceptional powers, experiences, and magical, suggestive abilities rules along with the Word. In the one, God's Word alone is binding; in the other, besides the Word, human beings

---

use of "Lord and Saviour" as a title for Christ was a direct challenge to the self-proclaimed divinity and cosmic-sovereignty of Caesar, who called himself "Lord and Saviour". Or, consider the following statement in Colossians, "And having disarmed the powers and authorities, [Christ] made a public spectacle of them, triumphing over them by the cross" (Col 2:15). As a final example, the book of Revelation contains a subversive yet devastating attack on the oppression and godlessness of the Roman Empire. See Gordon D. Fee, *Revelation* (Eugene, OR: Cascade, 2010).

[68] MacIntyre's evaluation of Nietzsche is insightful: "For it is in his relentlessly serious pursuit of the problem, not in his frivolous solutions that Nietzsche's greatness lies, the greatness that makes him *the* moral philosopher if the only alternatives to Nietzsche's moral philosophy turn out to be those formulated by philosophers of the Enlightenment and their successors" (*After Virtue*, 114). This acknowledgement of genuine insight into the problems of human existence, while simultaneously lacking helpfully constructive proposals, could characterize other existentialist thinkers such as Sartre and Camus as well.

bind others to themselves. In the one, all power, honor, and rule are surrendered to the Holy Spirit; in the other, power and personal spheres of influence are sought and cultivated.[69]

A second weakness is that the existentialist understanding of freedom is deficient. While it effectively articulates the individual's freedom *from* other people to satisfy one's own desires and goals, it lacks a corresponding emphasis that freedom is also *for* others. From a theological perspective, true freedom involves not just the liberty to do what one wants; it also involves a transformative movement toward others in selfless, sacrificial, and redemptive love. True freedom enables one to love and serve God and others as one should. It is epitomized by the way God exercises God's own freedom in being bound to human beings through covenant and by redeeming and uniting them in Christ.[70] Third, while Christian theology affirms existentialism's rejection of the oppressive manipulation of truth and authority, it cannot endorse existentialism's tendency to abolish all appeals to truth and authority structures. From a theological perspective, these forces are not inherently oppressive but only become so when they are abused. Existentialists fail to make this distinction and thus create an impoverished and reductionist account of these realities, leading to a model of community that naively rejects the importance of authority and governance (will not authority assert itself in some form anyway?). Moreover, its rejection of transcendent truth undermines its commitment to freedom. On the basis of existentialist epistemology, such a commitment is either groundless (as in Sartre) or self-motivated (as in Beauvoir) and thus volatile. One could choose with Sartre to respect the freedom of others, but if such respect for others does not serve one's agenda one could just as consistently side with Nietzsche in choosing the path of manipulative self-assertion by employing one's sovereign freedom to subject others to one's own will.

The Self-Preserving Animal of Sociobiology

A third influential attempt to describe what it means to be human comes from sociobiology or evolutionary psychology, as represented by Edward O. Wilson. According to Wilson, modern scientific discoveries about the evolution of human beings and other creatures have created two great dilemmas for human existence and spirituality. First, "No species, ours included, possesses a purpose beyond the imperatives created by its genetic history."[71] Or, put differently, "The species lacks any goal external to its own biological nature."[72] For Wil-

---

[69] Bonhoeffer, *Life Together*, 39–40.
[70] Dietrich Bonhoeffer, *Creation and Fall: A Theological Exposition of Genesis 1-3*, vol. 3 *Dietrich Bonhoeffer Works*, trans. Douglas Stephen Bax (Minneapolis: Fortress, 1997), 63.
[71] Edward O. Wilson, *On Human Nature* (Cambridge, MA: Harvard University Press, 2004), 2.
[72] Wilson, *On Human Nature*, 3.

son, human beings are simply biological entities and every aspect of human nature, development, values, beliefs, and behaviour (e.g., aggression, sex, altruism, religion) can be explained by genetic influence without the need to invoke non-material explanations or reflections. Wilson does not deny the influence of culture and society on individual people, but he insists that the parameters of such influence are predetermined by genes. As Wilson forcefully puts it, "genes hold culture on a leash."[73] All of human existence is rooted in biological evolution and can be explained in terms of natural selection; whatever qualities and characteristics we presently observe about human beings developed because they enhanced the preservation of the species. For example, Wilson says that the brain exists because it promotes the survival and multiplication of the genes that direct its assembly. Moreover, the human mind "is a device for survival and reproduction, and reason is just one of its various techniques."[74] Even complex historical and cultural phenomena, such as philosophies and religions, can be explained by their potential to preserve biological life. "Religions, like other human institutions, evolve so as to enhance the persistence and influence of their practitioners."[75] All religions serve the goal of collective self-aggrandizement.[76] Wilson recognizes that his observations are potentially dangerous, because they undermine the transcendent beliefs and goals that have held together and organized traditional societies.[77]

This recognition leads to the second dilemma for human existence and spirituality. Sociobiology tells us that religion and morality evolved because innate censors and motivators existing in the brain deeply and unconsciously impacted the formulation of religious and ethical premises (due to their species enhancing qualities). If this is the case, there is no such thing as transcendent religious truths or moral values and we must choose what should be maintained and what should be abandoned—we must choose our morality.[78] Even so, Wilson does not surrender morality to personal whim or preference, but insists that sociobiology can provide not just a descriptive explanation but also normative prescriptions for ethics based on scientific empirical observations.[79] His basic moral premise is that ethics should serve the preservation of the species. "Human behaviour . . . is the circuitous technique by which human genetic material

---

[73] Wilson, *On Human Nature*, 167.
[74] Wilson, *On Human Nature*, 2. For a trenchant philosophical critique attempts to explain the human mind fully in materialist terms, see Thomas Nagel, *Mind and Cosmos: Why the Materialist Neo-Darwinian Conception of Nature Is Almost Certainly False* (New York: Oxford University Press, 2012).
[75] Wilson, *On Human Nature*, 3.
[76] Sociobiology is, in many ways, a pseudo-scientific counterpart to Nietzschean philosophy. One can discern parallels between sociobiology and Nietzsche, especially concerning the theme of self/species-preservation as the ultimate good.
[77] Wilson, *On Human Nature*, 4.
[78] Wilson, *On Human Nature*, 4–7.
[79] Stephen J. Pope, "Engaging E.O. Wilson: Twenty-Five Years of Sociobiology: E.O. Wilson as a Moralist," *Zygon* 36 (June 2001): 233.

has been and will be kept intact. Morality has no other demonstrable ultimate function."[80] Whatever increases our potential for survival is good; whatever threatens it is bad. Sociobiology can help us to distinguish these scientifically.

Type 5: An instrumental good for its members
Wilson does not devote much attention to human community, but a sociobiological model of community can be inferred from his discussion of altruism and kin selection. The social bonds in this model of community are ultimately biological in nature. From an evolutionary perspective, human community is an instrumental good for its members and promotes their potential for survival and reproduction. Of course, most contemporary people do not see themselves joining a community in order to preserve their genes or multiply their offspring, but these basic instincts presently operate at a subconscious level, having been formulated and deeply engrained over thousands of past generations. Thus, according to Wilson, human relationships and community are ultimately self-serving and are designed to safeguard the preservation and progeny of individuals. One objection commonly raised against Wilson is the problem of altruism. If relationships and community are basically self-serving, how does one explain the sacrificial and charitable qualities and behaviours that characterize many human beings? Wilson's response is that there are two kinds of altruism. Soft-core altruism is easily explained by the predictions of natural selection as being selfish, calculating, and as expecting reciprocal benefit or reward.[81] People are good and charitable toward others because they want others to be good and charitable to them (though self-deception and lack of self-awareness often mask such egocentric motivations). Sometimes this self-serving altruism is more obvious, as when corporations publicly support charities or causes as marketing strategies or when individuals give in order to receive tax benefits. Hard-core altruism, which is irrationally and unilaterally directed toward others without a desire for reciprocation or concern for social reward or punishment, is more difficult to explain. For example, why would someone risk her life to save a complete stranger without regard for personal benefit or social recognition? Wilson explains that such behaviour likely evolved through kin selection, which is a kind of natural selection operating on entire groups to ensure the survival of one's close relatives.[82] Individual acts of self-sacrifice for loved ones in the past led to the preservation of altruistic tendencies in entire groups,

---

[80] Wilson, *On Human Nature*, 167.
[81] Wilson, *On Human Nature*, 155–56.
[82] Wilson, *On Human Nature*, 155. Such evolution took place as individuals with a genetic disposition toward 'hard-core' altruism sacrificed their lives in order to save their family or tribe, thereby extinguishing their own individual genetic contribution but simultaneously ensuring the spread of the altruistic tendency through the survival of the next generation (e.g., nephews and nieces with similar genes). For a helpful explanation of kin selection, see J. Philippe Rushton, "Altruism and Society: A Social Learning Perspective," *Ethics* 92 (April 1982): 428–29.

which were passed on to future generations and continue to have sub-conscious effects on human behaviour in the present. Wilson argues that most human altruism is soft-core or directly self-oriented, which provides a sociobiological basis for a social contract model of community and society.[83]

There are two primary strengths of a sociobiological model of community. First, its basic assumption is that community should protect and nurture human survival and propagation. This is a helpful reminder to ecclesial communities that their existence is meant to serve both the creation mandate and the redemption mandate. One should not be elevated above the other, as when efforts to feed the hungry and promote justice are regarded as simply a pretext for evangelism or, alternately, when spirituality is regarded as simply a pretext for social activism. Conversely, both serve God's holistic intentions for the world.[84] Second, like the social contract model it contains valid insights concerning the selfish orientation of human beings, which we ignore to our peril. Community always involves varying degrees of negotiation, mediation, and conflict resolution concerning the differing personal goals and ambitions of individual members. Therefore, wise communities are aware of this and create just authority structures as well as healthy checks and balances that provide accountability for those in leadership.

One weakness of this model is that, like the social contract model, it views social bonds as being ultimately self-serving. Thus, it cannot adequately sustain a Christian understanding of personhood and practice of community, which is built upon a love that goes beyond personal altruism and is rooted in and empowered by God's other-centred *agape* love.[85] Despite certain advocates of the health and wealth gospel or the church growth movement, the ultimate purpose of Christian community is not collective self-aggrandizement as Wilson suggests. Rather, it is union with others in Christ by the Spirit and formation into Christ's image, which includes a *cruciform* (i.e., self-sacrificial) pattern of worship and discipleship (e.g., Matt 17:24; Mark 9:33–37; Phil 2:5–11). Second, a sociobiological approach cannot provide an adequate basis for social ethics. While its scientific observations might provide some helpful and relevant in-

---

[83] Wilson, *On Human Nature*, 158–64. Wilson argues that the tendency toward individual self-preservation is a good thing and provides a more stable basis for society than 'hard-core' group preservation. Better to have many self-motivated individuals contract together to pursue their goals under common limitations than to have whole groups at war with each other.

[84] Dietrich Bonhoeffer, *Ethics*, vol. 6 *Dietrich Bonhoeffer Works*, trans. Reinhard Krauss, Charles C. West, and Douglas W. Stott (Minneapolis: Fortress, 2005), 153–70; John Stott, ed., *Making Christ Known: Historic Mission Documents from the Lausanne Movement 1974–1989* (Grand Rapids: Eerdmans, 1996), 24, 28; Miroslav Volf, *Work in the Spirit: Toward a Theology of Work* (Eugene: Wipf and Stock, 2001), 99–102.

[85] Sociobiology seems unable to distinguish between reciprocal love and selfishness; in essence, it reduces all love to lustful desire (not necessarily in a sexual sense, but in the sense of desiring another for one's own personal benefit).

sights into how human nature is changing and developing, "scientific accounts of evolution, human behaviour, neurochemistry, and genetics will always 'underdetermine' ethics."[86] For one thing, self-preservation is not always a good guide to action. At a communal or group level, a self-preserving mindset could lead to an institutionalism that continues to promote the status quo, for better or for worse. Or it could lead to a preoccupation with institutional growth while ignoring the cultivation of more important values and virtues. Moreover, genetic drives and predispositions are not always a helpful guide to healthy relationships or ethical actions. For example, genetic influences have been linked to the over-consumption of fatty foods, dangerous thrill-seeking behaviour, some forms of sexual deviancy, and alcoholism, but such influences are usually not determinative. Human beings are significantly complex creatures that can (and often should) choose to ignore their genetic tendencies.[87] Finally, the sociobiological approach suffers from epistemological deficiencies, including unexamined assumptions and commitments that lead to reductionist explanations of complex realities.[88] Moreover, its epistemological naivety sometimes leads it to posit explanations that seem too convenient and excessively simplistic. For example, if a sociobiologist observed that infants cry mostly at night, she could explain such behaviour as an adaptive advantage to inhibit competing pregnancies. However, if she observed that infants cry mostly during the day, she could explain it as a genetic advantage to hide the infant from predators.[89] It seems that for every set of observations a sociobiological conjecture is readily at hand. As one critic sharply warns, "a theory so protean that it can account for all observations about life may be little more than a veiled truism."[90] While a sociobiological description in some cases explains too much, in other cases it explains too little due to its reductive-naturalistic assumptions. For example, at the discovery of a biological mechanism regulating moral reasoning a sociobiologist might conclude that human values, ideals, and aspirations are simply adaptive advantages that serve biological self-preservation. However, it could just as easily be the case that certain moral values or laws pre-date human biology and pervade the nature of things (i.e., if God designed the cosmos with certain purposes and goals in mind). If such were the case, one would expect

---

[86] Pope, "Engaging E.O. Wilson," 237–38.
[87] See James C. Peterson, *Changing Human Nature: Ecology, Ethics, Genes, and God* (Grand Rapids: Eerdmans, 2010), 68, 70–71, 73–76, 183, 191, 195, 198.
[88] Stephen Pope exposes two such unexamined assumptions: (1) the methodological assumption that morality can be sufficiently analyzed and explained by the methods of the biological sciences; and (2) the (Humean) assumption that morality is largely a matter of emotions or "intuition based on emotion" (Pope, "Engaging E.O. Wilson," 234–35).
[89] Peterson, *Changing Human Nature*, 72. Peterson credits the example to John C. Avise, *The Genetic Gods: Evolution and Belief in Human Affairs* (Cambridge, MA: Harvard University Press, 1998), 155–56.
[90] Tom Bethell, "Against Sociobiology," *First Things* (January 2001): 19.

that natural selection would favour the evolution of biological capacities that enable moral reasoning.

Being Human as Caring-For Others

With roots in the ethics of care, this view sees the human being primarily as a caring person and human community as concentric circles of care. According to Nel Noddings, relationships are at the heart of what it means to be human and reciprocal caring is the corresponding framework for ethics. Noddings asserts that the category of "relation" is ontologically basic for human beings, though she explains that this claim is based not in metaphysical or theological speculation but in phenomenological observations about human existence.[91] She writes, "Taking *relation* as ontologically basic simply means that we recognize human encounter and affective response as a basic fact of human existence."[92] According to Noddings, caring is the one universal human reality because all people want to be cared for (even if they themselves do not care for others). The impulse toward caring is rooted in one's immersion in natural caring relationships, beginning with a child's early relationship to its parents. Through such basic formative relationships a person gradually learns both to receive and give what Nodding calls "natural care".[93] This natural caring impulse ought to direct the way people think about and treat others. When facing a situation in which caring does not come naturally or is difficult, one must then draw upon what Noddings calls "ethical care". Ethical care is based in and empowered by natural care and allows one to extend the caring relation beyond natural inclinations by drawing on the memories and feelings associated with one's experience of natural caring relationships. Noddings explains, "Because we . . . have been immersed in relations of care since birth, we often naturally respond as carers to others. When we need to draw on ethical caring, we turn to an ethical ideal constituted from memories of caring and being cared for."[94] While natural caring is part of the basic experience of being human, ethical caring must be taught and cultivated through role modeling, dialogue (as empathetic relating, not debate), practice through care-giving experiences (e.g., tending to guests, caring for small children, community service, etc.), and what Noddings calls "confirmation" by mentors and teachers (e.g., calling out the best in someone,

---

[91] Nel Noddings, *Educating Moral People: A Caring Alternative to Character Education* (New York: Teachers College Press, 2002), 21. Noddings writes, "It does not depend on gods, or eternal verities or an essential human nature, or postulated underlying structure of human consciousness. Even its relational ontology points to something observable in this world—the fact that 'I' am defined in relation, that none of us could be an 'individual', or a 'person', or an entity recognizably human if we were not in relation." (15)

[92] Nel Noddings, *Caring: A Feminine Approach to Ethics & Moral Education* (Los Angeles: University of California Press, 1984), 4.

[93] By *natural* Noddings does not mean biological, but the basic formative caring relationships that one experiences during infancy and childhood.

[94] Noddings, *Educating Moral People*, 15.

always giving them the benefit of the doubt).[95] These strategies for moral education encourage "engrossment", in which one empathizes with another's concrete situation and comes to understand what that person is feeling and experiencing.[96] They also encourage what Noddings calls "displacement of motivation", in which the one-caring adopts and promotes the goals of the one cared-for.[97] In sum, for Noddings genuine human existence is about caring and being cared for.

Type 6: Concentric circles of care
In a model of community based on the ethics of care, people are bound together in concrete relationships of giving and receiving care. One's community of "cared-fors" is multi-layered and involves a kind of hierarchy of care defined by four concentric circles, which are differentiated by proximity of relationship to the one-caring.[98] In this model one is most committed to one's *intimate others*, those falling in one's innermost circle such as one's spouse, family, and close friends. These relationships trump all other ethical relations (special dilemmas arise when conflicts occur within this circle). Moving outward, one is committed in a more limited way to people for whom one has *personal regard*. These may include one's larger friendship group, co-workers, and acquaintances. Three considerations guide one's responsibility here, including one's own feelings, the expectations of other persons, and the nature of situational relationships (i.e., what one owes a boss in comparison to a teacher or a coach is partially determined by the nature and purpose of the relationship: one owes one's boss integrity and quality of work, one's teacher respect and diligence, and one's coach commitment to attending practices). The third concentric circle includes *potential others* for whom one is prepared to care. These are either people one has yet to meet in the future or those connected through a "chain of relationships" to others in one's inner circle of care (e.g., a wife's friend, a friend's mother, etc.). The final, outer circle includes *strangers*. Noddings argues that we have no real responsibility to care for strangers, other than being open and receptive to the possibility that strangers could move inward in our concentric circles of care. This is because, for Noddings, genuine caring must always be concrete (involving actual personal relationships) and reciprocal rather than ideal and paternalistic. We cannot "care-for" everyone abstractly and we are not morally obligated to do so, but we can "care-about" everyone in the qualified sense of being open and receptive.[99] An interesting outcome of this view is that Noddings insists that we have no ethical obligation to care-for

---

[95] Noddings, *Educating Moral People*, 15–20; See also *Caring*, 121–24.
[96] Noddings, *Caring*, 9, 18–19, 30–35, 112–13.
[97] Noddings, *Caring*, 112–13; Raja Halwani, "Care Ethics and Virtue Ethics," *Hypatia* 18 (Fall 2003): 162–63.
[98] See Noddings, *Caring*, 46–47.
[99] For Noddings's explication of this distinction between caring-for and caring-about, see *Caring*, 18, 112–13 and *Educating Moral People*, 86–88.

starving children in Africa. While our concern for them might be positive, beneficial, and honourable, it is too abstract to count as genuine caring-for and is not morally obligated (though we might care-about such people as strangers and demonstrate unusually generous support).[100]

An account of being human and being in community based on the ethics of care has some compelling strengths. First, its recognition of the primacy of relationships deeply resonates with the Christian tradition, in which love for God and others is central. As we will see in the next chapter, relationships have constitutive significance in a theological account of being human. This emphasis on relatedness, encounter, receptivity, and responsiveness provides a needed corrective to rationalistic and individualistic conceptions of community and ethics. Moreover, Noddings's claim that relationships are ontologically basic finds further grounding in the doctrine of the Trinity. From a trinitarian perspective, not only is the category of relationship ontologically basic for human beings, more fundamentally it is deeply embedded in the structures of ultimate reality, being intrinsic to the nature and character of the triune God.[101] Second, a community of care model has important implications for spiritual and ethical formation. Specifically, it encourages us to focus on forming and cultivating *people in their concrete contexts*, rather than indoctrinating them with abstract rules and principles. While not rejecting the place of rules and principles altogether, a community of care model aims to foster a caring environment of formative relationships, which begins to shape the way people treat and respond to others. Third, a community of care model recognizes the importance of emotions for human development, life, and ethics. It reminds us that we are

---

[100] See Noddings, *Caring*, 86. Noddings identifies two criteria to guide decisions concerning our obligation to care for others: (1) the existence of or potential for a present relationship; and (2) the dynamic potential for growth in the relationship, including the potential for increased reciprocity or even mutuality. The first establishes an absolute obligation and the second prioritizes one's obligations.

[101] Noddings herself might object to grounding her theory this way, finding trinitarian doctrine too abstract and speculative (and, granted, in some cases debates about the Trinity have degenerated into abstract speculation). Actually, the doctrine arose as the early church reflected on its concrete experiences of God's actual dealings with human beings, especially though the Incarnation, life, death, and Resurrection of Jesus Christ and through God's ongoing presence with them since the Pentecostal outpouring of the Holy Spirit. Concerning the development of trinitarian doctrine and its concrete relevance for Christian life, see for example: David Coffey, *Deus Trinitas: The Doctrine of the Triune God* (New York: Oxford University Press, 1999); Stanley J. Grenz, *Rediscovering the Triune God: The Trinity in Contemporary Theology* (Minneapolis: Fortress, 2004); Catherine Mowry LaCugna, *God For Us: The Trinity and Christian Life* (New York: HarperSanFrancisco, 1993); Ted Peters, *God as Trinity: Relationality and Temporality in Divine Life* (Louisville: Westminster John Knox, 1991); Karl Rahner, *The Trinity* (New York: Crossroad, 2004); James B. Torrance, *Worship, Community & the Triune God of Grace* (Downers Grove: InterVarsity Press, 1996); and Thomas F. Torrance, *The Christian Doctrine of God: One Being Three Persons* (New York: T & T Clark, 1996).

emotional beings, not just rational robots, and that our emotions are to be cultivated and channelled rather than repressed or ignored. This recognition that we are emotional beings is a good reminder to ecclesial communities as they shape their worship and liturgy and develop their strategies for discipleship and spiritual formation.[102]

Probably the greatest weakness of a community of care model is its treatment of the stranger, as explicated by Noddings's notion of concentric circles of care. In ethical terms, in the caring model proximity of relationship always trumps degree of need. However, from a Christian perspective, these must be held in close balance. Undoubtedly, our first priority is to love God and to care for those whom God has entrusted to us. However, we are also called to demonstrate care for our ecclesial community, which involves a social bond that transcends natural or biological family relationships, socio-political ties, and the sharing of common interests and benefits (e.g., Gal 3:26–28). Moreover, Christian care explicitly extends to those who are different and especially to those who are in need.[103] From a Christian perspective, Noddings's view lacks a commitment to addressing and overcoming social and systemic injustices. For example, who will have the proximity and the means to care for the underprivileged if people are responsible only for those in their own socio-economic or geographic circles? In contrast, Christianity expands the concept of proximity by redefining our understanding of the neighbour, the stranger, and the alien.[104] A second weakness of the model is that the criterion of care does not by itself help us to identify precisely which relationships or forms of community are healthy or morally praiseworthy. All that matters is the caring relation between people in the circle. But what if an individual in our circle or even an entire community is complicit in evil? The mafia looks after its own and honour exists even among thieves, but should one really befriend the mafia

---

[102] To make the point, Noddings quotes C.S. Lewis's response to educators in his time who, in fear of the influence of propaganda, were teaching children to set emotions aside in favour of critical and calculating rational thought. Lewis writes, "For every one pupil who needs to be guarded from a weak excess of sensibility there are three who need to be awakened from the slumber of cold vulgarity. . . . [B]y starving the sensibility of our pupils we only make them easier prey to the propagandist when he comes. For famished nature will be avenged and a hard heart is not infallible protection against a soft head." (Quoted in Noddings, *Educating Moral People*, 42).

[103] See Nicholas Wolterstorff, "Can Human Rights Survive Secularization?" parts I and II, *Perspectives* 23, no. 3 (March 2008): 10–14, and no. 4 (April 2008): 12–17.

[104] Christine Pohl points to examples such the Good Samaritan, the "least of these" in Matthew 25, the early church's practice of ministry to widows and orphans, and the church's status-transcending celebration of the Eucharist, in order to show that one's neighbour includes people very different from us and otherwise considered to be strangers. Pohl also points back to Israelite law (e.g., Exod 23), which legislates protection of and provision for foreigners. See her book, *Making Room: Recovering Hospitality as a Christian Tradition* (Grand Rapids: Eerdmans, 1999).

or join the circle of thieves?[105] Thus, as Raja Halwani points out, "something is needed to regulate and to ward off the possibility of such moral corruption."[106] A third weakness of a community of care model has to do with motivation. If caring for others provides the foundation for relationships, for community, and for ethics, what happens if one simply does not care about or empathize with other people? Noddings's answer is that when natural care is lacking one must invoke ethical care, but why would someone do this? If care is the only basic ontological reality, and if one has no recourse to other more basic ethical criteria (e.g., transcendent moral imperatives or fundamental virtues), what would motivate a person to exercise ethical care? In contrast, a Christian perspective prioritizes love while also recognizing that love is not merely a human possibility, but is deeply grounded in the love of God, empowered by the Spirit of God, and cultivated within the body of Christ, which is the community of faith. This is important because God's redemptive, reconciling love is at the heart of a Christian understanding of community.[107]

Impact of contemporary views of personhood on the church

Stanley Hauerwas observes that the church is constantly being tempted to imitate the false politics of the world, especially when false worldly narratives about human existence and purpose begin to take the place of those embodied in Scripture and the Christian tradition.[108] If Hauerwas's observation is correct then it is reasonable to ask: How have the dominant rival conceptions of human personhood and community discussed above impacted the way Christians understand and practice ecclesiology? The analysis provided above already gives a partial answer and what follows below provides some concrete examples. It is important to note that the following comparison is intended to be typological and does not assume a one-to-one correspondence between proposed types and particular ecclesial communities or church movements. It is quite likely that specific churches and movements combine one or more of the proposed types. Moreover, we should acknowledge forthrightly that all of the types have both positive and negative features. The typology is therefore intended as a tool for analyzing and evaluating conceptual differences and for generating awareness of probable practical tendencies and their related strengths and weaknesses.

---

[105] See Psalm 1.

[106] Halwani, "Care Ethics," 163. Halwani picks up on Victoria Davion's criticism that engrossment and motivational displacement are problematic if the one being cared-for is evil. See her article, "Autonomy, Integrity, and Care," *Social Theory and Practice* 19, no. 2 (1993): 161–82.

[107] E.g., 2 Cor 5:16–21; Eph 2:11–18; 1 John 4:7–21.

[108] Stanley Hauerwas, *In Good Company: The Church as Polis* (Notre Dame: University of Notre Dame Press, 1995), 8.

Social Contract and the Attractional Church

The main feature of an "attractional" model of church is that it is designed to appeal to potential and existing members on the basis of the benefits it offers them.[109] There are two basic versions of the attractional church. One version, as represented by many seeker and independent churches, is analogous to a social contract understanding of community. It involves an implicit contractual agreement in which religious consumers offer faithful attendance and financial giving to the church organization in exchange for religious goods and services they receive from it. Such a consumerist orientation creates a tendency for churches to cater to the self-actualizing goals of its patrons. This approach is indebted to modernist values and epistemological assumptions, such as rationalism, individualism, and the doctrine of progress. It has led attractional churches to under-emphasize history, tradition, corporeal aspects of worship (liturgy, art, architecture, multisensory expression, etc.) and tangible and emotional experiences of the Spirit. Of course, if an attractional church were to perceive these as being important to potential members it would emphasize them, but this is to treat them as instrumental rather than intrinsic goods. The second version of the attractional church is analogous to the Kantian notion of community as a group joined together by a common sense of duty under the moral law. Representatives of this version include many conservative churches that distance themselves from the world in order to maintain and promote traditional values and lifestyles. This approach is less consumerist in its orientation, but attractional nevertheless because it envisions the church as an instrumental aid to the moral and spiritual formation of individuals.

The primary strengths of the consumerist attractional type include its ability to draw large numbers and secure basic commitment, its adaptive flexibility, and its relevance to the lives of contemporary people. The primary strengths of the conservative attractional type include its ability to secure group conformity and the sense of security and convention it provides for its members. The weakness of both versions of the attractional church include excessive individualism lacking an understanding of the church as a mystical union of believers deeply united in the Spirit (and as an intrinsic and not merely an instrumental good), an inward focus lacking due emphasis on social justice and the pursuit of Christ's kingdom purposes in and for the world, and a truncated approach to spirituality failing to balance Scripture *and tradition,* reason *and experience of the Spirit.*

Self-Defining Existentialism and the Emerging Church

A key feature of the existential church type is the priority it gives to authenticity and self-expression (or self-assertion), along with a rejection of rationalism and collectivism. This church type is non-institutional and non-hierarchical. It

---

[109] For a helpful discussion and critique of the attractional church model, see Michael Frost and Alan Hirsch, *The Shaping of Things to Come: Innovation and Ministry in the 21st Century* (Grand Rapids: Baker, 2013).

finds unity not primarily in common assent to doctrines, but in shared experiences and values. It communicates truth not in abstract propositional statements, but through artful expression and concrete pragmatic action. One contemporary movement that represents this type is the Emerging Church.[110] While the movement is diverse, it is possible to identify some of the dominant values and practices common to its proponents in North America. The Emerging Church is committed to: (1) a postmodern expression and practice of Christianity; (2) a kingdom approach to discipleship, mission, and evangelism; (3) an ecumenical openness to exploring and combining the best of diverse Christian ecclesial traditions, and (4) a sustained critique of modern North American Christianity.[111] The Emerging Church shares some common affinities with the existential church type, including its stress on individual freedom, authenticity, and expression, its epistemological suspicion of abstract and propositional truths, and its resistance of oppressive systems and collectives.

Combined with its Christian convictions, these existential commitments contribute many of its strengths. To cite just one example, the Emerging Church writers are critical of the seeker sensitive movement for capitulating to a modern, consumerist mindset in its evangelism strategies.[112] As Brian McLaren writes, *"Postmodern people don't want a God shrunken to fit modern tastes."*[113] In contrast, the Emerging Church movement is "a retrieval of the deep theological tradition of wrestling with the intellectual and spiritual difficulties inherent in the Christian faith."[114] Its leaders envision a different kind of church, one that is relevant precisely because it is authentic, one that is evangelistic precisely because it is distinctively and unapologetically Christian. However, its affinities with existentialism also lead to some weaknesses. These include trendiness

---

[110] For a more detailed exploration and assessment of the emerging church, see my article "John Wesley in Conversation with the Emerging Church," *Asbury Theological Journal* 63 (Spring 2008): 75–93. See also Jeff Keuss, "The Emergent Church and Neo-correlational Theology after Tillich, Schleiermacher and Browning," *Scottish Journal of Theology* 61, no. 4 (2008): 450–61.

[111] See Dan Kimball, *The Emerging Church: Vintage Christianity for New Generations* (Grand Rapids: Zondervan, 2003); Eddie Gibbs and Ryan K. Bolger, *Emerging Churches: Creating Christian Community in Postmodern Cultures* (Grand Rapids: Baker, 2005); Tony Jones, *The New Christians: Dispatches from the Emergent Frontier* (San Francisco: Jossey-Bass, 2008); 70–72; Brian D. McLaren, *The Secret Message of Jesus: Uncovering the Truth that Could Change Everything* (Nashville: W. Publishing Group, 2006) and *Everything Must Change: Jesus, Global Crises, and a Revolution of Hope* (Nashville: Thomas Nelson, 2008).

[112] Kimball distinguishes the best innovators of the seeker approach (e.g., Rick Warren) from those who employ a one-size-fits-all church strategy. See also Jones, *The New Christians*, 71.

[113] Brian D. McLaren, *More Ready Than You Realize: Evangelism as Dance in the Postmodern Matrix* (Grand Rapids: Zondervan, 2002), 52.

[114] Jones, *The New Christians*, 109.

and elitism (in some cases almost a Nietzschean sense of superiority),[115] radical individualism,[116] carelessness or cynicism toward truth and authority,[117] and a tendency among its adherents to express freedom in terms of liberation *from*—but not *for*—their former evangelical heritage through "narratives of disaffiliation."[118]

Self-Perpetuation and the Church Growth Movement

The main feature of the self-perpetuating church type is that the primary focus is on church preservation and growth, akin to the species and group preserving orientation posited at the centre of sociobiology. This driving focus parallels the sociobiological explanation of religious community as collective self-aggrandizement. A representative example of this type is the church growth movement, which advocates efficiency, progress through goal fulfillment, measurable growth, and the use of business models to plan and execute strategic vision and mission, programming, governance, and marketing. Time, energy, and resources are directed toward whatever contributes to the growth of the church; whatever does not contribute to organizational growth is treated as being of lesser importance. This approach has several strengths, including effective strategic planning and administration, high impact and efficiency in executing its plans, large numbers and financial leverage due to economies of scale,

---

[115] See Scott Bader-Saye, "The Emergent Matrix," *Christian Century* 121, no. 24 (2004): 20; Andy Crouch, "The Emergent Mystique," *Christianity Today* 48, no. 11 (2004): 37; Philip Harrold, "Deconversion in the Emerging Church," *International Journal for the Study of the Christian Church* 6 (March, 2006), 86.

[116] For example, some emerging churches practice 'mosaic' worship gatherings, in which individuals are free to wander and express themselves in whatever ways suit them (e.g., painting or sculpting, listening to music, prayer walking, labyrinths, etc.).

[117] For example, Brian McLaren mines a wide spectrum of traditions and theologies in order to construct his own blend of Christian orthodoxy. While his spirit of creativity and charity is inspiring, in several instances he misrepresents the traditions from which he claims to draw. For example, McLaren is clearly not a Calvinist or a fundamentalist, yet he claims these titles for himself by redefining their meaning (even revising the acronym TULIP with words representing his own views). See Brian D. McLaren, *A Generous Orthodoxy* (Grand Rapids: Zondervan, 2004). As another example, Tony Jones writes, "Whereas traditional groupings of Christians are either bounded sets (for example, Roman Catholicism or Presbyterianism—you know whether you're in or out based on membership) or centered sets (for example, Evangelicalism, which centers on certain core beliefs), emergent Christians do not have membership or doctrine to hold them together. The glue is relationship" (Jones, *The New Christians*, 56). Jones is not shallow and his point is well taken: relationships are essential to Christian faith and love is the essence of God's character. However, in response to his statement, surely Christian life together is a certain kind of relationship, one with specific shared commitments, beliefs, values, and goals?

[118] Philip Harrold, "Deconversion in the Emerging Church," 84–86. Harrold cites examples of people referring to their transition to Emerging Church contexts as "outgrowing", "wrestling with", "disentangling from", or "being wrenched out of" traditional church contexts.

valuable insights concerning consumer psychology, and proficiency in casting vision and leading change.

The greatest weakness of the self-perpetuating type is a tendency toward theological superficiality, combined with a pragmatic and uncritical adoption of business models to run the church and direct its priorities. Consequently, churches representative of this type tend to place intrinsic value on instrumental goods such as growth, efficiency, and change, while placing instrumental value on intrinsic goods such as spiritual formation, virtue cultivation, and social justice. In so doing, they prioritize organizational church growth over kingdom growth (or at the very least equate them).[119] Of course, churches of this type sometimes promote and foster these latter goods, but they tend to regard them as instrumentally valuable for meeting needs and thus contributing to the bottom line of organizational growth. Moreover, they believe that such kingdom goods will be achieved as an indirect outcome of the growth of the church (rather like the capitalist belief in the invisible hand of the market, which combines and directs individual self-interests toward the common good). However this reverses the New Testament view, as evident in Jesus's kingdom parables, that kingdom growth logically precedes and creates authentic church growth (just as God's reign always precedes and guides faithful stewardship).[120] Moreover, the New Testament depicts the church as the sign, foretaste, and instrument of the eschatological kingdom of God.[121] This basic weakness of the self-perpetuating type leads to other problems, such as a tendency toward homogeneity rather than unity-in-diversity (the result of niche marketing strategies) and a truncated view of mission (the focus is church expansion).[122]

---

[119] Hauerwas makes the rather stinging charge that "Current 'church growth' strategies seem intent on proving that you can get people to come to church whether or not God exists." Stanley Hauerwas, *In Good Company: The Church as Polis* (Notre Dame: University of Notre Dame Press, 1995), 4. Hauerwas is not speaking about the intentions of church growth advocates, but is pointing out the inherent connection between media and message (i.e., draining uncomfortable Christian content creates a secularized message fostering a secularized church).

[120] On this matter see George E. Ladd, *A Theology of the New Testament*, ed. Donald A. Hagner (Grand Rapids: Eerdmans, 1993), 110–17.

[121] Darrell L. Guder, ed., *Missional Church: A Vision for the Sending of the Church in North America* (Grand Rapids: Eerdmans, 1998), 101, 104, 106; Lesslie Newbigin, *The Gospel in a Pluralist Society* (Grand Rapids: Eerdmans, 1989), 229.

[122] Kevin Vanhoozer notes that C. Peter Wagner promotes the "homogeneous units principle" as an important key to church growth in his book *Our Kind of People: The Ethical Dimensions of Church Growth in America* (Atlanta: John Knox, 1979). Vanhoozer comments, "Such pragmatism is clear and simple, but it results in a design for living together as church that is ultimately subevangelical and sub-Protestant to the extent that it bears witness to (*pro* + *testare*) something less than the truth of the gospel (*euangelion*), namely, that we have been made one people 'in Christ.'" Kevin J. Vanhoozer, *The Drama of Doctrine: A Canonical-linguistic Approach to Christian Theology* (Louisville: Westminster John Knox, 2005), 439.

Church as a Community of Care

In the caring church type, the focus is on being a loving and inclusive caring community.[123] Like the concentric circles of care model promoted by the ethics of care, the church is envisioned as a large family or close friendship network, in which the inner social life of the community is of primary importance. Accordingly, the community prioritizes efforts toward strengthening relationships and community involvement while devoting less attention to teaching doctrine or involvement in mission. It is likely to be strong in pastoral care and counselling but may be week in the areas of preaching, teaching, and evangelism. Its social bonds are primarily emotional or sentimental and its tendency is to bring together people who are already like-minded and like-hearted (it is more important to get along than to argue the finer points of theology or politics).

One strength of this type is that it provides a caring environment that prioritizes relationships and practical care for its members. A second strength is that it focuses on people primarily as relational beings, rather than as units of an organization, participants in church programs, or consumers of religious goods and services. A third strength is that its relational approach has appeal for contemporary people in postmodern culture who are longing for personal connection, a safe place to belong and ask questions, and support in navigating life and raising children. One weakness of the caring type is an under-emphasis on truth and doctrine, leading to a sentimental sociality that neglects an emphasis on the church as a *kingdom* community dedicated to following Jesus's teachings and seeking first God's kingdom of justice and righteousness (Matt 6:33; see chapter 8). A second weakness is group insularity and inwardness, leading to the neglect of strangers and outsiders and possibly (given the first weakness) the development of exclusive social cliques within the group. A third weakness is that this type lacks a strong sense of mission and a passion to seek and promote justice in and for the world, beyond its own insular social network.

Concluding Summary: Two Problems to Address

The existence of rival and sometimes incommensurable accounts of being human and being in community in contemporary culture fosters at least two major problems, both of which distort our understanding of human sociality and ethical discernment and responsibility. The first problem is reductionism. Contemporary accounts tend to describe the human being in "nothing but" terms within the confines of rationalism, emotivism, biological determinism, or sentimentalism. The second problem is that the coexistence of these rival contemporary accounts leads to the polarization of key issues and the creation of false dualisms in our understanding and practice of community and ethics. With respect to community, we find ourselves caught between individualism and collectiv-

---

[123] The sentimental church for the like-hearted bears some affinity to Avery Dulles's 'mystical communion' church type (Dulles, *Models*, chapter 3).

ism, self-fulfillment and service to others, freedom and authoritarianism, and inwardness versus outward focused in orientation (e.g., discipleship vs. evangelism, community relational formation vs. missional impact). Similarly, concerning ethics, we struggle to integrate personal, social, and global ethics, and find ourselves caught in polarities and dualisms, such as individual freedom versus biological determinism, rationalist rule following versus emotivist relativism (corresponding with foundationalist and existentialist epistemologies), and personal piety versus social justice. Furthermore, dualisms also confuse and frustrate the church's role in impacting culture (e.g., sacred versus secular, syncretism versus withdrawal, triumphalism versus passive defensiveness, and individual soul-saving versus societal transformation).

What is needed to remedy the situation is a holistically nuanced and theologically thick description of what it means to be human (uniting theory and praxis), one which clarifies and integrates the intrinsically social-personal and ethical-spiritual character of genuine, redeemed human existence as the *new humanity in Christ*. My proposal is that such an account would contribute to a better understanding of Christian community and ecclesiology. It would clarify the nature of the church's inner sociality and its outward mission of partnering with God to transform individuals, society, and the world, in light of God's imminent and in-breaking new creation. Thus, in the chapters that follow I will offer not simply a new and improved church type to be added to the others, but a comprehensive theological framework for understanding eccesiology in light of theological anthropology.

Part II: Theological Anthropology in Trinitarian Perspective

CHAPTER 3

The Human Person as a Relational Creature

It is really the God-relationship that makes a human being a human being
(Søren Kierkegaard)[1]

Introduction

From a theological perspective, what is most distinctive about human beings is that they are created to be in communion with God.[2] What makes human beings most fully and uniquely human is not something they possess in and of themselves, for example some essential nature distinguishing them from other non-human creatures. Rather, what makes them fully and uniquely human is that *God relates to them* in a special way as Creator, Reconciler, and Consummator.[3] This unique relationship with God grounds and sustains human identity,

---

[1] Søren Kierkegaard, *Concluding Unscientific Postscript to Philosophical Fragments*, vol. 1, ed. Howard V. Hong and Edna H. Hong (Princeton: Princeton University Press, 1992), 244.

[2] This idea is well supported throughout the historic Christian tradition. For example, see: Athanasius, *On the Incarnation of the Word* 4.4–6, 5.1, in *NPNF2-04: Athanasius: Select Works and Letters*, ed. Philip Schaff and Henry Wace (Edinburgh: T & T Clark, 1891), 38; Clement of Alexandria, *The Instructor* III.1 in *ANF02: Fathers of the Second Century: Hermas, Tatian, Athenagoras, Theophilus, and Clement of Alexandria (Entire)*, ed. Philip Schaff (Grand Rapids: CCEL, 2004), 271; Augustine, *The Confessions of St. Augustine*, trans. John K. Ryan (New York: Doubleday, 1960), 44; Anselm, *Proslogium* (chapter 1) in *Proslogium; Monologium; An Appendix in Behalf of the Fool by Gaunilon; and Cur Deus Homo*, trans. Sidney Norton Deane (Chicago: Open Court, 1926), 4–5.

[3] However, as James Peterson points out, human beings do possess an emergent capacity that makes a relationship with God possible. As Peterson puts it, "The biology of *Homo sapiens* is continuous with other hominids and the rest of life. Yet in *Homo sapiens* we find emergent capabilities that constitute a unique being. It is this being to whom God introduces God's self, making possible the bearing of the *imago Dei*, the image of God." James C. Peterson, "*Homo Sapiens* as *Homo Dei*: Paleoanthropology, Human Uniqueness, and the Image of God," *Toronto Journal of Theology* 27, no. 1 (2011): 17. So, God's relating to humans does indicate that they are distinct from the other creatures in their emergent capacities (consciousness, reasoning, morality, etc.). The point I am making is that God's relational purposes for human beings (as God's

purpose, and authentic existence in the world.[4] As Miroslav Volf argues, if God's relation to human beings is "the key to their humanness," then their communion with God is "the key to their true identity". Thus, "They are truly themselves when they are in communion with the Creator and Redeemer through the Spirit."[5] This primary relationship with God constitutes human beings as relational creatures that live in openness and receptivity toward the world and partial fulfilment in the relationships they enjoy with God and fellow human beings.[6] Moreover, given this relational constitution, human existence is intrinsically *ethical* existence because a right relationship with God fosters an orientation that is attuned to God's purposes and priorities, leading to a way of living that promotes the well-being of self, others, and world. This chapter will explicate the relational character of human existence as being grounded in the love of God and reflecting the dynamic and ecstatic life of the Trinity. It will then explore some implications that this relational anthropological view has for Christian life and ethics.

Trinitarian Love is God's Essential Nature

One God, three persons

The New Testament declares that God is love (1 John 4:8). In attesting to this, Scripture is not just telling us that love is merely an aspect of God's character or a description of how God normally acts (though both of these statements are true), but more fundamentally that love defines God's essential nature. Since love is God's essential nature, Luther argued that love properly determines God's disposition and actions toward human begins, while wrath is God's "alien work" and is always at the service of God's love. As Luther puts it, "For love's anger (wrath) seeks and wills to sunder the evil that it hates from the good that it loves, in order that the good and its love may be preserved."[7] Now if love is God's *essential* nature then it must be true that love has always characterized God, even before the creation of human beings or even heavenly creatures. If love is essential to God's nature, then love is constitutive of the divine

---

covenant partners) preceded their development. God did not choose us because we were rational, but made us rational in order to make us covenant partners.

[4] Stanley J. Grenz, *Theology for the Community of God* (Grand Rapids: Eerdmans, 1994), 127, 140–43. Grenz writes, "With Adam (or 'homo sapiens') and solely with Adam, God enters into a special relationship or covenant. In this covenant God declares a new intention for creation, namely, that this creation—Adam and his offspring—fulfil a special destiny by being related to God in a way unique from all other aspects of the universe that God has made" (149).

[5] Miroslav Volf, *Work in the Spirit: Toward a Theology of Work* (Eugene: Wipf and Stock, 2001), 133.

[6] T.F. Torrance, *Calvin's Doctrine of Man* (London: Lutterworth, 1949), 35.

[7] Quoted in Dennis Ngien, *The Suffering of God According to Martin Luther's Theologia Crucis* (Eugene, OR: Wipf and Stock, 1995), 107.

life itself and God is eternally a loving Being.[8] As an essentially loving Being, God exists not as an isolated individual deity but in the eternal communion of Father, Son, and Holy Spirit. Thus, the One God exists as three subsisting persons; and, as three divine persons-in-relation, the Father, Son, and Holy Spirit subsist eternally as the One God. Of course, our knowledge of God's trinitarian existence as Father, Son, and Holy Spirit derives not from abstract theological speculation about the word *love*, but from the biblical declaration that "God is love" interpreted by the historic Christian tradition in the light of the scriptural narratives that record the incarnation, life, death, resurrection, and ascension of Jesus Christ and the coming of the Holy Spirit at Pentecost. In other words, it is not that we first theorize a general idea about what love is and then project it onto God (as Feuerbach would have it). Rather, God through the person of Jesus Christ uniquely reveals God's Self to us and thereby demonstrates and imparts Love to us in the Holy Spirit.[9] The biblical writers began to reflect on the reality and implications of the Incarnation for their understanding of God, as they moved from the monotheism of the Old Testament to an emerging proto-trinitarian theology in the New Testament, which the early church fathers subsequently explicated and developed.[10]

The insight that God is love led Augustine to formulate his mutual love model of the Trinity. According to Augustine's mutual love model, the Father eternally generates the Son (without beginning or end) and the Holy Spirit proceeds from the Father and the Son and subsists as their mutual love.[11] Augus-

---

[8] John D. Zizioulas, *Being as Communion: Studies in Personhood and the Church* (Crestwood: St. Vladimir's Seminary Press, 2002), 46.

[9] For example, see the following passages: John 17:26; Rom 5:5; Gal 5:22; Eph 3:16–19; 2 Tim 1:7; 1 John 3:16, 4:10–12. Theologically, this statement depends on the affirmation that the Son and the Spirit are of one being or substance (*homoousion*) with the Father. See Thomas F. Torrance, *The Christian Doctrine of God: One Being Three Persons* (New York: T & T Clark, 1996), 80, 98, 127.

[10] It is beyond the scope of the present book to recount in detail the historical development of the doctrine of the Trinity, explaining how the early church came to interpret Scripture with the aid of tradition, reason, and experience of the Risen Christ through the Holy Spirit. Concerning such themes, I recommend the following books: Lewis Ayres, *Nicaea and Its Legacy: An Approach to Fourth-Century Trinitarian Theology* (Oxford/New York: Oxford University Press, 2004); David Coffey, *Deus Trinitas: The Doctrine of the Triune God* (New York: Oxford University Press, 1999); Grenz, *Theology*, 53–71; Wolfhart Pannenberg, *Systematic Theology*, vol. 1. (especially chapter 5), trans. Geoffrey W. Bromiley (Grand Rapids: Eerdmans, 1991); and Torrance, *The Christian Doctrine of God*.

[11] See Steven M. Studebaker, *Jonathan Edwards' Social Augustinian Trinitarianism in Historical and Contemporary Perspectives* (Piscataway, NJ: Gorgias, 2008), 109–34, "Integrating Pneumatology and Christology: A Trinitarian Modification of Clark H. Pinnock's Spirit Christology," *Pneuma* 28, no. 1 (2006): 12, and "Jonathan Edwards's Social *Augustinian* Trinitarianism: an Alternative to a Recent Trend," *Scottish Journal of Theology* 56, no. 3 (2003): 272. Note that Augustine does not here depersonalize the Holy Spirit, as the Spirit's role is active not passive. See Augustine,

tine begins his discussion with a reflection on the nature of love as depicted in 1 John 4:16: "God is love, and those who abide in love abide in God, and God abides in them." He discovers that love implies a Trinity of relationships and can serve as something of an analogy for the Triune God: "There you are with three, the lover, what is being loved, and love. And what is love but a kind of life coupling or trying to couple together two things, namely lover and what is being loved?"[12] This analogy does not espouse tritheism, as if there are three gods loving each other, but rather illustrates that God *is* love and as such exists in complexity and differentiation. In contrast, human beings image God in this manner only in a partial sense, for, as Augustine says, "it is not the case that anyone who loves himself is love except when *love* loves itself".[13] For the human individual, love is not its own subject, but only gains transcendence in the encounter with another human person. However, Augustine implies that there is inter-subjectivity within God, because in God (and in God alone) "love loves itself".[14] Love takes on such an all-encompassing reality as to be a transcendent Subject.[15]

To depict simultaneously the essential unity of God and the inter-relatedness of Father, Son, and Spirit, the Greek fathers of the early church employed the concept of *perichoresis*. This term was first used by Gregory of Naziansus to express the way in which the divine and human natures in the one person of Christ co-inhered without the integrity of either being diminished. In subsequent Cappadocian theology, *perichoresis* came to depict the mutual indwelling, co-inhering, or inter-penetrating of Father, Son, and Holy Spirit.[16] As Catherine Mowry LaCugna explains it, *perichoresis* illustrates that the three persons "mutually inhere in one another, draw life from one another, 'are' what they are by relation to one another."[17] According to T.F. Torrance, this move

---

The Trinity XV/5.36, vol. 5 *The Works of Saint Augustine: A Translation for the 21st Century*, trans. Edmund Hill, ed. John E. Rotelle (New York: New City, 1991), 424.

[12] Augustine, *The Trinity* VIII/5.14 (255).

[13] Augustine, *The Trinity* IV/1.2 (272). Emphasis added.

[14] Augustine, *The Trinity* IV/1.2 (272).

[15] Identifying the Spirit as the bond of Love shared between the Father and the Son is not unique to Augustine or even to the Western tradition. For example, we find this connection in Athenagoras of Athens, Athanasius (who says that the Spirit constitutes the union between Father and Son), Basil (the Spirit is the communion of the Father and Son, the bond of their union), Gregory of Nazianzus (the Spirit is the "intermediate" between Father and Son), and Epiphanius (the Spirit is "in the midst" of the Father and Son as the "Bond" of the Trinity). See Torrance, *The Christian Doctrine of God*, 167.

[16] See Torrance, *The Christian Doctrine of God*, 88–102. Torrance writes, "In the perichoretic Communion of the Father, Son and Holy Spirit who are the one Being of God, Unity and Trinity, Trinity and Unity mutually permeate and actively pass into one another" (179).

[17] Catherine Mowry LaCugna, *God For Us: The Trinity and Christian Life* (New York: HarperSanFrancisco, 1993). Quoted in Stanley J. Grenz, *The Social God and the Re-*

had deep and far reaching implications not only for the Christian understanding of God but also for the Christian understanding of the human person, with ripple effects influencing the development of modern conceptions of personhood.[18] This new understanding of personhood distinguished Christian thinking from classical Greek ontology in which being (*ousia*) had been conceived as something static and unchanging, as for example in Aristotle's distinction between *substances* and *accidents* and his restriction of *relation* to the latter category. Conversely, by admitting the category of *relation* into the concept of *being* the Cappadocians reconceived being itself (*ousia*) in dynamic and relational terms. In the new Christian understanding, "With God, Being and Communion are one and the same" and being could now be conceived as being-in-relation.[19] Torrance summarizes,

> It was in connection with this refined conception of *perichoresis* in its employment to speak of the intra-trinitarian relations in God, that Christian theology developed what I have long called its *onto-relational* concept of the divine Persons, or an understanding of the three divine Persons in the one God in which the ontic relations between them belong to what they essentially are in themselves in their distinctive *hypostases*. Along with this there developed out of the doctrine of the Trinity the new *concept of person*, unknown in human thought until then, according to which the relations between persons belong to what persons are.[20]

In the Christian view both God and human beings are conceived in relational and personal terms. Both God and human beings are regarded as persons-in-relationship (though, as we will discuss shortly, there are important limitations to this correspondence between divine and human persons).

God's redemptive mission is grounded in God's nature as love
In recent years many theologians have attempted to recover an emphasis on missiology by articulating its significance for our understanding of God, Christian life, and ecclesiology. For example, the missional church literature describes God as a missional or sending God. Just as the Father sent the Son and the Spirit into the world to accomplish the *missio Dei* (mission of God), so now God sends the church into the world as "God's instrument for God's mission."[21] While this renewed emphasis on mission is welcome and helpful, it

---

lational Self: A Trinitarian Theology of the Imago Dei (Louisville: Westminster John Knox, 2001), 317.

[18] Zizioulas makes the even stronger claim that the person "as a concept and as a living reality is purely the product of patristic thought" (*Being as Communion*, 27).

[19] Torrance, *The Christian Doctrine of God*, 104. See also Zizioulas's discussion in *Being as Communion*, 27–46.

[20] Torrance, *The Christian Doctrine of God*, 102.

[21] Darrell L. Guder, ed., *Missional Church: A Vision for the Sending of the Church in North America* (Grand Rapids: Eerdmans, 1998), 6–8.

runs the risk of making missional ecclesiology too functional and pragmatic. It is important to remember and assert that God's redemptive mission is grounded more fundamentally in God's nature as love. God's mission to redeem the world flows from God's prior love for creation. As the first letter of John states, "God's love was revealed among us in this way: God sent his only Son into the world so that we might live through him" (1 John 4:9). God's love for creation is rooted, in turn, in the other-centred, ecstatic, perichoretic love that constitutes God's triune being and reflects the fullness and over-flowing quality of the divine life. That such love essentially characterizes the Trinity means that God created the world and human beings as a free act of divine self-giving. Likewise, out of the same love, God acts redemptively to heal and restore human beings when they defy God's intentions and suffer the consequences of sin. Finally, through loving personal interaction with creation and covenant partnership with human beings, God is drawing all things toward eschatological consummation and fulfilment. God therefore demonstrates and enacts the loving being and character of the Trinity in creating, reconciling, and transforming all things through Christ in the Spirit.[22]

Trinitarian Love is Constitutive of the Human Person

The imago Dei and being in relationship

According to Stanley Grenz, "no assertion moves us closer to the heart of our human identity and our essential nature than does the declaration, 'We are created in the divine image.'"[23] Due to the importance and intricacy of the concept of the *imago Dei*, theologians have for centuries debated its precise meaning. Three general approaches represent the dominant views that theologians have proposed. The first, which Grenz calls the "structural" approach, describes the image of God as referring to some capacity or endowment that humans possess inherently, such as rationality or freedom of the will.[24] The second approach is the relational interpretation of the *imago Dei*, which claims that human beings reflect God's image by being in relationship with God and other human be-

---

[22] This all depends on their being a correspondence between God's being and God's act, the demonstration of which is one of the most important contributions of trinitarian theology. Torrance writes, "If there is no real bond *in God* between the economic Trinity and the ontological Trinity, the saving events proclaimed in the economy of the Gospel are without any divine validity and the doctrine of the Trinity is lacking in any ultimate divine truth. The trinitarian message of the Gospel tells us that the very contrary is the case, for in Jesus Christ and in the Holy Spirit we really have to do with the *Lord God himself* as our Saviour" (*The Christian Doctrine of God*, 7–8). This highlights the significance of Rahner's now famous axiom that the "'economic' Trinity is the 'immanent' Trinity and the 'immanent' Trinity is the 'economic' Trinity." See Karl Rahner, *The Trinity* (New York: Continuum, 2001), 22.

[23] Grenz, *Theology*, 168.

[24] Grenz, *The Social God and the Relational Self*, 142–60.

ings.²⁵ A third major approach interprets the image of God as a task or vocation to be accomplished or as a goal or destiny to be reached.²⁶ In my view, each of these approaches has biblical roots and contributes something meaningful to our understanding of what it means for human beings to be created in the image of God. Saint Anselm brings these themes together nicely in his prayer: "Lord, I acknowledge and I thank thee that thou hast created me in this thine image, in order that I may be *mindful* of thee, may *conceive* of thee, and *love* thee" (emphasis added).²⁷ While all three views are important, there is a sense in which the relational interpretation takes *theological* precedence.²⁸ A right relationship with God orients and enables human beings to enjoy healthy and life-giving relationships with other human beings, to employ their reason in the service of genuine truth and thus to attain not merely rationality but wisdom, and to exercise responsibly their vocation to sustain, restore, and improve themselves and their world as faithful stewards of God's creation. In this chapter, I will explore the meaning and significance of the relational interpretation of the *imago Dei*; in chapters four and five I will explicate the rational and vocational interpretations.

Historical roots of the relational view

The relational interpretation of the *imago Dei* goes back to medieval and patristic thinkers, such as Anselm, Augustine, and Athanasius.²⁹ Its more immediate historical roots are in the thought of the Protestant Reformers Martin Luther and John Calvin, both of whom interpreted the *imago Dei* in terms of being in a right moral and spiritual relationship with God.³⁰ According to Luther, the righteousness that is connected to the image of God is dynamic and active, rather than a static possession of the human person, because righteousness is not something that humans possess in and of themselves but consists in being mor-

---

[25] Grenz, *The Social God and the Relational Self*, 162–77.
[26] Grenz, *The Social God and the Relational Self*, 177–82.
[27] Anselm, *Proslogium* (chapter 1), 4–5.
[28] Many exegetes believe that the immediate context of Genesis 1:26–27 favours the vocational view because the passage closely associates the image of God with the calling to exercise stewardship over the earth and its creatures. This argument is surely correct in its observation that the vocation to exercise stewardship is crucially linked with the divine image, yet it fails to account for the fact that the very notion of stewardship entails and depends upon a unique *relationship* between the steward and the King. It is in virtue of their special relationship to God that human beings can serve as appropriate vice regents, a relationship which enables both human reasoning (awakened by God's Word-address) and faithful stewardship (reflecting God's character and purposes). Thus, while vocation helps to specify the content of the relationship and thus clarify one aspect of the *imago Dei*, it is neither theologically prior to nor fully conceptually determinative.
[29] See footnote 2.
[30] See Grenz, *The Social God and the Relational Self*, 162–69.

ally and spiritually justified before God.[31] For Luther the *imago* is not just the capacity to know and love God but the right ordering and functioning of human reason and will, which results from justification and enables human beings *actually* to know and love God.[32] In their created, pre-fallen state, Adam and Eve were naturally justified before God and exercised their freedom and reason in openness toward and trust in God. Luther believed that the image of God was distorted in the Fall, when human beings were corrupted and their relationship with God was became distorted. The image is regained only through saving faith in Jesus Christ by which they are justified by grace and receive Christ's own righteousness, an "alien" righteousness that is imputed to them.

While Luther's understanding of the *imago* was implicitly relational, Calvin was explicit in interpreting the image of God as referring to a relationship with God.[33] Like Luther, Calvin stressed the dynamic quality of the *imago* but associated it with the actual act of reflecting God as an intelligible response to God's Word. Specifically, Calvin proposed that human beings image God when they reflect God's glory and character with integrity and thus genuinely resemble their Creator. When human beings live in such a manner God looks at them and sees God's own image, as if God were gazing into a mirror. Thus, imaging

---

[31] The so-called Finish interpretation of Luther emphasizes that Christ is really present in faith, which highlights the link between justification and union with Christ leading to a more participatory view of righteousness than the traditional forensic interpretation allows. See, for example, Tuomo Mannermaa, *Christ Present in Faith: Luther's View of Justification*, ed. Kirsi Stjerna (Minneapolis: Fortress, 2005). While interesting and potentially fruitful for understanding the link between justification and sanctification, this position has not yet obtained general consensus in Luther scholarship. Whether it does so still remains to be seen. (See: Carl E. Braaten, "The Finnish Breakthrough in Luther Research," *Pro Ecclesia*, 5 [Spring 1996]: 141–43; see also Matt Jenson's review of the book in the *International Journal of Systematic Theology* 7 [Oct. 2005]: 482–85). One objection raised by critics is that it does not adequately account for Luther's historical context (e.g., his polemic against Rome concerning the selling of indulgences, the authority of the Pope, the critical law-gospel distinction, etc.). Another is that Mannermaa's interpretation relies too heavily on Luther's commentary on Galatians in isolation from Luther's other works. For our present purposes, it is perhaps best to see Luther emphasizing both forensic righteousness and transformation in union with Christ. Luther explores both of these themes, and their interrelation, in his treatise *On Christian Liberty*, trans. W.A. Lambert and Harold J. Grimm (Minneapolis: Fortress, 2003).

[32] Bayer argues that for Luther "the human being is human *insofar as* he is justified through faith — *in that* he is justified by faith." He explains that Luther envisioned human uniqueness as being grounded in a faith relationship to God, in particular by being consciously (in faith) dependent on God for life and sustenance, rather than subsisting on their own strength. Oswald Bayer, *Martin Luther's Theology: A Contemporary Interpretation*, trans. Thomas H. Trapp (Grand Rapids: Eerdmans, 2008), 155–58.

[33] Grenz, *Theology*, 166.

or mirroring God depends on being properly oriented toward God.[34] Primarily, Calvin has individual human beings in mind, each reflecting the divine image by responding in faith and love to God.[35] However, his doctrine of the *imago Dei* has implications for interpersonal relationships as well, because the properly aligned God-human relationship grounds inter-human relationships and enables such relationships to reflect God's glory. Calvin writes, "Because men have been created for such intercourse and communion with God, they have intercourse and society among themselves so that their life in community, characterized by rectitude [meaning constant dependence upon God], may image the glory of God."[36] With Luther, Calvin maintained that the image of God was distorted by the Fall. In their fallen state, human beings are alienated from God and live in a state of pervasive depravity. For Calvin, restoration of the image is given in and through Christ, who as the Word of God and the second Adam is the perfect image of God.

In summary, the Reformers contribute two insights to our relational interpretation of the *imago Dei*: first, the image of God refers to a dynamic relationship rather than a static possession; second, imaging God means reflecting God's glory and moral character in one's own life. Although human sin distorts and corrupts the image of God in human beings, it never completely destroys it. Human beings constantly turn away from God, but God perseveres in lovingly pursuing human beings.[37]

---

[34] Torrance clarifies that "strictly speaking, it is God who images Himself in man, and that means that He graciously embraces man as His child in Christ the express Image of his glory. It is as man answers this gracious decision in love and faith that he bears the image of God." Torrance, *Calvin's Doctrine of Man*, 35 (original italics removed).

[35] Calvin argues that "though the divine glory is displayed in man's outward appearance, it cannot be doubted that the proper seat of the image is in the soul." He goes on to argue that "our definition of the image seems not to be complete until it appears more clearly what the faculties are in which man excels, and in which he is to be regarded as a mirror of the divine glory." Calvin then highlights knowledge, righteousness, and holiness and infers that "the image of God was manifested by light of intellect, rectitude of heart, and the soundness of every part." And finally, the image "is properly the internal good of the soul." See John Calvin, *Institutes of the Christian Religion* I.XV.3–4 (Grand Rapids: Eerdmans, 1989), 162–65.

[36] Quoted from Torrance, *Calvin's Doctrine of Man*, 51 (with Torrance's italics removed).

[37] This affirmation is strengthened by an emphasis on God's prevenient grace (divine grace preceding human decision), which establishes the possibility of saving faith, and by a corresponding emphasis on the universal scope of the Spirit's mission in drawing people to the Risen Christ. See Clark H. Pinnock, *Flame of Love: A Theology of the Holy Spirit* (Downers Grove: InterVarsity Press, 1996), Clark H. Pinnock, *Most Moved Mover: A Theology of God's Openness* (Grand Rapids: Baker, 2001), and Jürgen Moltmann, *The Spirit of Life: A Universal Affirmation*, trans. Margaret Kohl (Minneapolis: Fortress, 2001).

In the modern period, the first theologian to develop the personal and person-constituting implications of the *imago Dei* was Dietrich Bonhoeffer in his book *Creation and Fall*.[38] In contrast to many traditional attempts to ground the image of God in innate human capacity or potential, Bonhoeffer innovatively interpreted the *imago Dei* in terms of an *analogia relationis* (an analogy of relationship).[39] Bonhoeffer unpacks his relational analogy in two directions. First, the analogy describes the vertical relationship that human beings have with God, a relationship which is characterized by genuine freedom and reciprocal love. Bonhoeffer writes, "To say that in humankind God creates the image of God on earth means that humankind is like the Creator in that it is free."[40] This freedom should not be understood as a substance or quality that humans possess in and for themselves, but as something they have *for God and for others* by virtue of their relationship with the Creator. He notes that God demonstrates this other-oriented kind of freedom, God's own freedom, in freely binding Godself to human beings in covenant love.[41] In addition, the quality of life that the Holy Spirit imparts to human beings (by the Spirit's life-breath) constitutes and continually opens their genuine freedom to love and worship God, so that: "In the free creature the Holy Spirit worships the Creator; uncreated freedom glorifies itself in view of created freedom. The creature loves the Creator, because the Creator loves the creature."[42] Thus, the vertical dimension of the *imago Dei* means that God created human beings in freedom so that they could freely reciprocate God's love. As Bonhoeffer asserts, "only such an image, in its freedom, would fully praise God, would fully proclaim God's glory as Creator."[43] Moreover, since the image is a relation and not a possession, it exists only insofar as humanity points to or illustrates God's love and character. Bon-

---

[38] Dietrich Bonhoeffer, *Creation and Fall: A Theological Exposition of Genesis 1–3*, ed. John W. de Gruchy, trans. Douglas Stephen Bax, vol. 3, *Dietrich Bonhoeffer Works* (Minneapolis: Fortress, 1997). The book is based on Bonhoeffer's 1932 lectures at Berlin and was published the following year. The classic academic treatment of the centrality of sociality in Bonhoeffer's thought is Clifford J. Green, *Bonhoeffer: A Theology of Sociality* (Grand Rapids: Eerdmans, 1999). See also his recent essay, "Sociality, Discipleship, and Worldly Theology in Bonhoeffer's Christian Humanism," in *Being Human, Becoming Human: Dietrich Bonhoeffer and Social Thought*, ed. Jens Zimmermann and Brian Gregor (Eugene, OR: Pickwick, 2010), 71–90.

[39] Bonhoeffer, *Creation and Fall*, 65. Incidentally, Karl Barth appropriated Bonhoeffer's *analogia relationis* in his 1942 Doctrine of Creation. See Barth, "The Work of Creation," vol. 3/1 of *Church Dogmatics: The Doctrine of Creation* (London: T & T Clark, 2009).

[40] Bonhoeffer, *Creation and Fall*, 62.

[41] Bonhoeffer writes, "it is the message of the gospel itself that God's freedom has bound itself to us, that God's free grace becomes real with us alone, that God wills not be free for God's self but for humankind. Because God in Christ is free for humankind, because God does not keep God's freedom to God's self, we can think of freedom only as a 'being free for . . .'" (*Creation and Fall*, 63).

[42] Bonhoeffer, *Creation and Fall*, 64.

[43] Bonhoeffer, *Creation and Fall*, 61.

hoeffer asserts that the analogy or likeness "must be understood very strictly in the sense that what is like derives its likeness *only* from the prototype, so that it always points us only to the prototype itself and is 'like' it only in pointing to it in this way."[44]

Second, the *imago Dei* as a relational analogy describes the horizontal relationships that human beings enjoy with one another. This observation stems from Bonhoeffer's reflection on Genesis 1:26–27, which brings the concept of the *imago Dei* into close proximity with the creation of human beings as male and female. Bonhoeffer writes, "And God created them man and woman. The human being is not alone. Human beings exist in duality, and it is in this dependence on the other that their creatureliness consists."[45] While the vertical relationship with God constitutes the human creature as a relational being, it does not yet bring the human being to fulfilment and completion. This does not indicate a deficiency in the Creator-creature relationship, rather it reflects God's deliberate design for human beings. In creating human beings in the duality of male and female, God intended that they live together in reciprocal love and interdependence.[46] As such, the lone figure of "the man" or "Adam" in Genesis 2 represents a not-yet-fully-human creature yearning for completion.[47] God created Adam to find this completion outside of himself in relationship to another (i.e., Eve).[48] This ecstatic nature, this yearning for completion in the other, is embodied in the human's physical and sexual constitution. As Grenz observes, human sexuality points to the essentially other-orienting and mutually completing character of human existence as male and female. He writes,

---

[44] Bonhoeffer, *Creation and Fall*, 65.
[45] Bonhoeffer, *Creation and Fall*, 64.
[46] Clifford Green summarizes Bonhoeffer's position: "Since God's being is being-for-humanity, so human relationships image this in one person 'being-free-for-the-other' in love." Clifford Green, "Human Sociality and Christian Community," in *The Cambridge Companion to Dietrich Bonhoeffer*, ed. John W. de Gruchy (Cambridge: Cambridge University Press, 1999), 117.
[47] Alistair I. McFadyen, *The Call to Personhood: A Christian Theory of the Individual in Social Relationships* (Cambridge: Cambridge University Press, 1990), 32. As Ray Anderson expresses it, "Adam is not a 'completed human' by virtue of being an example or instance of individuated humanity, even in relation to God. Rather, being related to God and being determined by God, Adam cannot be complete without encountering himself in the other as one who is 'bone of his bone and flesh of his flesh.' There is a differentiation of creatureliness itself which is constitutive of the human, not merely differentiation between the human and the non-human, or even differentiation between the human and God." Anderson, *On Being Human*, 48.
[48] Wolfhart Pannenberg, *Anthropology in Theological Perspective*, trans. Matthew J. O'Connell (Edinburgh: T & T Clark, 1999), 43–79. See also Grenz, *Theology*, 130–32, 139–43, and F. LeRon Shults, *Reforming Theological Anthropology: After the Philosophical Turn to Relationality* (Grand Rapids: Eerdmans, 2003), 90–91, 236–37.

At the heart of human sexuality is embodiment, which includes the sexed body that marks a person as male or female and out of which other aspects of human existence emerge. Bound up with embodiment is the sense of incompleteness, coupled with the drive for completeness, that together lead to bonding. Sexuality, therefore, is the dynamic that draws human beings out of their individual isolation into relationships with others.[49]

The creation of Eve from Adam's own human flesh means that she is a unique and special gift; she is one with Adam as a being-in-relationship, an equal partner and co-ruler over creation. Consequently, the fact that Eve is created from Adam's flesh does not elicit pride in Adam but profound joy and humility, as demonstrated by Adam's grateful exclamation, "This is now bone of my bones and flesh of my flesh!" (Gen 2:23). Bonhoeffer writes, "Adam knows that he is bound in a wholly new way to this Eve who is derived from him. This bond is best described in the expression: he now belongs to her, because she belongs to him. They are now no longer without each other; they are one and yet two."[50] Adam and Eve are united together as "one flesh" (Gen 2:24), yet they retain their individuality and uniqueness.[51] They encounter each other in unity and distinction and exist both for-each-other and over-against each other. They complete each other's humanness. To be clear, Bonhoeffer's point that is not that the image of God is fulfilled in male-female marital relations, but that the basic male-female duality that we observe in Genesis illustrates the way we are called to relate, specifically by being free-for-others in other-centred love and joined together in a communion that is built upon the distinction of persons.

In addition, Bonhoeffer expounds humanity's freedom to rule over creation from the *analogia relationis*. While freedom over against other human beings should be understood as freedom *for* one another, freedom over against the created world should be understood as freedom *from* creation (i.e., humanity's dominion over it).[52] This is not a freedom devoid of responsibility or care for creation—indeed, stewardship and service are inseparable:

> [T]his freedom to rule includes being bound to the creatures who are ruled. The ground and the animals over which I am lord constitute the world in which I live, without which I cease to be. It is my world, my earth, over which I rule. I am not free from it in any sense of my essential being, my spirit, having no need of nature, as though nature were something alien to the spirit. On the contrary, in my

---

[49] Grenz, *The Social God and the Relational Self*, 301. For Grenz's full discussion of human sexuality and its relation to the *imago Dei* see pp. 267–303. See also Ray S. Anderson, *On Being Human: Essays in Theological Anthropology* (Pasadena: Fuller Seminary Press, 1982), 104–29.
[50] Bonhoeffer, *Creation and Fall*, 97.
[51] Bonhoeffer, *Creation and Fall*, 98.
[52] Bonhoeffer, *Creation and Fall*, 66.

whole being, in my creatureliness, I belong wholly to this world; its bears me, nurtures me, holds me.[53]

Thus, Bonhoeffer's relational approach to the *imago Dei* focuses on human relationships with God and other human beings, but it also has implications for faithful stewardship of the earth and the non-human other. His view is consistent with the one I will develop in chapter five, which states that human beings are called to sustain, restore, and improve themselves and their world.

Imago Dei *and the Trinity*

Bonhoeffer's analysis adds a personal and person-constituting aspect to the *imago Dei* and thus contributes a new dimension to the relational view espoused by Luther and Calvin. Bonhoeffer rightly grounds his theological reflection on the incarnation and Christology. However, his explication is not yet fully trinitarian. A trinitarian interpretation of the *imago Dei* reasons that if God exists eternally in communion as Father, Son, and Holy Spirit, then human beings image God not merely as individuals but as persons in communion. Grenz articulates the view clearly as follows:

> As the doctrine of the Trinity asserts, throughout all eternity God is community, namely, the fellowship of Father, Son, and Holy Spirit who comprise the triune God. The creation of humankind in the divine image, therefore, can mean nothing less than that humans express the relational dynamic of the God whose representation we are called to be.[54]

While a trinitarian theology of the *imago Dei* takes its initial cue from Genesis 1:26–27, it does not depend exclusively on the exegesis of this passage. Rather, in light of a canonical approach to Scripture, which attests to God's economic and progressive self-revelation to us as Father, Son, and Holy Spirit, it employs a trinitarian hermeneutic to the reading of all of Scripture, including the first two chapters of Genesis. Thus, it affirms *theologically* that the God of Genesis is indeed the Trinity—Father, Son, and Holy Spirit. Specifically, a trinitarian interpretation of the *imago Dei* is an extension of New Testament Christology, especially the declaration that only Jesus Christ, the Son of God, reflects God's image fully and with complete integrity (2 Cor 4:4; Col 1:15; Heb 1:3). Human beings come to reflect God's image only by being in relationship with God "in Christ", whereby they are gradually transformed by the Spirit into Christ's image as they put on the new self that is created to be like God (Rom 8:29; 1 Cor 15:49; 2 Cor 3:18; 1 John 3:2; Eph 4:24; Col 3:9–10).

Furthermore, being "in Christ" means being in communion with others who are also "in Christ", bound in the Spirit to one another as members of Christ's

---

[53] Bonhoeffer, *Creation and Fall*, 66.
[54] Grenz, *Theology*, 179.

The Human Person as a Relational Creature

Body, the church (Rom 12:4–5; 1 Cor 12:12–13; Eph 4:4–6). As Grenz argues, "Only in fellowship with others can we show forth what God is like, for God is the community of love".[55] Miroslav Volf somewhat playfully puts it this way:

> Because the Christian God is not a lonely God, but rather a communion of the three persons, faith leads human beings into the divine *communio*. One cannot, however, have a self-enclosed communion with the triune God—a 'foursome,' as it were—for the Christian God is not a private deity. Communion with this God is at once also communion with those others who have entrusted themselves in faith to the same God. Hence one and the same act of faith places a person into a new relationship both with God and with all others who stand in communion with God.[56]

Thus, from a New Testament perspective, being in the image of God means more specifically being in the image of Christ, which entails a relationship with Christ and with other human beings who are "in Christ" in the bond of the Spirit. Though we do not yet experience the full measure of the communion that God ultimately intends for us, we can by faith in Christ and participation in his Body experience it now in some measure, as a foretaste and deposit of what is to come. As Volf argues, "Present participation in the trinitarian *communio* through faith in Jesus Christ anticipates in history the eschatological communion of the church with the triune God."[57] Several passages in Scripture support this view, depicting our final redemption in relational terms. For example, Jesus uses the image of a banquet to describe the final coming together of God with all of God's people (Matt 8:11–12, 22:1–14; Luke 14:15–24). The book of Revelation portrays all believers collectively as Christ's bride yet at the same time as individuals attending the wedding feast of the Lamb (Rev 19:6–9; 21:2, 9ff; 22:17). Moreover, it portrays the final dwelling place of the redeemed as a city filled by God and characterized by love, peace, wisdom, honour, and glory (Rev 21:22–27). In addition, God's eschatological kingdom will bring together people from every tribe, language, people, and nation (Rev 6:9).

I have been advocating a trinitarian, relational interpretation of the *imago Dei*, however it is important to clarify that human beings do not reflect the divine image simply by being in a group with others. For example, a group of workers forming a single crew and working on a common project is not a fitting analogy for the Trinity, but an overly simplistic form of social trinitarianism lurking dangerously close to tritheism or polytheism.[58] The trinitarian

---

[55] Grenz, *Theology*, 179.
[56] Miroslav Volf, *After Our Likeness: The Church as the Image of the Trinity* (Grand Rapids: Eerdmans, 1998), 173.
[57] Volf, *After Our Likeness*, 129.
[58] While Gregory of Nyssa's work *On Not Three Gods* is sometimes regarded as espousing such simple form of social trinitarianism, such is a misinterpretation of his argument. Gregory's purpose is to disprove tritheism by arguing that the unity of di-

view is not simply a reactionary move away from individualism toward collectivism. Rather, it points to the exocentric nature of each and every human being, which cries out for relational completion in God and others. In the trinitarian interpretation of the *imago Dei* that I am espousing, the image of God belongs neither to the human being as an individual nor to human beings as a group, but to the intrinsic sociality of the human being, to the human *person-in-relation* who is bound to others "in Christ" by the Spirit. What I am proposing, therefore, is a modified form of social trinitarianism that proceeds not simply from Trinity to human community, but from Trinity through theological anthropology and soteriology to ecclesial community.[59]

Openness to the world, exocentricity, and relationality
Wolfhart Pannenberg observes that a primary characteristic of human existence is openness to the world.[60] In distinction from much of the animal world (though not in absolute distinction), human beings can transcend the givenness of their natural environment, stretch toward ever expanding potential, and reach for infinite possibilities. They have the ability to change themselves and the world around them. They are continually on the move, continually self-defining and world-defining. Corresponding with this openness to the world is the human capacity for self-consciousness and self-transcendence. As Kierkegaard puts it, the human self is a *relation*; it is a *self relating to itself*. The human self is a synthesis in which a subject (I) relates to itself as an object (me).[61] This means that human self-identity is both dialectical (actively and passively being and becoming) and temporal (oriented to past, present, and future). It is both a gift to be received and a goal to be attained. Thus, the human being is characterized by what Pannenberg calls "exocentricity", a term which defines the self's relational constitution as being both centred and other-oriented. As F. LeRon Shults explains it, "'Exocentric' refers to the idea that to be a self involves a being centred outside oneself through the mediation of knowing (and

---

vine operations infers a unity of nature. All of God's actions have their origin in the Father, proceed through the Son, and are perfected in the Holy Spirit. See Lewis Ayres, "On not three people: The fundamental themes of Gregory of Nyssa's Trinitarian theology as seen in To Ablabius: On Not Three Gods," *Modern Theology* 18 (Oct. 2002): 445–74. See also Miroslav Volf, "Being as God Is: Trinity and Generosity," in *God's Life in Trinity* (Minneapolis: Fortress, 2006), 5–7.

[59] Volf argues similarly in *After Our Likeness*, 199–200. Moreover, he argues that the analogy between Trinity and church must be conditioned by the doctrines of creation (we correspond only in creaturely fashion) and eschatology (we will experience fully communion with God and one another only at the *eschaton*). For a good critique of more simplistic forms of social trinitarianism, see John L. Gresham, Jr., "The Social Model of the Trinity and its Critics," *Scottish Journal of Theology* 46, no. 3 (1993): 325–43.

[60] Pannenberg, *Anthropology*, 43–79; cf. Grenz, *Theology*, 130–32.

[61] Søren Kierkegaard, *The Sickness Unto Death: A Christian Psychological Exposition for Edification and Awakening*, trans. Alastair Hannay (London: Penguin, 1989), 43.

being known by) the other, while at the same time being centrally organized by the agency of the ego."[62] In its inner centeredness the self is relatively stable. In its other-orientation the self is malleable and subject to adaptation and change. All of this means that humans are by nature constituted as relational beings that gain their identity through a continual, dialectical negotiation of the self with itself, the world, and other human selves—a process which Miroslav Volf calls "differentiation".[63] One's true identity, therefore, is neither exclusively one's inner essence (who I am inside, my soul) nor one's outer relations (what others and the world make of me), but a kind of ongoing journey or quest of being and becoming as it navigates identity and otherness, stability and change, initiative and receptivity, individuality and sociality. Practically speaking, our relationships shape and affect who we are essentially as persons, though they are not fully determinative of our identity or personhood.[64] For example, becoming a husband and a father does not merely provide me with a new set of associations with corresponding responsibilities and tasks; it fundamentally changes my personal identity in an essential but not fully determinative way.[65]

Theologically, what constitutes human beings in their creatureliness as self-conscious, transcendent, exocentric, relational beings is the personal address of God's Word.[66] Human beings are uniquely the creatures to whom God intelligibly and lovingly speaks and from whom God desires an intelligible and loving response. God created human beings to be self-transcending relational creatures who "come into themselves" both by receiving their identity as a gracious gift from God and by actively responding to God's call to define and shape their lives in faithful response to God's Word.[67] Thus, in one sense human beings do not create themselves because only God gives and orients life. The same Word of address that constitutes them as relational beings also constitutes them as responsible beings, who are accountable before God for their lives and

---

[62] Shults, *Reforming Theological Anthropology*, 90.

[63] Miroslav Volf, *Exclusion and Embrace: A Theological Explanation of Identity, Otherness, and Reconciliation* (Nashville: Abingdon, 1996), 64–66.

[64] Volf, *After Our Likeness*, 186.

[65] Volf provides a similar example in *Exclusion and Embrace* (66). The distinction "essential but not fully determinative" is important; for example, too many women throughout history have had their identities over-determined by their relational orientation as wife and mother.

[66] Anderson, *On Being Human*, 35–37; Bonhoeffer, *Creation and Fall*, 40–42; McFadyen, *The Call to Personhood*, 22.

[67] Recall Calvin's important observation that genuine God-knowledge and genuine self-knowledge mutually correspond and arise together. Calvin, *Institutes* I.I.1–3, 37–39; cf. Augustine, *Confessions*, 44. Earlier, Clement of Alexandria had written, "It is then, as appears, the greatest of all lessons to know one's self. For if one knows himself, he will know God; and knowing God, he will be made like God". (Clement, *The Instructor* III.1, 271). For an insightful and practical approach to spiritual formation grounded in this truth, see David G. Benner, *The Gift of Being Yourself: The Sacred Call to Self-Discovery* (Downers Grove: InterVarsity Press, 2004).

who encounter in both God and others ethical claims and limits on their existence.[68] In a limited sense, though, human beings do create themselves because God's creational intent was to give them the freedom to love and serve God with heart, soul, mind, and strength. As McFadyen puts it, "It is the divine intention that human beings shall be free in relation to Godself as God's dialogue-partners."[69]

Love and the Relational Ethical Dimension

In a Christian worldview, theology and ethics, while distinct, are closely related and interwoven in such a way as to be mutually implying and enriching.[70] Faith and action go hand in hand. The Christian life involves a dialectic of moving between believing and obeying, receiving and giving, in stillness and in action: "*only the believers obey, and only the obedient believe*."[71] When Jesus called his disciples, he did not merely beckon them to "listen to me" or "believe what I believe" but rather to "*follow me*" (of course, following Jesus required and assumed basic trust, belief, and a desire to learn and grow). In Paul's letters the indicatives of God's love and grace precede the imperatives of obedience and faithful living, yet in order for Christians to understand God's love and grace fully they must begin to walk in it (e.g., Gal 6:7–10; Eph 4:17–32, 5:15–20; Phil 3:12–16; Col 3:12). Similarly, the first letter of John prioritizes God's love and grace over human merit (4:9–10), yet it also stresses that genuine fellowship with God and others requires "living in the light" (1:7), renouncing sin (1:8–10), and obeying God's commands (2:3–6). Thus, as Bonhoeffer notes, "Christian community is not an ideal we have to realize, but rather a reality created by God in Christ in which we may participate."[72] "All Christian thinking, speaking, and organizing must be born anew out of . . . prayer and [righteous] action."[73] Accordingly, in this section we are not leaving theology behind

---

[68] Dietrich Bonhoeffer, *Sanctorum Communio: A Theological Study of the Sociology of the Church*, ed. Clifford J. Green, trans. Reinhard Krauss and Nancy Lukens, vol. 1, *Dietrich Bonhoeffer Works* (Minneapolis: Fortress, 1998), 45–55.

[69] McFadyen, *The Call to Personhood*, 20.

[70] Hauerwas argues that theological claims are already ethical claims. "For theology is a practical activity concerned to display how Christian convictions construe the self and world. Therefore, theological claims concerning the relation of creation and redemption are already ethical claims, since they situate how one works methodologically." Stanley Hauerwas, *The Peaceable Kingdom: A Primer in Christian Ethics* (Notre Dame: University of Notre Dame Press, 1983), 55.

[71] Dietrich Bonhoeffer, *Discipleship*, ed. Geffrey B. Kelly and John D. Godsey, trans. Barbara Green and Reinhard Krauss, vol. 4, *Dietrich Bonhoeffer Works* (Minneapolis: Fortress, 2001), 63 (emphasis original).

[72] Dietrich Bonhoeffer, *Life Together*, ed. Geffrey B. Kelly, trans. Daniel W. Bloesch and James H. Burtness, vol. 5, *Dietrich Bonhoeffer Works* (Minneapolis: Fortress, 1996), 38.

[73] Dietrich Bonhoeffer, *Letters and Papers from Prison*, ed. Eberhard Bethge (New York: Simon & Schuster, 1997), 300.

but developing the implications of our relational theological anthropology for Christian ethics.

God's reconciling love opens the human heart for reconciliation with God and others

The fall of human beings into sin, as depicted in Genesis 3, means that human beings have corrupted their relationship with God and have become alienated from God. As the Genesis narrative shows, the fall into sin has a fundamentally relational aspect because it is rooted in mistrust or disbelief and an arrogant desire for autonomy from God. Mistrust is apparent when Adam and Eve begin to question God's Word to them: "You may eat any fruit in the garden except fruit from the tree of the knowledge of good and evil. If you eat of its fruit, you will surely die" (Gen 2:17).[74] Instead, they trust the deceiving word of the serpent and their own capacity to discern what is best without relying on God. Their arrogant desire for autonomy is demonstrated by their yielding to the temptation of eating from the forbidden tree in order to become like God (Gen 3:4). In their created state, Adam and Eve were designed to live as exocentric beings that receive their life-breath and find their own individual identities outside themselves in God. Now, they yield to the temptation to be *as autonomous individuals* their own source of life and identity, their own source of the knowledge of good and evil.[75] Bonhoeffer infers that the human being "now lives out of its own resources, creates its own life, is its own creator; it no longer needs the Creator, it has itself become creator, inasmuch as it creates its own life. Thereby its creatureliness is eliminated, destroyed. Adam is no longer a creature."[76] Of course, human beings do not have it within themselves to be their own creator, their own source of life and identity; hence, God's Word proves to be true: "You will surely die." Adam and Eve immediately sense that something is wrong, and in their shame they flee and hide from God (Gen 3:7–8). Moreover, their initial unbelief leads to greater mistrust, denial, and blame,

---

[74] See Dietrich Bonhoeffer, *Creation and Fall*, 105–109, and *Temptation*, trans. Kathleen Downham (London SCM, 1955), 16.

[75] Dietrich Bonhoeffer, *Ethics*, ed. Clifford J. Green, trans. Reinhard Krauss, Charles C. West, and Douglas W. Stott, vol. 6, *Dietrich Bonhoeffer Works* (Minneapolis: Fortress, 2005), 277, 299–338. Bonhoeffer argues that faith in Christ reorients us toward trusting God as the source of all goodness. He writes, "We experience and recognize ethical reality not by craftiness, not by knowing all the tricks, but only by standing straightforwardly in the truth of God and by looking to that truth with eyes that it makes simple [einfältig] and wise" (*Ethics*, 78). Christian ethics primarily involves formation in Christ, not in an expansion of *our* (i.e., autonomous) knowledge of good and evil, our "knowing good and evil in disunion with the origin" as Bonhoeffer puts it (*Ethics*, 308). "The question of the good becomes the question of participating in God's reality revealed in Christ" (*Ethics*, 50). "Thereby we are turned away from any abstract ethic and toward a concrete ethic. We can and should speak not about what the good is, can be, or should be for each and every time, but about *how Christ may take form among us today and here*" (*Ethics*, 99; emphasis original).

[76] Bonhoeffer, *Creation and Fall*, 115.

as they begin to accuse each other and even God of wrongdoing (Gen 3:12–13). In response to their disobedience, God shows them love and mercy (Gen 3:21). However God also allows them to live with the consequences of their sin, namely their alienation from God and from each other as depicted by their banishment from the Garden of Eden in Genesis 3:23–24 and by the escalating tension and hatred between human beings in Gen 4–11.

Bonhoeffer observes that by usurping God's place as the centre and source of life, freedom, and truth, human beings sinfully place themselves in the centre.[77] This has serious and far-reaching consequences. As Bonhoeffer graphically describes it,

> Because the fall of humankind is both inconceivable and finally inexcusable in God's creation, the word *disobedience* fails to describe the situation adequately. It is rebellion, the creatures stepping outside of the creature's only possible attitude, the creature's becoming creator, the destruction of creatureliness, a defection, a falling away from being safely held as a creature. As such a defection it is a *continual* fall, a *plunging down* into a bottomless abyss, a state of being let go, a process of moving further and further away, falling deeper and deeper. And in all this it is not merely a *moral lapse* but the destruction of creation by the creature. The extent of the fall is such that it affects the whole created world.[78]

In their fallen orientation, human beings now redefine their God-given freedom as freedom-for-self and unwittingly become slaves to sin. Henceforth, their existence is no longer characterized by freedom *for* God but by enslavement to self in subjugation to their own corrupt nature. Likewise, they no longer exist in freedom for other human beings, but now seek to dominate and rule over others. Furthermore, they no longer freely rule creation, but are now ruled by it and exist in hostility toward it. In sum, freedom has been turned on its head and corrupted.

To describe the sinful condition, Bonhoeffer draws upon Luther's observation that humans have a *cor curvum in se*, a heart turned in upon itself. Instead of living in genuine exocentricity they now become radically self-centred or "wrongly centred" as Miroslav Volf puts it.[79] In this fallen, self-enclosed state, human beings experience disorientation, alienation, and distortion in their relations to themselves, others, and the world. Concerning their identity and personal groundedness, human beings experience a disruption of the self's integrity. Consequently, they struggle to know and find themselves and desperately attempt either to construct themselves through accomplishments and achieve-

---

[77] Bonhoeffer, *Creation and Fall*, 115–22. Bonhoeffer pursues an existential reading of the Fall, rather than a moralistic one.

[78] Bonhoeffer, *Creation and Fall*, 120. See, in this light, Rom 1:18–32.

[79] Volf, *Exclusion and Embrace*, 69. See also Pannenberg's discussion of sin as "centrality" in *Anthropology*, 80–153.

ments (pseudo-immanence through dominance) or distract themselves from the problem by losing themselves in relationships and experiences (pseudo-transcendence through self-abandonment).[80] Kierkegaard referred to this condition as "despair". He argued that despair appears in two basic forms, either in "not wanting to be oneself" or in "wanting to be oneself" (i.e., one's ideal self).[81] Ultimately, though, the root of despair is "not wanting to be oneself", because even in wanting to be one's ideal self one desires to *become* in the future *what one is not* in the present. Hence, even the desire to become one's *true* self is nevertheless a desire not to be one's *actual* self. For Kierkegaard, this disruption in the synthesis of the self is the result of human alienation from God and thus can be remedied only through faith in God. By faith, the self is freed to be itself by living genuinely before God. Only by faith can the human self rest, "grounded transparently in the power that established it."[82]

In their self-enclosed state, human beings also experience alienation from each other, leading to the destructive patterns that Miroslav Volf labels "exclusion". According to Volf, exclusion appears in two basic forms, both of which result from a distortion of our created exocentricity and differentiation. First, we can exclude others by placing ourselves in a position of sovereign independence from them. In this case, the other "emerges either as an enemy that must be pushed away from the self and driven out of its space or as a nonentity—a superfluous being—that can be disregarded and abandoned."[83] This perhaps represents the most obvious way that we exclude others. We see them as being too different, too foreign, too other from us. As such, they are a threat to our own security, a rival to our own ambition for dominance and influence, a competitor in our own quest for wealth and power. The second, less obvious way that we exclude others is by failing to take their otherness seriously enough. In this case, we fail to see the other truly as an *other* that stands overagainst us making an ethical claim on us. We thus assimilate the other into our own views and ideologies, our own motives and desires, our own goals and ambitions. In Kant's language, we fail to treat other persons as ends in themselves and see them merely as means to our own ends. Moreover, by so doing we fail to allow others the space they need truly to be themselves. As Bonhoeffer observes, we attempt to fashion others into our own image rather than seeing them as reflecting God's image in their own unique way. Bonhoeffer accordingly warns:

> God does not want me to mold others into the image that seems good to me, that is, into my own image. Instead, in their freedom from me God made other people

---

[80] See Henri J.M. Nouwen, *In the Name of Jesus: Reflections on Christian Leadership* (New York: Crossword, 1989).
[81] Kierkegaard, *The Sickness Unto Death*, 43–51.
[82] Kierkegaard, *The Sickness Unto Death*, 44. Or, as Bonhoeffer puts it, they are freed once again to be genuine creatures of their Creator (*Ethics*, 94).
[83] Volf, *Exclusion and Embrace*, 67.

in God's own image. I can never know in advance how God's image should appear in others. That image always takes on a completely new and unique form whose origin is found solely in God's free and sovereign act of creation.[84]

By assimilating others into our own image, we fail to acknowledge their difference and thereby suppress their individuality, thus disregarding their distinctive value and dignity as human beings.

In addition to alienating persons from themselves and others, the self-enclosed state also alienates human beings from the natural world.[85] Scripture alludes to this in its description of God's curse on the land in Genesis 3 (and unfolding throughout the book), which results in difficulty in tending and working the land, famine and droughts, and escalating conflict in terms of ownership rights, imperialism, and war. In the New Testament, the apostle Paul says that all of creation is experiencing the impact of the curse of sin and is groaning in anticipation of its final redemption and re-creation (Rom 8:19–22). Human alienation from the creation can lead to the exclusionary treatment of the natural environment, whereby humans assert their dominance over nature and treat it merely as a means for human-oriented ends (e.g., a profit-driven disregard for the environment, which in turn threatens all forms of life including human life). Alternatively, the distorted relationship between human beings and the natural world can foster an inappropriate sense of human oneness with creation that downplays the uniqueness of human beings as God's rightful stewards, leading them to abnegate their responsibilities to care for creation by sustaining, restoring, and improving it.

In response to human sinfulness, rebellion, and alienation, God's reconciling love opens the human heart for restored communion with God, others, and the natural world. In his epistle to the Romans, Paul writes, "Therefore, since we are justified by faith, we have peace with God through our Lord Jesus Christ" (Rom 5:1). Elsewhere, Paul writes that through Christ "God was pleased to reconcile to himself all things, whether on earth or in heaven, by making peace through the blood of his cross" (Col 1:20). Jesus understood that a crucial aspect of his mission was to reconcile human beings to a restored relationship with God and each other. Accordingly he prayed that they would all be one "just as you and I are one, Father—that just as you are in me and I am in you, so they will be in us, and the world will believe you sent me" (John 17:21). Jesus came to unite us to the Father and thereby to unite us together as fellow human beings. In order to do this, Jesus took our alienated condition upon himself and, by means of the cross, suffered rejection, humiliation, hatred, violence, foresakenness, and death at the hands of and in solidarity with fellow

---

[84] Bonhoeffer, *Life Together*, 95.
[85] Grenz, *Theology*, 207. See also Volf's discussion of "Spirit, Work, and Environment" in *Work in the Spirit*, 141–48.

human beings.⁸⁶ Even his closest friends abandoned him. Yet even while hanging on the cross Jesus demonstrated God's love and forgiveness, crying "Father, forgive them; for they do not know what they are doing" (Luke 23:34). And in the very midst of his loneliness and rejection, Jesus created community: "When Jesus saw his mother and the disciple whom he loved standing beside her, he said to his mother, 'Woman, here is your son.' Then he said to the disciple, 'Here is your mother.'" (John 19:26–27) Moreover, in overcoming the alienating power of sin on the cross, Jesus overcame the destructive power of exclusion by "disarming the principalities and powers" of spiritual and structural/systemic evil (Col 2:15; Eph 6:12) and by demonstrating God's judgment against divisive social barriers, such as racial, socio-economic, and gender inequality: "There is no longer Jew or Gentile, slave or free, male or female. For you are all one in Christ Jesus" (Gal 3:28).

The liberating presence and redemptive activity of the Holy Spirit are essential in inaugurating and realizing our reconciliation with God and one another in Christ. Specifically, the Holy Spirit brings healing to our self-enclosed hearts (*cor curvum in se*) and opens them to be free for God and others once again. The Spirit reverses our egocentricity and reorients us to be centred *extra se in Christo*, outside of ourselves in Christ. As Volf says, our new centre is a de-centred centre.⁸⁷ This is because, "The Spirit enters the citadel of the self, de-centers the self by fashioning it in the image of the self-giving Christ, and frees its will so it can resist the power of exclusion in the power of the Spirit of embrace."⁸⁸ Henri de Lubac expressed a similar notion when he wrote, "He [the Spirit] creates in man new depths which harmonize him with the 'depths of God', and he projects man out of himself . . . he makes universal and spiritualizes, he personalizes and unifies."⁸⁹ The Christian now lives within what Alan Torrance calls the "I, yet not I, but Christ" dynamic of Christian existence.⁹⁰ Torrance is referring to Paul's words in Galatians 2:19–20: "I have been crucified with Christ nevertheless I live, yet not I, but Christ who lives in me. And the life I live in the flesh I live by faith in the Son of God, who loved me and gave himself for me."⁹¹ Importantly, it is the Holy Spirit who enables one to live this "I, yet not I, but Christ" dynamic, because it is the Spirit who brings

---

⁸⁶ For a profound treatment of this theme, see Jürgen Moltmann, *The Crucified God: The Cross of Christ as the Foundation and Criticism of Christian Theology*, trans. R.A. Wilson and John Bowden (New York: Harper & Row, 1974).

⁸⁷ Volf, *Exclusion and Embrace*, 71. See also Grenz, *The Social God and the Relational Self*, 325–26.

⁸⁸ Volf, *Exclusion and Embrace*, 92.

⁸⁹ Henri de Lubac, *Catholicism, Christ and the Common Destiny of Man*, trans. Lancelot Sheppard (San Francisco: Ignatius, 1988), 339.

⁹⁰ Alan J. Torrance, *Persons in Communion: An Essay on Trinitarian Description and Human Participation* (Edinburgh: T&T Clark, 1996), 363.

⁹¹ Cf. Col 2:9–10: "For in Christ the fullness of God lives in a human body, and you are complete through your union with Christ".

human beings into union with Christ. Our reconciliation with God and others is therefore a *pneumatological event* in which the Spirit takes an active and integral role. This pneumatological affirmation is consistent with the mutual love model of the Trinity discussed at the beginning of this chapter, which identified the Holy Spirit as the bond of love between the Father and the Son and as the one who binds together the Son's two natures (divine and human) in the incarnation and resurrection.[92] This latter bond forms the basis of Christ's capacity to be the sole priest and mediator for fallen and alienated human beings before God. It allows Christ to receive and take to himself all of creation, to reconcile and redeem it by means of the cross and the resurrection, and finally to offer it back to the Father as the New Creation.[93] Moreover, in the mutual love model, the Spirit plays a parallel role in human redemption by acting as the bond of love between God and redeemed human beings, whom the Spirit brings into union with Christ (the Spirit comes to indwell human beings, thereby placing them "in Christ" who is "in" the Father).[94] This union with Christ in the Spirit grounds and enables all of Christian life and ministry—being and doing, knowing and worshiping, loving and serving. As Luther puts it, "A Christian lives not in himself, but in Christ and in his neighbour. Otherwise he is not a Christian. He lives in Christ through faith, in his neighbour through love."[95]

Miroslav Volf employs the analogy of "embrace" to help clarify the meaning of reconciliation.[96] He analyzes four acts in the drama of embrace and then suggests four key features of the embrace as a whole. The first act is the *opening of one's arms*. Opening one's arms signifies to another a desire for connection, initiates the creation of space in oneself for the other to enter safely, and is a gesture of invitation. The second act is *waiting*. The significance of waiting is that it underscores the importance of both initiative and reciprocity. Waiting entails that one has taken the first step, but also that one does not force oneself on the other. It requires patience and the willingness to put oneself on the line and risk rejection. As such, it is not an "act of invasion" but preserves the free-

---

[92] Steven Studebaker explains the Spirit's identity as the bond of love between the Father and Son as follows: "[T]he Son is a subject who loves the Father. The Father and the Son in their concordant love for one another bring forth the Holy Spirit. The personal identity of the Holy Spirit is the objectification of the Father's and Son's mutual love. As mutual love, the Holy Spirit's primary characteristic is union. The Spirit is the love that indissolubly unites the Father and the Son. The identity of the Holy Spirit as mutual love does not depersonalize the Spirit. The Spirit is a unique divine person whose activity is that of uniting the other two divine persons." Studebaker, "Integrating Pneumatology and Christology," 12. See also Grenz, *The Social God and the Relational Self*, 327.

[93] The theme of creation, fall, and redemption, corresponding to incarnation, cross, and resurrection, is a constant theme in Bonhoeffer's theology. For a summary, see Bonhoeffer, *Ethics*, 157–59, and *Letters and Papers from Prison*, 381–82.

[94] See John 14:16–20; 17:21.

[95] Luther, *On Christian Liberty*, 62.

[96] For his analysis, see *Exclusion and Embrace*, 140–47.

dom and dignity of the other. The third act is the *closing of the arms*. In this stage reconciliatory love is accepted and reciprocated by the other. In closing one's arms, one does not strangle the other but embraces the other gently. This signifies that in the embrace of reconciliation neither party should be assimilated by the other. They are embraced and accepted precisely in their alterity as *other*. Act four is the *reopening of the arms*. This act signifies that the embrace has preserved the unity-in-diversity character of genuine Christian reconciliation. It ensures that boundaries are respected and prevents an unhealthy co-dependency or enmeshment. Truly loving another means embracing but not owning them. It means ultimately being able to relinquish them into the hands of God, who is their relational centre and the ground of their identity and personhood. Volf goes on to say that the embrace as a whole is characterized by the *fluidity of identities* (persons are mutually impacted yet appropriately differentiated), *non-symmetricity* (in reconciliation both parties are not necessarily equally guilty; however, following in the way of the Crucified Christ still means embracing the guilty other), *under-determination of the outcome* (one waits patiently without any guarantee that the embrace will take place), and *risk* (in initiating reconciliation, one could be misunderstood, despised, or even violated).

God's transforming love and abundant communion with God and others
As the previous section demonstrated, growing together into maturity in Christ is not simply about self- or group-improvement, but involves transformation by the Spirit. More profoundly, it involves participating in the divine life as we share by the Spirit in the Son's relationship with the Father.[97] Thus, growing in Christ consists not only in imitating him but also involves the spiritual reality of Christ being formed in us by the Spirit.[98] "For it is God who is at work in you, enabling you both to will and to work for his good pleasure" (Phil 2:13). We now press on toward the goal of knowing and being like Christ, sharing in his suffering and experiencing the power of his resurrection, yet we are able to do so only because Christ has already taken hold of us and is drawing us toward that goal (Phil 3:12–14). Sharing in the divine life is a consequence not merely of our individual faith (though it includes it) but points to the fact that through the incarnation, death, resurrection, and ascension of Christ, God has done something radically and comprehensively new. As Paul says, "if anyone is in Christ there is a new creation" (2 Cor 5:17). In Christ God reconciled all things

---

[97] For the practical implications of our participation in the divine life, see James B. Torrance, *Worship, Community & the Triune God of Grace* (Downers Grove: InterVarsity Press, 1996). Bonhoeffer stressed participation in the reality of God as the essence of Christian existence. See Sabine Dramm, *Dietrich Bonhoeffer: An Introduction to His Thought*, trans. Thomas Rice (Peabody, MA: Hendrickson, 2007), 39, 42, 46.

[98] Both of these are major themes in Bonhoeffer's work. The imitation of Christ is central in *Discipleship* while the notion of Christ being formed in us is central in *Ethics*.

to Godself (Col 1:20) and is now in the process of making all things new (Rev 21:5). The promise of Scripture is that God is going to complete the good work that has already begun (Phil 1:6). This includes the reconciliation, restoration, and fulfillment of human relationships with God and with other human beings. In anticipation of the final return of Christ, God's transforming love is drawing human beings into ever fuller, holistic, and abundant communion with God and others. "God is love, and all who live in love live in God, and God lives in them. And as we live in God, our love grows more perfect" (1 John 4:16–17). God is creating a new humanity in Christ by the Spirit. To foreshadow what I will later say in the ecclesiology section, Christians receive a down-payment of God's transformative love and a foretaste of sharing in the loving, ecstatic communion of the Trinity through their life together in the community of faith. As Grenz eloquently puts it,

> [T]he Spirit brings the ecclesial community to fulfill the divinely given mandate to be the prolepsis of the new humanity as the *imago dei*, which is the goal of the biblical salvation-historical drama. . . . Thereby, it truly becomes a fellowship of those whose relationships are being transformed by the power of the indwelling Spirit to reflect as far as possible in the midst of the brokenness of the present the eschatological community modeled after the fullness of love present within the dynamic of the triune God.[99]

What will the fully realized community of God look like? Scripture gives us only gleanings, hints, and snapshots. We do know that we will be reunited in fellowship with fellow human beings whom Christ has redeemed (1 Thess 4:13–18; 2 Thess 2:1). We also know that God intends this new community to include as many people as possible and accordingly is patiently waiting for all to come to faith, not wanting any to perish (2 Pet 3:9). From the picture of the heavenly city painted in Revelation 21–22, we know that we will see God's face, experience the joy of God's full presence and love, and finally rest in the deep knowledge that we belong to God. We will know God and others as they truly are, and in turn we will be deeply known, understood, and accepted. Hence, our relationships with God and others will be characterized by unreserved trust and transparency. There will no longer be any tears, sorrow, pain, or death; no more sin, no lying, cheating, abuse, hatred, or violence. Instead, we will live in peace, security, prosperity, and everlasting joy with God and others in the new creation.

General implications for Christian ethics

I now conclude this chapter by suggesting, very briefly, some implications that a relational understanding of human personhood has for Christian ethics.

---

[99] Grenz, *The Social God and the Relational Self*, 335.

First, a relational view of personhood underscores the centrality of love for Christian ethics. To repeat Luther's statement, "A Christian lives not in himself, but in Christ and in his neighbour. Otherwise he is not a Christian. He lives in Christ through faith, in his neighbour through love."[100] This reflects Jesus's pronouncement that the greatest two commandments are to love God with all of one's heart, mind, soul, and strength, and to love one's neighbour as oneself (Mark 12:29–31). Of course, knowing precisely *how* to love another person in various concrete situations requires wisdom, discernment, and theological-ethical reflection in the context of a loving community of faith.[101] But for now, suffice it to say that loving God and others is the top priority. A second, related implication is that we should be focused primarily on forming *people* according to the image of Christ in their situated lives and concrete contexts, not just on formulating and indoctrinating rules, principles, axioms, or formulas to solve abstract moral quandaries.[102] Jesus himself emphasized the importance of having a transformed heart, the cultivation of which leads one to love God and others reflexively. He argued that good works flow from a good heart, just as good fruit flows from a good tree (Luke 6:43–45). While rules, principles, and abstract reasoning do play a role in a comprehensive relational Christian ethics, they must be placed within the larger framework of worldview and character formation.[103] Third, the intrinsically relational nature of human personhood requires that we be equally concerned with personal *and* social ethics. The individual person is inherently social, while society is composed of individual or differentiated persons. Accordingly, Christian ethics is irreducibly personal-social in character. This means that Christians ought to be concerned both for personal morality *and* for interpersonal harmony, in both the church and society, by fostering healing, forgiveness, reconciliation, and peace. They ought to strive tirelessly both for individual holiness *and* for communal, social, and structural/systemic justice. Fourth, a Christian love-ethic entails loving and advocating for those who are other or different from oneself, including the poor, the hungry, the weak, the abused, those who suffer from mental and physical disabilities, the lonely, the sick, the downtrodden, the socially marginalized or outcastes, the prisoners, and even the enemy. Fifth, caring for the other means caring for people dispersed throughout the world. In his parable of the Good Samaritan, Jesus radically expanded the concept of one's neighbour to

---

[100] Luther, *On Christian Liberty*, 62.

[101] To pursue this in more detail, see: Richard A. Burridge, *Imitating Jesus: An Inclusive Approach to New Testament Ethics* (Grand Rapids: Eerdmans, 2007); Richard B. Hays, *The Moral Vision of the New Testament: Community, Cross, New Creation: A Contemporary Introduction to New Testament Ethics* (San Francisco: HarperSanFrancisco, 1996); and Glen Stassen and David Gushee, *Kingdom Ethics: Following Jesus in Contemporary Context* (Downer's Grove: InterVarsity Press, 2003).

[102] Bonhoeffer, *Ethics*, 99.

[103] Stassen and Gushee, *Kingdom Ethics*, 100–107. See also Dallas Willard, *Renovation of the Heart* (Colorado Springs: NavPress, 2002).

include those who are very different from oneself, whether by race or ethnicity (Jew vs. Samaritan), religion (pure Jew vs. godless Samaritan), social status (sacred priest vs. lay traveler) or place of origin (Judea vs. Samaria; see also John 4:21–24). In a globalized context, faithfulness to the way of Jesus requires expanding the concept of neighbour even further. Christian ethics, therefore, will include global ethics, which highlights not only the relational character of personhood and ethics but also the universality of the church as Christ's Body extending throughout the world and God's universal intent to reconcile all things in Christ (Col 1:20).[104] Finally, in recognition of our relationship to the earth as God's faithful stewards, Christian ethics involves humane and responsible treatment of non-human creatures and the environment.

---

[104] The theological foundation for a global ethic is the assumption and reconciliation of all of humanity in Christ (Bonhoeffer, *Ethics*, 85, 94; Torrance, *The Christian Doctrine of God*, 161, 250).

CHAPTER 4

The Human Person as a Rational Creature

Introduction

The previous chapter envisioned human beings as relational creatures whom God invites to participate in the divine *communion* of Father, Son, and Holy Spirit by drawing them to share in the ecstatic love of God. What I want to say in this chapter reflects a similar pattern: Human beings are rational creatures whom God invites to participate in the divine *conversation* of Father, Son, and Holy Spirit by drawing them to share in the wisdom and *Logos* of God. By participating with God in this way, human beings are invited to discern the creational designs and purposes of the Father, through the wisdom of the Son, in the illumination and empowerment of the Spirit. Theologically and ethically, this perspective emphasizes the aspect of human purpose and destiny that concerns *knowing* God and other human beings and *understanding* God's created world.

Creation as intelligible trinitarian conversation

"In the beginning . . . God *said* . . ." (Gen 1:1, 3; emphasis added).

"In the beginning was the Word . . . All things were made through him, and without him nothing was made that was made" (John 1:1, 3).

"God created all things through Christ and for Christ. He is before all things, and in him all things hold together." (Col 1:16–17)

"The Spirit searches all things, even the deeps things of God. . . . No one knows the things of God except the Spirit of God" (1 Cor 2:10, 11).

Scripture depicts the creation of the world as a kind of divine conversation, in which the trinitarian God calls creation into existence and then creation responds obediently to God's call.[1] In this conversation, God the Father (*Thought or Mind*) speaks creation into being by means of God the Son (the Father's in-

---

[1] The notion of creation as divine conversation occurs in Luther. See, for example, *Luther's Works* 1.9, ed. Jaroslav Pelikan (St. Louis: Concordia, 1958). See also Jens Zimmermann's discussion of Luther in his *Recovering Theological Hermeneutics: An Incarnational-Trinitarian Theory of Interpretation* (Grand Rapids: Baker Academic, 2004), 51–57; cf. Oswald Bayer, *Martin Luther's Theology: A Contemporary Interpretation*, trans. Thomas H. Trapp (Grand Rapids: Eerdmans, 2008), 95–105.

telligible *Word*) in the dynamic and animating life-power of God the Holy Spirit (*Breath*, Lord and Giver of Life). All of creation responds to God's speech and displays God's glory and purposive creativity, but human beings respond in a unique way. Human beings are special in that God's Word comes to them in the form of a personal and personalizing intelligible address, which calls forth a reciprocal intelligible response. God not only creates human beings by means of the divine *Logos*; God also invites human beings to share in the divine *Logos* in and through the illuminating power and animating *Breath* of the Spirit. Just as God's Word constitutes human beings as relational creatures who respond to God's love in receptivity and reciprocity, so God's Word simultaneously constitutes human beings as rational creatures, with the intelligence and freedom not merely to parrot God's speech but actually to converse with God as genuine conversation partners. God creates humans in and for love, to be in relationship with God, Father, Son, and Spirit. Yet growing in love includes growing in one's knowledge of the other. Accordingly, God's ecstatic love confronts human beings as God's intelligible and self-revelatory Word and illuminating Spirit, which invites an intelligible and responsible answer. In reciprocal love to God and in basic trust in God, human beings are created to live their lives as an ongoing conversation with God. The characteristic that describes this way of life is what Scripture calls wisdom.

Rational and ethical as mutually defining

Imago Dei, *morality, and rationality*

In chapter three we observed that the image of God refers to three things, namely a relationship, a capacity or structure, and a vocation or calling, though it was suggested that the relational aspect stands out as primary. Luther and Calvin interpreted the *imago Dei* in moral and spiritual terms as being in a right relationship with God by reflecting God's glory and character. In order to do that, however, human beings must be endowed with freedom and reason, because reflecting God's character implies not just mimicking God's actions or following God's rules but being the kind of people who reflect God's goodness in their whole being—in their thoughts, affections, intentions, and actions. It means being the kind of people whose lives demonstrate a holistic love for God and fellow human beings. *This includes loving God and others with their minds.* In light of this, theologians such as Augustine were correct to argue that one aspect of the *imago Dei* is the operation of human reasoning, which implies that human beings are like God in that they are rational creatures.[2]

---

[2] See Grenz's discussion of Augustine in Stanley J. Grenz, *The Social God and the Relational Self: A Trinitarian Theology of the Imago Dei* (Louisville: Westminster John Knox, 2001), 152–57. Augustine followed the reverse pattern and suggested that we cannot love what we do not know, though he acknowledged a circularity (he called it a vicious circle) in the relationship between knowing and loving. See Augustine, *The Trinity* VIII/3.6, trans. Edmund Hill, part I, vol. 5, *The Works of Saint Au-*

Augustine was not the first to suggest that the divine image consists in human rationality. Many earlier theologians had already done so (some more explicitly than others), including Justin Martyr, Irenaeus, Clement of Alexandria, Athanasius, and Cyril of Jerusalem, but Augustine's view became the most influential.[3] In his volume on *The Trinity*, Augustine searches for images of the triune God in creation and finally arrives at the human mind. He proposes that the human mind images God in the act of memory, understanding, and will.[4] Augustine places the emphasis on the activity of the mind (i.e., he means the mind active in the reasoning process, not simply the capacity for rationality or thought), because this demonstrates the unity of the Trinity by showing the simultaneous interaction of three inseparable and mutually implying operations.[5] "These three then, memory, understanding, and will, are not three lives but one life, not three minds but one mind."[6] In Augustine's psychological analogy of memory, understanding, and will, there is no clear way to establish which function is prior and which is subordinate.[7] The action of one implies the joint action of all three. Augustine counsels supreme caution when thinking about trinitarian analogies and, accordingly, refuses to identify any of the trinitarian persons with memory, understanding, or will.[8] His overall point is that the reasoning process within a human being images the tri-unity of God by demonstrating the joint operation of three relations in one Being. In time, others built on Augustine's reasoning to argue that the image of God is located in the individual human's use of reason, though Augustine himself had said that the human rational nature images God most clearly when it *remembers, knows, and loves God*. In Augustine's view, which is representative of the broader patristic

---

gustine: A Translation for the 21st Century, ed. John E. Rotelle (New York: New City, 1991), 245–46. Thus, Grenz comments, "For Augustine, then, the seat of the divine image in the human person is the soul in its intellectual dimension, insofar as the goal of the image is knowledge of God. Yet in Augustine's estimation, knowledge of God is to be accompanied by love for God" (Grenz, *The Social God and the Relational Self*, 155). While the relationship between knowing and loving is something of a chicken-and-egg problem, I maintain that loving takes priority, because knowing and being known presuppose the loving will to self-revelation or self-disclosure. In other words, it is true that we cannot love God without knowing God but it is also true that we could not begin to know God without God's self-disclosure to us in revelation, which is in turn prompted by God's ecstatic nature as a Being who loves and who is Love.

[3] See Grenz, *The Social God and the Relational Self*, 143–52.
[4] Augustine, *The Trinity* X/4.17–18 (pp. 298–99).
[5] Augustine, *The Trinity* XIV/2.9–10 (pp. 377–78).
[6] Augustine, *The Trinity* X/4.18 (p. 298).
[7] See Augustine, "Sermon 52," in *Sermons III: On the New Testament*, trans. Edmund Hill, part III, vol. 3, *The Works of Saint Augustine: A Translation for the 21st Century*, ed. John E. Rotelle (New York: New City, 1991), 59–62.
[8] Augustine, "Sermon 52," 62. However, he does assign places to the trinitarian persons in his mutual love model because he believes that Scripture warrants it by revealing that "God is love" (1 John 4:16).

tradition, genuine rationality is oriented toward God and responsive to God's purposes and will. For Augustine and patristic theology, rationality, awareness of God, and ethical responsibility before God are deeply intertwined. As Jens Zimmermann states, for the patristics:

> [E]ternal truth was concretely embodied in the historical figure of Jesus the Messiah, and access to this truth was no longer intellectual but relational, no longer primarily cognitio but communio, not an ascent of the mind but participation in the divine life through a personal encounter with the risen Christ. Hence, for the first time in ancient philosophy, reason was intrinsically shaped as ethics, because the Logos itself had embodied divine love within history for human beings.... [9]

Many centuries later, the philosopher Immanuel Kant articulated a view of the human person that combined both reasoning and morality, but without Augustine's emphasis on grounding and orienting rationality in and to God (i.e., the divine Logos/Word). Kant suggested that the human mind is inherently structured by certain formal concepts present within it (such as space and time), which correspond to universal categories of reason. These structures enable human beings to make rationally coherent and consistent judgements about the world and their place in it. Moreover, on account of their inherent capacity for rationality, human beings have direct access by means of *a priori* reasoning to the universal moral law without requiring the mediation of experience (according to Kant, the senses "merely furnish the 'raw data' that the mind systematizes").[10] For Kant, there is a correspondence between the human mind and the fundamental structuring of reality, both of which are constituted by and oriented to universal reason and the moral law. In a very real sense for Kant, then, morality is built into the very fabric of the universe. Consequently, Kant linked rationality and morality together in his view that "the goal of the moral dimension of human life is to become as rational as possible."[11] However, by removing the classical Christian emphasis on the personal orientation of human rationality to God, including the dialectical relation of self-knowledge and God-knowledge (as found in Augustine, Anselm, Aquinas, Calvin, etc.), Kant created a fissure separating faith from reason and ethics. For Kant, God is the abstract postulate of ethics, not the concrete and revelatory foundation for ethics.

From a theological perspective, Kant's view must finally be rejected because it individualizes and depersonalizes the nature of human moral existence. It does this by failing to account for human beings as relational persons before God, who encounter in God and other human beings concrete moral claims on

---

[9] Jens Zimmermann, *Incarnational Humanism A Philosophy of Culture for the Church in the World* (Downers Grove: IVP Academic, 2012), 86-87.
[10] Grenz, *The Social God and the Relational Self*, 74.
[11] Grenz, *The Social God and the Relational Self*, 75.

their own existence.[12] Yet Kant's approach does yield a legitimate insight, namely that there is a moral law (God's law) and hence morality pervades the structure of reality. Three interrelated theological observations lend support to Kant's insight. First, God created the world as an integrated whole and declared it "good". Goodness is a natural quality of creation because God created the world to be good and because God's glory and goodness continually fill and pervade it (e.g., Ps 19:1–4; Isa 6:3). Second, at the climax of creation God created human beings and then declared the whole of creation to be "very good". There is a strong sense in the creation account that God created the world *for* human beings, meaning not that everything else has only instrumental value but that human beings have a special and unique place in it.[13] Conversely, in the fallen or sinful state of alienation from and rebellion against God there is a moral disruption in the natural order of things. Not only does sin negatively impact the moral existence of human beings before God and others, it also creates moral ambiguity and distortion in the relation of human beings to the natural world. As Genesis three records, the curse affects the spiritual world (the devil/demonic), human beings, and the natural world (the ground or land is also cursed). It does not totally remove God's presence and sustaining care from the world, without which the universe would spin out into chaos and destruction, but it does introduce a rupture characterized by moral ambiguity and distortion.[14] Third, it is possible for human beings to discern right and wrong, even if such discernment is only partial and ambiguous. Human beings still have limited access to God's moral law, which is written on their hearts (Rom 2:15), even as they fail to live by it consistently due to the corruption of their passions, mind, and will (Rom 1, 7). In sum, human beings are by God's design moral and rational beings, though because of sin both their morality and rationality are distorted and corrupted.

---

[12] Kierkegaard says, "This notion of the single human being before God never occurs to speculative thought; it only universalizes particular humans phantastically into the human race. It was exactly for this reason that a disbelieving Christianity came up with the ideas that sin is sin, that it is neither here nor there whether it is before God. In other words, it wanted to get rid of the specification 'before God,' and to that end invented a new wisdom, which nevertheless, curiously enough, was neither more nor less than what the higher wisdom generally is – the old paganism." Søren Kierkegaard, *The Sickness Unto Death: A Christian Psychological Exposition for Edification and Awakening*, trans. Alastair Hannay (London: Penguin, 1989), 115.

[13] By way of analogy, what a person makes or creates often has intrinsic value to them but such value pales in comparison to the value of their children.

[14] As Bonhoeffer says, "All things appear as in a distorted mirror if they are not seen and recognized in God." Dietrich Bonhoeffer, *Ethics*, ed. Clifford J. Green, trans. Reinhard Krauss, Charles C. West, and Douglas W. Stott, vol. 6, *Dietrich Bonhoeffer Works* (Minneapolis: Fortress, 2005), 48.

Breakdown of the conversation and the limits of human access to the moral law
We gain a better sense of the limits of human understanding of the moral law by exploring the epistemological implications of human corruption. Human corruption is the result of humanity's alienation from God and rebellion against God. Alienation from God includes estrangement from the divine Word, which means that human beings no longer share in the divine conversation in a pure and unambiguous way. In this breakdown of communication, human beings begin to value their own words over God's Word. In their rebellion from God, they attempt to raise their own reasoning to a place of supremacy and sovereignty over the mind of God.[15] Their once harmoniously intelligible conversation with God becomes a dissonant cacophony of prideful and irrational voices trying to dominate and capitalize on the exchange. This results in the corruption of their knowledge of God, of other human beings, and of the world. Alienated from the divine Word and left to their own words, human beings cannot engage in true theology; they can only engage in mythology because their thoughts and language are inadequate, distorted, and prone to idolatry. "Instead of seeing God, human beings see themselves."[16]

In his Christology lectures, Bonhoeffer argues that fallen humans elevate their own *logoi* (words) above God's *Logos* (Word), they even attempt to classify Christ according to human categories of understanding. Due to their fallenness and corruption, they cannot genuinely think outside of themselves and instead assimilate Christ according to their own assumptions and agendas. They mistakenly associate him with their own values and ideals, thereby claiming divine approval for their own *logoi*. Likewise, instead of seeing other people as genuine others they assimilate them into their own self-oriented thoughts, desires, and plans. On a larger social scale, this assimilative tendency leads to the creation of oppressive ideologies, systems, and regimes.[17] In light of this, Bonhoeffer argued that Jesus Christ came as the supreme Counter-*Logos* and declared all human *logoi* to be judged, dead, and in need of transformation.[18]

To elucidate the epistemological predicament created by human sin, Bonhoeffer expands Luther's concept of the *cor curvum in se* and develops its implications for human thinking. He argues that the distortion of human relationships has an epistemological counterpart characterized by a change in orienta-

---

[15] Bonhoeffer, *Ethics*, 299–304.
[16] Bonhoeffer, *Ethics*, 303.
[17] Bonhoeffer delivered his Christology lectures in 1933. Accordingly, Hitler's recent ascension to power looms in the background and occupies much of Bonhoeffer's thinking and writing.
[18] For Bonhoeffer's analysis of Christ as the Counter-*Logos*, see: Dietrich Bonhoeffer, "Lectures on Christology," in *Berlin: 1921–33*, vol. 12 *Dietrich Bonhoeffer Works*, ed. Larry L. Rasmussen, trans. Isabel Best and David Higgins (Minneapolis: Fortress, 2009), 300–10. For the relevance of Bonhoeffer's analysis to the problems of injustice and oppression, see my article "Bonhoeffer's Anti-Logos and its Challenge to Oppression," *Crux* 41, no. 2 (2005): 2–9.

tion from *being-for-God-and-others* to *being-for-self*. Just as sin creates within the human being a heart turned in upon itself, so also does it create a mind turned in upon itself.[19] Bonhoeffer writes, "It is clear now that, on its own, the I cannot move beyond itself. It is imprisoned in itself, it sees only itself, even when it sees another, even when it wants to see God."[20] The will to know has become a veiled will to power.[21] This is the epistemological implication of being "in Adam", by which Bonhoeffer means the state of being in sin. He explains,

> For 'in Adam' means to be in untruth, in culpable perversion of the will, that is, of human essence. It means to be turned inward into one's self, *cor curvum in se*. Human beings have torn themselves loose from community with God and, therefore, also from that with other human beings, and now they stand alone, that is, in untruth. Because human beings are alone, the world is 'their' world, and other human beings have sunk into the world of things (cf. Heidegger's '*Mitsein*', 'being-with'). God has become a religious object, and human beings themselves have become their own creator and lord, belonging to themselves.[22]

When human beings are alienated from God their participation in the divine *Logos* is impaired and their reasoning is distorted. As the New Testament puts it, they suffer from spiritual blindness and defilement of the mind (2 Cor 4:4; Tit 1:15), hence they become enemies of God in their minds (Col 1:21). Consequently, their natural ability to access and understand the moral law is impaired (Rom 1). To be clear, it is not that human beings lose their *capacity* for reasoning; they continue to be adept at logic, empirical observation, and connecting means to ends. Rather, by alienating themselves from the ground of all rationality (the divine *Logos*) the *orientation* of their reasoning loses its proper centre. Their systems of thought may pass the test of internal validity, but their overall worldview is deficient. Correcting the problem involves not the abandonment

---

[19] This enthronement of the self-enclosed "I" leads to the oppressive and dominating forms of the subject-object relation (and other corresponding binary oppositions) that rightfully concern postmodern writers. See Miroslav Volf's well-balanced comments in *Exclusion and Embrace: A Theological Explanation of Identity, Otherness, and Reconciliation* (Nashville: Abingdon, 1996), 60–64, 204–205.

[20] Dietrich Bonhoeffer, *Act and Being: Transcendental Philosophy and Ontology in Systematic Theology*, ed. Wayne Whitson Floyd, trans. H. Martin Rumscheidt, vol. 2 *Dietrich Bonhoeffer Works* (Minneapolis: Fortress, 1996), 45.

[21] Nietzsche's description of the mind's will to power is an apt description of the depraved will of the *sinful mind* (though it does not aptly describe *willing and knowing as such*, as Nietzsche believed). For example, "It always creates the world in its own image; it cannot do otherwise; philosophy is this tyrannical impulse itself, the most spiritual Will to Power, the will to 'creation of the world,' the will to the *causa prima*." Friedrich Nietzsche, *Beyond Good and Evil: Prelude to a Philosophy of the Future* (Mineolo: Dover, 1997), 6.

[22] Bonhoeffer, *Act and Being*, 137.

of human reason but its reorientation, so that it can understand all things *sub ratione Dei*.[23] As Kevin Vanhoozer suggests, we need theological wisdom to help us discern the ultimate meaning of things by seeing them in relation to God and God's kingdom.[24]

Redemption from captivity of the mind

Since the human mind is corrupted in the fallen condition, it is therefore in need of redemption. The Greek word that the New Testament uses for conversion (*metanoia*) implies a fundamental reorientation of one's thinking or one's mind. In addition to receiving a new status (justification) and a new way of living (growing in sanctification), a follower of Christ also begins to operate with a new worldview based on Christ and his teachings. That God wishes to redeem our minds is apparent in Jesus's command that we are to love God with our minds (Mark 12:29–31), in Paul's exhortation that believers be transformed by the renewing of their minds (Rom 12:1–2), and in the many New Testament passages that discuss the nature of Christian wisdom (e.g., 1 Cor 2, James 3). In addition, two significant New Testament events have broad theological implications for the renewing of the mind, namely the incarnation and Pentecost.

Incarnation and the realignment of rationality

God could have created human beings to be ethereal spirits, in which case redemption would mean being set free from the body. Or God could simply have destroyed the world and transported us directly to a non-material heaven. Instead, however, God's becoming one of us in the incarnation of Jesus Christ signifies God's desire to reaffirm human bodily existence even while transforming it. Many writers have noted that the incarnation represents a profound affirmation of the original goodness of the world. For example, Eric G. Flett asserts, "The assumption and redemption of the body by Christ, and the entirety of the created order with it, is the fullest affirmation of human corporeality that may be sought."[25] While the incarnation is not simply a blanket endorsement of every aspect of material existence or of worldly values (Jesus's incarnate life also included the judgment of the cross), it does demonstrate God's love for the world and God's intention to re-create and redirect it.[26] According to Bonhoef-

---

[23] I.e., in light of the relation of all things to God, as stressed by Pannenberg. See F. LeRon Shults, *The Postfoundationalist Task of Theology: Wolfhart Pannenberg and the New Theological Rationality* (Grand Rapids: Eerdmans, 1999), 17, 20, 83, 109–10, 169.

[24] Kevin J. Vanhoozer, *The Drama of Doctrine: A Canonical-linguistic Approach to Christian Theology* (Louisville: Westminster John Knox, 2005), 377.

[25] Eric G. Flett, "Priests of Creation, Mediators of Order: the Human Person as a Cultural Being in Thomas F. Torrance's Theological Anthropology," *Scottish Journal of Theology* 58, no. 2 (2005): 165.

[26] John Howard Yoder balances incarnation and the cross and distinguishes between metaphysical and confessional dualism in *The Royal Priesthood: Essays Ecclesiastical and Ecumenical*, ed. Michael G. Cartwright (Waterloo, ON: Herald, 1998), 62, 108–109. He writes, "The duality of church and world is not a slice separating the re-

fer, the incarnation grants renewed dignity and value to the world as it is restored to be what God originally intended. Bonhoeffer often commends what he calls the "worldliness" of Christianity, but in so doing he is not promoting an irresponsible, careless, or hedonistic attitude or lifestyle.[27] He is careful to distinguish between genuine and false forms of worldliness.[28] For Bonhoeffer, worldliness can be genuine only when it is grounded in the incarnation of Jesus Christ. Genuine worldliness and genuine faith coexist inseparably in and through Christ, who is the Centre and Mediator of all reality. As Bonhoeffer reflects in *Ethics*, "In Christ the reality of God meets the reality of the world and allows us to share in this real encounter . . . Christian life is participation in the encounter of Christ with the world."[29] Especially when paired with the bodily resurrection of Christ and the theme of new creation by the Spirit, the incarnation affirms the intrinsic value that God places on our bodily and material existence, including the world of nature, work, rest, leisure, beauty, and human expression through art and culture.[30]

This incarnational affirmation of holistic human existence includes intellectual endeavour and ought to dignify, encourage, and guide the Christian's pursuit of the life of the mind. In the incarnation, the second person of the Trinity (Jesus) fully assumed human existence in order to redeem human beings as

ligious from the profane, nor the ecclesiastical from the civil, nor the spiritual from the material. It is the divide on this side of which there are those who confess Jesus as Lord, who in so doing are both secular and profane, both spiritual and physical, both ecclesiastical and civil, both individual and organized, in their relationships to one another and to others." (108–109)

[27] For Bonhoeffer's incarnational commendation of worldliness, see *Letters and Papers from Prison*, ed. Eberhard Bethge (New York: Simon & Schuster, 1997), 280–82, 286, 300, 310–12, 325–29, 336–37, 341–47, 359–63, 369–70, 378–79. For his critical theological affirmation of "natural life", see *Ethics*, 171–81. Bonhoeffer goes on to discuss implications for several ethical issues, including natural law, the right to life, suicide, reproduction, and freedom of bodily life (181–217).

[28] In addition, as Clifford J. Green explains, Bonhoeffer's notion of worldliness does not convey the same meaning as the English word secular (the first English editions of Bonhoeffer's prison letters made this unfortunate translation error). Bonhoeffer uses the German words weltlich (worldly) and Diesseitigkeit (this-worldliness, as opposed to otherworldliness) to describe his world-embracing, incarnational vision of non-religious Christianity. Bonhoeffer uses the word säkular (secular) only once—and on that occasion he uses it pejoratively to criticize existentialists and psychotherapists as "the secularized offshoots of Christian theology". See Green, "Sociality, Discipleship, and Worldly Theology in Bonhoeffer's Christian Humanism," in *Being Human, Becoming Human: Dietrich Bonhoeffer and Social Thought*, ed. Jens Zimmermann and Brian Gregor (Eugene, OR: Pickwick, 2010), 86–90.

[29] Bonhoeffer, *Ethics*, 132.

[30] See Miroslav Volf, *Work in the Spirit: Toward a Theology of Work* (Eugene: Wipf and Stock, 1991), 88–92, 96. Volf highlights the importance of the Spirit in genuine worldliness: "Because the whole creation is the Spirit's sphere of operation, the Spirit is not only the Spirit of religious experience but also the Spirit of worldly engagement" (104).

whole creatures, materially and spiritually, body and mind.[31] Redemption includes God's act of restoring human beings to renewed participation in the intelligible conversation of the Trinity by sharing again in the divine *Logos*. Accordingly, the New Testament declares that "we have the mind of Christ" (1 Cor 2:16) and thus have access to "the wisdom of God" (1 Cor 2:6–12). In their book, *The Passionate Intellect*, Norman Klassen and Jens Zimmermann argue that the incarnation infuses scholarship and education with a renewed sense of purpose, which is to proclaim and celebrate the affirmation of the human being and of nature that is offered in the life, death, and resurrection of Jesus Christ. They write, "The quality, character, and direction of your scholarly pursuits are a witness to God and participate in God's new creation. By pursuing knowledge, you engage in the diligent study of nature and human nature for the sake of the kingdom and its restorative, redemptive work."[32] Klassen and Zimmermann further argue that an incarnational perspective encourages Christians humbly and graciously to affirm truth wherever it is found, including in the discoveries and achievements of their non-Christian colleagues and students throughout the spectrum of academic disciplines. Such knowledge is part of God's common grace and can serve the renewal of the mind. Richard Hughes expresses a similar perspective when he writes:

> Precisely because I am a Christian scholar, I seek to maintain an open classroom in which my students can raise any questions they wish. Precisely because I am a Christian scholar, I seek to nurture in my students a hunger and thirst for truth. Precisely because I am a Christian scholar, I encourage my students to critically

---

[31] According to T.F. Torrance, Christ's full assumption of humanity, his fully becoming human in every sense, was a pervasive theme amongst patristic theologians such as Athanasius, Gregory of Nazianzus, and Cyril of Alexandria. In particular, it was crucial to their soteriology because it grounded their view that "the unassumed is the unredeemed" (i.e., Christ cannot save what he does not incorporate through the incarnation). Thomas F. Torrance, *The Christian Doctrine of God: One Being Three Persons* (New York: T & T Clark, 1996), 250. See also Scot McKnight, who refers to this soteriology as "identification for incorporation," in his book *A Community Called Atonement* (Nashville: Abingdon, 2007). For a beautiful and graphic portrayal of the themes of assumption and incorporation, see the parable of the lord and servant in Julian of Norwich, *Showings*, trans. Edmund Colledge and James Walsh (New York: Paulist Press, 1978), chapter 51, 267–78.

[32] Norman Klassen and Jens Zimmermann, *The Passionate Intellect: Incarnational Humanism and the Future of University Education* (Grand Rapids: Baker Academic, 2008), 162. See also Jens Zimmermann, "The Passionate Intellect: Christian Humanism and University Education," *Direction* 37 (Spring 2008): 19–37. In addition, see: Deane E.D. Downey and Stanley E. Porter, eds., *Christian Worldview and the Academic Disciplines: Crossing the Academy* (Eugene: Pickwick, 2009); Richard T. Hughes, *The Vocation of a Christian Scholar: How Christian Faith Can Sustain the Life of the Mind* (Grand Rapids: Eerdmans, 2005); and Harry Lee Poe, *Christianity in the Academy: Teaching at the Intersection of Faith and Learning* (Grand Rapids: Baker Academic, 2004).

assess not only the perspectives of others, but their own perspectives as well. And precisely because I am a Christian scholar, I encourage my students to approach their studies with imagination and creativity.[33]

As Hughes emphasizes, a Christian perspective that is grounded in the incarnation not only allows but actively encourages us to raise questions, to engage critically, to collaborate with others, and to articulate and reformulate our ideas as we passionately seek after the truth.[34]

Pentecost and the Spirit's renewal of our minds
The biblical narrative does not conclude with the resurrection of Christ. His redemptive mission was not complete without his ascension to heaven, which gave way to the coming of the Holy Spirit at Pentecost. Jesus himself once told his disciples that his imminent departure would be for their benefit, because otherwise the Holy Spirit would not come (John 16:7). According to Jesus, the Holy Spirit is the divine Counsellor who leads followers of Jesus into all truth, teaches them all things, and reminds them of everything that Jesus taught (John 14:16–17, 26). On account of the Spirit's coming at Pentecost and continual indwelling, disciples have "the mind of Christ" and hence gain access to the wisdom of God. As Paul writes, "the wisdom we speak of is the secret wisdom from God . . . we know these things because God has revealed them to us by his Spirit, and his Spirit searches out everything and shows us even God's deep secrets" (1 Cor 2:7, 10). Moreover, "no one can know God's thoughts except God's own Spirit . . . and God has actually given his Spirit" (1 Cor 2:11, 12).

The Spirit enables our access to the mind of Christ, and thus to the wisdom of God, in several distinct ways. *The Spirit plays a crucial role in regeneration and conversion.* Believers are reborn of the Spirit (John 3:5–8), washed and given new life though the Spirit (Titus 3:5), confess that Christ is Lord by the Spirit's illumination (1 Cor 12:3), and receive assurance that they are God's children from the Spirit (Rom 8:16). *The Spirit is involved in the redemption of the human will.*[35] In Romans 7, Paul laments that he cannot observe God's law by his own strength and willpower; he does what he knows he should not do and fails to do what he knows he should do. He cries, "Oh, what a miserable person I am! Who will free me from this life that is dominated by sin?" (7:24) Yet immediately Paul exclaims with gratitude that God has delivered him through Christ by the Spirit. He devotes his next chapter to explaining the working of the Holy Spirit in the believer's life, "for the power of the life-

---

[33] Hughes, *Vocation of a Christian Scholar*, 7.
[34] For a survey of Christian scholars and teachers attempting to integrate their Christian worldview with their scholarship in a way that preserves the integrity of both, see my article "Teaching, Scholarship, and Christian Worldview: A Review of Recent Literature," *McMaster Journal of Theology and Ministry* 11 (2009–2010): 28–61.
[35] In place of the fallen, Nietzschean "will to power" or the Pauline will to sin, the Holy Spirit renews a will to love and serve God and others.

giving Spirit has freed you through Christ Jesus from the power of sin that leads to death" (8:2). *The Spirit renews our thoughts and attitudes.* Paul writes in Romans 8:5 that "those who are controlled by the Spirit *think about* things that please the Spirit" (emphasis added). Elsewhere he encourages believers to be united in the Spirit (Eph 4:3–4) and to maintain fellowship in the Spirit by emulating Christ's humility (Phil 2:1, 5–11). *The Spirit sanctifies believers and matures them in love and holiness.* In the New Testament, there is a link between growing in knowledge and wisdom and maturing in love and holiness, which is the Spirit's work of sanctification. For example, Jesus told his disciples that if they demonstrated their love for him by obeying his commands, he would ask the Father to send them the Holy Spirit (John 14:15–16). James says that genuine wisdom from above is pure, peace-loving, gentle, humble, impartial, sincere, and full of mercy and good deeds (Jas 3:17). And Peter argues that a life of moral excellence leads to deeper knowledge of God, which in turn leads to self-control, patient endurance, godliness, and finally to genuine love for everyone (2 Pet 1:5–7). (Notice that many of the qualities that James and Peter list correspond to the fruit of the Spirit recorded in Galatians 5:22–23.) *The Spirit gives special gifts* of knowledge, wisdom, discernment, visions, and prophetic insight and utterance whenever and to whomever the Spirit wills (e.g., Acts 9:10; 1 Cor 2:10–12; Eph 4:11–13; 2 Pet 1:20–21).[36] Furthermore, the Spirit empowers boldness in preaching and evangelism (Acts 4:8, 13, 29–31; 13:9; 1 Pet 1:11–12) and enables effectiveness in teaching (Acts 5:32; 6:10; 18:25), all of which disseminates and cultivates Christian wisdom. Finally, *the Spirit guides and directs believers into wisdom* by interceding before the Father on their behalf. Amazingly, the Spirit actually prays for (and in) believers when they themselves do not know what to pray (Rom 8:26–27).

The Christian life of wisdom
In this chapter, I have been arguing from a theological perspective that human beings are created, renewed, and transformed to be rational creatures before the Creator. In saying this, I am not thereby reducing human ethics and existence to *simply being just and rational.* As Alasdair MacIntyre has effectively demonstrated, such a reduction would beg the question "*Whose* justice? *Which* rationality?"[37] Conversely, I have brought rationality into a dialogical relationship with ethical existence and reoriented both to the eternal *Logos* of God, which comes to human beings in the form of a personal address. Thus, from a theological perspective, genuine rationality involves faithfully seeking the truth and responsibly living it out in light of the knowledge and presence of God. This means that genuine rationality and morality are oriented toward seeking and living what Scripture calls *wisdom.* The purpose of wisdom is to equip people

---

[36] See also: Acts 10:3, 7, 10–16; 16:9–10; 22:17–18; 1 Cor 12:8–11; and 2 Cor 3:14–17.

[37] Alasdair MacIntyre, *Whose Justice? Which Rationality?* (Notre Dame: University of Notre Dame Press, 1988).

to live out their fundamental *telos* of knowing and loving God and fellow human beings. Thus, *rational* and *ethical* are taken up into the biblical concept of wisdom and set within the context of the wisdom community (see chapter 7, which discusses the church as a wisdom community).

Faith and the rational ethical dimension

Building trust, growing in love and wisdom

"Fear of the Lord is the beginning of wisdom." (Prov 9:10)

"Perfect love drives out fear." (1 John 4:18)

Religious faith is not opposed to rationality; it is the doorway to a particular kind of rationality.[38] The Old Testament proclaims that fear or reverence for the Lord is the beginning of wisdom and knowledge (e.g., Ps 111:10; Prov 1:7). Proverbs three gives several reasons for this. First, wisdom comes from God because God is the source of all true wisdom. Thus, we are exhorted to trust God and to seek God's will rather than relying on our own understanding (Prov 3:5–6). Second, by wisdom God created the universe. Proverbs 3:19–20 says: "By wisdom the Lord founded the earth; by understanding he established the heavens. By his knowledge the deep fountains of the earth burst forth, and the clouds poured down rain." Since God created the universe by wisdom, the universe has a rational structure with consistent physical properties and laws. Moreover, God's moral law orients the purpose and destiny of human beings. Third, reverence for the Lord is the beginning of wisdom because God is completely trustworthy (Prov 3:11–12). God is always good, just, faithful, gracious, merciful, and righteous. Furthermore, God corrects and disciplines those whom God loves. God's moral laws are not arbitrary but reveal and address the truth of the human condition. Thus, reverence for God lived out in faithful obedience to God's commands leads to health, long life, satisfaction, fulfilment, and finding favour with God and people (generally or proverbially speaking).[39] Fourth, God is all powerful. Everything that God does reflects God's glory, majesty, and supreme justice. God's power and sovereignty should command our respect and elicit our contemplation, praise, and obedience. Further, as supreme Judge

---

[38] This reflects the classic Christian emphasis on faith seeking understanding. For example, Anselm writes, "And so, Lord, who dost give understanding to faith, give me, so far as thou knowest it to be profitable, to understand that thou are as we believe; and that thou are that which we believe." Anselm, *Proslogium* (chapter 1) in *Proslogium; Monologium; An Appendix in Behalf of the Fool by Gaunilon; and Cur Deus Homo*, trans. Sidney Norton Deane (Chicago: Open Court, 1926), 6.

[39] Such proverbial optimism is challenged and balanced within the wisdom corpus, particularly in Job and Ecclesiastes, with a stark acknowledgment of the injustice, unfairness, pain, and misery that often (and sometimes inexplicably) characterize human life.

God curses the wicked but blesses the upright, which should motivate us toward obedience (Prov 3:33–35).

While fear of the Lord is the beginning of wisdom, it is not the end of wisdom. Nor does it account for the full content of wisdom. The first letter of John says: "Perfect love drives out fear because fear has to do with punishment. But the one who fears has not been made perfect in love" (1 John 4:18 NIV). Fear of God is the beginning of wisdom, but love for God is the end or *telos* of wisdom. The law came through Moses, but grace and truth came through Jesus Christ (John 1:17). As the definitive revelation of God, the Word and true Image of God, Jesus Christ came to reveal the full extent of the Father's love. Accordingly, Jesus taught that the greatest two commandments are to love God with all of one's heart, mind, soul, and strength, and to love one's neighbour as oneself. The Apostle Paul similarly argues that loving one's neighbour summarizes all the commands of the Law (Gal 5:14). Since obeying God's commands ultimately has to do with loving God and others holistically in thought, word, and deed, the cultivation of wisdom aims toward the transformation of heart and character.

Command, character, and Christian ethics in a Trinitarian framework
Moral transformation takes place as we receive and obey God's commands, through the revelatory Word of the Son, in the love and power of the Holy Spirit. God's commands are the basis for theological ethics, because they reflect God's holiness, righteousness, and justice, as well as God's creative purposes for us and for creation. As Stanley Grenz argues, God has the prerogative to declare what it means to be human, precisely because God is the Creator and Origin of human life and existence.[40] God's commands, in turn, have their source and initiative in the Father's character and love for human beings and the created world. Our moral response to God is to reciprocate God's love, emulate God's character, and seek reverently to honour God with our lives.

Moral transformation occurs, secondly, through the revelatory Word of the Son. Jesus Christ, the Son of God, is the one who fully reveals God's love and character to us. The Gospel of John tells us that although no one has ever seen God, the Word (*Logos*) has made God known to us (John 1:18). This Word is Jesus Christ, the only Son of the Father. As such, Jesus Christ is the authoritative interpreter of God's commands. This is evident, for example, throughout the Sermon on the Mount when Jesus says several times concerning the Mosaic Law: "You have heard it said. . . . *But I say* . . ." (emphasis added). In speaking this way, Jesus implicitly claims to have the authority to interpret the Law definitively, an authority which outranked the Pharisees and the religious teachers. As Kevin Vanhoozer helpfully points out, Jesus authoritatively interprets the Old Testament Scriptures, while the apostles subsequently interpret Jesus's

---

[40] Stanley J. Grenz, *Theology for the Community of God* (Grand Rapids: Eerdmans, 1994), 140–43.

person and work according to the interpretive patterns that Jesus himself implemented. Consequently, according to the precedent set by Scripture itself, Christology becomes the key hermeneutical lens for interpreting and integrating the canon.[41] "Jesus is both the material and the formal principle of the canon: its substance and its hermeneutic."[42] For Christians, this means that Jesus Christ is the source of our knowledge of God and that faith in Jesus is the basis of our confidence in God's love and character.

Finally, moral transformation occurs in the love and power of the Holy Spirit. As discussed in the previous chapter, the Holy Spirit is the living, personalizing, and transforming power that is God's love. As such, the Spirit is both Person and Gift. As Person, the Spirit is the third member of the Trinity who unites the Father and Son together in perfect, ecstatic, perichoretic love. As Gift, the Holy Spirit is the one who comes to reside within those who trust in Christ, as a seal of their salvation and a deposit and foretaste of their final transformation in glory. The Holy Spirit is the one who fills believers with God's love (the Spirit *is* God's Love) and who writes God's Law onto their hearts. According to the Apostle Paul (notably in Rom 8, but elsewhere as well), the filling of the Holy Spirit in the life of the believer is the transformative power that regenerates and sustains, heals and sanctifies, guides and perfects the Christian's new life in Christ. Being filled with the Spirit means being filled with the very Love of God. Thus, it is the Spirit of God as Love who gradually drives out all fear and awakens the believer's faith to grow in personal and loving trust in God. It is the Spirit who renews the mind, renovates the heart, and invites us to respond by dedicating our lives to Christ. The Spirit also binds Christians together in the community of faith and equips each member to encourage and serve the others, so that they all "will be mature and full grown in the Lord, measuring up to the full stature of Christ" (Eph 4:13). Following Christ daily by obeying the Word of God in the power of the Spirit, within the context of the Christian community as one participates in its distinctive worship and practices, gradually leads to the cultivation of wisdom and the transformation of character (see chapters 7 and 8).

Theology as knowing God and cultivating biblical wisdom
If, as I have argued, wisdom combines rationality with personal ethical responsibility before God, then theology is crucial to the pursuit of Christian wisdom. By *theology*, I mean faithful, disciplined, prayerful, and doxological reflection on the *Logos* of God, as revealed in Christ by the Spirit primarily in Scripture but interpreted in light of the Christian Tradition, reason, and direct experience of God.

---

[41] See Vanhoozer, *The Drama of Doctrine*, 194–96.
[42] Vanhoozer, *The Drama of Doctrine*, 196.

Theology and the knowledge of God

The purpose of theology is to know God and to make Him known to others.[43] Knowledge of God is possible because God desires to be known and reveals himself in Word and Spirit.[44] In the very beginning, the Word existed with God, and was in fact one with God (John 1:1). Through the Word, all things were created and in the Word all things hold together (Col 1:15). This Word became flesh and dwelt among us (John 1:14). Although no one has ever seen God, the Word, who is the very expression of God, the very exegesis of God, has made God known (John 1:18). Thus, as Karl Barth proposes, the principal task of theology is to hear and respond to the Word of God.[45] This Word of God is the Lord Jesus Christ himself, the Son of God, who creates, arouses and challenges all human theological words.[46] Theology is dependent on Christ for its very existence and continuance. It is not primarily a creative act (i.e., our creation), but rather a "response and praise to the Creator."[47] It is not merely a formulation of our thoughts about God, but our response to God's self-revelation to us. God accomplished this revelation objectively in human history in Jesus Christ, who fulfilled the calling of Israel.[48]

Moreover, it is the Spirit of God who makes the hearing of the Word possible. To speak intelligibly is to expire one's breath, forming and shaping it with one's words. Similarly, the Father's speech to us is animated by the breath of the Holy Spirit and given articulate expression by the Word. The Father sends the Spirit to teach us all things and to remind us of the words of the Son (John 14:26). The Spirit enables us to experience this Word as a living reality. No one can understand the Word of God apart from the Spirit of God. In this respect, our knowledge and experience of God is no different from that of the first disciples of Jesus, who knew the truth only because God chose to reveal it to them through the Word in the Spirit (Matt 16:17; Luke 10:21–22; John 12:37–41). The Spirit of God also empowers us to become witnesses of the Word, and sends us to the ends of the earth to proclaim the good news (Acts 1:8). Theology serves this evangelistic ministry of the Spirit, striving to articulate the reality of God in a contextual and relevant way.

---

[43] Peter Jensen, "The Teacher as Theologian in Theological Education," *Reformed Theological Review* 50 (Sept.–Dec., 1991): 83.

[44] John Webster argues that "in all of their variety the biblical writings together constitute a unified divine act of communication—a single, though rich, complex and historically extended, divine word from which a coherent body of teaching can be drawn." John Webster, "Biblical Theology and the Clarity of Scripture," in *Out of Egypt: Biblical Theology and Biblical Interpretation*, ed. Craig Bartholomew, Mary Healy, Karl Möller, and Robin Parry (Grand Rapids: Zondervan / Milton Keynes: UK, 2004), 352.

[45] Karl Barth, *Evangelical Theology: An Introduction* (Grand Rapids: Eerdmans, 1963), 17.

[46] Barth, *Evangelical Theology*, 17.

[47] Barth, *Evangelical Theology*, 17.

[48] Barth, *Evangelical Theology*, 20.

The Human Person as a Rational Creature

Knowledge of God is deeply connected to knowledge of oneself; indeed, God-knowledge and self-knowledge arise and fall together.[49] Without knowledge of God, knowledge of oneself is distorted and ultimately impossible. To know God as Creator, Reconciler, and Perfecter is to know oneself as creature, sinner, and finite, dependent on God for one's existence in past, present, and future. Thus, knowing God means loving and obeying God. To reject knowledge of God is to conceive of *oneself* as creator, redeemer, and perfecter, *oneself* as the source of one's own life, salvation, and sustenance.[50] This is the condition of sin. However, the knowledge of God, made possible by Christ's saving work and the Spirit's quickening of the soul, renews both heart and mind and realigns our lives around God as the centre and source of our existence (Rom 12:1-2). This fundamental transformation of the mind, which leads to a reorientation of one's actions, is what the biblical authors call repentance.[51] Accordingly theology, which seeks to articulate the knowledge of God coherently and concretely in particular contexts, aims at *conversion*, or, as D.A. Carson puts it, at "worldview transformation" at both a personal and a communal level.[52] In this effort, theology's job is never finished, because it is continually pressed by changing contexts to articulate the knowledge of God clearly and faithfully as new situations, challenges, and advances in human knowledge develop.[53] Such knowledge is not merely the accumulation of information but the formulation of wisdom. Kevin Vanhoozer proposes,

> Doctrine has a cognitive component, for we must understand what God has done for our salvation . . . , but the thrust of Christian doctrine is not mere knowledge, but rather wisdom: we demonstrate our understanding by speaking and acting in

---

[49] Clement of Alexandria, *The Instructor* III.1 in *ANF02: Fathers of the Second Century: Hermas, Tatian, Athenagoras, Theophilus, and Clement of Alexandria (Entire)*, ed. Philip Schaff (Grand Rapids: CCEL, 2004), 271; Augustine, *The Confessions of St. Augustine*, trans. John K. Ryan (New York: Doubleday, 1960), 44; Anselm, *Proslogium*, 4–5; John Calvin, *Institutes of the Christian Religion* I.1, trans. Henry Beveridge (Grand Rapids: Eerdmans, 1989), 37–39.

[50] No one is naïvely ignorant of God, rather knowledge of God is suppressed by human pride (Rom 1:18). We are all guilty of this and in need of redemption.

[51] Mark J. Boda and Gordon T. Smith, eds., *Repentance in Christian Theology* (Collegeville, MN: Liturgical, 2006). The basic definition of repentance, which is a fundamental change in thinking leading to a fundamental change in behaviour and/or way of living, appears consistently throughout this book.

[52] D.A. Carson, "Systematic and Biblical Theology," in *New Dictionary of Biblical Theology*, ed. T.D. Alexander and B.S. Rosner (Downers Grove: InterVarsity Press, 2000), 102.

[53] I. Howard Marshall, *Beyond the Bible: Moving from Scripture to Theology* (Grand Rapids: Baker, 2004), 71. Marshall writes, theology "enables believers to develop the implications of their faith and to come to fresh insights to deal with new knowledge and the danger of false belief."

manners that correspond to reality as it is disclosed by (and being conformed to) Jesus Christ.[54]

Thus, the ultimate foundation for the knowledge of God, and hence for theology, is the Incarnate Word of God, who by the Spirit of God reveals the Father. As Clark Pinnock asserts, "Revelation is neither contentless experience (liberalism) nor timeless propositions (conservatism). It is the dynamic self-disclosure of God, who makes his goodness known in the history of salvation, in a process of disclosure culminating in Jesus Christ."[55]

There is a deep connection between the *Logos* of God and the Bible as the written Word of God.[56] Scripture as the authoritative written Word of God serves the divine *Logos* of God and derives its inspired power from the Spirit of God. Consequently, knowledge of Scripture is crucial for theological formation and for growth in Christian wisdom. Theologians falling within the historic Christian tradition have always agreed that Scripture is an important source for Christian belief and practice. Faithfulness to Scripture is particularly important to theologians adhering to the broad evangelical tradition, as I do. But what is the relationship between Scripture and Christian theology and ethics? There is a vast and growing amount of literature dedicated to this question, which I will not survey here.[57] It is beyond the scope of this chapter to offer a full-fledged hermeneutical theory. I will restrict my discussion to some reflections on reading Scripture *theologically* as a rational-ethical person, *in order to know God and cultivate wisdom.*

a)   Faithfulness to Scripture

---

[54] Kevin J. Vanhoozer, "Into the Great Beyond: A Theologian's Response to the Marshall Plan," in *Beyond the Bible*, 87–88.

[55] Clark H. Pinnock, *Flame of Love: A Theology of the Holy Spirit* (Downers Grove: InterVarsity Press, 1996), 226.

[56] T.F. Torrance, *Divine Meaning: Studies in Patristic Hermeneutics* (Edinburgh: T & T Clark, 1995), 6–13.

[57] See for example: A.K.M. Adam, Stephen E. Fowl, Kevin J. Vanhoozer, and Francis Watson, *Reading Scripture with the Church: Toward a Hermeneutic for Theological Interpretation* (Grand Rapids: Baker Academic, 2006); Richard A. Burridge, *Imitating Jesus: An Inclusive Approach to New Testament Ethics* (Grand Rapids: Eerdmans, 2007); Stephen E. Fowl, *Engaging Scripture: A Model for Theological Interpretation* (Oxford: Blackwell, 1998); Stephen E. Fowl and Gregory Jones, *Reading in Communion: Scripture and Ethics in Christian Life* (Grand Rapids: Eerdmans, 1991); Anthony C. Thiselton, *The Hermeneutics of Doctrine* (Grand Rapids: Eerdmans, 2007); Vanhoozer, *The Drama of Doctrine*; Kevin J. Vanhoozer, Craig G. Bartholomew, Daniel J. Treier, and N.T. Wright, *Dictionary for Theological Interpretation of the Bible* (Grand Rapids, MI: Baker Academic, 2005); Francis Watson, *Text, Church and World: Biblical Interpretation in Theological Perspective* (Grand Rapids: Eerdmans, 1994) and *Text and Truth: Redefining Biblical Theology* (Grand Rapids: Eerdmans, 1997).

Scripture as the written Word is a penultimate or secondary foundation for theology in the sense that it serves the Living Word of God and depends on the Spirit of God for its inspired power and authority. It is secondary in the sense that it is not a member of the Trinity.[58] Scripture is God's primary and authoritative means of communicating the knowledge of God to human beings. The writers of the Old and New Testaments are the primary witnesses of God's words and actions in history.[59] As such, the biblical writers claim ultimate authority over all human speech concerning God and are sought after to measure the authenticity of all subsequent God-talk or theologizing. Accordingly, theological discourse can never be elevated above the biblical witnesses. Theology serves the written Word of God at a fundamental level.[60] Thus, as J.I. Packer stresses, devotion to Scripture is a necessary element of loyalty to Christ.[61] This is in contrast both to those who appeal to church tradition as the final authority and to those who elevate human reason to such a position (Packer cites Catholicism as an example of the former and Liberalism as epitomizing the latter).[62] Kevin Vanhoozer proposes a more nuanced comparison, contrasting his dramatic canonical-linguistic approach to theology with reductionist approaches, including theology as collecting and systematizing biblical propositions (e.g., Hodge; C.F. Henry), as witness to present and personal revelation (e.g., Barth), as the expression of religious experience (e.g., Schleiermacher), and as speech about church practices and traditions (e.g., Lindbeck).[63] Vanhoozer aims to incorporate the insights of Lindbeck's cultural-linguistic model over-against propositionalism, in order to emphasize the importance of the interpretive community's traditions and practices, while simultaneously maintaining (against Lindbeck) the ultimate authority of Scripture as God's self-

---

[58] T.F. Torrance writes, "whereas in Jesus Christ the divine Word and human word are united within one Person, that is, hypostatically, in the Bible the divine Word and the human word are only united through dependence upon and participation in Christ, that is, sacramentally." Torrance, *Divine Meaning*, 7.

[59] The biblical authors are more than just witnesses of something external to them. They are participants by the Spirit in God's revelatory speech and action. See Vanhoozer, *The Drama of Doctrine*, 5.

[60] Barth, *Evangelical Theology*, 31.

[61] J.I. Packer, *Fundamentalism and the Word of God* (Grand Rapids: Eerdmans, 1958), 21. As Stassen and Gushee demonstrate, Jesus himself affirmed the authority of the Scriptures (*Kingdom Ethics*, 84–90). Likewise, Packer observes that Jesus explicitly acknowledged the authority of the Old Testament as the foundation for his ministry (i.e., Matt 5: 17–20; Luke 4:18–21, 24:44). Similarly, the Apostles proclaimed that Christianity is the fulfillment of Scripture. Finally, the early church regarded the apostolic teaching and the Old Testament scripture as two complementary components of God's Word.

[62] Packer, *Fundamentalism*, 46, 58–62.

[63] Vanhoozer, *The Drama of Doctrine*, 4–7. Vanhoozer describes his work, over-against both conservatism and postliberalism, as a postconservative, canonical-linguistic theology and a directive theory of doctrine that roots theology more firmly in Scripture while preserving an emphasis on practice (xiii).

communicative Word, which refers beyond itself and the Christian community to the reality of God.[64] My own view corresponds closely with Vanhoozer's proposal.

b)   Illumined by the Holy Spirit

Only God can reveal God's Self directly: God is the source of revelation (the Father), the content of revelation (the Son), and the recipient of revelation (the Spirit indwelling the believer). As Barth says, "Revelation is therefore summons and empowerment."[65] God shares God's very life with us by giving us the Spirit, who resides within us and writes the Word of God onto our hearts.

The Holy Spirit operates on at least two levels in mediating the knowledge of God we receive through the Scriptures. First, the Holy Spirit is the author of Scripture. Paul writes in 1 Timothy 3:16, "All scripture is inspired by God and is useful for teaching, for reproof, for correction, and for training in righteousness." The Holy Spirit is the one who *inspired* Scripture (past action), who animated and spoke it into being. This does not mean that the Spirit dictated the words of Scripture to the biblical authors, but rather the Spirit breathed the communicative presence of God into their hearts and minds and guided their written articulation as they expressed the Word of God through their own literary capacity and creativity. The Holy Spirit is also the one who vivifies and applies Scripture to its hearers and readers (a present, even presenc*ing* action). The Spirit impresses Scripture onto their minds and renders it clear.[66] Moreover, by the power of the Spirit, Scripture gains a performative function—it actually accomplishes something in the hearer or reader. In this sense, an encounter with Scripture is a faith-*event*: something transpires; something happens. By this encounter with God through the Scriptures, believers are taught, rebuked, corrected, trained in righteousness, and generally equipped for every good work (1 Tim 3:16–17).

Second, the Holy Spirit directly speaks, guides, and empowers Christians in their daily thinking and acting (illumination). In this work, the Spirit does not contradict the Word of God (the Spirit remains consistent with what has already been revealed), but the Spirit may disturb and stir up one's current *understanding or interpretation* of past revelation. While the Word is embodied, giving form and structure, the Spirit is fluid and tends to disrupt systems and structures with God's dynamic presence. The implication of this for theology is that true theology is about a relationship. It is the fruit of one's communion with the

---

[64] Articulating a similar concern, Clark Pinnock writes, "Revelation is not primarily existential impact or infallible truths but divine self-revelation that both impacts and instructs. The mode of revelation is self-disclosure and interpersonal communication" (Pinnock, *Flame of Love*, 226).

[65] Webster, "Biblical Theology," 376.

[66] John Webster writes, "the coherent teaching that Scripture sets forth can be discerned by the Spirit-directed use of interpreted reason in the communion of saints." Webster, "Biblical Theology," 353.

Living God and must be pursued in the context of faith and prayer and expressed in reverence, adoration, joy, longing, lamentation, expectation, and perseverance—in short, it must be an expression of holy love.[67] As Gregory of Nyssa said, "concepts create idols. Only wonder understands".[68] Flowing from *communion with God*, theology is knowable yet provisional, true yet finite, dependable yet contextual, and for the present yet open to the future.

c)   *Situated within the Christian tradition*

Christianity is a faith that rests on historical truth claims.[69] "If Christ has not been raised, then our proclamation has been in vain and your faith has been in vain," the apostle forcefully asserts (1 Cor 15:14). The church, as the community of God stretching back in history to the time of Christ and the apostles, is a witness to the historical events recorded in Scripture. The early church fathers are particularly important, not only because of their temporal proximity to the biblical authors, but also because of the nature of the early Christian witness and the development of the canon. Previous to the finalization of the canon, the early fathers appealed to three inter-related and mutually supporting sources of theological authority: (1) Scripture; (2) tradition, as embodied in the orthodox, *catholic* church; and (3) ecclesial authority, vested in the office of bishops who traced their theology to the witness of the apostles and the churches established by the apostles. Tertullian's *Prescription Against the Heretics* serves as an apt example of the role of tradition and ecclesial authority during the patristic era:

> But if there be any (heresies) which are bold enough to plant themselves in the midst of the apostolic age, that they may thereby seem to have been handed down by the apostles, because they existed in the time of the apostles, we can say: Let them produce the original records of their churches; let them unfold the roll of their bishops, running down in due succession from the beginning in such a manner that [that first bishop of theirs] bishop shall be able to show for his ordainer and predecessor some one of the apostles or of apostolic men,—a man, moreover, who continued stedfast [sic] with the apostles.[70]

Once the canon was finalized (around 367 AD) theologians could appeal to Scripture as the final authority for theological reflection and doctrinal formulation. As Ron Highfield describes it, canonization was the process of concentrat-

---

[67] For a wonderful introduction to theology that emphasizes this point, see Kelly M. Kapic, *A Little Book for New Theologians: Why and How to Study Theology* (Downers Grove: IVP Academic, 2012).

[68] Quoted from Jürgen Moltmann, *The Spirit of Life: A Universal Affirmation*, trans. Margaret Kohl (Minneapolis: Fortress, 2001), 73.

[69] N.T. Wright, *The Resurrection of the Son of God* (Minneapolis: Fortress, 2003).

[70] Tertullian, *The Prescription Against the Heretics* XXXII, in *ANF03: Latin Christianity: Its Founder, Tertullian*, ed. Philip Schaff and Allan Menzies, trans. Peter Holmes, (Grand Rapids: Christian Classics Ethereal Library, public domain), 258.

ing the church's sources of authority (Scripture, tradition, office) into a single focus (the finalized canon). Henceforth, the great Christian theological Tradition became an ongoing conversation about the meaning and implications of Scripture for the knowledge of God and for the life and mission of the church. As Kevin Vanhoozer points out, the Reformation notion of *sola scriptura* does not rule out tradition as a legitimate source for theology. Rather, "To practice sola scriptura is to treat Scripture alone as the 'norming norm' and tradition as the 'normed norm'". [71] Church tradition has provisional ministerial authority but not ultimate authority, which is reserved for Scripture.

As a Living Tradition, Christianity changed and developed over time as it encountered different historical and cultural contexts and sought to bear witness to the gospel and clarify its meaning and significance within those contexts.[72] Using a dramatic analogy, Vanhoozer helpfully likens the biblical canon to the authoritative script of a play and the great church Tradition to faithful historical performances, guided by theological wisdom, that instantiate the script in particular and contextual ecclesial traditions. This theological wisdom enables faithful improvisation, guided by theological *phronesis* or practical reasoning that is sustained by relevant virtues (see below concerning *phronesis* and virtue).[73] This means that tradition holds an important place in theological reflection and articulation, and hence also for biblical exegesis. Theologians must be in conversation with other theologians, both past and present, as well as with creeds, confessions, and other historical Christian narratives and accounts of the past. The church's commission is to reflect theologically on the Word of God, engaging in exegesis, church history, dogmatics, ethics, and so forth (aided by its theologians), in order to proclaim God's Word faithfully and intelligibly in contemporary contexts.

Theology's foundation upon tradition means that it must *primarily* serve the church (not just professional academic theologians).[74] This does not require theology to be subservient to or at the disposal of the church—mere ecclesial propaganda as it were. Theology serves the church because the church is dependent on the Word for its existence and understanding and applying the Word requires theology. In other words, theology serves the church in order to help sustain the church's life. In serving the church in this way, theology claims a degree of autonomy (but not separation) in order to call the church to faithfulness in doctrine and practice. Furthermore, in serving the church, theology must aim to speak to the richness and variety of the whole people of God. It

---

[71] Vanhoozer, *The Drama of Doctrine*, 234.
[72] See Andrew F. Walls, *The Missionary Movement in Christian History: Studies in the Transmission of Faith* (Maryknoll, N.Y.: Orbis, 1996).
[73] Vanhoozer, *The Drama of Doctrine*, 152.
[74] John Webster writes, "The sphere of the clarity of Holy Scripture is the church, the creature of the Word of God; by the Word the church is generated and preserved, and by the Spirit the church sets forth the clear Word of God in traditions of holy attentiveness." Webster, "Biblical Theology," 369.

should promote, inform, and equip all believers in the use of their distinct abilities and spiritual gifts, and show them how each one fits into God's redemptive activity.

d)   Aided by reason

The emphasis I have placed on revelation does not negate the necessary and helpful place of reason in theology.[75] As Lesslie Newbigin argued, "It is not (as so often said) a question of reason versus revelation. It is a question of the data upon which reason has to work."[76] Indeed, "reason can only work with the data that it is given."[77] It is a means, not an end; it is a tool, not a final product. Because God is the Creator and source of truth, all truth is God's truth. God desires that we love God not only with our affections, but also with our minds. God has created a reasonable world, a phenomenal reality with a rational structure, even though reason alone cannot account for the wholeness of reality.[78]

At least two implications follow for theology. First, theology should be coherent and consistent. God's promises and God's actions are trustworthy and dependable. Therefore, our reflection on what God has revealed and enacted should be rational, even as it glories in wonder. Here, there is much to be learned in dialogue with such disciplines as philosophy, mathematics, physics and other abstract sciences. Second, theology should be consistent with empirical reality. In other words, it should be verifiable through experience and rational inquiry. Hence, theology can benefit from the insights of the social sciences, the human sciences, and the arts. To be clear, I am not saying that theology can always be immediately verifiable, or that it always corresponds perfectly with empirical experience (which is itself open to various interpretations). What I am suggesting is that a disjuncture between theology and empirical inquiry should occasion a pause; it should unveil an opportunity for further

---

[75] Pannenberg offers a helpful critique and modification of Barth's view of revelation, which Pannenberg argues is too limited (i.e., as present/existential, personal, I-Thou revelation) and fails to account for the breadth and complexity of revelation as we actually observe it in Scripture. Pannenberg surveys five different types of revelatory experiences recorded in the Bible. See Wolfhart Pannenberg, *Systematic Theology*, vol. 1, trans. Geoffrey W. Bromiley (Grand Rapids: Eerdmans, 1988), chapter 4, esp. 206–11.

[76] Lesslie Newbigin, *Truth to Tell: The Gospel as Public Truth* (London: SPCK, 1991), 24.

[77] Newbigin, *Truth to Tell*, 20.

[78] Alvin Plantinga speaks of the "design plan" of the human mind, appealing to the doctrine of creation to argue that God formed the world to be rational and the human mind to interact rationally and truthfully with it (though this relationship is distorted by human corruption). See his *Warrant and Proper Function* (New York: Oxford University Press, 1993). Vanhoozer explains Plantinga's view as follows: "God has created human beings so that their cognitive faculties will yield true beliefs, given optimal conditions and proper functioning. Plantinga argues that we are warranted in holding a belief if it is the product of reliable belief-forming cognitive mechanisms (e.g., perception, memory). Vanhoozer, *The Drama of Doctrine*, 302.

questioning, hypothesizing, reflecting and, if necessary, reformulating. For example, Copernicus's heliocentric theory of the solar system presented a growth opportunity for both science and theology. The dialogical relationship between empirical reasoning and theology goes both ways. Sometimes science will question the expositions of theology because they do not seem to fit the facts; at other times theology will question science regarding its assumptions and interpretations of the facts.[79]

Reading Scripture as a theological-ethical practice

Interpretation is an inherently ethical activity
In recent years, an increasing number of theologians and biblical scholars have stressed that biblical interpretation is an inherently ethical activity. This means that ethics is not simply the product of interpretation; ethics also informs and guides interpretation. The process is not strictly linear in either direction but dialogical, a hermeneutical process of faith seeking greater understanding and wisdom (and thus open to correction). Thus, reading Scripture is a *theological-ethical practice*, one that is both formative for one's ongoing personal transformation and social ethical engagement and, at the same time, is informed by one's present ethical beliefs, assumptions, core values, commitments, heart desires, and preferred mode(s) of practical reasoning. Given the theological anthropology I have been developing, this is not surprising: if biblical interpretation is a *human* practice and if being human involves— intrinsically and inescapably—an ethical dimension, then the interpretive task must also be considered an ethical task.

In the writings of the biblical authors, doctrine and ethics cannot be separated practically (even while they can be differentiated logically). Jesus implied as much when he said that one should aim not merely to hear the Word, but to hear *and* obey it (Luke 11:28). Elsewhere, he asserted that those who hear his words but do not obey them are foolishly building their lives upon a precarious foundation, while those who hear and obey him are wisely building upon a sure and stable foundation (Luke 7:26–27). Likewise, the letter of James tells us that anyone who hears the Word but does not obey it is like a man who sees his reflection in a mirror but immediately forgets what he looks like when he walks away. James calls this way of thinking self-deception and contrasts it with a truly blessed life that comes from obeying God's Word (Jas 1:22–25). Second Timothy 3:16–17 teaches the inspiration of Scripture and especially emphasizes what the inspired Word accomplishes ethically in its hearer/reader, namely teaching, reproof, correction, and training in righteousness, "so that everyone who belongs to God may be proficient, equipped for every good work". In ad-

---

[79] For a succinct summary of the dominant contemporary approaches to relating theology and science, including his own brief proposal, see John Polkinghorne, *Science and the Trinity: The Christian Encounter with Reality* (New Haven, CT: Yale University Press, 2004), chapter 1.

dition, the structure and theology of the Pauline epistles maintain an intimate connection between God's gracious initiative in Christ and the ethical response that God's grace calls forth in those who are now "in Christ" (e.g. Rom 6; Eph 2:8–10; Phil 2:5–11, 3:12–14).[80]

If biblical interpretation is an inherently theological-ethical activity of knowing God and cultivating wisdom, what kind of ethical framework is most fitting and what kinds of methodological implications does this have for interpreters? I suggest that the approach that best accounts for the depth and variety of Scripture is a character or virtue ethics framework.[81] One reason for this is that a character framework can appropriate insights from other ethical approaches. For instance, it can employ consequentialist reasoning to weigh pros and cons and to ask questions about the common good. It can employ Kantian reasoning in order to articulate general ethical principles. Or it can listen to divine commands with an expressed desire to obey the will of God. However, at its most comprehensive level, its focus is not on following commands or articulating rules and principles, but on *forming ethical people*—the kind of people who desire God's good and chose to act ethically.

A second reason is that a character ethics approach to exegesis resonates well with the approach that Jesus took. Jesus recognized the important but limited place for rules (e.g., John 14:15) but emphasized the transformation of the heart. We see this in Jesus's teaching, for example in the following analogy:

> No good tree bears bad fruit, nor does a bad tree bear good fruit. Each tree is recognized by its own fruit. People do not pick figs from thorn bushes, or grapes from briers. The good man brings good things out of the good stored up in his

---

[80] Burridge argues that Paul's imperatives of obedience always flow out of his indicatives of grace (*Imitating Jesus*, 105–7).

[81] Joseph Kotva argues that virtue theory offers an ethical framework that is notably suited to Christian convictions, modes of reasoning, and ongoing moral reflection. In addition, it: (1) helpfully resists reductionist pressures by providing an integrated, multi-faceted account of the moral life; (2) helps us explores themes absent from Scripture and theology (e.g., friendship); it informs our reading and use of Scripture (particularly the Bible's role in the moral life); and (4) virtue theory and Christian convictions are mutually edifying (Christian thought can help correct and enrich virtue theory, especially with an emphasis on grace and a richer account of the human telos informed by Christology, anthropology, creation, revelation, etc.). See Joseph J. Kotva, Jr., *The Christian Case for Virtue Ethics* (Washington, D.C.: Georgetown University Press, 1996), especially chapter 7. Others promoting a virtue approach (in different variations) include Burridge, *Imitating Jesus*; Fowl, *Engaging Scripture*; Vanhoozer, *The Drama of Doctrine*; Stanley Hauerwas, *A Community of Character: Toward a Constructive Christian Social Ethic* (London: University of Notre Dame Press, 1981); Richard B. Hays, *The Moral Vision of the New Testament: Community, Cross, New Creation: A Contemporary Introduction to New Testament Ethics* (San Francisco: HarperSanFrancisco, 1996); and Daniel J. Treier, *Virtue and the Voice of God: Toward Theology as Wisdom* (Grand Rapids: Eerdmans, 2006).

heart, and the evil man brings evil things out of the evil stored up in his heart. For out of the overflow of his heart his mouth speaks (Luke 6:43–45).

Jesus argues that good works flow from a good heart like good fruit flows from a good tree. A few worm-infested apples do not make a whole tree bad, but an infected root spoils all of the fruit. In the same way, a person whose heart has been made good may still have some rough edges, but gradually their whole life is renewed and transformed from the inside-out.[82] Jesus's stress on character formation is also apparent in his decision to call a group of disciples to follow him and learn from him. As Richard Burridge argues, the gospels encourage their readers to imitate the words and deeds of Christ within an inclusive Christian community.[83] Likewise, the Apostle Paul encourages his readers to imitate the example of Christ (Phil 2:5–10) as well as his own example (1 Cor 4:16). Neither Jesus nor Paul promotes mindless mimicking; what they endorse is learning from the Lord and from other disciples what it means to live in accordance with Christ's death and in hope of his resurrection.[84] These exhortations to imitate Christ and others support the emphasis in character ethics on the importance of training and mentoring for equipping people to act wisely and consistently in complex and novel situations.[85] In addition, the New Testament emphasis on learning from others fits well with a character ethics stress on the formative role that communities play in ethical development (see chapter 8).[86]

Moreover, a character ethics approach can account for the diversity seen in the various types of ethical claims the Bible makes. In their book *Kingdom Ethics*, Glen Stassen and David Gushee argue that four levels of ethical reasoning can be observed in Scripture, including immediate judgements, rules, princi-

---

[82] Martin Luther comments on this passage and provides a similar analogy: A well constructed building does not make its builder good, rather a good builder produces well constructed buildings. See Martin Luther, *On Christian Liberty*, trans. W.A. Lambert and Harold J. Grimm (Minneapolis: Fortress, 2003), 39–40, 46.
[83] Burridge, *Imitating Jesus*, 388–94.
[84] Fowl discusses the importance of imitating Christ and other Christian exemplars for forming Christian character in *Engaging Scripture*, 190–96.
[85] Learning a trade is a good example of this. While an electrician must study the basic rules and principles about electricity, such knowledge is not sufficient. The student must also learn to be an electrician by spending thousands of hours in practice as an apprentice under the guidance of a mentor. Through such practice and guidance, the apprentice gradually acquires a tacit sense for how to make decisions, apply knowledge, and employ skills that are intrinsic to the trade. In a similar way, biblical interpretation does not tell us how we should respond in every situation (the Bible simply does not address explicitly many of the issues that modern people face), but it forms equips our hearts and minds to respond appropriately and faithfully.
[86] See Alasdair MacIntyre, *After Virtue: A Study in Moral Theology* (Notre Dame: University of Notre Dame Press, 1984), 191, 215–25.

ples, and basic convictions.[87] At the level of immediate judgment, a moral decision applies to one particular case and the decision maker provides no reasons for the judgment. For example, someone might say something like, "I don't know why it is wrong; I just know that it is wrong." Often such judgments are based upon underlying rules, principles and convictions, but are made instinctually in a given moment. To focus exclusively on immediate judgments is to endorse an emotivist (i.e., stressing preference) or an existentialist (i.e., stressing decision) ethics approach.[88] Moral judgment at the rules level consists in creating and obeying rules, which are direct commands and prohibitions that apply not just to one particular case (as with immediate judgments) but to all similar cases. An example of this is the commandment "You shall not murder," a rule that Jesus quoted favourably in the Sermon on the Mount. If one's moral focus is on rules alone one falls prey to legalism, which is essentially detaching rules from their underlying principles and theological/philosophical frameworks.[89] The next level of moral reasoning is principles, which have two characteristics. While rules explain and critique immediate judgements, principles explain and critique rules. Also, principles are more general than rules and do not tell us specifically what to do. If one makes principles the sole focus of ethics, one falls into what Stassen and Gushee call "principlism". There are two main problems with principlism. First, it rejects the legitimacy of rules, yet Jesus clearly endorsed some rules; hence, principlism could lead us to ignore the direct commands of Christ. Second, sometimes principles conflict with other principles; hence, their resolution requires deeper theological/philosophical commitments and basic convictions.[90] The final level of reasoning consists of basic convictions, which are ultimate commitments embedded within theological/philosophical narratives and frameworks. Basic convictions provide the basis for formulating, evaluating, and applying principles and rules. According to Stassen and Gushee, God's character, actions, and will constitute the basic conviction level for Christians.

Each of these four modes of judgment can be correlated roughly with a corresponding level of interpretive engagement. One could legitimately read Scripture at an immediate judgment or instinctual level, as do many Christians in

---

[87] Glen Stassen and David Gushee, *Kingdom Ethics: Following Jesus in Contemporary Context* (Downers Grove: InterVarsity Press, 2003), 100–107.

[88] Stassen and Gushee call a fixation at the level of immediate judgement a "situation ethics approach". Such an approach assumes that actions in themselves are neither right nor wrong and that situations are far too complex to speak generally about specific moral rules. Thus, situation ethics rejects the articulation and application of universal moral rules (*Kingdom Ethics*, 107–8). I have avoided the term "situation ethics," which might restrict the discussion to the views of Joseph Fletcher who coined the term. My intention is not to discuss Fletcher but to describe a type of approach that avoids general rules and principles in favour of immediate judgments made in unique contexts and circumstances.

[89] Stassen and Gushee, *Kingdom Ethics*, 109–11.

[90] Stassen and Gushee, *Kingdom Ethics*, 111–13.

their daily devotional reading, but a fixation on this level would promote a radical reader-response approach (akin to emotivist or existentialist ethics). One could read Scripture on the level of applying exegetical rules and methods, but without underlying principles and convictions such efforts would be in danger of becoming mechanistic and question-begging (akin to legalism). One could read Scripture on the level of hermeneutical principles or lenses, but a fixation at this level would lead to suppressing the uniqueness of particular texts in favour of broad, overarching norms and patterns (akin to principlism).[91] Finally, one could read Scripture on the level of basic convictions, but without also integrating personal response, exegetical methods, and hermeneutical insights, such an approach runs the risk of reading abstract theological ideas into the text (promoting "system addicts", to borrow a phrase from Trevor Hart).[92] In contrast to a narrow focus on just one of these, a character ethics approach provides the overall framework in which all four of these modes of judgment can be employed appropriately, according to their contexts.[93] All four levels are important and useful, grounded and unified in their witness to the revelatory presence and address of the Living Christ through the Holy Spirit.[94] All four serve the more comprehensive goal of holistic transformation of the reader(s) by the Spirit into the image of Christ. A character ethics approach thus accounts for the complexity of the interpretive endeavour. It underscores the fact that good interpretation requires not merely the acquisition of skills but also, more importantly, the cultivation of interpretive virtues and the exercise of practical reasoning or *phronesis*.

Virtues and biblical interpretation
A character approach to biblical exegesis requires the cultivation of virtues. According to Alasdair MacIntyre, virtues are human qualities that meet three

---

[91] John Webster expresses the concern that a preoccupation with hermeneutical issues will distract readers from their responsibility to be obedient: "[T]he task of the church is best understood not as speaking meaningfully but as speaking obediently, that is, speaking in a manner appropriate to the fact that God is not a mute reality to be called into presence by language or practice, but the eternally creative and active Word." John Webster, *Barth's Moral Theology: Human Action in Barth's Thought* (Grand Rapids: Eerdmans, 1998), 125.

[92] Trevor Hart, "Systematic – In What Sense?" In *Out of Egypt: Biblical Theology and Biblical Interpretation* (Grand Rapids: Zondervan, 2004), 341.

[93] Burridge, *Imitating Jesus*, 390.

[94] Burridge, *Imitating Jesus*, 25–29, 78. Burridge's suggestion captures the uniqueness of Christian ethics as a personal and communal (i.e., ecclesial) response to the Living God who became man, the Word made flesh. It also emphasizes the crucial importance of holding together *who* Christ is with *what* he said and did. To separate these is to make concrete Christian faith and discipleship into an (un-Christian) abstraction that is foreign to the New Testament. Finally, it highlights the communal (and ecclesial) nature of ethical formation and judgment. Jesus did more than teach with words and deeds; He also created a new community within which his example and teachings could be learned and practiced.

criteria. First, a virtue is a quality necessary for achieving the goods internal to what MacIntyre calls "practices".[95] A practice is a complex and coherent form of a socially established human activity, the excellent pursuit of which leads inherently to the attainment of the goods that are uniquely related to and acquired through it.[96] Second, a virtue must be holistic, contributing to the good of a whole human life and not merely something peripheral to human existence.[97] A virtue is not simply an ability or skill limited to a particular task or activity; rather, it is an underlying character trait that is comprehensive in scope. Third, virtues can be conceived only within a received living tradition.[98] A living tradition is a "socially embodied argument" that is based upon a particular conception of the *telos* of human life and plays a constitutive role in identity formation. According to MacIntyre, one can never seek the good in isolation from others, not least because one's ethical worldview depends on the formative role others play. Social traditions and virtues are interdependent: traditions shape the understanding of virtues, while the virtues animate and sustain traditions.

One implication for biblical interpretation that we can draw from MacIntyre's analysis is that exegesis alone, especially when narrowed to exegetical method, does not qualify as a complex ethical practice; it is merely a skill. By themselves, exegetical methodologies are too narrow and reductionistic to be considered practices in MacIntyre's full sense, especially those claiming to be purely objective or descriptive. This observation challenges the idea that one can interpret the Bible simply by applying the right rules and methods of interpretation to Holy Scripture in a purportedly value-neutral and non-theological manner. Such methodologies might well provide useful and interesting insights, but they do not amount to the theological-ethical *practice* of biblical interpretation. The latter requires cultivating and indwelling interpretive virtues, which are those qualities necessary for achieving the goods that are internal to the practice of biblical interpretation.[99] Another implication we can draw from

---

[95] MacIntyre, *After Virtue*, 191.
[96] MacIntyre cites the game of chess as an example of a practice. Virtues of chess are those qualities that enable practitioners to attain the goods internal to playing the game. Internal goods are those which derive naturally and uniquely from the practice itself. Thus, a financial reward for winning a chess tournament is not an internal good, because both winning and money can be pursued in other ways. At the level of practice alone, MacIntyre's conception of virtue is closely related to an intrinsic orientation (both desire and effort) toward excellence.
[97] MacIntyre, *After* Virtue, 215–19.
[98] MacIntyre, *After Virtue*, 220–25.
[99] While a full discussion of such virtues would require a more extensive treatment, we might begin by citing three fundamental Christian virtues, namely faith, hope, and love/charity. Fowl argues for the primacy of charity or love (Fowl, *Engaging Scripture*, 86–91). He is careful to stress that these virtues do not eliminate interpretive disagreements in the church (which can be healthy), but foster the kind of context in which disagreements can best be articulated, debated, and provisionally resolved. In

MacIntyre's discussion is that biblical interpretation, as an intrinsically ethical activity, can be practiced faithfully only within a received, living social tradition that teaches and embodies a particular conception of the *telos* of human life.[100] MacIntyre's observation can be applied to highlight the significance of the church as a necessary context for the practice of biblical interpretation.[101]

Practical reasoning (phronesis) and biblical interpretation
In his preface to the *Brazos Theological Commentary on the Bible*, R.R. Reno suggests that theological interpretation depends not primarily on employing particular exegetical methodologies but on being the kind of person that has cultivated wisdom through spiritual, theological, and ecclesial formation. In particular, Reno argues that such people are trained in the Nicene tradition, by which he means "a pervasive habit of thought" and "the animating culture of the church in its intellectual aspect."[102] Stephen Fowl endorses a similar view when he argues for the priority of character in theological interpretation. In his approach, rules, methods, and skills are tools that interpreters with well-formed character employ through *phronesis* or practical reasoning. Such reasoning does not naively aspire to absolute purity or objectivity, as in rationalism, but involves "a pattern of thinking, feeling, and acting" in appropriate ways. According to Fowl, a Christian's employment of *phronesis* is appropriate when it conforms to Christ, especially to the pattern of his death and resurrection.[103] One of the primary tasks of practical reasoning is acquiring accurate vision, which allows one to see things in proper perspective and alignment.[104] For ex-

---

addition to Fowl's suggestions, since biblical interpretation is a pneumatological event, one would expect its intrinsic virtues to include the fruit of the Spirit: love, joy, peace, patience, kindness, generosity, faithfulness, gentleness, and self-control (Gal 5:22–23). Such qualities fit MacIntyre's criterion that virtues must be holistic, contributing to the whole of life and not merely peripheral or isolated activities disconnected from life. Finally, as Vanhoozer argues, proper interpretation involves being apprenticed by the canon itself though canonical practices of interpretation, especially the patterns and precedents set by Jesus and then Paul (*The Drama of Doctrine*, part 3, chapters 9–10).

[100] In this book I maintain that the *telos* of human life has three basic dimensions that correspond to the meaning of human personhood—relational, rational, and eschatological.

[101] Francis Watson argues that the church is the preliminary reading community within which Holy Scripture is located (*Text, Church and World*, 13). See also Fowl, who argues that understanding the Spirit's work is a matter of communal discernment and debate, which occurs over time and is often shaped by prior interpretations of Scripture as well as by beliefs and practices (*Engaging Scripture*, 114).

[102] R.R. Reno, "Series Preface," in *Brazos Theological Commentary on the Bible: Matthew* (Grand Rapids: Brazos Press, 2006), 12. This is because doctrine is most powerful when it is a habit of the mind, not merely the repetition of abstract propositions.

[103] Fowl, *Engaging Scripture*, 190–96.

[104] Fowl cites Jesus's discussion of the eye as a lamp to the whole body, which brings light to one's whole life (Matt 6:22–23; Cf. Luke 11:34–36). See *Engaging Scripture*, 75–83.

ample, drawing on the book of Philippians, Fowl contrasts the *phronesis* of those whose citizenship is in heaven with the *phronesis* of those who are preoccupied with worldly concerns. He then discusses the significance of baptism, eucharist, catechism, and liturgy for the formation of a *phronesis* that "knows the power of Christ's resurrection" and "shares in his sufferings".[105]

Recently, a number of theologians have proposed performance models, usually musical or dramatic, to depict the integration of *phronesis*, virtue, and exegetical proficiency.[106] Kevin Vanhoozer proposes a "canonical-linguistic" model that depicts the theological task as participating in God's theo-drama. In this model, "Doctrine helps the people of God to participate fittingly in the drama of redemption, and so to be true and faithful witnesses to God's incarnate wisdom."[107] For, "If theology is about the speech and action of the triune God and the church's response in word and deed, then doctrine is best viewed as direction for the church's fitting participation in the drama of redemption."[108] His desire is to move theology beyond mere theoretical knowledge and reorient it toward Christian wisdom, which unites theory and practice.[109] He explains, "The canonical-linguistic approach to theology has as its goal the training of competent and truthful witnesses who can themselves incarnate, in a variety of situations, the wisdom of Christ gleaned from indwelling canonical practices and their ecclesial continuations."[110]

In Vanhoozer's dramatic analogy, God is the *playwright*, the gospel corresponds to *God's theo-drama* (God's redemptive speech and actions culminating in Christ), the biblical canon is the authoritative *script*, the Holy Spirit is the *director* of the play (with pastors and elders serving as *assistant directors*), and doctrine is *direction or stage prompts* that enable the actors to perform the script and improvise faithfully upon it.[111] In this scheme, the role of the theologian corresponds to the role of the *dramaturge*, who in theatrical contexts is the person responsible for helping the director (in the church's case, the assistant directors—pastors and leaders) to make sense of the script both for the actors (the congregation) and the audience (the world to which the gospel is proclaimed and demonstrated).[112] Vanhoozer notes that this twofold responsibility

---

[105] Fowl, *Engaging Scripture*, 196, 200–2.
[106] For example: Hans Urs von Balthasar, *Theo-drama: Theological Dramatic Theory*, vols. 1–4 (San Francisco: Ignatius, 1998–94); Samuel Wells, *Improvisation: The Drama of Christian Ethics* (Grand Rapids: Brazos, 2004).
[107] Vanhoozer, *The Drama of Doctrine*, 25.
[108] Vanhoozer, *The Drama of Doctrine*, 31.
[109] Vanhoozer, *The Drama of Doctrine*, 13.
[110] Vanhoozer, *The Drama of Doctrine*, 25.
[111] Vanhoozer, *The Drama of Doctrine*, 107, 243–44.
[112] The Holy Spirit, as the main Director, plays a crucial role in the drama: "*The Holy Spirit is both the author of the script and the one who guides the church's contemporary performance—its improvisatory variations—on the script.* The Spirit employs doctrine, too, to serve the church insofar as it helps in understanding the theo-drama. *The drama of doctrine consists in the Spirit's directing the church rightly to partici-*

of the dramaturge parallels the twofold task of theology, namely exegetical *scientia* (interpretive skills, methods, techniques, etc.) and practical *sapientia* (wisdom for life and missional context).[113] He contrasts the way his dramaturge model depicts the relationship of theologian to Scripture with other influential models, including the theologian as scientist (e.g., Hodge), as poet (e.g., Barr, McFague), and as ethnographer (e.g., Lindbeck).[114]

Vanhoozer's notion of theology as a dramatic enterprise fruitfully combines *knowing* (propositional, tacit, communal), *doing* (personal ethical agency), and *being* (cultivating virtue to enable the faithful exercise of practical reasoning in alignment with canonical patterns). Moreover, it retains an emphasis on biblical authority, while recognizing the crucial roles that tradition, community, and church practices play in genuine theological reflection and formation. Finally, Vanhoozer's approach provides a fitting model for engaging in theological interpretation of the Bible as an ethical practice. It encourages us to read Scripture in order to know and love God and to participate fittingly and faithfully in God's ongoing story through the cultivation of biblical-theological wisdom. To recall what was said earlier in the chapter, the heart of biblical wisdom is living one's life as an ongoing conversation with God and thinking about all things rationally in relation to God and in obedience to God.

Concluding summary

This chapter depicted the human person as a rational creature, whom God creates, redeems, and transforms to participate in the divine *Logos* and thus to share in the wisdom of God. This view of the human person suggests at least four general implications for Christian ethics.

First, Christian ethics is informed by faith seeking understanding. It prioritizes both knowing God and understanding God's created world, with the intention of seeking to comprehend, teach, pursue and enact God's purposes in and for the world. Second, Christian ethics affirms the life of the mind. This reflects God's creative intent that human beings delight in discovering and participating in God's designs for the natural world. Understanding God's created world in a coherent and comprehensive way requires that Christians engage not only religious studies and theology, but also the sciences, the social sciences, the arts, and the humanities. Affirming and cultivating the life of the mind reflects

---

pate in the evangelical action by performing its authoritative script" (102; emphasis original).

[113] In part three of the book, Vanhoozer outlines six features of the canonical-linguistic approach. The first three concern the *sciential* aspects of the theologian's task (with relation to the biblical text): postpropositionalist, postconservative, and postfoundational. The second three concern the sapiential aspects of the theologian's task: prosaic (contextual, *in* but not *of* the world), phronetic (employing theological *phronesis* to deliberate well about what God has done in Jesus Christ and what our fitting response should be), and prophetic (sound judgment and faithful and relevant witness).

[114] Vanhoozer, *The Drama of Doctrine*, 244–47.

God's ethical intent that human beings not merely conform to rules or submit to authorities and traditions, but become the kind of people who can "test and discern" God's will because they have a renewed mind and a renovated character. Third, as important as affirming the life of the mind is, Christian ethics also affirms that human beings are more than their minds. Human beings are *whole persons*. Cultivating and shaping the mind is just one aspect of holistic character formation, which also includes fostering virtues and shaping passions, loyalties, perceptions, practical reasoning (or *phronesis*), and the basic convictions that make up one's worldview.[115] Finally, Christian ethics seeks to be rooted in Scripture, illuminated and empowered by the Holy Spirit, in dialogue with tradition, and coherently synthesized by reason.

This approach acknowledges and promotes the authority of Scripture for Christian orthodoxy and orthopraxy, but also underscores the dynamic interplay of accessing the Scriptures *with* minds renewed by the Spirit and *supported by* the human quest for truth, including the wisdom of other believers both past and present (i.e. ecclesial traditions, biblical scholars, theologians, pastors and church leaders). It also highlights the primary purpose of engaging Scripture, namely to grow in our love and knowledge of God, which then orients our thoughts, prioritizes, commitments, and responsibilities with respect to God, other human beings, and the natural world.

---

[115] See Stassen and Gushee, *Kingdom Ethics*, 59–61.

CHAPTER 5

The Human Person as an Eschatological Creature

Introduction

In this chapter we will explore the idea that human beings are eschatological creatures, invited to participate in the divine *commission* or vocation by sharing in the reign of God. Theologically and ethically, this perspective highlights the importance of *hope* for a trinitarian theological anthropology and emphasizes the aspect of human purpose and destiny that concerns serving as God's stewards and representatives by sustaining, restoring, and improving creation in faithful partnership with God. The chapter begins with a discussion of the human being as called by the Father for a mission and purpose, followed by a discussion of the destructive implications of human corruption for that mission and purpose. It then describes restoration in Christ and transformation by the Spirit in the context of saving human beings from a purposeless and self-destructive destiny and thereby renewing and realigning them in their calling to serve God's purposes. Finally, it explores the role of hope in the eschatological dimension of Christian ethics within the context of the new creation and the vocation to serve the kingdom of God in the power of the Spirit. It concludes with some general implications for sustaining, restoring, and improving the world as steward-priests of the new creation.

Called by the Father for a purpose and mission

Creation, imago Dei, *and calling*

Created to advance and develop over time
Human beings are creatures of change and have in many ways advanced over time. They have accumulated knowledge, developed artistry and craftsmanship, travelled and explored the world, and built cultures and civilizations. Since the advent of modern science, they have greatly augmented their understanding of the natural world and achieved rapid technological innovation, with ripple effects leading to previously unfathomable advances in health and medicine, media and communications, global travel and trade, and the widespread accessibility of information through the Internet. Of course, not all development has been positive. As sinful creatures, human beings also have employed their technological skills and knowledge to devise ever new and innovative ways of deceiv-

ing, cheating, controlling, enslaving, and killing each other. Thus, the ongoing development of scientific knowledge and technological proficiency continually gives rise to new ethical questions and concerns that previous generations of humans did not have to face. Nevertheless, change and advancement are inherent features of human existence. Every established culture or tradition has to negotiate change in order to survive, even while trying to maintain faithfulness to its treasured history and values. For Christians, this means faithfully translating and adapting the ancient apostolic faith for present conditions and contexts.

The negotiation of change often leads to conflict and disagreement, because for most people change is threatening and difficult even when it is mostly positive; all change involves a degree of risk and ambiguity concerning outcomes and implications. Christian theologians have long debated whether development was part of God's original creative intent for humanity. One influential view maintains that human beings were created in a state of original righteousness, maturity, and perfection. This view is often attributed to Augustine and the so-called Western theological tradition,[1] but it should be noted that while Augustine generally supports the original righteousness and perfection view, he also depicts creation as being analogous to a seed that God planted and imbued with the latent potentiality to grow and develop over time.[2] Some proponents of the ideal origins view argue that redemption means restoring human beings to their original state of perfection, which they forfeited wholly or in part through the Fall. More persuasive is the alternate view of Irenaeus and Athanasius that God created human beings not in a state of full maturity and perfection, but in a state of infancy from which they would advance and develop over time.[3] Irenaeus argued that the creation of human beings in the image of God points not to a static quality or possession but to a dynamic reality toward which they are moving.[4] Eric Osborn explains, "While Adam is in one sense perfect, the possibility of further perfection is set before him."[5] The imago Dei is present in hu-

---

[1] Stanley J. Grenz, *The Social God and the Relational Self: A Trinitarian Theology of the Imago Dei* (Louisville: Westminster John Knox, 2001), 177–78.
[2] Augustine, *The Literal Meaning of Genesis* 5.23.44, trans. Edmund Hill, ed. John E. Rotelle, vol. 13 *The Works of St. Augustine* (New York: New City, 2002), 299.
[3] See Patrick Franklin, "Understanding the Beginning in Light of the End: Eschatological Reflections on Making Theological Sense of Evolution," *Perspectives on Science and Christian Faith* 66, no. 3 (Sept. 2014): 156–58.
[4] Irenaeus, *Against Heresies* IV/11.1–2; 38.1–4; V/8, 10, 15, in *The Apostolic Fathers with Justin Martyr and Irenaeus*, ed. Philip Schaff (Grand Rapids: Eerdmans, 2001). See also: Julie Canlis, "Being Made Human: the Significance of Creation for Irenaeus' Doctrine of Participation," *Scottish Journal of Theology* 58, no. 4 (2005): 434–54; James C. Peterson, *Changing Human Nature: Ecology, Ethics, Genes, and God* (Grand Rapids: Eerdmans, 2010), 6, 25, 127, 171; Matthew C. Steenberg, *Irenaeus on Creation: The Cosmic Christ and the Saga of Redemption* (Boston: Brill, 2008); F. LeRon Shults, *Reforming Theological Anthropology: After the Philosophical Turn to Relationality* (Grand Rapids: Eerdmans, 2003), 235–42.
[5] Eric Osborn, *Irenaeus of Lyons* (Cambridge: Cambridge University Press, 2001), 85.

man beings at the dawn of creation but awaits further development and ultimately eschatological consummation. The implication of this is that the advancement of human knowledge, culture, and productivity are part of God's creative intent for human beings. As J. Richard Middleton argues,

> The Bible itself portrays the move from creation to eschaton as movement from a garden (in Genesis 2) to a city (in Revelation 21–22). Redemption does not reverse, but rather embraces, historical development. The transformation of the initial state of the earth into complex human societies is not part of the fall, but rather the legitimate creational mandate of humanity. Creation was never meant to be static, but was intended by God from the beginning to be developmental, moving toward a goal.[6]

Correspondingly, Irenaeus argues that Jesus Christ, the prototypical human being, became incarnate *as an infant* in order to recapitulate genuine human existence and so to take all of sinful humanity into himself and direct it toward maturity and fulfilment.[7] In an Irenaean developmental view, human redemption involves not simply restoring human beings to a prelapsarian state of original perfection, but redeeming them in Christ and thereby restoring them to a right relationship with God, and then transforming and directing them toward a future destiny of maturity and glory. Thus, the incarnation inaugurates God's final goal for mature humanity. In support of Irenaeus's view, Scripture records not only that Jesus was born as an infant in humble circumstances, but also that he *grew* in wisdom, in stature, and in favour with God and people (Luke 2:52). The writer of Hebrews tells us that Jesus "had to be made like his brothers and sisters in every way, in order that he might become a merciful and faithful high priest in service to God, and that he might make atonement for the sins of the people." The author goes on to explain that "because he himself suffered when he was tempted, he is able to help those who are being tempted" (Heb 2:17–18). And the apostle Paul writes, "God made him who had no sin to be sin for us, so that in him we might become the righteousness of God" (2 Cor 5:21). From a biblical point of view, neither creation nor redemption is a static state. Rather, both creation and redemption reflect God's eschatological purposes of directing human beings toward their *telos* as dynamic and developing creatures, gradually being transformed into the image of Christ.[8]

---

[6] J. Richard Middleton, "A New Heaven and a New Earth: The Case for a Holistic Reading of the Biblical Story of Redemption," *Journal for Christian Theological Research* 11 (2006): 76.

[7] Irenaeus, *Against Heresies* IV/38.2, 4.

[8] Human beings are dynamic creatures that God has placed in his developing creation, within which humans serve as stewards, priests, and gardeners to care for creation and draw out its latent potential. See Franklin, "Understanding the Beginning in Light of the End," 154–58.

The Human Person as an Eschatological Creature

In addition to its resonance with Scripture, Irenaeus's dynamic view of the human person fits well with modern scientific discoveries about human personhood and development, especially in anthropology and biology. First, as Pannenberg and others have observed, human beings are inherently exocentric creatures that define their identity in ongoing dialogical openness and receptivity to the world around them.[9] In chapter 3, we employed this observation to argue that human beings are inherently relational creatures; we now observe that their exocentricity also implies that they are inherently future-oriented, present-transcending creatures that continually discover new possibilities for their existence in the world.[10] Second, Irenaeus's view fits with modern insights about the brain's role in hard wiring moral development, thus linking morality with our concrete biological embodiment. This has important implications for Christian spirituality and character formation.[11] Third, Irenaeus's view resonates with contemporary scientific views that promote a holistic, non-reductive understanding of human biological existence (e.g., body *and* soul, brain *and* mind, instinctual doing *and* consciousness of being, etc.) with the aid of such notions as complexity theory, emergence, supervenience, and top-down causation.[12] Fourth, an Irenaean view is compatible with modern evolutionary theory concerning human origins and development (but does not necessarily require it) and lends support to synthetic, interdisciplinary theological frameworks, such as theistic evolution, evolutionary creation, or biologos.[13]

---

[9] Wolfhart Pannenberg, *Anthropology in Theological Perspective*, trans. Matthew J. O'Connell (Edinburgh: T & T Clark, 1999). J. Wentzel Van Huyssteen notes the Pannenberg's notion of exocentricity or human self-transcendence "summarizes a broad consensus among contemporary anthropologies." See Huyssteen, *Alone in the World? Human Uniqueness in Science and Theology* (Grand Rapids: Eerdmans, 2006), 140.

[10] Philip Hefner (in dialogue with Pannenberg) similarly writes, "To be a person is not fully contained in our physic-biological behavior but rather also requires the marshalling of that behavior in response to the demand from our world to actualize our authentic possibilities within it." Hefner, "Imago Dei: The Possibility and Necessity of the Human Person," in *The Human Person in Science and Theology*, ed. Niels Henrik Gregersen, Willem B. Dress, and Ulf Görman (Grand Rapids: Eerdmans, 2000), 86.

[11] See Paul N. Markham, *Rewired: Exploring Religious Conversion* (Eugene: Pickwick, 2007). For a summary, see my review of Markham's book in *Perspectives on Science and Christian Faith* 60 (December 2008): 274–75.

[12] Niels Henrik Gregersen, "God's Public Traffic: Holist Versus Physicalist Supervenience," in *The Human Person in Science and Theology*, ed. Niels Henrik Gregersen, Willem B. Dress, and Ulf Görman (Grand Rapids: Eerdmans, 2000), 153–88; Markham, *Rewired*, 103–21; Heffner, "Imago," 73–94.

[13] "Evolutionary Creation" is the term Denis Lamoureux uses to describe his position. See Denis O. Lamoureux, *Evolutionary Creation: A Christian Approach to Evolution* (Eugene, OR: Wipf and Stock, 2008). Francis Collins uses the term "biologos" to describe his own approach to integrating evolution with Christian theism. See Francis S. Collins, *The Language of God: A Scientist Presents Evidence for Belief* (New York: Free Press/Simon & Schuster, 2006); Peterson, *Changing Human Nature*, 2–6;

Imago Dei *as commission and task*

In the previous two chapters we observed the relational and rational aspects of being made in God's image. Presently, we will consider the eschatological character of the *imago Dei*, which associates the image of God in human beings with their purpose and calling to function as stewards of the earth and priests of creation, as well as with their orientation toward their final transformation into the image of Christ by the Holy Spirit.

Many biblical commentators and theologians have pointed out that the declaration in Genesis 1 that human beings are made in God's image occurs together with their given mandate to rule over the earth.[14] Genesis 1:26 records: "Then God said, 'Let us make human beings in our image, in our likeness, so that they may rule over the fish in the sea and the birds in the sky, over the livestock and all the wild animals, and over all the creatures that move along the ground.'" Moreover, Genesis 2:15 describes the human task as working and protecting the garden and Psalm 8:3–8 says that God made human beings to be rulers over God's created works. In light of such texts, Middleton asserts that "the fundamental human task is conceived as the responsible exercise of power on God's behalf over the non-human world."[15] Middleton explains that in the ancient Near Eastern culture, ruling over the earth had to do primarily with the development of agriculture and animal husbandry (the basis of human societal organization), but also included by extension the advancement of culture, technology, and civilization.[16]

As Middleton's statement suggests, human dominion does not involve free license to dominate creation by exploiting or abusing the earth or other creatures, but is limited by two qualifications. First, human beings are to exercise their dominion in responsibility before God, because creation is first and foremost *God's* creation and humans are accountable to God in their role within it. Second, human beings are not given absolute rule but exercise their dominion on God's behalf. This means that their ruling must faithfully represent God's purposes and goals for creation. Human rule of the earth thus amounts not to sovereign kingship but faithful stewardship. Human beings are God's representatives and vice regents, appointed to rule God's creation according to

---

Huyssteen, *Alone in the World*, 139–58. The Biologos Forum is the name of Collins's website that discusses the relationship between science and Christian faith (http://www.biologos.org/).

[14] Stanley J. Grenz, *The Social God and the Relational Self*, 196–97 and *Theology for the Community of God* (Grand Rapids: Eerdmans, 1994), 174, 177–78; J. Richard Middleton, "A New Heaven and a New Earth," 80–81 and *The liberating Image: the Imago Dei in Genesis 1* (Grand Rapids: Brazos, 2005).

[15] Middleton, "A New Heaven and a New Earth," 81. Similarly, Dallas Willard writes: "In creating human beings God made them to rule, to reign, to have dominion in a limited sphere. Only so can they be persons." Dallas Willard, *The Divine Conspiracy: Rediscovering Our Hidden Life in God* (New York: HarperSanFrancisco, 1998), 21.

[16] Middleton, "A New Heaven and a New Earth," 81.

God's prerogatives. A third qualification, not mentioned by Middleton, is that genuine human dominion is eschatologically conditioned. Faithful stewardship means not only exercising dominion on God's behalf, but also confidently and joyfully anticipating the final return of the King (Rev 11:15).

The idea that reflecting God's image includes faithful stewardship gains further support by Scripture's portrayal of the universe as God's palace-temple, in which God places human beings and commissions them to be steward-priests. One important representative text is Isaiah 66:1: "Heaven is my throne, and the earth is my footstool. Where is the house you will build for me? Where will my resting place be?"[17] Reflecting on this text, Rikki E. Watts asks, "Where does one find a throne and a footstool if not in a palace, and what is the palace of Yahweh if not a temple?"[18] In his article, Watts provides a fascinating comparison of several key details in Genesis 1 with other Ancient Near Eastern creation accounts, identifying both striking similarities and significant differences.[19] He suggests that the depiction of creation as a palace-temple is unsurprising when one considers the contextual realities of the ancient world as well as the ancient belief that the actions of kings paralleled the cosmic activity of the gods. He explains that the greatest threat to ancient, settled agricultural existence was chaos resulting from wars, lawlessness, or flooding. In such ancient societies it was the king who defeated enemies and provided protection, who upheld the

---

[17] In addition to this text, John Walton observes that 1 Kings 8:28 and Isa 6:3 (cf. Exod 40:34) also depict the cosmos as a temple. John H. Walton, *The Lost World of Genesis One: Ancient Cosmology and the Origins Debate* (Downers Grove: InterVarsity Press, 2009), 84.

[18] Rikki E. Watts, "Making Sense of Genesis 1," paragraph 47, online article for the American Scientific Affiliation: http://www.asa3.org/ASA/topics/Bible-Science/6.02Watts.html; also published as "On the Edge of the Millennium: Making Sense of Genesis 1" in *Living in the LambLight: Christianity and Contemporary Challenges to the Gospel*, ed. Hans Boersma (Vancouver: Regent College, 2001), 129–51. Watts also notes that the Old Testament is full of architectural imagery in its description of creation, speaking for example of the foundations of the earth, the pillars of the earth and of the heavens, the heavens' windows, the stretching out of the heavens like a canopy or tent, and containing storehouses (paragraph 46). See also Rikk E. Watts, "The New Exodus/New Creational Restoration of the Image of God: A Biblical-Theological Perspective on Salvation," in *What Does it Mean to be Saved? Broadening Evangelical Horizons of Salvation*, ed. John G. Stackhouse, Jr. (Grand Rapids: Baker Academic, 2002), 15–41.

[19] Watts clarifies that his point is not that Genesis 1 is identical with other Ancient Near Eastern accounts, or even that Genesis borrows from them (which is possible, but not necessary to assume). Rather, he is "simply interested in trying to understand what issues a second-millennium B.C. culture might have been interested in" ("Making Sense of Genesis One," paragraph 17). John Walton makes a similar point in his re-reading of the Genesis text in light of Ancient Near Eastern literature: "I am not suggesting that the Israelites are borrowing from these ancient literatures. Instead the literatures show how people thought in the ancient world, and as we examine Genesis, we can see that Israelites thought in similar ways." Walton, *The Lost World*, 79.

law, and who supervised the construction of barriers to restrain the floods. Moreover, upon establishing his kingdom and entering into victorious rest, the king would build a palace for himself and a temple for his nation's deity. This pattern resembles the Genesis account of God differentiating, restraining, and ordering creation to function as God's palace and temple, in which God comes to dwell and rule on the day of Sabbath rest.[20] Watts finds additional support for the palace-temple depiction of creation in the forming of humanity in the image of God. In the Ancient Near East, the last thing placed within a temple was the image of the deity, who was then invoked to indwell the temple as a resting place and authority centre.[21] Similarly, in Genesis 1 God forms the human being in God's own image as the culminating act of creation and then (in Gen 2) breathes the divine Spirit into the human creature to invoke life and call it into blessing (Sabbath rest) and dominion.

Of course, there are also important differences between the Genesis account and other Ancient Near Eastern myths. For instance, the idea that human beings bear the divine image appears only in Genesis 1 and in some Egyptian texts.[22] However, in Egyptian literature only a single individual acts as the god's ruling representative—specifically the king. Moreover, ancient kings frequently placed images of themselves throughout their territories to symbolize their power and sovereignty.[23] In contrast, Genesis teaches that all human beings are intended to reflect God's image and consequently to serve equally as God's stewards or vice regents over creation.[24] Thus, as Stanley Grenz points out, the Genesis narrative served as a critique of Ancient Near Eastern theology and ideology by universalizing the divine image and thereby safeguarding the dignity and equality of every human being.[25] The ethical implication of this, as

---

[20] See also Walton's comments about the meaning of the seventh day Sabbath rest in relation to the cosmos as God's temple. Walton, *The Lost World*, 72–92.

[21] Walton notes that the purpose of a temple in the ancient world was not primarily to be a place where people gathered for worship (like modern churches), but rather a "home" and "headquarters" or "control room" for the deity. (*The Lost World*, 75).

[22] Watts writes, "Unlike the Babylonian traditions, the Egyptians grant a special role to humans. According to the Great Hymn to Atum, the god 'created mankind and distinguished their nature and made their life'. We also find the making of man from clay with either Khnum being seen as a potter molding humanity on his wheel (Great Hymn to Khnum) or Ptah molding humanity with his hands. In the Instruction of Amenemope, 'Man is clay and straw, and God is his potter' and in a few texts there is even the idea that humanity is made in the image of the god, as per the Instruction of King Merikare: 'They are his [Re] own images proceeding from his flesh'. The Egyptian word used here (*snnw*) is often written with a determinative in the shape of a statue. This is similar to Genesis 1's notion of humanity being made from the dust of the earth in Elohim's image (*tselem*), a word which initially meant a piece cut from an object and which would be entirely appropriate for a piece of clay cut for a sculpture." Watts, "Making Sense of Genesis 1," paragraph 30.

[23] Watts, "Making Sense of Genesis 1," paragraph 49.

[24] Watts, "Making Sense of Genesis 1," paragraph 36.

[25] Grenz, *The Social God and the Relational Self*, 200–202.

Watts strongly puts it, is that "any act of abuse against another human being is an act of high treason against the God whose image we bear and to whose kingship and sovereignty we therefore inherently bear witness."[26]

In his recent books *The Lost World of Genesis One* and the more detailed *Genesis One as Ancient Cosmology*, John Walton lends further support to the idea that Scripture depicts creation as God's palace-temple and human beings as Gods steward-priests.[27] Walton convincingly argues that Genesis 1 should be interpreted not as an account of the material origins of creation, but as an account of God establishing creation's proper functioning and purpose. Similarly, Richard Middleton observes, "The underlying picture is of God as a cosmic ruler of a harmonious, well-functioning realm."[28] Walton's argument progresses through several propositions. First, Genesis 1 is representative of ancient cosmology. Second, ancient cosmology operates with a functional ontology and thus is function-oriented.[29] In a functional ontology, something is thought to exist not because of its material properties (as in a modern materialist ontology) but because it has a function in an ordered social and cultural system. Within such a perspective, to create something is not merely to give it material substance; the actual creative act consists in assigning it a functioning role.[30] To exist, therefore, is to have a function. As Walton puts it, "cosmic creation in the ancient world was not viewed primarily as a process by which matter was brought into being, but as a process by which functions, roles, order, jurisdiction, organization and stability were established."[31] Third, the Hebrew word for "create" (*bārā'*) used in Genesis 1 concerns function and the word for "beginning" (*rēšît*) refers to a period of time rather than a single point in time. Accordingly, Walton suggests that Gen 1:1 should be rendered: "In the initial period, God created by assigning functions throughout the heavens and the earth, and this is how he did it."[32] Fourth, Genesis 1 describes the beginning state of creation as being non-functional. This is evident in its description of the primal state in terms of functional nonexistence in its use of the words *tōhû* and *bōhû* and by the presence of primal cosmic waters, which is the classic form that nonexistence takes in the functionally oriented ancient world.[33] Moreover, from this perspective, God's declaration "it is good" means that what has just been

---

[26] Watts, "Making Sense of Genesis 1," paragraph 55.
[27] John H. Walton, Genesis 1 as Ancient Cosmology (Winona Lake, IL: Eisenbrauns, 2011). For a recent summary of Walton's basic position, see his essay "Reading Genesis 1 as Ancient Cosmology," in *Reading Genesis 1–2: An Evangelical Conversation*, ed. J. Daryl Charles (Peabody, MA: Hendrickson, 2013), 141–69.
[28] Middleton, *The Liberating Image*, 70.
[29] Walton, *The Lost World*, 26–27; *Genesis 1 as Ancient Cosmology*, 43.
[30] Walton, *The Lost World*, 26–27.
[31] Walton, *The Lost World*, 53.
[32] Walton, *The Lost World*, 38–46.
[33] Walton argues that the hermeneutical presuppositions of traditional interpreters led them to translate these words with conceptually material terms (e.g., "formless and void") rather than with functional terms. Walton, *The Lost World*, 47–49.

created (i.e., given function) is in fact functioning properly. The repeated use of this phrase throughout the account leading up to the culminating "it is very good" after the creation of human beings expresses the functional readiness of creation for the arrival of humans.[34]

Walton's next three propositions (five through seven) concern the functional role of the seven days of creation.[35] In the first three days God establishes *functions*. On day one God declares "Let there be a period of light", separates the light from darkness, calling the former "day" and the latter "night", and thereby creates time.[36] On day two God separates cosmic space into waters below (sea) and a firmament above, which is a solid canopy-like structure to restrain the upper cosmic waters.[37] Day two thus concerns the functional creation of weather. On day three, God separates the terrestrial space (land from seas) so that the land could begin to serve the function of producing food (vegetation). So, in the first three days God establishes three great functions, which in the ancient worldview jointly provided the foundation for life—time, weather, and food.[38] These functions are reiterated in reverse order in Genesis 8:22, directly after the great flood, as an act of recreation and renewed blessing: "As long as the earth endures, seed time and harvest [food], cold and heat, summer and winter [weather], day and night [time] will never cease."

On days four through six of the creation narrative, God installs *functionaries*: the sun moon and stars on day four to separate day from night, mark the seasons, and provide light to the earth; living creatures of the seas and birds of the sky on day five to carry out their own function of increasing and multiplying to fill the waters and the earth; and wild animals, livestock, and ground creatures on day six to spread out across the land. Most importantly, on the sixth day God creates human beings in God's own image to fulfill a unique role. Human beings are to function not just in relation to their origin (land, sea, etc.) or their kind (the call to reproduce). They are to function in a multifaceted way in relation to the world (to rule over it), to God (as vice regents), and to each other as embodied persons (male and female).[39] Human beings are created to reflect the divine image partly by executing their god-like function of ruling over creation. Walton notes that at this point the Genesis account differs in per-

---

[34] Walton, *The Lost World*, 51.
[35] Walton, *The Lost World*, 55–71.
[36] Walton asks us to notice that this description is functional rather than material, as it makes no scientific sense to separate light from darkness or simply to call light (as such) "day".
[37] Walton argues that translating expanse/firmament with the word "sky" is inaccurate and misleading, being motivated not by the text but by concordist hermeneutics. Walton, *The Lost World*, 51 (for Walton's critique of concordism, see pp. 16–19).
[38] Walton, *The Lost World*, 59–60. Walton demonstrates that other Ancient Near Eastern texts also prioritized the importance of these three foundational functions.
[39] Walton elsewhere notes that God's assertion that "it is not good for the man to be alone" in Genesis 2 is a functional judgment, meaning that the human condition without the woman was not yet functionally complete (*The Lost World*, 51).

spective from other Ancient Near Eastern myths. While most of the ancient world viewed creation as serving the gods (and many depict humans as slaves of the gods), in Genesis creation is established not for God's benefit but for humanity's benefit.[40]

Finally, on day seven God "rests" from creative activity and thereby takes up residence in the cosmic palace-temple that is God's creation. Walton argues that the language of resting points unambiguously to a temple context. He writes, "Deity rests in a temple, and only in a temple." Consequently, "Without hesitation the ancient reader would conclude that this is a temple text and that day seven is the most important of the seven days."[41] According to Walton, the seventh day is most important because of the significance of divine temple rest. In the ancient world, a temple was constructed so that a deity could have a centre for its rule. The significance of day seven in the Genesis account, then, is that God comes to indwell creation and thus to fill and rule over it.[42] "In short, by naming the functions and installing the functionaries, and finally by deity entering his resting place, the temple comes into existence. . . ."[43] In light of Walton's analysis, Genesis 1 describes not the material origins of creation but the functional inauguration of creation, depicted in terms of the construction of God's cosmic palace-temple and the installation of human beings as God's steward-priests to rule and care for it. As we will explore later in this chapter, human beings fulfill their creative function and commission, and in this way reflect God's image, by sustaining, restoring, and improving creation in faithful partnership with God. Moreover, this commission has an eschatological dimen-

---

[40] Moreover, ancient accounts usually depicted people offering up all of creation to the gods, but in Genesis people represent God to the rest of creation (Walton, *The Lost World*, 67–69).

[41] Walton, *The Lost World*, 72. To illustrate the functionally operative yet incomplete state of creation at the end of the sixth day, Walton employs a business analogy: "In days four to six the functionaries are installed in their appropriate positions and given their appropriate roles . . . they are assigned their offices (cubicles), told to whom they will report, and thus given an idea of their place in the company. Their workday is determined by the clock, and they are expected to be productive. Foremen have been put in place, and the plant is now ready for operation. But before the company is ready to operate, the owner is going to arrive and move into his office" (71).

[42] Walton, *The Lost World*, 75. For additional support, Walton appeals to Psalm 132, which unites in one place the ideas of divine rest, temple, and enthronement. He writes, "God's 'ceasing' (*šābat*) on the seventh day in Genesis 2:2 leads to his 'rest' (*nûḥa*), associated with the seventh day in Exodus 20:11. His 'rest' is located in his 'resting place' (*měnûḥâ*) in Psalm 132, which also identifies it as the temple from which he rules" (74).

[43] Walton, *The Lost World*, 89. Walton argues that the seven days of creation depict the inauguration of a cosmic temple. He compares this account with the inauguration of the tabernacle in Exodus 35–40. The construction of the tabernacle progresses from an initial material building phase in chapters 25–39 to a final inauguration/creation phase in chapter 40, at which point the glory of the Lord fills it.

sion, because the task of sustaining, restoring, and improving creation is ongoing and leads toward a final fulfilment or *telos*, which is the new creation.

Usurpation and the distortion of the commission

The reality of sin in the lives of human beings impacts their relationships (see chapter 3), their knowledge of God and understanding of God's purposes (see chapter 4), and their commission to be steward-priests of God's creation. Concerning the latter, in Genesis 3 we observe that the threefold function of human beings with respect to God, others, and the world is distorted by sin and the curse that sin carries with it. After Adam and Eve partake of the forbidden fruit, God pronounces judgement and describes the consequences of their disobedience. First, the fact that Adam and Eve have disobeyed God's explicit command out of their desire to be "like God" demonstrates the corruption of their role as God's representative vice regents. Sin has corrupted their hearts and led them to prioritize their own desires and plans over God's. Second, sin distorts the proper functioning of the relationship between Adam and Eve. According to God's original intent Adam and Eve would have functioned as equal co-rulers of creation (Gen 2), but due to the corrupting power of sin their relationship is now characterized by a mixture of pathological desire and a twisted will to rule over each other. Third, the human vocational function with respect to nature is disrupted. Genesis 3 depicts this disruption as impacting both the man and the woman; the woman experiences it in the form of pain during childbearing and the man experiences it in the form of toil and difficulty in working the earth. Moreover, this disruption of proper functioning (i.e., of God's intended order) leads to servitude—the woman to the man from whom she was formed and the man to the ground from which he was formed. God's original intent was for men and women to rule creation faithfully through their vocation and work, by caring for one another and for non-human creatures, by raising families, and by building cultures, societies, and civilizations. However, sin now disrupts this proper functional ordering of the cosmos and causes human beings to be *ruled by* creation rather than exercising appropriate dominion over it.

We can explore the destructive impact of sin on human existence further by reflecting on the nature of sin not just as disobedience to God but, more insidiously, as rebellion against God. In his theological reading of Genesis 3, Bonhoeffer suggests that the placement of the tree of the knowledge of good and evil at the centre of the garden represents the centrality and authority of God's Word and command for genuine human existence.[44] It reflects God's intent that human beings be oriented toward God in openness, basic trust, and dependence. In the language of Pannenberg, God created human beings to be exocentric creatures that find their centre outside of themselves in God. As their defining centre, God is the ground of their identity and the source of their very life

---

[44] Dietrich Bonhoeffer, *Creation and Fall: A Theological Exposition of Genesis 1-3*, ed. John W. de Gruchy, trans. Douglas Stephen Bax, vol. 3, *Dietrich Bonhoeffer Works* (Minneapolis: Fortress, 1997), 83–88.

(Bonhoeffer notes that the tree of life is also at the centre of the garden). When Adam and Eve eat the forbidden fruit they transgress their boundary or limit as God's creatures and reject the sufficiency of God's Word and providence for their existence.[45] Bonhoeffer explains,

> Thus for their knowledge of God human beings renounce the word of God that approaches them again and again out of the inviolable center and boundary of life; they renounce the life that comes from this word and grab it for themselves. They themselves stand at the center. This is disobedience in the semblance of obedience, the desire to rule in the semblance of service, the will to be creator in the semblance of being a creature, being dead in the semblance of life.[46]

The serpent's claim that Adam and Eve would become "like God" by knowing good and evil is cunningly deceptive, because it introduces a subtle distortion of their calling to be stewards and co-rulers of creation. Indeed God did create Adam and Eve to reflect God's image, but in their twisted desire to be "like God" they transgressed their creaturely limit and attempted to usurp God's unique place as the centre and authority of their existence. Thus, the ultimate character of their action was malevolent and led to increasing degrees of corruption, disruption, and finally spiritual death (Gen 3–11). As Bonhoeffer reflects, "Humankind-sicut-deus [like God] is dead, for it has cut itself off from the tree of life; it lives out of its own resources, yet it cannot live. It is compelled to live, yet it cannot live. That is what death means."[47]

At least three consequences follow from the sinful attempt of human beings to usurp God's rightful place. First, we experience a threefold distortion of our identity and purpose. We forget that we were meant to be stewards of God's creation and instead enthrone ourselves as sovereign kings. Consequently, we begin to exploit the world and other human beings to serve our own purposes as we construct our own personal kingdoms. Moreover, we forget that we were meant to be priests of God's creation, representing God within the created world by shaping and guiding it to glorify God and serve God's purposes. Instead, we fall into an idolatrous quest for our own glory and honour. We begin to covet the praise and worship of other human beings and seek to influence others to serve us, sometimes even using religion as propaganda to justify and solidify our own place of honour and privilege (e.g., Jesus's critique of the reli-

---

[45] Bonhoeffer writes that in sinfulness, the human being "now lives out of its own resources, creates its own life, is its own creator; it no longer needs the Creator, it has itself become creator, inasmuch as it creates its own life. Thereby its creatureliness is eliminated, destroyed. Adam is no longer a creature." Bonhoeffer, *Creation and Fall*, 115.

[46] Bonhoeffer, *Creation and Fall*, 117.

[47] Bonhoeffer, *Creation and Fall*, 135.

gious leaders in Mark 12:38–40).[48] In addition, we forget that all of creation is God's palace-temple and is therefore sacred and intended to serve and glorify God. Instead, we divide up creation into spheres and create false dichotomies that separate religion/faith from everyday life (e.g., sacred–secular, inward–outward, or private–public). This restricts or confines our devotion and allegiance to God to certain fragments of our existence. As Bonhoeffer reflects, "The displacement of God from the world, and from the public part of human life, led to the attempt to keep his place secure at least in the sphere of the 'personal,' the 'inner,' and the 'private.'"[49] Perhaps this tendency is most acute in the modern age, though impurity of heart is a perennial temptation. Against this tendency,

> The Bible does not recognize our distinction between the outward and the inward. Why should it? It is always concerned with *anthrōpos teleios*, the *whole* man, even where, as in the Sermon on the Mount, the decalogue is pressed home to refer to 'inward disposition.' That a good 'disposition' can take the place of total goodness is quite unbiblical.[50]

Human beings are meant to serve and glorify God holistically and comprehensively, living their whole lives with consistency and integrity before God as steward-priests of God's palace-temple creation. The sinful tendency to displace God from the centre of our lives to the periphery thoroughly distorts our intended identity and purpose.

Second, in place of locating our identity and purpose outside of ourselves in God, we pursue a self-constructed identity and a self-directed destiny. We become literally dis-oriented, because we are alienated from our Creator, who is our true source and centre of meaning. Consequently, we fall prey to anxiety as we attempt desperately to make something of ourselves or, alternately, to despair in our failure to achieve our goals or meet the expectations of others.

---

[48] Marx and Nietzsche perceived this often present aspect of religion clearly, even if myopically and one-sidedly. For a Christian critique of this kind of religion, see Dietrich Bonhoeffer, "Lectures on Christology," in *Berlin: 1921–33*, vol. 12 *Dietrich Bonhoeffer Works*, ed. Larry L. Rasmussen, trans. Isabel Best and David Higgins (Minneapolis: Fortress, 2009), 300–10 and Ralf K. Wüstenberg, *A Theology of Life: Dietrich Bonhoeffer's Religionless Christianity* (Grand Rapids: Eerdmans, 1998).

[49] Dietrich Bonhoeffer, *Letters and Papers from Prison*, ed. Eberhard Bethge (New York: Simon & Schuster, 1997), 344. Elsewhere Bonhoeffer writes that the division of the world into such spheres fallaciously assumes there are realities which lie outside the reality of Christ. This creates a possibility of living one's life in either: (a) a spiritual existence which has no part in secular existence; or (b) a secular existence which can claim autonomy for itself and exercise this right of autonomy in its dealings with the spiritual sphere. See Dietrich Bonhoeffer, *Ethics*, vol. 6 of *Dietrich Bonhoeffer Works*, ed. Clifford J. Green, trans. Reinhard Krauss, Charles C. West, and Douglas W. Stott (Minneapolis: Fortress, 2005), 47–75.

[50] Bonhoeffer, *Letters and Papers from Prison*, 346 (emphasis original).

Moreover, in our disorientation we are oblivious to God's eschatological purposes and plans for us. Lacking a genuine and compelling vision of God's future, we ascribe infinite and eternal value to what is finite and temporary. Alienated from God's liberating Spirit, who brings God's eschatological future into the present and directs us to our true destiny, we become closed-off, ruled, and enslaved by the tyranny of our own past and present.

Third, rebellion from God leads us into a downward spiral of meaninglessness, purposelessness, and ultimately nonexistence. Bonhoeffer vividly describes the effects of human sinful rebellion as follows:

> As such a defection it is a *continual* fall, a *plunging down* into a bottomless abyss, a state of being let go, a process of moving further and further away, falling deeper and deeper. And in all this it is not merely a *moral lapse* but the destruction of creation by the creature. The extent of the fall is such that it affects the whole created world.[51]

Bonhoeffer's description receives support from John Walton's observations concerning the effects of sin as portrayed by the flood account in Genesis 6–8. At the beginning of Genesis God separated and restrained the ominous cosmic waters, which in the functional ontology of the ancient world represented purposelessness and nonexistence. Throughout the unfolding creation account, God brings increasing differentiation, purpose, and order to creation, culminating with the creation of human beings and the indwelling of God's own presence and glory in creation (God's Sabbath palace-temple rest). After the entrance of sin the proper functioning of creation is disrupted and the world, particularly human life and society, gradually regresses into disorder, chaos, wickedness, violence, and destruction. Whereas initially God was pleased with creation and declared that "it is good" (i.e., it is functioning properly), now God is grieved by the dysfunctional and corrupt state of creation and even regrets having made human beings (Gen 6:6). So God decides to send a great flood to cover the earth and destroy all living things, including human beings with the exception of Noah and his family (Gen 6:11–22). Walton describes the flood in relation to God's creational purposes as follows: "In Genesis, after the cosmos is ordered, a crisis leads God to return the cosmos to an unordered, nonfunctional state by means of a flood. Here the cosmic waters are let loose from their boundaries and again the earth becomes non-functional."[52] Thus, the pattern Walton identifies is that sin is a disruption God's intended purposes for creation and as such incurs God's judgment and leads toward the degenerative undoing of creation.

---

[51] Bonhoeffer, *Creation and Fall*, 120. Stanley Grenz describes sin in terms of a struggle of cosmic forces (*Theology*, 210).
[52] Walton, *The Lost World*, 60.

In the New Testament, the Apostle Paul in his letter to the Romans likewise describes the downward spiral of human sin and evil (1:18–32). Paul says that God gave human beings over to suffer the consequences of their dysfunctional, rebellious, and destructive behaviours and describes their resulting existence as a kind of living death (in 7:5 Paul says that they bear the fruit of death) leading ultimately to spiritual death (Rom 5:12–14; see also Jas 1:13-15 and Gal 6:8). Instead of enjoying the dignity, honour, and satisfaction of their intended vocation as steward-priests to rule and care for creation, human beings become slaves to sin (John 8:34; Rom 6:23; Gen 4:7) and are conformed to the sinful patterns of this world (Rom 12:2).

Saved from a purposeless and self-destructive destiny

Recreated in the image of Christ

As mentioned earlier, the creation of human beings in the image of God points not to a static quality or possession but to a dynamic reality toward which they are moving. This image was present in human beings at creation in embryonic form as a promise of what would later be realized more fully through their union with Christ in the Spirit.[53] It would reach full maturity only at the final resurrection and is therefore ultimately an eschatological reality.[54] Thus, Athanasius argues that human beings were created "by nature corruptible, but destined, by grace following from partaking in the Word, to have escaped their natural state, had they remained good."[55] Similarly, Irenaeus writes,

> [T]he Word of God was made man, assimilating Himself to man, and man to Himself, so that by means of his resemblance to the Son, man might become precious to the Father. For in times long past, it was *said* that man was created after the image of God, but it was not [actually] *shown*; for the Word was as yet invisible, after whose image man was created, Wherefore also he did easily lose the similitude. When, however, the Word of God became flesh, He confirmed both these: for He both showed forth the image truly, since He became Himself what was His image; and He re-established the similitude after a sure manner, by assimilating man to the invisible Father through means of the visible Word.[56]

Irenaeus links the recreation of sinful human beings in the image of Christ to Christ's redemptive work of recapitulation, whereby Christ assimilated or "took up [humanity] into himself" and thereby restored human beings by means of his

---

[53] Irenaeus, *Against Heresies* V/16.2 (544); Osborn, *Irenaeus* , 79, 92.
[54] Grenz, *Theology for the Community of God* , 172–73; and *The Social God and the Relational Self*, 147–48, 177.
[55] Athanasius, *On the Incarnation of the Word* 5.1, in *NPNF2–04: Athanasius: Select Works and Letters*, ed. Philip Schaff (New York: Christian Literature, 1892), 38.
[56] Irenaeus, *Against Heresies* V/16.2 (544).

incarnation, life, death, resurrection, and ascension.[57] Jesus Christ came to "recapitulate" human existence—being born as an infant, growing into adulthood, and then dying a human death—in order to live the truly genuine and faithful human life that sinful men and women had failed to live.[58] Though this work of recapitulation, Christ "accustomed" humanity to God and God to humanity.[59] By means of his redemptive work, Christ defeated the work of evil one, suffered our fate, and rescued us from a destiny of purposelessness and destruction.[60] In addition, he incorporated us into his own life of faithfulness before the Father, demonstrated how we ought now to live as creatures renewed in his image, and pointed the way forward to our eschatological future as mature image bearers. He has therefore given us a renewed purpose and destiny.[61] As Eric Flett puts it, "That human beings are created in the image of God means that they are christologically determined and oriented towards the future, where the consummation of that determination lies."[62]

The New Testament explicitly teaches that Jesus Christ is uniquely and preeminently the image of God (2 Cor 4:4; Col 1:15). Since Jesus Christ uniquely, truly, and fully reflects God's image, he is therefore the prototypical human being who teaches and demonstrates what it means to be authentically human.[63]

---

[57] Irenaeus, *Against Heresies* III/16.6 (442–43). Osborn observes that the concept of recapitulation pervaded the theology of the second century, being found in Justin, Clement, and Tertullian (*Irenaeus*, 97). For a thorough explication of Irenaeus's doctrine of recapitulation see Osborn, *Irenaeus*, chapters 5 and 6 (97–140).

[58] For Irenaeus's many comments about recapitulation, see *Against Heresies* II/22.4; III/16.6, 21.10, 23.1; V/12.4, 14.1, 19.1, 21.1.

[59] Osborn observes that one of the major themes in Irenaeus is that of "accustoming", noting that "the first purpose of the economy was to accustom man to God and to accustom God to man." The incarnation marks a new and particularly significant phase in the process of accustoming, as "in Christ, man is able to see God, to contain God, to accustom himself to participate in God while God is accustomed to live in man" (2.30.3). Osborn, *Irenaeus*, 80, 81.

[60] Irenaeus, *Against Heresies* V/21.1 (548).

[61] Shults writes: "What is most true about human nature is not its primordial past but its eschatological future, an arriving determination that addresses us and calls us to spiritual union with God in Christ" (*Reforming Theological Anthropology*, 242).

[62] Eric G. Flett, "Priests of Creation, Mediators of Order: the Human Person as a Cultural Being in Thomas F. Torrance's Theological Anthropology," *Scottish Journal of Theology* 58, no. 2 (2005): 175.

[63] Hauerwas argues that we should not equate being a Christian with being human. He writes, "Such a position is bound to use Christ to underwrite the integrity of the 'natural', since he is seen as epitomizing the fulfillment of the human vocation . . . this seems to be very bad advice – as Mark Twain observed, the worst advice you can give anyone is to be himself . . . ." Stanley Hauerwas, *The Peaceable Kingdom: A Primer in Christian Ethics* (Notre Dame: University of Notre Dame Press, 1983). But Hauerwas is here assuming a static or essentialist anthropology, in which case his criticism is correct. If, however, we are speaking of human beings not in essentialist terms but in eschatological terms of "new humanity in Christ by the Spirit," Hauerwas's criticism does not apply.

As Stanley Grenz says, "In his risen glory, Jesus Christ now radiates the fullness of humanness that constitutes God's design for humankind from the beginning."[64] Accordingly, he is the "firstborn among many brothers and sisters", the "firstborn of all creation", and the "firstborn from among the dead" (Rom 8:29; Col 1:15, 18). Moreover, Jesus Christ is the one in whose image all redeemed human beings are destined to be conformed. As Paul writes, "For those God foreknew he also predestined to be conformed to the image of his Son" (Rom 8:29). Grenz rightly observes that this verse does not concern speculation about the status of one's personal faith and election, but is rather a powerful affirmation of God's plan for humanity in the new creation. The sense of the verse, therefore, is that "believers *will indeed* be brought into conformity to the Son, in union with whom they, in fact, already live through the Spirit."[65] While our former sinful disposition reflected the image of Adam (representing sinful humanity), our redemption means that we will reflect the image of the Risen Christ who is the true human being.[66]

Reoriented and realigned to serve Christ our Lord and King as his steward-priests

Being recreated to reflect the image of the Risen Christ in the power of the Spirit involves being reoriented and realigned to serve Christ as Lord and King. This is not just a personal matter of one's private faith, but involves an allegiance to Christ that claims all of one's existence in the world. As Bonhoeffer asserts, "Jesus claims for himself and the Kingdom of God the whole of human life in all its manifestations."[67] Moreover, "In Christ we are invited to participate in the reality of God and the reality of the world at the same time, the one not without the other."[68] Jesus Christ is the Lord of all reality, and in Christ all the scattered pieces of our fragmented and conflicted lives are reconciled, united together, and reoriented as we strive to seek first Christ's kingdom (Matt 6:33) with pure hearts (Matt 5:8; 6:21) and a clear and focused vision (Matt 6:22–23). As we seek him earnestly in the power of the Spirit, Christ teaches us and realigns our values and priorities. He gives all that we are, have, and do new meaning and direction. Our relationships, our work, our passions and dreams, our finances and resources, our plans and agendas are all redirected to serve Christ and his kingdom. All of this occurs not merely by our own strength, power, or ingenuity, but by the Spirit's work of drawing us (along

---

[64] Grenz, *The Social God and the Relational Self*, 231.

[65] Grenz, *The Social God and the Relational Self*, 227 (emphasis added).

[66] As Paul writes, "And just as we have borne the image of the earthly man [Adam], so shall we bear the image of the heavenly man [Christ]" (1 Cor 15:49).

[67] Bonhoeffer, *Letters and Papers from Prison*, 342.

[68] Bonhoeffer, *Ethics*, 55. Bonhoeffer continues, "What matters is *participating in the reality of God and the world in Jesus Christ today*, and doing so in such a way that I never experience the reality of God without the reality of the world, nor the reality of the world without the reality of God" (emphasis original).

with our gifts and abilities) into the kingly and priestly ministry of Jesus Christ himself, who by the same Spirit works in us and through us.[69]

Consequently, God's original intention that we be steward-priests of God's palace-temple creation is reaffirmed, but with renewed gratitude, focus, hope, and power, because of our union with Christ by the Spirit and our glorious eschatological destiny. In Christ, we are a "chosen people, a royal priesthood, a holy nation, God's special possession" so that we "may declare the praises of him who called [us] out of darkness into his wonderful light" (1 Pet 2:9).[70] With his shed blood, Jesus Christ the Lamb of God has purchased for God "members from every tribe and language and people and nation" and "made them to be a kingdom of priests to serve our God, and they will reign on the earth" (Rev 5:9–10). As steward-priests of God's new creation, redeemed human beings work toward and eagerly anticipate the final transformation of creation into God's eschatological cosmic city-palace-temple, the New Jerusalem (Rev 21), at which point God will come to dwell fully with human beings and rule in eternal justice, truth, and peace.[71]

Transformation by the Spirit into the likeness of the Son

In chapter three we explored the Spirit's ministry in drawing human beings into ever fuller, holistic, and abundant communion with God and others. In chapter four we observed the Spirit's role in redeeming human beings from the captivity of their minds and leading them to cultivate wisdom by enabling access to the mind of Christ. Presently we will briefly consider the Spirit's role in renewing and transforming human beings to be Christ's eschatological steward-priests.

---

[69] As Paul declares, "It is God who works in you to will and to act according to his good purpose" (Phil 2:13).

[70] Middleton notes that this verse serves as a continuation of the Abrahamic calling of God's people to mediate God's blessing to the world. Middleton, "A New Heaven and a New Earth," 85.

[71] Rikki Watts observes several features identifying the New Jerusalem as God's eschatological temple: "One striking feature is the absence of any Temple (Rev 21:22). The odd cube shape of the city might explain this. The only other biblical objects in a similar setting that are cube-shaped are the Holy of Holies in the Tabernacle (10 cubits, probably) and Solomon's temple (20 cubits; 1 Kgs 6:20; 2 Chr 3:8; cf. the Holy Place in Ezekiel's temple, 500 cubits square, Ezek 42:16-20; 45:2). If so, then this suggests that the reason there is no temple in the New Jerusalem is because the city itself has become, not just the Temple, but the very Holy of Holies (cf. also Ezek 45:2-3). But what about the surprising size of the city: 12,000 stadia (approximately 1,500 miles) along each axis? The significance of these dimensions might lie in the observation that the size of the city corresponds to that of the then-known Greek world, while the height emphasizes the co-mingling of heaven and earth. In other words, the climax of the new creation is not the abandonment of the earth, but instead the coming of Yahweh himself to the earth to dwell among us." Watts, "Making Sense of Genesis 1," paragraph 48.

The Apostle Paul argues that our gradual conformity to the image of Christ is achieved not simply by human effort, but is made possible by the transformative and empowering work of the Spirit. For example, to the Corinthians he writes, "And all of us, with unveiled faces, seeing the glory of the Lord as though reflected in a mirror, are being transformed into the same image from one degree of glory to another; for this comes from the Lord, the Spirit" (2 Cor 3:18). Scripture teaches that the transformation of the believer is already underway, even though it is not yet complete, because the Spirit of the new age has already broken into the old. The Spirit is a down payment or seal of the glory to come (2 Cor 1:22; 5:4; Eph 1:13–14). The Spirit is the first instalment of the believer's inheritance in the kingdom of God (Rom 8:15–17; 14:17; 1 Cor 6:9–11; Gal 4:6–7). In addition, the New Testament indicates that we should expect a moral transformation when the Spirit of holiness comes into a person's life (Rom 8:1ff; 1 Cor 6:9–11; Gal 5:16ff). Accordingly, it encourages us to live in the power of the Spirit, to walk in the Spirit, and to be led by the Spirit in all that we think, say, and do (Rom 8:4–6, 14; Gal 5:16, 18, 25).

Jesus himself was totally dependent upon the Spirit's power and guidance for his own calling and ministry as the Lord, Messiah, and founder of God's eschatological kingdom. Jesus possessed the Holy Spirit without measure (John 3:34) and lived his entire life immersed in the Spirit's presence. The Spirit effected his birth (Matt 1:18-25; Luke 1:35), anointed him at his baptism (Matt 3:16-17; Mark 1:10-11; Luke 3:22; John 1:33), led him into the desert to face temptation (Matt 4:1; Mark 1:12; Luke 4:1), and inspired his mission of proclaiming good news to the poor, proclaiming freedom for the prisoners, recovering sight for the blind, setting the oppressed free, and proclaiming the year of the Lord's favour—the eschatological dawning of the kingdom (Luke 4:16–20). By the Spirit, Jesus accomplished his ministry of healing, teaching, confronting, reconciling, and even raising people from the dead. Indeed, by the Spirit's power Jesus himself was raised from the dead and amazingly *this same Spirit now dwells within his followers* (Rom 8:11) and empowers the ministry of the church. This is apparent throughout the book of Acts, in which the church ministers in the power of the Spirit just as Jesus had. In and by the Spirit, Christ continues to be present and active within the church and in the lives of believers (Rom 8:9; Gal 4:6; Phil 1:19). The church can function effectively as Christ's body only by being filled with the life-giving Spirit. Without the Spirit, the body of Christ would be inanimate, dead.

In particular, two aspects of the Spirit's ministry contribute to the transformation of redeemed persons and equip them to be faithful and effective steward-priests of the new creation. First, as we grow in Christ we begin to manifest the fruit of the Spirit: love, joy, peace, patience, kindness, goodness, faithfulness, gentleness and self-control (Gal 5:22). Miroslav Volf explains that the fruit of the Spirit concerns general Christian character, thus it is God's intent

The Human Person as an Eschatological Creature

that all believers bear the fruit of the Spirit.[72] As Spirit-led character traits, the fruit of the Spirit comes neither automatically nor by meritorious earning but results through a process of spiritual-character cultivation in which believers cooperate with the Spirit—or better yet *participate* in the Spirit's gracious work. They do this by "living with" and "keeping in step with the Spirit" (Gal 5:25) and by crucifying "the sinful nature with its passions and desires" (Gal 5:24, 16–21). As James Peterson remarks, this process is a marathon rather than a sprint and accordingly requires sustained effort, disciplined training, and ongoing practice.[73] Through such spiritual-character formation in the Spirit, believers gradually attain to genuine freedom in Christ (Gal 5:1, 13).

Second, the Holy Spirit uniquely bestows individual believers with particular spiritual gifts, in order to equip them to serve God and others in their specific, concrete life circumstances (Rom 12; 1 Cor 12; Eph 4). While the Spirit gives spiritual gifts to edify and empower the church, such gifts are not necessarily restricted to ecclesial settings. For example, the gift of evangelism is inherently directed outside the church as a ministry to unbelievers. Volf argues that the Spirit equips believers with spiritual gifts to help them pursue not only their ecclesial ministry but also their worldly calling or vocation. He writes,

> All functions of the fellowship—whether directed inward to the Christian community or outward to the world—are the result of the operation of the Spirit of God and are thus charismatic. The place of operation does not define charisms, but the manifestation of the Spirit for the divinely ordained purpose.[74]

For example, Scripture records that the Holy Spirit inspired craftsmanship (Exod 35:2–3; 1 Chron 28:11–12) and anointed judges and kings to fulfill their appointed tasks (Judges 3:10; 1 Sam 16:13; 23:2; Prov 16:10). Yet it is not appropriate to attribute everything that a Christian does to a spiritual gift. According to Volf, the difference between the fruit of the Spirit and the gifts of the Spirit is that the former has to do with cultivating and exhibiting Christian character, while the latter concerns insights and abilities that the Spirit enables for specific and concrete tasks and situations. Both of these fundamental aspects of the Spirit's work are crucial to the Christian's calling to serve as Christ's steward-priests in the world. Through spiritual-character formation, Christians cultivate the fruit of the Spirit and increasingly operate in genuine freedom (for God and others), wisdom, and faithful consistency even as they face ever novel and challenging life situations. Moreover, through the Spirit's gracious charismatic gifting, believers receive special abilities (physical, men-

---

[72] Miroslav Volf, *Work in the Spirit: Toward a Theology of Work* (Eugene: Wipf and Stock, 2001), 111.
[73] Peterson, *Changing Human Nature*, 41.
[74] Volf, *Work in the Spirit*, 111–12.

tal, psychological, spiritually discerning, etc.) to accomplish specific tasks that God places uniquely before them.

Hope and the eschatological ethical dimension

New Creation

Miroslav Volf asserts that "at its very core, Christian faith is eschatological".[75] As such, Christian faith is oriented toward and directed by "the end" or "the final things". But what does it mean for Christian faith to be eschatological and what kind of end does it envision?

First, in contrast to both over-realized eschatology and under-realized eschatology, Scripture promotes *inaugurated* eschatology. In over-realized eschatology, for instance in some (but not all) forms of postmillennialism, the eschatological kingdom of God is something that is either fully present in human society or, more often, something that is fully possible within the present order of things.[76] The danger of over-realized eschatology is that it tends to be too optimistic about human progress and thus naive concerning the continuing influence of evil in the unfolding of history. Such confidence, once commonplace in the period following the Enlightenment, plunged dramatically during the twentieth century, which included two World Wars, several brutal totalitarian regimes, the rise of technologically proficient international terrorism, and the moral corruption of secular western societies. Conversely, in under-realized eschatology, for example Dispensationalism, God's eschatological kingdom is pushed completely into the future. The danger of this perspective is that it downplays the importance of present transformation and thereby trivializes the ethical, kingdom teachings of Jesus, especially those found in the Sermon on the Mount. It views these teachings as standards binding not for the present but only for the end time when Christ will come to set up his permanent kingdom.[77]

---

[75] Volf, *Work in the Spirit*, 79.

[76] Scripture refutes over-realized eschatology in passages such as Luke 19:11 and Acts 1:6–8. It is important to recognize that postmillennialists such as Jonathan Edwards and John Wesley were quite aware of human depravity and did not place their faith in the notion of human progress. Their post millennial hope stemmed from God's creativity and relentless grace, not naive trust in human ability or historical advancement.

[77] Craig S. Keener, *A Commentary on the Gospel of Matthew* (Grand Rapids: Eerdmans, 1999), 160. Another danger is that such a perspective can lead to inaction, apathy, or absorption in fantasizing about the future. In Acts 1:10–12, two angels appeared to the disciples who were staring up at the sky after Jesus's ascension. They scold, "why do you stand here looking into the sky? This same Jesus, who has been taken from you into heaven, will come back in the same way you have seen him go into heaven." The passage can be read as a subtle critique of under-realized eschatology (as if to say: "stop daydreaming and get on with your mission!"), especially when combined with Jesus's statement in verse 8 that they were to be his witnesses in Jerusalem, and in all Judea and Samaria, and to the ends of the earth. Conversely, verses 6–8 can serve as a critique of over-realized eschatology: here Jesus refutes his disciples' expectation that he would now restore the kingdom of God to Israel. The

In contrast to these two extremes, inaugurated eschatology views God's kingdom as being *already* present but *not yet* fully consummated. As such, it claims our allegiance, strengthens our faith and hope, directs our vision of the future, and hence guides our present ethical action.[78] Yet because it is a dynamic and expectant reality, rather than a static and fully achieved one, it relativizes the goodness of the present order and encourages us always to seek God's kingdom in greater fullness and depth. This inaugurated eschatological viewpoint best fits the New Testament's teaching concerning the kingdom of God. For example, Miroslav Volf notes that the kingdom prayer in Matthew's gospel (Matt 6:9–13) is a prayer for God's rule to be increasingly realized over all the earth. Moreover, Jesus's declaration that the meek will inherit the earth (Matt 5:5) points toward the establishment of God's kingdom *on this earth*, rather than placing hope in some distant and ethereal heaven.[79] Several other passages also underscore the present-yet-future character of the kingdom of God. Jesus often says that the kingdom of God is "near", "advancing", "at hand", "among you", "within you", and something that his disciples would experience in the present life.[80] In Matthew 12:28, Jesus says "if I drive out demons by the Spirit of God, then the kingdom of God *has come upon you*."[81] At the same time, Jesus is not hereby claiming that his presence and actions demonstrate the full consummation of the kingdom; for, demonic power and evil continue to have influence in the present world.[82] Rather, he is claiming that his actions demon-

---

pericope as a whole discourages both triumphalist activism and passive speculation, and instead encourages faithful witness to the rule of the King in and by the power of the Spirit.

[78] Bonhoeffer writes, "It is not with the beyond that we are concerned, but with this world as created and preserved, subjected to laws, reconciled, and restored. What is above this world is, in the gospel, intended to exist for this world; I mean that, not in the anthropocentric sense of liberal, mystic pietistic, ethical theology, but in the biblical sense of the creation and of the incarnation, crucifixion, and resurrection of Jesus Christ." Bonhoeffer, *Letters and Papers from Prison*, 286.

[79] Volf, *Work in the Spirit*, 94. In addition, Middleton argues that the term "heaven" simply "does *not* describe the Christian eschatological hope." He continues, "Not only is the term 'heaven' never used in Scripture for the eternal destiny of the redeemed, but continued use of 'heaven' to name the Christian hope may well divert our attention from the legitimate biblical expectation for the present transformation of our *earthly* life to conform to God's purposes. Indeed, to focus our expectation on an otherworldly salvation has the potential to dissipate our resistance to societal evil and the dedication needed to work for the redemptive transformation of this world." Middleton, "A New Heaven and a New Earth," 96. On this theme, see also N.T. Wright, *Surprised by Hope: Rethinking Heaven, the Resurrection, and the Mission of the Church* (New York: HarperOne, 2008).

[80] Matt 3:2; 4:17; 10:7; 11:12; Mark 1:15; 9:1; Luke 9:27; 10:9, 11; 17:21; 21:31.

[81] Emphasis added. See also Luke 11:20.

[82] Jesus elsewhere indicates that the fullness of the kingdom is a future reality. For example, "I tell you the truth, I will not drink again of the fruit of the vine until that day when I drink it anew in the kingdom of God" (Mark 14:25; cf. Luke 22:16, 18). Jesus

strate the presence and power of the kingdom as a foretaste and deposit of what is to come later in fullness. Since for Jesus the kingdom of God is an inaugurated reality, Jesus intended that his teachings be taught and practiced in the present lives of his followers even as they also point toward a future fulfillment of perfection and completion.[83]

Second, the end has to do with the transformation of the present world into the new creation, rather than its annihilation or destruction.[84] In his book, *Work in the Spirit*, Volf contrasts these two views, which he regards as the two dominant perspectives concerning the continuity or discontinuity of the present age in relation to the age to come. He analyzes the implications of each approach for the value of human work and cultural involvement (and by extension all human activity in the world). According to Volf, in the annihilation view human action in the present world has only earthly significance and is devoid of ultimate significance.[85] Of course, as Volf points out, human action could still indirectly serve certain eternal goals, such as edifying faith, fostering sanctification, and promoting Christian service. For example, human work could serve to purify one's soul of idleness or lust in preparation for heavenly perfection.[86] However, if human action is only a kind of prerequisite for faith, sanctification, or Christian service, then its results "are eschatologically insignificant independent of their direct or indirect influence on the souls of men and women."[87] In terms of ultimate significance, they are instrumentally helpful but not intrinsically valuable. To clarify further, Volf argues that it is "logically compatible" to affirm that the world will be annihilated while simultaneously striving to improve the conditions of the present life as part of one's duty to love and serve one's neighbour. However, such an approach is "theologically inconsistent" because belief in the eschatological destruction of the world is not consonant with a theological affirmation of the goodness of creation. Volf writes, "It makes little sense to affirm the goodness of creation and at the same time ex-

---

also describes the kingdom of God as the final banquet or feast at the end of time (Luke 13:29; 14:15).

[83] Matt 5:13–20; 7:24–27; 28:20; John 8:31–32; 14:23–24.

[84] According to Irenaeus, it is not the world *per se* that will be annihilated or destroyed in the age to come, but only that which is corrupted by evil and sin. He writes, "For neither is the substance nor the essence of the creation annihilated (for faithful and true is He who has established it), but 'the *fashion* of the world passeth away' (1 Cor 7:31) – i.e. 'those things among which transgression has occurred, since man has grown old in them'" (*Against Heresies* V/36.1; 567, emphasis original).

[85] Volf, *Work in the Spirit*, 90–91.

[86] As another example, Volf imagines that if the great composer J.S. Bach were an annihilationist he could still attribute significance to his musical creativity and composition, perhaps out of a desire to edify his audience spiritually and thereby glorify God.

[87] Volf, *Work in the Spirit*, 90.

The Human Person as an Eschatological Creature

pect its eschatological destruction."[88] Correspondingly, without a theologically grounded affirmation of the inherent value and goodness of creation, "positive cultural involvement hangs theologically in the air."[89] As a result, Christians who believe in the destruction of the world tend to shy away from social and cultural involvement, a response which for them is *theologically consistent* though not logically necessary in a strict sense.[90]

In contrast to the annihilationist view, a transformative eschatology implies that the results of the cumulative actions of human beings have intrinsic value and gain ultimate significance.[91] This is because they are *directly* related to the new creation, not just indirectly associated with it as instrumentally beneficial. Volf suggests metaphorically that noble human actions will become the "building materials" from which the glorified world will be constructed. Not that a transformative, new creation view grants *carte blanche* approval to every kind of human action. God's judgement remains on all evil and destructive behaviour. Instead, all action that contradicts the new creation is meaningless, while all action that corresponds to it is ultimately meaningful.[92] Having acknowledged that important qualification, the transformative view affirms that human achievements in serving and creating whatever is good, true, and beautiful, will be taken up, cleansed, perfected, and thereby assimilated into God's new creation—all on the basis of Christ's redemptive work and the Spirit's regenerative and transformative activity. This approach best fits the biblical portrayal of new creation (see below). It also provides a much stronger incentive than the annihilationist position for social and cultural involvement, because it affirms the

---

[88] Volf, *Work in the Spirit*, 96. Volf overstates his point here. There is nothing theologically inconsistent with affirming that God can create something of value without intending it to endure eternally. An orchid can bloom beautifully only to then wither. However, Volf's general argument still holds as a critique of the eschatological destruction view because the latter has its basis in God's judgement rather than in God's originally intended purpose for creation. Withering is part of a flower's intended design, but eschatological destruction was not God's original purpose for creation. A better analogy would depict the eschatological transformation of the earth, for instance the metamorphosis of a caterpillar into a butterfly, the process of giving birth, or the growth of a seed into a tree. The key is to maintain an appropriate degree of both continuity and discontinuity. Perhaps the best analogy for new creation is the Christian doctrine of the resurrection of the body. Romans 8:20–24 depicts the transition to new creation in terms of labour pains giving way to new birth and applies the analogy both to the whole creation and to our individual human bodies. Thus, to alter Volf's argument, belief in the eschatological destruction of the world is not consonant with a theological affirmation of *the Resurrection*. In chapters six through eight, I suggest a threefold model of cultural engagement defined in terms of cross (cruciform engagement), incarnation (incarnational engagement), and resurrection (moving in God's power to realize new possibilities).

[89] Volf, *Work in the Spirit*, 91.

[90] See also Peterson, *Changing Human Nature*, 32–33.

[91] Volf, *Work in the Spirit*, 91–92.

[92] Volf, *Work in the Spirit*, 121.

intrinsic and continuing value of human action with respect to the new creation. As Middleton argues,

> Whereas a dualistic [discontinuous] understanding of redemption typically devalues the good world God created and encourages an aspiration to transcend finitude, the biblical worldview leads to an affirmation of the goodness of creation, along with a desire to pray and work for the redemption of precisely this world (including human, socio-cultural institutions) that earthy life might be restored to what it was meant to be.[93]

In a new creation model, our noble efforts will not be wasted but transformed and redeployed to build and shape God's new world. Volf adds that this view not only affirms present achievement but also provides inspiration and encouragement to those whose creative, moral, or vocational efforts are not appreciated by other human beings. God sees and appreciates them. Even more affirming, God is employing them for God's own good, eternal purposes.

Volf's transformative, new creation eschatology aptly captures the New Testament's teaching concerning the destiny of the world.[94] The New Testament authors affirm that God is not planning to destroy the world but to renew and transform it. In Romans 8:21, Paul writes, "the creation itself will be liberated from its bondage to decay and brought into the freedom and glory of the children of God." Commenting on this passage, F.F. Bruce contends that "these words of Paul denote not the annihilation of the present material universe on the day of revelation, to be replaced by a universe completely new, but the transformation of the present universe so that it will fulfill the purpose for which God created it."[95] In Ephesians 1:9-10, Paul teaches that God's mysterious plan of salvation is "to bring all things in heaven and on earth together under one head, even Christ." In Colossians 1:19-20, Paul writes that God was pleased to reconcile all things to Godself by making peace through his shed blood. In Revelation, the Risen Christ himself declares "I am making everything new!" (Rev 21:5). Such transformation has already begun, because as Paul writes, "If anyone is in Christ there is a new creation" (2 Cor 5:17). Yet it is also a coming reality for which all of creation longs and thus "has been groaning as in the pains of childbirth right up to the present time" (Rom 8:22). In Acts, while preaching to a crowd Peter says that Jesus will remain in heaven "until the time comes for God to restore everything, as he promised long ago through his holy prophets" (3:21). Volf notes that this new creation hope corresponds to the earthly hopes of the Old Testament prophets (e.g., Isa 11:6–10;

---

[93] Middleton, "A New Heaven and a New Earth," 75.
[94] See also Middleton's sketch of the biblical new creation plot ("A New Heaven and a New Earth," 80–91).
[95] F.F. Bruce, *The Epistle of Paul to the Romans: An Introduction and Commentary* (Grand Rapids: Eerdmans, 1963).

65:17–25), but also and more importantly to the Christian doctrine of the resurrection of the body.[96] As Paul says directly after speaking of creation's longing for redemption in Romans 8, "Not only so, but we ourselves, who have the firstfruits of the Spirit, groan inwardly as we wait eagerly for our adoption, the redemption of our bodies" (v. 23). Thus, Peter says that "we are looking forward to a new heaven and a new earth, the home of righteousness" (2 Pet 3:13). In summary, the New Testament describes the transition from the present order to the new creation variously in terms of liberation, bringing together, reconciling, making peace, making new, restoration, adoption, redemption, and transition to a new heaven and earth, not in terms of the destruction or annihilation of creation.[97]

Serving the kingdom of God in the power of the Spirit
Volf argues that a new creation perspective leads to a theological view of human action as cooperation with the Spirit of God.[98] He writes, "Christian life is life in the Spirit of the new creation or it is not Christian life at all. And the Spirit of God should determine the whole life, spiritual as well as secular, of a Christian."[99] First, we cooperate with God by preserving and shaping the creation that God entrusted to us. For example, Volf observes such cooperation in Genesis 2:5, which says that there had not yet been rain upon the earth because there was no man to till the ground. The text alludes to an intended design of cooperation between God who sends rain and human beings who cultivate the ground, plant seed, and harvest crops—thus serving the preservation of God's creation. Recalling also Walton's functional framing of the Genesis account, according to God's design creation is incomplete without the ruling presence of human beings for its ongoing preservation and cultivation.

Second, we cooperate with God's Spirit in transforming creation.[100] This transformative activity includes the essential elements of preserving creation just mentioned and places them within an eschatological framework of God's new creation. In one important sense, human beings do not *in and of themselves* make the new creation (see below), because ultimately new creation is God's gift. In Revelation 21, the New Jerusalem comes down to us from heaven at God's appointed time and prerogative. Thus, realizing God's new creation involves expecting, waiting, longing, and receiving. But this neither implies nor

---

[96] Volf, *Work in the Spirit*, 95.
[97] See Middleton's helpful summary table in "A New Heaven and a New Earth," 90. He concludes that biblical salvation is restorative (God is repairing what went wrong with creation, not taking us out of it to live in heaven) as well as comprehensive and holistic (God intends to restore "all things", which includes our bodies and not just our souls). Middleton also responds effectively and persuasively to problem texts, such as John 14:1–3, 2 Cor 5:1–10, 1 Thess 4:13–18, and Matt 24:37–41; cf. Luke 17 (pp. 91–96).
[98] Volf, *Work in the Spirit*, 98.
[99] Volf, *Work in the Spirit*, 79.
[100] Volf, *Work in the Spirit*, 99–104.

requires passivity or inactivity on our part, because Scripture also exhorts us to seek the kingdom actively and to work toward its fulfilment diligently (e.g., Matt 6:33; 25:14–30). The key theological concept, which transcends the two extremes of ambitious achievement and passive (or even lazy) complacency, is *participation*. By participating in and with the Spirit of God human action actually contributes to the eschatological kingdom, which will arrive in fullness through God's final action. Moreover, in keeping with the scope of new creation, such transformation is not limited to the private lives of individuals or even the inner ecclesial life of the church. It aims more broadly to impact human culture and society, to promote the flourishing of non-human life, and to preserve and nurture the health of the earth. As Volf contends, "Because the whole creation is the Spirit's sphere of operation, the Spirit is not only the Spirit of religious experience but also the Spirit of worldly engagement."[101]

An eschatological qualification of teleological ethics

Christian ethics has a strong teleological orientation, being shaped by a compelling vision that human life is infused with purpose and directed toward a specific destiny, namely the new creation. As Volf asserts, "New creation is the end of all God's purposes with the universe, and as such, either explicitly or implicitly is the necessary criterion of all human action that can be considered good."[102] However, as the biblical language of new creation implies, Christian ethical existence is not just teleological but, more specifically, eschatological. Christian theology thus stipulates an eschatological qualification of teleological ethics.

This eschatological qualification safeguards two crucial theological affirmations. First, it affirms the finality of God's gracious initiative and revelatory Word over all notions of historical necessity along with their corresponding human ideologies (whether utopian optimism or fatalistic pessimism). This means that the progressive movement of history is not merely evolutionary (in a self-enclosed sense) but is open and potentially responsive to God's ongoing initiative.[103] As Volf argues, the new creation as portrayed in Scripture does not "result [merely or primarily] from the action of intrahistorical forces pushing history toward ever-superior states."[104] Volf explains, "Although we must af-

---

[101] Volf, *Work in the Spirit*, 104. Volf also says that "the Spirit strives to lead both the realm of nature (*regnum naturæ*) and the realm of grace (*regnum gratiæ*) toward their final glorification in the new creation (*regnum gloria*)." (119)

[102] Volf, *Work in the Spirit*, 81.

[103] Denis O. Lamoureux helpfully distinguishes between "teleological evolution" (which includes not just random chance but also divine purpose) and "dysteleological evolution" (mere random chance, atheistic metaphysic). See his book *I Love Jesus and I Accept Evolution* (Eugene, OR: Wipf and Stock: 2009), 3–6.

[104] Volf, *Work in the Spirit*, 84. I have modified Volf's original statement, which reads: "A truly *new* creation can never result from the action of intrahistorical forces pushing history toward ever-superior states." As it stands, the statement is too much of a generalization. The point is not that nothing genuinely new ever transpires, but that

firm the continuity between present and future orders, that affirmation should not deceive us into thinking that God's new creation will come about in linear development from the present order of things."[105] Moreover, God's intention that creation be open to ongoing divine initiative means that authentic historical development is receptive to God's revelatory Word and is framed by the larger story of God's dealings with humankind in creation, redemption, and eschatological transformation. This is not to downplay the significance of historical action, but to emphasize the mysterious and surprising role of God's sovereignty within it. The Word and Spirit of God legitimize and protect the world's genuine freedom and present existence while simultaneously qualifying and redirecting both toward God's ultimate future end.[106] An eschatological perspective therefore implies that both the present and the future are valued and affirmed. To some degree the present exists for the sake of the future, but God's future also exists for sake of the present and is already invading and transforming it through the liberating presence and power of the Spirit. As Bonhoeffer puts it, God makes use of the "penultimate", the things before the last, for the sake of the "ultimate". God preserves the present age and the things of this world in order to speak God's ultimate justifying Word in God's own ordained time. Consequently, we must value and affirm both penultimate and ultimate intrinsically, yet theologically God's ultimate reality takes final and determinative precedence.[107]

---

the biblical new creation is contingent upon God's intervention and not merely the result of human efforts or historical processes, even while involving human participation by the Spirit.

[105] Volf, *Work in the Spirit*, 84.

[106] Accordingly, Bonhoeffer argues that Jesus Christ is the centre of human history. He argues that history lives between promise and fulfillment (just as human beings live between law and gospel), however corrupted by sin it cannot fulfill its promise (just as sinful human beings cannot fulfill the law). History finds its true meaning and destiny only in the incarnation, life, death, and resurrection of Jesus Christ. Just as Christ take a *pro me* posture toward human beings in redemption, so he also stands *for the world* as its representative and as Lord of its history. Dietrich Bonhoeffer, "Lectures on Christology," 324–27.

[107] For Bonhoeffer's discussion of the penultimate and ultimate, see *Ethics*, vol. 6 of *Dietrich Bonhoeffer Works*, ed. Clifford J. Green, trans. Reinhard Krauss, Charles C. West, and Douglas W. Stott (Minneapolis: Fortress, 2005), 146–70. The ultimate is the free justifying Word of God. It is ultimate or final because it comes from God alone (i.e., by means of His self-revelation) and is not preceded logically by anything. Bonhoeffer writes, "Through its content it is a *qualitatively* ultimate word. There is no word of God that goes beyond God's grace. There is nothing greater than a life that is justified before God. Because it involves a compete break with everything penultimate, with all that has gone before; because it is never the natural or necessary end of a way already pursued but rather the complete condemnation and devaluation of that way; because it is God's own free word that can never be forced from God by anything whatsoever; therefore it is the irretrievably ultimate word, the ultimate reality" (149). However, paradoxically, this Word of God is also ultimate in

The second theological affirmation that is preserved by an eschatological qualification of teleology is the reality of God's ongoing, intimate involvement with creation. An eschatological new creation orientation is guided not simply by teleological principles that are intrinsic to or latent within creation, but more significantly by the activity, power, and personal presence of God's Spirit. As Ted Peters suggests, God's eschatological new creation is a pull from the future, not merely a push from the past.[108] Consequently, it requires not only that we emphasize the dynamic and changing quality of creation (including human beings) *in principle*, but that we actually conceive the *telos* itself dynamically as continually unfolding before us as God's purposive will and personal act. Eschatology goes beyond teleology (as such) because it concerns the personal in-breaking of God's Spirit into our present reality to shape present circumstances and guide the future outcomes. Thus, the human *telos* is not just a theoretical and abstract idea, but a personal reality in which we participate with the Holy Spirit. This dynamic approach corresponds to the biblical conception of the eschatological kingdom of God. As Dallas Willard nicely puts it, the kingdom of God is *the range of God's effective will*.[109] As such, God's present-yet-coming kingdom is not primarily a thing, a system, or a movement, but essentially concerns *God's active and present reign*. Accordingly, redeemed human beings enter into God's kingdom and serve its extension through their participation by the Spirit in the ministry of the Son (who is King and High Priest) as steward-priests of the new creation.

New Creation and the call to sustain, restore, and improve as steward-priests
Human beings are called to sustain, restore, and improve creation in faithful partnership with God.[110] From the beginning, God intended that human beings play a crucial role within the developing creation.[111] Scripture regards human activity as essential to the full flourishing of God's good creation.[112] Thus, it is

---

the sense of time. Thus: "Something penultimate always precedes it, some action, suffering, movement, intention, defeat, recovery, pleading, hoping—in short, quite literally a span of time at whose end it stands. . . . There is a time of God's permission, waiting, and preparation; and there is an ultimate time that judges and breaks off the penultimate" (150–50).

[108] Ted Peters, *Anticipating Omega: Science, Faith, and Our Ultimate Future* (Göttingen: Vandenhoeck & Ruprecht, 2006), 12, 14.

[109] Willard, *The Divine Conspiracy*, 25.

[110] Peterson, *Changing Human Nature*, 23–35.

[111] Paul S. Evans, "Creation, Progress, and Calling: Genesis 1–11 as Social Commentary," *McMaster Journal of Theology and Ministry* (2011–2012): 77; cf. Middleton, *The Liberating Image*, 89–90, 204–12.

[112] It should be noted that other parts of creation also contribute to the unfolding and development of the created order. For example, as Paul Evans notes, in Genesis 1:11 the earth is called to "bring forth" plants and is thus clearly "participating in bringing forth new creatures" (Evans, "Creation," 83, note 53). Similarly in Genesis 1:20, God commands, "Let the waters bring forth swarms of living creatures", and in verse 24, "Let the earth bring forth living creatures of every kind."

the nature of human beings to impact and shape the created world in which they are placed and of which they themselves are an integral part: "Dust you are and to dust you shall return" (Gen 3:19).[113] Their impact on creation is inevitable, so the salient question becomes: what kind of impact will it be? As Peterson helpfully points out, "The question is not whether we will shape our surroundings; it is whether we will do so consciously and conscientiously. Our past and present give us a starting point but not a goal. The key guide is not what we have been, but what we should be."[114] As gardeners in God's sacred garden, human beings are called to cultivate and improve the natural environment, the non-human creaturely world, and even themselves. Improvement of the natural environment includes such things as caring for the earth, reducing pollution, responsible forestry, and conserving water and energy. However, it also includes making the natural world more liveable for human beings, for example by constructing water wells for the poor, designing better and more efficient ways to farm and harvest crops, building shelters, homes, and cities, and using tools and technology to improve the quality of life.[115] Improvement of the non-human creaturely world includes such things as caring for endangered species, intervening in the spread of disease, population control, and preventing the cruel treatment and exploitation of animals. Responsible self-improvement includes a range of life-enhancing changes, from correcting and improving vision and hearing, to curing sickness through innovations in natural/organic health care and pharmaceutical advancement, to improving the body's immune system through immunization and healthier lifestyles, to the eradication of disease (e.g., past examples include small pox and polio), to surgery, and perhaps even genetic intervention.[116]

Human beings are called to exercise dominion over all of creation, yet creation is enormous and the needs are seemingly endless. As finite beings we must set priorities and make wise choices within those priorities. Two biblical metaphors provide broad guidance in setting our priorities for care and service of creation. First, scripture depicts human beings as priests of creation (Gen 1; 1 Pet 3:9; Rev 5:9–10). As priests they function as God's representatives and thus aim to discern, communicate, and equip others to achieve God's creative, re-

---

[113] Peterson helpfully reflects, "Beavers build a dam across a stream to create a lake to protect their lodges and make trees more accessible for food. They transform the ecosystem in which they live. That is their nature. Human beings build a dam across a river to protect their homes and provide easier access to water and irrigated food crops. That is part of our nature. Our actions can be destructive of ourselves and the rest of God's world, but they are not inherently destructive or unnatural simply because they bring about change." Peterson, *Changing Human Nature*, 32.

[114] Peterson, *Changing Human Nature*, 10.

[115] See Peterson, *Changing Human Nature*, 52–64.

[116] For an intriguing and informed argument in favour of genetic intervention, stemming from a detailed analysis of the salient biomedical and theological issues, see Peterson, *Changing Human Nature*, 80–98. As the book unfolds, Peterson provides helpful guidelines for safe and responsible genetic intervention and improvement.

demptive, and eschatological purposes. Yet since part of God's purposive will is for human beings to live in freedom and responsibility, the priestly role of discerning, communicating, and equipping others to achieve God's purposes aims not to control others through rules and coercive power but to help others to appreciate and cultivate godly values and character (rules and limited coercive governmental power have their proper place within this broader mandate). Knowledge of both God's person/character and God's world (i.e., scientific knowledge of how things work) are paramount to this priestly task.

Second, Scripture depicts human beings as stewards of God's creation. Matthew 25 includes three parables that set broad parameters for how followers of Jesus should prioritize and employ their time and resources while awaiting Christ's return.[117] The first parable (the ten virgins) exhorts Jesus's followers to be ready for his imminent return. It reminds us that our time to serve and represent our Master may be quite long, but we must remain vigilant in active and faithful service in the meantime. The second parable, which is the parable of the talents, describes what we should be doing as we remain vigilant in active and faithful service. Specifically, we should be using our remaining time to multiply and employ our God-given resources. Each of us has a different mix of talents, gifts, wealth, and resources. The primary issue is not what we have, but how we use what we have. God expects us to invest all that we are and have in the extension of God's kingdom, to the very best of our ability. The key notion here is investment, which means that we are expected not simply to use our gifts or spend and enjoy our resources, but to exercise active creativity and ingenuity to multiply them for God's service. What kind of investment will multiply our gifts and resources for God's service and kingdom? The final parable of the sheep and the goats answers this question. In this parable, God's people are recognized as those who used their time and resources to care for the needs of fellow human beings, especially those who are vulnerable or who are alienated from others (i.e., the hungry and thirsty, the homeless, the naked, the sick, and those in prison). In summary, we are to serve as God's stewards by our active faithfulness to Christ in the alignment of our priorities and goals, as demonstrated by our efforts to employ and multiply our gifts and resources in his service, which especially includes caring for other human beings in need.

Finally, as faithful priests and stewards of God's new creation we align ourselves under God's primary commands, which are to love God with all of our heart, mind, soul, and strength, and to love our neighbours as ourselves. Our charge is to be priests and stewards over all of creation, but in light of the Great Commandments our priority is to serve God and fellow human beings. God loves all of creation, which includes the entire *cosmos* and not just human beings (John 3:16).[118] But God loves human beings in a special and unique way as

---

[117] I am here drawing insights from Peterson's discussion of Matthew 25 in *Changing Human Nature*, 33–35.

[118] Peterson, *Changing Human Nature*, 15.

unique image bearers and covenant partners. By God's creative design we are stewards and priests of creation, but even more importantly we are God's beloved children created to be in relationship with God and one another (see chapter 3).[119] Thus, while our mandate includes caring for everything that God has made, our top priority is to love God by caring for and serving other human beings.

Concluding Summary

This chapter concludes my theological reflections on anthropology in trinitarian perspective. Following chapters three and four, which respectively depicted human persons as relational and rational creatures, this chapter depicted human persons as eschatological creatures that are created, redeemed, reoriented, and transformed to be God's steward-priests of creation/new creation. I then discussed the eschatological-ethical dimension of human existence in terms of serving the kingdom of God in the power of the Spirit and proposed an eschatological qualification of teleological ethics. I ended with some reflections on the continuing call to sustain, restore, and improve the world in light of the dawning new creation. We now move forward to the constructive section on ecclesiology, which builds upon the insights developed in this section and draws out implications for the church as relational, rational, and eschatological communities of the new humanity.

---

[119] See also R. Paul Stevens, *The Other Six Days: Vocation, Work, and Ministry in Biblical Perspective* (Grand Rapids: Eerdmans; Vancouver: Regent College, 2000), 89–104.

Part III: The Church as Communities of the New Humanity

CHAPTER 6

The Church as Relational Communities of Love

Introduction

The church as communities of the new humanity

The aim of this book is to explore the significance of theological anthropology for ecclesiology. I began in chapter 1 by describing our contemporary culture's confusion concerning what it means to be human. I argued that our inability to define what it means to be human has devastating long-term implications, including the dissolution of community, the disintegration and dichotomization of personal and social ethics, and the collapse of social and global justice. In chapter 2, I provided an overview of six dominant typological ways of construing community, based on conflicting views of the human person that are implicitly (and sometimes explicitly) operative in contemporary culture, and then related each type to present expressions of the church. I observed that all of these contemporary types share two common problems, namely reductionism and dualism. Moreover, any ecclesiology that uncritically adopts the contemporary assumptions about being human will consequently struggle to articulate coherently the nature of the church's sociality and the intrinsic relation of the church to personal, social, and global ethics. I suggested that what is needed to understand and frame ecclesiology properly is a theologically and practically thick account of what it means to be human, which clarifies and integrates the intrinsically social-personal and ethical-spiritual character of genuine, redeemed human existence. In chapters 3–5, I offered such an account, describing human beings as relational, rational, and eschatological creatures to whom God relates by creating, reconciling, and transforming them, thereby drawing them to participate in God's own triune life and mission. The present chapter marks the beginning of the third and final section, which in parallel with the previous three chapters will construct an ecclesiology that depicts the church as relational, rational, and eschatological communities of the new humanity. I will not attempt to say everything that can be said about the church, but will restrict my focus to what are in my view the most significant and relevant implications of viewing ecclesiology in light of theological anthropology.

Before we progress further, it is appropriate to pause and ask whether the New Testament provides warrant for referring to the church as the new humanity. I believe that it does, but it is important to point out that the description of the church as the new humanity is less the result of finding such terminology in proof texts than it is an overall hermeneutical framework that brings together several themes and trajectories of Scripture. Nevertheless, several New Testament texts taken together provide an initial precedent for such terminology and a starting point from which a more developed theology of the church as the new humanity can emerge.

First, the New Testament describes Jesus Christ as the new human being. Romans 5:12–21 and 1 Corinthians 15:45–49 depict Christ as the second Adam, the one who lived a uniquely genuine and faithful human existence before God and thus made possible the renewal and redemption of all human beings. Moreover, Scripture teaches that while human beings were created to reflect God's image, Jesus Christ is the only human being ever to reflect God's image fully and perfectly (2 Cor 4:4; Col 1:15; Heb 1:3). Christ is therefore the prototypical human being in whose image redeemed human beings are being renewed and transformed (Rom 8:29; 1 Cor 15:49; 2 Cor 3:18; 1 John 3:2). Second, the New Testament depicts redeemed persons as renewed human beings "in Christ" by the Spirit, both personally as new men and women and corporately as the new humanity, which is the church. In terms of personal renewal, Romans 5 says that because we are "in Christ" we now live in triumph over sin and death (Rom 5:17). Romans 6 goes on to teach that in baptism we were united with Christ in his death, burial, and resurrection. We have therefore died to sin and have been given a new kind of life, a life that is "in Christ" and immersed in the Spirit (Rom 8). Ephesians 4:24 instructs believers to put on the "new human", which has been created according to the likeness of God in righteousness and holiness. Colossians 3:10 likewise instructs believers to put on the "new human", which is being renewed in knowledge according to the image of its creator.[1] In terms of corporate renewal, Galatians 3:27–28 says that we were united in Christ at baptism and made like him; consequently, there is no longer a distinction between Jew and Gentile, male and female, slave and free, as all are one in Christ. Romans 12:5 says that we who are many are one body in Christ and 1 Corinthians 10:17 likewise says that we are one bread and body in Christ. In Ephesians 2:14–15, Paul argues that Christ has brought peace between Jews and Gentiles, having abolished their enmity in his flesh and created in himself one new person (the church). In summary, by means of his redemptive work Christ has achieved for human beings their objective renewal, reconciliation, righteousness, holiness, and peace. Christ has thereby disclosed and enabled a new way to be human; moreover, he has created "in" and for himself a new humanity (the church).

---

[1] The *NLT* speaks of the "new nature" and Eugene Petersons renders the phrase simply "new life." *Holy Bible, New Living Translation* (Wheaton: Tyndale House, 1996); Eugene Peterson, *The Message: The New Testament in Contemporary English* (Colorado Springs: NavPress, 1993).

The church as relational communities of love

In chapter three I described the human being as a relational creature invited to participate in the communion of the Trinity by sharing in the ecstatic love of God. However, in their sinfulness human beings reject this intended communion with God and, as a consequence, turn in upon themselves and experience alienation from God and other human beings. Accordingly, Christ's redemptive work includes a relational objective, which is to reverse the *cor curvum in se* (heart turned in upon itself), renew human openness to God and others, and thus make a way for reconciliation and peace. Since human redemption involves the *reconciliation* of human beings with both God and other human beings, it is an inherently social reality that aims to establish genuinely life-giving *relationships* with God and other human beings. The church is the community that God establishes to embody and promote God's reconciliatory purposes among human beings. It is the place where redeemed and reconciled human beings live with and for each other "in Christ" in the unity and power of the Holy Spirit. And it is the community that seeks, in and by Spirit, to draw all human beings into its fellowship, in its reconciliatory mission of attaining peace and extending God's family to the entire human race. It thus serves the advancement of God's one, new humanity. Its concrete embodiment takes a multiplicity of forms and thus does not destroy cultural and racial diversity (recall from chapter 5 that cultural expression is part of the human mandate), though it does seek by God's grace and power to redeem and transform sinful forms of cultural expression (e.g., ethnocentricity). The church is therefore both a means *and* an end, both an instrument *and* a goal. It is a means/instrument because it serves God's mission and message of reconciliation. Yet it is also an end/goal because it embodies and experiences that which it serves and proclaims. By God's grace it already *is* what it is becoming, existing as a proleptic sign and foretaste of its ultimate eschatological destiny—a community of human beings living in perfect communion with God and others in the new creation.[2] This chapter will unpack the theme of the church as relational communities of love, first by exploring the church's inner community life and then by suggesting implications for the church's engagement with the world.

Inner community life of the church

The theological basis of Christian community

Union with each other in Christ by the Spirit
Christian community is not fundamentally a human achievement, but is an objective reality "in Christ" that is increasingly realized subjectively "in the Spir-

---

[2] See also my comments below, in light of Bonhoeffer, that Christian community in the church is not an ideal to be accomplished by human effort, but a divine *reality* in Christ in which we are invited to participate by the Spirit.

it."³ By the power of the Spirit, Jesus Christ has achieved on our behalf reconciliation with God and other human beings.⁴ Because of Christ's work, we now have communion with each other through our union with Christ in the fellowship of the Spirit.⁵ Accordingly, Dietrich Bonhoeffer argues that Christian community is not a human ideal, but a divine reality in Christ.⁶ It is not a "dream world" defined by cozy feelings, "blissful experiences", or "exalted moods", in which everyone behaves exactly as we would like. Rather, genuine Christian community is messy; it brings us into fellowship with real human persons who are different from us, who possess different gifts and passions than we do, who are sometimes emotionally and spiritually wounded because of their past experiences, and who struggle with various sins and temptations. Pursuing true community involves undergoing a process of disillusionment concerning our own ideals, which are actually an impediment to genuine community. Only then can we break through to the fellowship that Christ establishes in the Spirit.⁷ Bonhoeffer writes,

> Every human idealized image that is brought into the Christian community is a hindrance to genuine community and must be broken up so that genuine community can survive. Those who love their dream of a Christian community more than the Christian community itself become destroyers of that Christian community even though their personal intentions may be ever so honest, earnest, and sacrificial.⁸

What Bonhoeffer is pointing out is that by pursuing an idealized dream of Christian community, we are in danger of excluding the actual people that God has put in our lives. We either exclude them from the start because they do not

---

³ This is not to endorse a radical separation of the objective work of Christ and the subjective work of the Spirit. Indeed, the Spirit enabled Christ to complete his objective work and was fully operative in every moment on every level. Moreover, it is *Jesus Christ* whom believers subjectively encounter in the Spirit. My point here is simply that Christian community is something created objectively on our behalf, which we enter and realize more fully over time. It thus follows the same New Testament indicative-imperative pattern as justification and sanctification, grace and works, and the transformation of heart and character/life.

⁴ Rom 5:1; 2 Cor 5:18–21; Eph 2:14, 16, 19; Col 1:19–22; 1 Pet 2:10; 1 John 4:9–12.

⁵ 1 Cor 12:4, 13; 2 Cor 13:13; Eph 4:3–4; Phil 2:1.

⁶ Dietrich Bonhoeffer, *Life Together*, vol. 5 of *Dietrich Bonhoeffer Works*, ed. Geffrey B. Kelly, trans. Daniel W. Bloesch and James H. Burtness (Minneapolis: Fortress, 1996), 35–38.

⁷ Bonhoeffer argues that Christian community is empowered and led by the Holy Spirit, not by human emotion, charisma, or strategic intelligence, and political manoeuvring. In addition, it is characterized by spiritual (*agape*) love, rather than emotional and self-centred (*eros*) love. Bonhoeffer, *Life Together*, 38–40, 42–44.

⁸ Bonhoeffer, *Life Together*, 36.

fit our idealized picture (perhaps our desired demographic?), or we gradually become frustrated and angry with others when they fail to meet our expectations of them. Sometimes, we fall into despair and then doubt whether pursuing Christian community is even worthwhile. As Bonhoeffer says, we "first become accusers of other Christians in the community, then accusers of God, and finally the desperate accusers of [ourselves]."[9] Bonhoeffer warns that even pastors must exercise caution in this regard, being vigilant in resisting the temptation to complain about their congregations. "Congregations have not been entrusted to them in order that they should become accusers of their congregations. . . ." When they "begin to make accusations against it, they had better examine themselves first to see whether the underlying problem is not their own idealized image, which should be shattered by God."[10] Instead, Bonhoeffer encourages pastors to intercede for their congregations before God with faith and gratitude. To clarify, Bonhoeffer is not rejecting efforts to make plans for the community or to set goals concerning its spiritual growth or mission. The New Testament is full of exhortations encouraging the church toward spiritual growth and mission. What he is cautioning against is our sinful tendency of desiring to fashion others into our own image and subjecting them to our own plans and agendas (in this case plans and agendas concerning our ideal Christian community). Such idealizing betrays either a desire to control others (a will to power) or an unhealthy tendency toward enmeshment or co-dependency, which desires and needs others for one's own self-fulfillment in a way that does not sufficiently respect their otherness and integrity as unique persons whom God is fashioning according to God's own image.

To guard against such idealizing, Bonhoeffer emphasizes that we find genuine Christian community *only in and through Christ*. He writes,

> I have community with others and will continue to have it only through Jesus Christ. The more genuine and the deeper our community becomes, the more everything else between us will recede, and the more clearly and purely will Jesus Christ and his work become the one and only thing that is alive between us. We have one another only through Christ, but through Christ we really do *have* one another. We have one another completely and for all eternity.[11]

Bonhoeffer develops three implications of this affirmation.[12] First, Christians need others in community for the sake of Jesus Christ. By God's intended design, the gospel message comes not directly from God to us individualistically; rather, it comes to us interpersonally through other human beings who proclaim

---

[9] Bonhoeffer, *Life Together*, 36.
[10] Bonhoeffer, *Life Together*, 37–38.
[11] Bonhoeffer, *Life Together*, 34.
[12] Bonhoeffer, *Life Together*, 31–33.

it to us and thereby draw us unto into community with Christ and each other. Our need for Christian community thus reflects the thoroughly relational character of human existence—from creation, through redemption, to eschatological transformation. Furthermore, Christians constantly need other believers to speak Christ's word to them, in order to receive encouragement, nourishment, hope, and assurance. Second, a Christian comes to others only through Jesus Christ. Bonhoeffer reminds us that Christ himself is our peace; it is only in him that we are one body. He writes, "He is the mediator, not only between God and human persons, but also between person and person, and between person and reality."[13] Christ alone is our Mediator, which means that Christ *unites us together* in himself but also that Christ *comes between us* in order to preserve our unique identity and otherness. Since we come into genuine communion with others only through Christ, it is Christ to whom we are primarily accountable and whom we ultimately seek to honour in our relationships. Accordingly, Christ's mediation preserves both genuine community and genuine individuality. Explaining further, Bonhoeffer argues that Christ has abolished all immediacy in human relationships. All seemingly immediate or direct relationships are built upon an illusion; it is only through Christ's mediation that genuine relationships with others are possible.[14] Bonhoeffer writes,

> Ever since Jesus called, there are no longer natural, historical, or experiential unmediated relationships for his disciples. Christ is the mediator between son and father, between husband and wife, between individual and nation, whether they can recognize him or not. There is no way from us to others than the path through Christ, his word, and our following him. Immediacy is a delusion.[15]

In and by the Spirit, Christ comes in between us to bind us together, to preserve our legitimate separateness, and to direct our first love and loyalty to God. As Volf expresses it, God's relation to every human person "keeps the human being as person either from dissolving in the stream of its multiple relationships, or from disintegrating into 'a transtemporal society' of 'moments of selfhood.'"[16] Third, Christian community is found only in and through Christ because Christians are elected and accepted in Christ together with the whole church from eternity (Eph 1). In the incarnation, cross, and resurrection, Christ took us into himself and made us his Body. According to God's eternal plan, we are elected *together in Christ* from all eternity and one day will live *togeth-*

---

[13] Bonhoeffer, *Life Together*, 33. See also Dietrich Bonhoeffer, *Discipleship*, vol. 4 of *Dietrich Bonhoeffer Works*, ed. Geffrey B. Kelly and John D. Godsey, trans. Barbara Green and Reinhard Krauss (Minneapolis: Fortress, 2001), 94–99.
[14] Bonhoeffer, *Discipleship*, 93–94.
[15] Bonhoeffer, *Discipleship*, 95.
[16] Miroslav Volf, *After Our Likeness: The Church as the Image of the Trinity* (Grand Rapids: Eerdmans, 1998), 183.

er with Christ in eternal community. Bonhoeffer is here describing election in Barthian terms, but one could affirm that believers are elected together in Christ regardless of one's interpretation of the election of individuals (e.g., Calvinist, Arminian, Wesleyan).

Participating in the Trinity
As I argued in the previous section, we do not create or achieve Christian community because we are *already* in community in Christ by the Spirit, but this does not imply that we should be passive or inactive concerning it. By God's grace and power we can *participate* in what God is doing to establish community among us. We can participate by seeking it, proclaiming it, living it out, and inviting others to join it by pointing them to its true foundation and head, Jesus Christ. The New Testament speaks of Christians experiencing the *koinōnia* of the Holy Spirit, a word which is often translated "fellowship" but also includes the idea of partnership or participation.[17] To experience the fellowship of the Holy Spirit is not just to commune with the Spirit, individually and corporately; it is actually to *participate* in the Spirit and thereby to experience communion with God and each other. The same Spirit who proceeds as the mutual love between the Father and the Son, thus completing or perfecting the ecstatic and perichoretic relational unity of the Trinity, also unites Christian brothers and sisters together by drawing them to share in the divine Love, and thereby to participate in God's own trinitarian life.[18] By participating in the Spirit, Christians share together in the trinitarian love of the Father, Son, and Holy Spirit. As Grenz puts it, "Through the Spirit, we participate in the love that lies at the heart of the triune God himself."[19] Or as James Torrance exclaims, "By sharing in Jesus' life of communion with the Father in the Spirit, we are given to participate in the Son's eternal communion with the Father"

---

[17] I. Howard Marshall, *New Testament Theology: Many Witnesses, One Gospel* (Downers Grove: InterVarsity Press, 2004), 290.

[18] By using the words completing and perfecting I do not mean to imply that the Spirit came into existence after the Father and Son; indeed the procession of both the Son and the Spirit are eternal. Rather, the Spirit's uniting activity as Love *eternally* completes and perfects the love of the Father and Son. In any case, the focus on *perichoretic* union shifts the discussion from essential origins to eternal relations. See Thomas F. Torrance, *The Christian Doctrine of God: One Being Three Persons* (New York: T & T Clark, 1996), 175–80. Later Torrance writes, "Properly understood, then, when it is said that the Spirit proceeds from the Father and the Son, or from the Father through the Son, what is meant is that the Spirit proceeds from the Community of Being of the Father and the Son, or from the Communion (Κοινωνία) between the Father and the Son which the Holy Spirit himself is, and the three Divine Persons are in their eternal perichoretic relations with each other" (192).

[19] Stanley J. Grenz, *Theology for the Community of God* (Grand Rapids: Eerdmans, 1994), 484. See also Volf, *After Our Likeness*, 128–29.

and hence in the trinitarian life of God.[20] Through their sharing and participating together in the love of the Trinity, Christian brothers and sisters have unity in the Spirit and the church community begins to reflect the communion of the triune God.

In this sense, the church community images the Trinity and God's own trinitarian life becomes a model for human relationships in the church. For example, from a trinitarian perspective Christian unity should not be confused with uniformity or homogeneity; genuine Christian oneness is unity-in-diversity and genuine Christian community is built upon the distinctiveness of individual persons-in-relationship.[21] While the church should not be conceived as a uniform collective, neither should it be conceived as a mere association of individuals. Trinitarian fellowship means that our bond goes much deeper than formal associative or contractual ties. Being bound together in the Spirit, we have become united in a way that is analogous (but not identical) to the unity of Father and Son. As Jesus prayed to the Father, "My prayer for all of them is that they will be one, just as you and I are one, Father—that just as *you are in me* and *I am in you*, so *they will be in us*, and the world will believe you sent me" (John 17:21; emphasis added).[22] Volf argues that the nature of Christian unity is obscured in both Catholicism, which tends toward uniformity, and typical Free Church models, which tend to envision the church as a group of already converted and saved Christians uniting into an associative fellowship by *their own* covenant with each other.[23] In place of both the former, which corresponds

---

[20] James B. Torrance, "The Doctrine of the Trinity in Our Contemporary Situation," in *The Forgotten Trinity*, ed. Alasdair I.C. Heron (London: BCC/CCBI Inter-Church House, 1989), 7. Quoted in Stanley J. Grenz, *The Social God and the Relational Self: A Trinitarian Theology of the Imago Dei* (Louisville: Westminster John Knox, 2001), 325.

[21] Volf, *After Our Likeness*, 192–98. See also Dietrich Bonhoeffer, *Sanctorum Communio: A Theological Study of the Sociology of the Church*, vol. 1 of *Dietrich Bonhoeffer Works*, ed. Clifford J. Green, trans. Reinhard Krauss and Nancy Lukens (Minneapolis: Fortress, 1998), 60, 83, 89–94; *Life Together*, 81–83.

[22] Consequently, Volf writes, "The correspondence between the trinitarian and ecclesial relationships is not simply formal. Rather, it is 'ontological' because it is soteriologically grounded. Jesus' high priestly prayer . . . presupposes communion with the triune God, mediated through faith and baptism, and aims at its eschatological consummation." Volf, *After Our Likeness*, 195.

[23] But see Brian Hamilton, "The Ground of Perfection: Sattler on the 'Body of Christ,'" in *New Perspectives in Believers Church Ecclesiology*, ed. Abe Dueck, Helmut Herder, and Karl Koop (Winnipeg: CMU, 2010), 143–60. While Hamilton acknowledges that an associative conception of the church unfortunately characterizes much of the believers church tradition, the tradition also includes voices that promote a more participatory model of church and ethics. For example, central to the theology of Michael Sattler was the theme of union with Christ by incorporation into the Body of Christ, which for Sattler theologically grounded both Christian community and Christian ethics.

more closely to monotheism (or subordinationism), and the latter, which corresponds more closely to tritheism, Volf sets out to construct a trinitarian Free Church ecclesiology that takes seriously a trinitarian, participatory model of church unity-in-diversity in Christ by the Spirit.

It is important to stress that the church images the Trinity metaphorically, not literally. Miroslav Volf, who endorses the notion of the church as the image of the Trinity, acknowledges, "It does not seem that the conceptualization process proceeds simply in a straight line from above (Trinity) to below (church and society) and that social reality is shaped in this way."[24] Volf qualifies the correspondence between church and Trinity with three observations.[25] First, in contrast to divine unity, human beings need to cultivate a will for unity and a covenant to bind them together. Second, ecclesial communion is not yet full and consummated. Third, human beings do not indwell other persons, as do the divine persons (and as the Spirit does in humans). As I argued in the preceding paragraph, is it only by virtue of our participation in the Spirit's uniting love and presence that Christians become united in Christ. It is possible for us to be together "in Christ" only because the Spirit is "in" each of us. As Volf argues, "It is not the mutual perichoresis of human beings, but rather the indwelling of the Spirit common to everyone that makes the church into a communion corresponding to the Trinity, a communion in which personhood and sociality are equiprimal."[26] The Holy Spirit opens Christians to one another and allows them to become what Volf calls "catholic persons", who in their individual uniqueness both give and receive, both influence and are shaped, in their relationships with others.[27] Consequently, the church does not reflect the image of the Trinity simply because it is a community that tries to imitate the triune relationships.[28] It reflects the image of the Trinity because it is comprised of individual exocentric human beings whom the Spirit of God indwells and thereby frees to love and serve God and others genuinely. Just as God created individual human beings in the divine image to be other-centred and to find their fulfilment in relationship with God and other human beings (see chapter 3), so now God redeems and transforms human beings to cultivate relational fulfilment with God and others in the church community (though complete fulfilment awaits escha-

---

[24] Volf, *After Our Likeness*, 194.
[25] Volf, *After Our Likeness*, 207–11.
[26] Volf, *After Our Likeness*, 213.
[27] Volf, *After Our Likeness*, 212. See also Grenz, *The Social God and the Relational Self*, 326, 334.
[28] As I noted in chapter 3, what I am proposing is a modified form of social trinitarianism, which proceeds not simply from Trinity to human community but from Trinity through theological anthropology and soteriology to ecclesial community.

tological consummation).²⁹ This model of trinitarian-ecclesial correspondence provides a theological framework to support Luther's assertion that "a Christian lives not in himself, but in Christ and in his neighbour. Otherwise he is not a Christian. He lives in Christ through faith, in his neighbour through love".³⁰ As Luther observed, this notion of living "in Christ" and "in" one's neighbour has important implications for practical Christian life and ethics, as we will discuss later in the chapter.

One implication of the foregoing discussion of Christian life as participating together in the life of the Trinity is that Christian soteriology must be conceived relationally rather than merely individualistically. As Bonhoeffer asserts, "Whoever seeks to become a new human being individually cannot succeed. To become a new human being means to come into the church, to become a member of Christ's body."³¹ Volf explains that if salvation were to take place between God and the individual soul then it would be individualistic and functionalist. Consequently, church membership could not be an expression of what Christians *are*, but only a pragmatic implication of what they should *do*.³² Conversely, while Christian salvation certainly includes the redemption of individuals (an affirmation that preserves the importance of personal intimacy with and loyalty to God) it also necessarily has a corporate dimension. The same redemptive act that delivers human beings from sin and death also places them into communion with God and each other. They are therefore redeemed *together*, not in isolation. As the first letter of Peter portrays it, as we come to Christ God is building us "as living stones" into a spiritual temple and reconstitutes us as God's new people (1 Pet 2:5, 9–10). Accordingly, as Grenz writes,

> As this occurs, the church serves as a community of salvation. Thereby, it truly becomes a fellowship of those whose relationships are being transformed by the power of the indwelling Spirit to reflect as far as possible in the midst of the brokenness of the present the eschatological community modeled after the fullness of love present within the dynamic of the triune God.³³

Being in the church is *intrinsically* related to the believer's salvation; it is not just a secondary application—not because the church is an institutional dis-

---

[29] Grenz, *The Social God and the Relational Self*, 325–28, 334–36. Grenz writes, "The self emerges *extra se* in that participation 'in Christ' constitutes the identity of participants in the new humanity" (326).

[30] Martin Luther, *On Christian Liberty*, trans. W.A. Lambert and Harold J. Grimm (Minneapolis: Fortress, 2003), 62.

[31] Bonhoeffer, *Discipleship*, 219. Elsewhere Bonhoeffer argues, "For this much is certain: there is no community with Jesus Christ other than the community with his body! It is in this body alone that we are accepted and able to find salvation." (216)

[32] Volf, *After Our Likeness*, 172.

[33] Grenz, *The Social God and the Relational Self*, 335. See also Grenz, *Theology*, 481.

penser of salvation but because it is the community in which reconciliation is embodied and transformation takes place. It is the place in which redeemed human persons practice and live out concretely their restored relationships with God and others.

The church as the Body of Christ

One of the ways that the New Testament describes the corporate life of Christians is by depicting the church as the Body of Christ (Rom 12:3–8; 1 Cor 12:12–31; Eph 4:1–16; Col 1:15ff). According to George Ladd, this is the most distinctive Pauline metaphor for church and Guthrie views it as the most vivid and expressive one.[34] It is employed to convey several important truths. First, it depicts the oneness of the church in terms of unity-in-diversity.[35] On the one hand, although it is comprised of many members the church is essentially one. Every member is important and contributes to the functioning of the whole. Every member has been baptized into one Body and partakes in one Spirit. Just as the parts of the human body are linked together and function interdependently for the benefit of the entire body, so each member of the congregation is linked to the others and exists to serve the whole community. On the other hand, this oneness does not mean uniformity. The church is not a homogenous collective, but a community of distinct and inter-relating persons. Each person is uniquely called and gifted by the Holy Spirit to contribute to the congregation in some way. Every individual person is significant; in fact, each person's individuality or otherness enriches and edifies the group.[36]

The New Testament applies the body metaphor to the church both as a local congregation and as a universal entity.[37] In Paul's earlier letters the image refers to local congregations, but in Colossians and Ephesians it broadens in scope to include the church universal. Its application to the local congregation reflects the fact that each and every local congregation that meets the criteria for being a church is in fact fully a church.[38] Every congregation is a church in

---

[34] George E. Ladd, *A Theology of the New Testament*, ed. Donald A. Hagner (Grand Rapids: Eerdmans, 1993), 590; Donald Guthrie, *New Testament Theology* (Leicester: Inter-Varsity Press, 1981), 744.

[35] Marshall, *New Testament Theology*, 274–75.

[36] See Bonhoeffer, *Discipleship*, 220–21.

[37] Ladd, *Theology of the New Testament*, 592; Guthrie, *New Testament Theology*, 743; and Marshall, *New Testament Theology*, 462.

[38] Volf's defining criteria serve well: "Every congregation that assembles around the one Jesus Christ as Savior and Lord in order to profess faith in him publicly in pluriform fashion, including through baptism and the Lord's Supper, and which is open to all churches of God and to all human beings, is a church in the full sense of the word, since Christ promised to be present in it through his Spirit as the first fruits of the gathering of the whole people of God in the eschatological reign of God. Such a congregation is a holy, catholic, and apostolic church." Volf, *After Our Likeness*, 158 (original italics removed).

the full sense of the term because Christ is fully present to each by the Spirit.[39] Every church is therefore a microcosm of the whole rather than a part of the whole or, as Grenz puts it, every congregation is the "church in miniature" characterized by "all the lofty phrases used in the New Testament of 'the church.'"[40] At the same time, every genuine local congregation is related to every other local congregation and thus exists simultaneously as the church universal. Volf helpfully suggests that the tension between locality and universality is best resolved not in spatial terms such as a part-whole dynamic, but in eschatological terms of anticipation and fulfillment. He writes, "The local church is not a concrete realization of the existing universal church, but rather the real anticipation or proleptic realization of the eschatological gathering of the entire people of God."[41] All local churches are related in Christ because the same Spirit constitutes their existence and draws them toward their eschatological unity and catholicity. Volf argues that the church's catholicity parallels the catholicity of individual believers. Specifically, it is a spiritual catholicity attained in and by the Holy Spirit and characterized by openness toward all other churches (a kind of corporate exocentricity).[42] It is not an institutional catholicity guaranteed by ecclesiastical authority structures. As a defining mark of its existence, this catholic openness is an indispensable condition of a congregation's ecclesiality. A local church cannot claim to be a church in sectarian isolation from other churches.

Second, the image of the Body of Christ implies that all who serve by using their spiritual gifts are making an important contribution (Rom 12:3–8). There is no place in the church for spiritual elitism. While it is true that certain gifts are more foundational and formative for the whole community than others (1 Cor 12:27–31; Eph 4:11), each person is equal in value and dignity and should be treated with love and respect. In this regard, it is interesting to note that in both Romans 12 and 1 Corinthians 12–13, Paul follows his explanation of the proper functioning of spiritual gifts using the Body of Christ metaphor with a discussion of the primacy of love and humble service. What matters most is not the gift(s) one possesses (only God can be credited and glorified for that) but how one uses one's gift(s) to edify others as God leads and enables. Thus, Paul instructs church members to be self-aware, to know their own strengths and weaknesses and to exercise humility as they seek to make a contribution to the community (Rom 12). To do this, believers must appreciate the importance of

---

[39] Volf, *After Our Likeness*, 154–55.
[40] Grenz, *Theology*, 468.
[41] Volf, *After Our Likeness*, 140.
[42] Moreover, every congregation as a catholic community of the new humanity must be characterized by openness to all human beings, because Christ is the Saviour and Lord of all. See Volf, *After Our Likeness*, 156–58.

all of the gifts to the church community and seek guidance and mentoring from others as they learn to discern and use their own particular gifts.

The church as the Body of Christ thus lends support to the doctrine of the priesthood of all believers. The New Testament refers to the church as a "royal priesthood" and a "kingdom of priests", thereby universalizing the concept of priesthood and calling every believer into some kind of ministry. Properly speaking Christ alone is priest; when the term "priest" is applied to believers in the New Testament, it is always in the context of *all believers* who share vicariously in the priesthood of Christ (e.g., 1 Pet 2:5, 2:9; Rev 1:6, 5:10, 20:6). Moreover, the Old Testament distinctions of race, social status, and gender lose their significance as qualifying factors for priesthood.[43] Rather, the particular ministry to which a believer is called depends on her calling and gifting by the Holy Spirit.[44] By baptism and through the reception of the Holy Spirit, every believer becomes a priest, receives spiritual power and gifts, and is thereby called to minister in that power and giftedness both within and outside the church.[45]

Third, the image of the Body of Christ implies a close relationship with Christ, expressed in loyalty, obedience, and service to his desires and plans. In his earlier use of the image, in Romans and 1 Corinthians, Paul employs the body metaphor to describe the relationships between believers in terms of unity built upon diversity, mutual service, and loving interdependence. In his later letters, namely Colossians and Ephesians, he adds a new detail: Christ is the head of the body and thus the Lord of the church.[46] Christ is present in the church, yet he also transcends and surpasses it; the church is not simply an extension of the incarnation.[47] This development in Paul's use of the body meta-

---

[43] Stanley J. Grenz, "Biblical Priesthood and Women in Ministry," in *Discovering Biblical Equality: Complementarity Without Hierarchy*, ed. Ronald W. Pierce and Rebecca Merrill Groothuis (Downers Grove: InterVarsity Press, 2005), 278.

[44] As Paul writes, "Now there are different kinds of spiritual gifts, but it is the same Holy Spirit who is the source of them all . . . God manifests the Spirit through each person for the good of the entire church. . . . The Holy Spirit alone decides which gift a person should have" (1 Cor 12:4, 7, 11b).

[45] Miroslav Volf, *Work in the Spirit: Toward a Theology of Work* (Eugene: Wipf and Stock, 2001), 111–12. See also my article "Women Sharing in the Ministry of God: A Trinitarian Framework for the Priority of Spirit Gifting as a Solution to the Gender Debate," *Priscilla Papers* 22 (Autumn 2008): 14–15, 17.

[46] Bonhoeffer, *Discipleship*, 220.

[47] Guthrie, *New Testament Theology*, 746. In his early works, Bonhoeffer described the church in terms of "Christ existing as church-community." As his theology matured, he increasingly stressed Christ's otherness and transcendence over the community as its Counter-*Logos*, Lord, and Mediator, though he retained a strong incarnational emphasis on the presence of Christ in other human beings. He increasingly identified the church with its crucified Lord and portrayed it as a community of the cross. Moreo-

phor is probably in response to the rise of false teachers and heretical ideas, both of which tempted the churches to compromise their loyalty to Christ alone, their corresponding counter-cultural way of life, and their witness to the world.[48] Paul calls the church to remain faithful to its Lord.

In his discussion of the church as the Body of Christ, Bonhoeffer closely associates the presence of Christ with the church: "The church of Christ is Christ present through the Holy Spirit. . . . The life of believers in the church-community is truly *the life of Jesus Christ in them* (Gal 2:20; Rom 8:10; 2 Cor 13:5; 1 John 4:15)."[49] Moreover, since the church serves a *crucified* Lord it must therefore be a community of the cross, which is devoted to a cruciform pattern of discipleship and self-giving. He writes, "In the community of the crucified and transfigured body of Jesus Christ, we take part in Christ's suffering and glory. Christ's cross is laid upon the body of the church-community."[50] Christ said that his disciples would have to deny themselves daily, pick up their cross, and follow him (Matt 10:38; 16:24; see also Phil 2:5–11). Fittingly, Christians are baptized into Christ's death so that they can begin to share in his resurrection life (Rom 6; Phil 3:10–11). In his discussion of the Body of Christ in Romans 12, Paul says that Christians are called to offer their own bodies as living sacrifices to God and to care for others through mutual service, hospitality, forgiveness, and non-retaliation (they must deny themselves personal vengeance and instead commit to conquering evil with good). God promises to use their humility, weaknesses and dependency on God to accomplish God's own glorious purposes (2 Cor 11:16–33). Christians are also called to share each other's burdens (Gal 6:2), to give to those in need (Matt 5:42; 1 Cor 16:1–4; 2 Cor 8:1–15; 9:1–15; Eph 4:28), to endure humiliation for the sake of the gospel (1 Cor 1:18–2:5), and to suffer for the sake of righteousness, justice, and truth (Matt 5:10–12; 2 Thess 1:1–18; 1 Pet 3:13–22; 4:12–19). Just as Christ suffered vicariously for us, so we are called to a ministry of "vicarious repre-

---

ver, he shifts his focus from Christ simply "existing as church community" to Christ taking concrete form in the church.

[48] In the case of Colossians, Marshall suggests that Paul was confronting a misleading philosophy (and its teachers), which combined certain Jewish elements together with Asian religion. One aspect of this religion was a belief in spiritual powers which threatened human life and needed to be placated through worship and ascetic practices. In response (Col 1–2), Paul presents Christ as the creator of all that exists and the supreme ruler over all powers, spiritual or otherwise, which he disarmed by means of the cross. Christ is the head of the Church, and supports it, holds it together, and makes it grow. Therefore, Paul exhorts the Colossians to "continue to live in him, rooted and built up in him, strengthened in the faith as you were taught, and overflowing with thankfulness" (Col 2:6b–7). See Marshall, *New Testament Theology*, 366–69.

[49] Bonhoeffer, *Discipleship*, 221.

[50] Bonhoeffer, *Discipleship*, 221.

sentative action" by suffering with and for others.[51] In so doing, by the grace and power of the Spirit we bring the concrete presence of Christ to other human beings. As Luther put it, we become "little Christs" to them.

Relational ministries of the church

Viewing the church as a relational community of love highlights several important relational ministries to which the church is called. First, the church is called to the ministry of reconciliation. It is to be the community ruled by the love and peace of Christ, which comes between members to resolve their differences and settle their conflicts (Col 4:15). It is therefore a community of confession and forgiveness. Jesus told his disciples that they would receive forgiveness as they themselves forgave others who offended them and Paul says that we are to extend mercy and forgiveness just as we have received mercy and forgiveness from God (Matt 6:14; Col 4:12–13). As a community of justified sinners, rather than an idealized utopia of perfect people, the church consists of people who have received forgiveness and acceptance in Christ and who extend that same forgiveness and acceptance to others. As Bonhoeffer says, the church is "the community of those who have truly experienced God's costly grace, and who thereby live a life worthy of the gospel which they neither squander nor discard."[52] It is not thereby a place that avoids conflict or downplays the hurt caused by sin; rather, it aims to resolve conflict truthfully, lovingly, and graciously.[53] Sometimes discipline is necessary, as when the church has to stand by a victim and against an unrepentant offender, but such discipline should be offered in love and in hope of repentance and reconciliation (Matt 18:15–20; Jas 5:19–20).[54] It is also a community of social reconciliation, one which breaks down dividing walls that separate people and divide them into hierarchical classes of privileged and unprivileged, according to their race, nationality, gender, and socio-economic status (Gal 3:26–28; Jas 2:1–9). As Paul writes to the Corinthians, we must no longer evaluate others by what the world thinks of them, but instead see them in light of the new creation as brothers and sisters in Christ (2 Cor 5:16–17).

---

[51] Vicarious representative action is a theme in Bonhoeffer (e.g., *Discipleship*, 90, 222).

[52] Bonhoeffer also writes, "The community of saints is not the 'ideal' church-community of the sinless and perfect. It is not the church-community of those without blemish, which no longer provides room for the sinner to repent. Rather it is the church-community that shows itself worthy of the gospel of the forgiveness of sins by truly proclaiming God's forgiveness, which has nothing to do with forgiving oneself." Bonhoeffer, *Discipleship*, 269.

[53] This includes working with experienced experts (doctors, therapists, mental health experts, lawyers, etc.) when facing more serious situations.

[54] As Bonhoeffer notes, it is important to proclaim both forgiveness and repentance, both faith and obedience together as one reality in following Christ (*Discipleship*, 269; see also Bonhoeffer's discussion of cheap and costly grace, 43–56).

The Church as Relational Communities of Love

Second, the church is called to the ministry of mutual edification. As previously discussed, the church as the Body of Christ promotes the priesthood of all believers. It actively seeks to discern the gifts and abilities of its members and encourage people to serve accordingly. Some forms of service focus on the worship gathering and everything involved in making it happen. Other forms of service take place in the daily life of the community, such as one-on-one mentoring and discipling, small group ministry, hospitality, encouragement, spiritual friendship and accountability, and actively welcoming and integrating new members into the community. In the context of mutual edification, the role of the pastor is to be a shepherd and an equipper. As a shepherd, the pastor personally knows and cares for the flock. As part of their care, pastors are aware of the needs and struggles of their congregants (so far as congregants are willing to confide) and seek appropriately and discerningly to be catalysts for care in the congregation by drawing others into ministry according to their gifts and maturity. In this way, pastoral care becomes not a solitary affair but a communal ministry. This requires pastors to be, primarily, equippers that strategically train all of God's people in the congregation for ministry in order to build up and edify the whole Body of Christ (Eph 4:12). Pastors are not primarily chaplains that care for many but without needing to develop a coherent strategy for leadership, ministry training and deployment.

Third, the church is called to the ministry of bearing one another's burdens.[55] This includes providing for those in need by sharing our resources and giving financially (Acts 2:43–47; 4:32–37; Matt 5:42; 6:1–4; 1 Cor 16:1–4; 2 Cor 8:1–15; 9:1–15; Eph 4:28). It includes bearing one another's emotional burdens by encouraging one another, strengthening each other's faith, and genuinely loving each other with actions and not just words (Rom 12:9; Col 4:16–17; 1 John 3:18; 4:11–12). It includes bearing each other's weaknesses and sinfulness by exhorting each other to holiness and keeping each other accountable (Matt 18:15–20; Rom 14; Gal 6:1–2; Heb 12:14–17). Moreover, it involves caring for the lonely, the sick, the elderly, and the oppressed (Matt 25:31–46; Acts 6:1–4; 1 Tim 4:1–16). It is important to remember that bearing the burdens of others is not a service that we perform paternalistically. As Murphy David of the Open Door ministry cautions: "Without supper, without love, without table companionship, justice can become a program that we *do* to other people."[56] Properly speaking, bearing the burdens of others is *Christ's* ministry in which we humbly participate by the Spirit. Moreover, it is a formative practice that gradually shapes us to be more like Christ, when pursued with the right motivation and attitude. Finally, bearing the burdens of others can be a source of joy, because

---

[55] See Bonhoeffer, *Life Together*, 100–103.
[56] Quoted in Christine D. Pohl, *Making Room: Recovering Hospitality as a Christian Tradition* (Grand Rapids: Eerdmans, 1999), 74.

in so doing we share in the sufferings of Christ by participating in his priestly ministry.[57]

Fourth, the church is called to a cruciform pattern of discipleship. It is called to be a community of the cross, which lives counter-culturally because of its loyal dedication to its crucified Lord (Matt 5–7; Rom 12:1–2). It will be characterized by distinct values and priorities, which align with God's kingdom purposes. It will aim to model God's character and pursue God's will in its life and mission. It will hold a different view of who is valuable and truly blessed (Matt 5:1–12), who is wise (1 Cor 1:18–31; Jas 3:13–18), who is successful (Matt 6:19–21; Luke 12:13–34; 18:18–30), and who is genuinely holy, righteous, and full of faith (Matt 6:1–18; Mark 7:1–23; Luke 7:1–10; 36–50; 9:46–48; John 4:43–54). Moreover, it will model a different approach to leadership, namely servant leadership characterized by humility, grace, and self-giving (Matt 20:20–28; Mark 9:33–37; 10:35–45; Phil 2:5–11). As a counter-cultural community of the cross, it will live in the midst of the world as salt, light, a city set on a hill (Matt 5:13–16), and a colony of citizens of heaven (Phil 3:17–21) or "resident aliens".[58] Sometimes it will be called to suffer persecution, as a result of living in faithfulness to Christ in a hostile environment (Matt 5:10–12; John 15:18–27; 1 Pet 4:12–19).

Constitutive and formative relational practices

The church is equipped for its relational ministry through constitutive and formative practices. Primary among these are the constitutive ministries of the Word and the sacramental ordinances.[59] The ministries of the Word, baptism, and the Lord's Supper are constitutive for the church's existence, in other words they are its definitive marks, because they are fundamental to the crea-

---

[57] Bonhoeffer, *Life Together*, 102.

[58] See Stanley Hauerwas and William H. Willimon, *Resident Aliens: Life in the Christian Colony* (Nashville: Abingdon, 1993).

[59] The term "sacramental ordinance" is my own, reflecting my belief that these two constitutive and sustaining church rites are both sacramental and ordained. Their being sacramental means that they mediate God's presence and grace. In this view many things are sacramental, for example marriage, the church, and creation (see Robert W. Jenson, *Systematic Theology: Vol. 2: The Works of God* [New York: Oxford University Press, 1999], 251). Their being ordinances means that Christ himself specifically initiated and set apart baptism and the Lord's Supper to be special covenantal (Calvin), converting (Wesley), acts of commitment (Grenz). As sacramental ordinances, these practices draw believers into participating in deep mysteries in which God is at work. At the same time, they are a faithful response to Christ's specific commands: "Go and make disciples . . . baptizing them . . ." (Matt. 28:19); and "Do this in remembrance of me . . ." (Luke 22:19). In sum, I am using the term "sacrament" to stress mystery and participation in God's gracious activity and "ordinance" to stress the obedient faith response of the believer.

The Church as Relational Communities of Love

tion and extension of the church.[60] The proclamation of the Word (preached and witnessed) calls people to God and brings them together as a fellowship of the Word. Baptism marks their new birth (or regeneration) and their entrance into the fellowship, while the Lord's Supper sustains their communal life as the Body of Christ. These central ministries form and shape the church to be relational, rational, and eschatological communities of the new humanity, but here I will just touch briefly on their relational significance (see chapters 7 and 8 for their rational and eschatological significance respectively). The relational aspect of the ministry of the Word takes two forms. First, it takes the form of the preached Word, which addresses the congregation with the gospel of reconciliation. Preachers announce the good news that by God's grace people can be reconciled to God and to one another. Second, it takes the form of personal address, as Christian brothers and sisters share in the ministry of the Word by speaking God's Word to one another in order to teach, edify, encourage, correct, and rebuke each other in love. Bonhoeffer argues that Christians need other Christian brothers and sisters to speak God's Word to them because "the Christ in their own hearts is weaker than the Christ in the word of other Christians. Their own hearts are uncertain; those of their brothers and sisters are sure."[61] The ministry of the word is inherently relational, because it brings God's Word to us objectively; it comes from outside of ourselves from another and thus has a special power to cut through the darkness, doubt, and selfishness of our own self-enclosed hearts. One's subjective internal thoughts and feelings can obscure one's understanding of God's Word and will. An apt word from a wise Christian brother or sister provides helpful perspective, increased accountability, and perhaps even Spirit inspired guidance.

What about the sacramental ordinances? The relational significance of baptism is that through baptism believers ratify their union with Christ, thus affirming their trust and loyalty to Christ as Saviour and Lord, and come into communion with the counter-cultural community of faith. While believers' union with Christ is ratified in baptism, their union with other believers in the community of faith is ratified by entering into covenant with them.[62] The relational significance of the Lord's Supper is that believers regularly celebrate the real presence of Christ with them and the resulting communion they enjoy with one another "in Christ" by the Spirit.[63] Moreover, they remember and celebrate

---

[60] Volf, *After Our Likeness*, 152–53. Grenz refers to the sacraments as "community acts of commitment". For Grenz, baptism is the seal of Christian identity and depicts union with Christ, the forgiveness of sins, the transfer of loyalties, and entrance into the church. The Lord's Supper is a continual reaffirmation of Christian identity and loyalty to Christ. See Grenz, *Theology*, 511–40.
[61] Bonhoeffer, *Life Together*, 32.
[62] For the importance of community covenants, see Grenz, *Theology*, 480.
[63] Many Baptist theologians (and others in the tradition of congregational polity and ordinances) have moved closer to a sacramental understanding of baptism and the

God's act of *making peace* with and between them through the shed blood of Christ. Thus, "In receiving Christ's broken body and spilled blood, we, in a sense, receive all those whom Christ received by suffering."[64] In addition, the Lord's Supper as Holy Communion is a constant reminder that believers are to care for and support one another by sharing what they have with those in need (1 Cor 11:17–34). It thus reinforces the nature of the church as a community that breaks down dividing social, cultural, and economic walls of separation.[65]

Lord's Supper in the sense that these are not just statements of a believer's beliefs or symbols of an absent Christ. Rather, they are deep spiritual mysteries in which believers participate by the Holy Spirit in something that God is doing and in which Christ is really present in a special way (not least in that the gospel is embodied by them). For example, Thomas Finger, referring to his approach as "communal presence", writes, "The Eucharist . . . conveys Jesus' real, communal and memorial presence as a primary manifestation of grace birthing the new creation in visible communal form." Thomas N. Finger, *A Contemporary Anabaptist Theology: Biblical, Historical, Constructive* (Downers Grove: InterVarsity Press, 2004), 208. See also: Grenz, *Theology*, chapter 19; Donald G. Bloesch, *The Church: Sacraments, Worship, Ministry, Mission* (Downers Grove: InterVarsity, 2002), 149–75; and Clark H. Pinnock, *Flame of Love: A Theology of the Holy Spirit* (Downers Grove: InterVarsity Press, 1996), 113–47. In my view, we should reject false dichotomies that force us to choose between symbol and real presence, between remembrance of the past and celebration of present blessings, and between theological affirmations and ethical implications. A participatory model embraces each of these perspectives and provides them with an overarching framework that is sufficiently theological, Christological, and pneumatological—and hence fully trinitarian. Moreover, it accounts for the varied biblical concepts and metaphors associated with the sacramental ordinances. For example, Scripture depicts the Lord's Table as: "breaking of the bread" (Acts 2:42; Luke 24:30-31, 45), emphasizing the presence of the Risen Christ in the church; the Lord's "last supper" (1 Cor. 11:17-24; Matt. 22:1-14; Luke 14:15-24; Rev. 19:6-9), emphasizing our remembrance of God's past saving deeds (the cross, but also alluding to the Exodus and Passover) and their future completion (the eschatological banquet); "eucharist" (John 6:11; 1 Cor. 11:24), emphasizing our present offering of praise and thanksgiving; and "communion" (1 Cor. 10:16), emphasizing the mystical bond of our fellowship with Christ and other believers as we participate in the body and shed blood of Christ.

[64] Miroslav Volf, *Exclusion and Embrace: A Theological Explanation of Identity, Otherness, and Reconciliation* (Nashville: Abingdon, 1996), 129. See also Stanley Hauerwas, *In Good Company: The Church as Polis* (Notre Dame: University of Notre Dame Press, 1995), 40.

[65] Note that Paul's stern rebuke and warning to the Corinthians that some were partaking of the supper in an unworthy fashion and were thus incurring God's judgement on themselves (11:27–30) concerned their greediness and their failure to make sure everyone had enough to eat (see 11:17–22). His exhortation for believers to "examine themselves" does not refer primarily to a moment of private, inner confession (though in might lead to such examination by way of *application*); it refers rather to social sin against the Body of Christ and their need for repentance and reconciliation.

In addition to the church's constitutive practices, several other formative practices sustain the relational life of the church. One such practice is worship. Worship is a broad subject that concerns all of one's life (Rom 12:1) and can be discussed from many different angles. As a relational practice, however, worship draws believers together before God in the Spirit to rest in God's presence and to offer praise, adoration, and thanksgiving unto God. As James B. Torrance defines it, "worship is the gift of participating by the Spirit in the incarnate Son's communion with the Father."[66] It therefore serves to increase the community's intimacy with God and fills them with wonder over who God is and what God has done for them in Christ. In addition, the genuine practice of worship preserves the relational integrity of believers before God. In other words, genuine worship can be offered only by communities that are characterized by life-giving, holy, and God-honouring relationships between members. Jesus instructed his disciples that if they go to the temple to offer a sacrifice to God but remember that they have a dispute with a brother or sister, they should first go and be reconciled to that person before giving their offering to God (Matt 5:23–24). Bonhoeffer comments strongly on this passage, asserting that "Contempt for others makes worship dishonest and deprives it of any divine promise. Individuals as well as church communities who intend to enter God's presence with contemptuous or unreconciled hearts are playing games with an idol."[67] Such worship is idolatrous because it involves violating God's explicit command to love our neighbour and thus means pushing the true God out of the mind of the worshipper. It is therefore dishonest and false. As the first letter of John says, "anyone who does not love does not know God" and "anyone who claims to love God but hates a Christian brother or sister is a liar" (4:8, 20). In addition to loving others, Scripture teaches that genuine worship involves pursuing just and righteous relationships and communal arrangements—economically, sexually, socially, and politically (e.g., Isa 1:12–17; Amos 5; Mic 6:8; Rom 12–14; 1 Cor 6:9–20; Eph 5–6; Col 3–4).[68] Thus, genuine worship as a relational practice involves coming before God to offer praise with honest and open hearts, as faithful servants who aim to live our entire lives as a sacrifice of worship unto God by loving God with all that we are and have and by loving our neighbours as ourselves.

A number of other practices also serve the relational formation of Christian communities, including the disciplines of solitude, confession, submission, service, and prayer in the modes of confession and absolution, supplication, and

---

This aspect of the Lord's Supper is reflected strongly in the Anabaptist tradition. See, for example, Finger, *A Contemporary Anabaptist Theology*, 202–207.

[66] James B. Torrance, *Worship, Community & the Triune God of Grace* (Downers Grove: InterVarsity Press, 1996), 30.

[67] Bonhoeffer, *Discipleship*, 123.

[68] See also Bonhoeffer, *Discipleship*, 264–65.

intercession.[69] I will highlight just two of these presently. The practice of solitude is important because genuine community involves a dialectic interplay between the individual and the group, corresponding to time spent being alone and time spent in community. As Bonhoeffer warns, "Whoever cannot be alone should beware of community. . . . Whoever cannot stand being in community should beware of being alone."[70] The practice of solitude allows the individual to centre herself in God and resist being assimilated and overshadowed by the identity of the community and the expectations of others. It also helps the community as a whole to guard against harmful co-dependency and enmeshment. On the other hand, the practice of solitude exists not for its own sake but is intended to build and strengthen the community. As argued throughout this chapter, the Christian life is not a solitary existence but involves life in community in the Body of Christ. Solitude and community are both important and mutually enriching. Emphasizing one over the other is unhealthy. As Bonhoeffer says, "Each taken by itself has profound pitfalls and perils. Those who want community without solitude plunge into the void of words and feelings, and those who seek solitude without community perish in the bottomless pit of vanity, self-infatuation, and despair."[71]

The practice of confession is important to the integrity of the Christian community because it helps to preserve its honesty before God as well as healthy relationships between members. Confession can be practiced both corporately in worship, through song and liturgy, and individually in the form of one Christian brother or sister confessing to another in an accountability relationship. Bonhoeffer emphasizes the second form of confession, because confessing to another Christian helps break sinful patterns and habits.[72] It does this by bringing secret sins into the light to be exposed and disarmed of their power.[73] Additionally, it prevents the confessor from self-delusion, ensuring that the Christian is actually confessing *to God* through another concrete and objective person in order to seek *transformation*, and is not just confessing to herself in order to absolve her own guilty conscience. Moreover, the practice of confession brings both the confessor and the confidant before God and reinforces the mediation of Christ between them and thus the church's nature as a community

---

[69] For a good discussion of these practices, see Richard J. Foster, *The Celebration of Discipline: The Path to Spiritual Growth* (New York: Harper and Row, 1978) and *Prayer: Finding the Heart's True Home* (New York: HarperSanFrancisco, 1992).

[70] Bonhoeffer, *Life Together*, 82 (italics removed).

[71] Bonhoeffer, *Life Together*, 83.

[72] For Bonhoeffer's discussion of confession, see *Life Together*, 108–16.

[73] Bonhoeffer writes, "Sin wants to be alone with people. It takes them away from the community. The more lonely people become, the more destructive the power of sin over them. . . . Sin wants to remain unknown. It shuns the light. In the darkness of what is left unsaid sin poisons the whole being of a person." But, "sin that has been spoken and confessed has lost all its power." Bonhoeffer, *Life Together*, 110.

of gospel reconciliation. It serves to renew and restore their community *in Christ*. Finally, the practice of confession leads to a true sense of forgiveness and assurance of one's salvation. The practice of genuine confession can therefore foster a community that is characterized by humility, gratitude, thanksgiving, and joy. Bonhoeffer suggests two precautions concerning the practice of confession. First, only those who practice confession themselves should hear the confessions of others. They must be humble and gracious, knowing personally the forgiving and restoring touch of God's grace in their own lives. Second, we must not make confession into a meritorious transaction in which the confessor is believed to score points with God, so to speak. Instead, we confess because we are assured in the gospel of God's redemptive work and loving will to forgive. In addition to Bonhoeffer's precautions, I would add further that it is important to choose for one's confidant a mature believer who is equally serious about pursuing holiness through God's grace. Moreover, as confession is an intimate matter one should avoid placing oneself and the other into temptation. For example, one should confess an addiction to someone other than a presently struggling addict (aside from therapeutic groups such as Alcoholics Anonymous). Or, if the confession is sexual in nature, one should probably confess to someone of the same gender.

The church engaging the world

God wants the church to be a community of love, characterized by life-giving relationships of care and mutual service. But God does not want the church to be insular. By God's design the church is called to be not only a community of redeemed Christians worshipping God and ministering to one another, but also an outward-oriented or exocentric community that reaches out to the world, extending the love of God and the hope of the gospel to all.[74] Just as the Holy Spirit turns the hearts of individual human beings outside of themselves toward Christ and other persons, so the Holy Spirit also turns the church community as a whole outside of itself toward the world in mission. The Christian faith is, at both the personal and corporate levels, inherently other-oriented. To extend Luther's dictum cited earlier: *the church lives not in itself, but in Christ and in the world. Otherwise it is not the church. It lives in Christ through faith, in the world through love.* Consequently, the church is inherently both ethical and missional. This means that its mission in and to the world is not something secondary or optional, but is constitutive of the church's very essence. In this final section of the chapter we will explore some implications of a relational conception of ecclesiology for the church's engagement in and for the world.

---

[74] Thus, there is an intra-ecclesial and extra-ecclesial exocentric orientation of the church. Intra-ecclesially, the members of the Body of Christ are oriented to serving and loving each other; extra-ecclesially, they are oriented to serving and loving the people of the world.

The church participating in Christ's priestly ministry

As ambassadors of reconciliation

All Christian ministry is properly *Christ's* ministry, in which Christians participate by the Holy Spirit. As a relational community, the church engages the world by participating in Christ's priestly ministry as ambassadors of reconciliation. A priest is someone who stands between God and other human beings and plays a mediatory role of representing God to people and representing people to God. A priest also has the task of making atonement on behalf of the people before God, thus reconciling the people with God. Strictly speaking, in the New Testament Christ alone is the great High Priest who makes atonement for human beings once and for all. Yet the church, as God's reconciled people reconstituted as the Body of Christ, participates in Christ's priestly ministry by God's grace and in the Spirit's presence and power. In this ministry, the church itself does not accomplish atonement on behalf of others (Christ has already done this), but in its "I, yet not I—but Christ" existence (Gal 2:20) it ministers "in Christ" and seeks to point people to Christ. The church is not the unique Mediator between God and human beings, but by the Spirit the church participates in Christ's ministry of mediation before the Father and thereby serves Christ as his representative in the world.[75]

In his second letter to the Corinthians, Paul writes:

> All this is from God, who reconciled us to himself through Christ, and has given us the ministry of reconciliation; that is, in Christ God was reconciling the world to himself, not counting their trespasses against them, and entrusting the message of reconciliation to us. So we are ambassadors for Christ, since God is making his appeal through us; we entreat you on behalf of Christ, be reconciled to God. For our sake he made him to be sin who knew no sin, so that in him we might become the righteousness of God (2 Cor 5:18–21).

In this passage Paul makes two sets of claims, one set concerning God and the other concerning Christians. With respect to God, he tells us that God has given us new life and that Christ made this gift of new life possible. In what theologians have often called "the great exchange", God made Christ who had no sin to be sin for us so that we could become God's righteousness (2 Cor 5:21). As Paul explains elsewhere, our old sinful self died with Christ so that we could rise again with Christ to new life by sharing in his resurrection (Rom 6). Moreover, God did not just stand by and watch from a distance but was "in Christ"

---

[75] This priest metaphor should not be pressed to the point of giving the impression that God is not active in people outside of the Christian community until the Christian shows up to mediate between them. Christ as High-Priest the is Mediator between all human beings. Christians are called to the special task of sharing explicitly in Christ's ministry.

reconciling people to Godself. Consequently, God no longer counts peoples' sins against them. With respect to Christians, Paul says that we are now Christ's ambassadors of reconciliation. As such, we have been commissioned to proclaim the good news that Christ has achieved reconciliation and to urge people to respond by turning to God to experience this reconciliation and receive new life in Christ. Thus, one of the ways that the church is called to engage the world is by being ambassadors of reconciliation in proclaiming the gospel and teaching people how to begin a saving relationship with God. The church does not accomplish this by its own power and ingenuity, but in and through the power of God's Word and Spirit. Just as God was "in Christ" reconciling the world to Godself, so God is now "in Christians" blessing their ministry of reconciliation with God's own presence and power by the Holy Spirit.

As the church for others
Another way that the church participates in the priestly ministry of Christ is by living sacrificially for others in the world. As Bonhoeffer argued, the church does not exist merely for itself; the church also exists for others. By its very constitution as an exocentric entity, Christ's church is a "church for others". Bonhoeffer's notion of the "church for others" arose from his fervent and disciplined meditation upon the mysteries of the incarnation and crucifixion of Jesus.[76] As he contemplated the full divinity and humanity of Christ, he realized that Jesus's weakness and suffering in finite, bodily, human existence was the supreme expression of the victory and supremacy of God. In his incarnation, life, death, and resurrection, Jesus demonstrates that the true nature of both God and humanity (in the *imago Dei*) is being-there-for-others.[77] Thus, Bonhoeffer refers to Christ as the "man for others." In his Outline for a Book, Bonhoeffer writes:

> It is only this "being there for others," maintained till death, that is the ground of his omnipotence, omniscience, and omnipresence. Faith is participation in this being of Jesus (incarnation, cross, and resurrection). Our relation to God is not a "religious" relationship to the highest, most powerful, and best Being imaginable—that is not authentic transcendence—but our relation to God is a new life in "existence for others," through participation in the being of Jesus. The transcendental is not infinite and unattainable tasks, but the neighbour who is within reach in any

---

[76] For a fuller treatment of Bonhoeffer's notion of the church for others, see my article "Bonhoeffer's Missional Ecclesiology," *McMaster Journal of Theology and Ministry* 9 (2007–2008): 116–17, 121–25.

[77] Jens Zimmerman notes that Bonhoeffer's stress on solidarity with others, especially "the least of these" (Matt 25), has deep roots in patristic theology. See his essay, "Being Human, Becoming Human: Dietrich Bonhoeffer's Christological Humanism," in *Being Human, Becoming Human: Dietrich Bonhoeffer and Social Thought*, ed. Jens Zimmermann and Brian Gregor (Eugene, OR: Pickwick, 2010), 33.

given situation. God in human form—not, as in oriental religions, in animal form, monstrous, chaotic, remote, and terrifying, nor in the conceptual forms of the absolute, metaphysical, infinite, etc., nor yet in the Greek divine-human form of "man in himself," but "the man for others," and therefore the Crucified, the man who lives out of the transcendent.[78]

Since the church's being and mission are created and defined by the being and mission of Christ, the fact that "Jesus is there only for others" implies that "The church is the church only when it exists for others . . . Its mission is to tell men of every calling what it means to live in Christ, to exist for others."[79] It accomplishes this mission by *being* the reconciled and free community of Christ and by *proclaiming* and *embodying* the gospel as it engages the world. It is crucial that the church not just proclaim the message (important as that is); it must also *be the message* by embodying it in its own life. As God's ambassadors Christians are called to represent God both in their speech and in their actions. As Bonhoeffer points out in his discussion of the Sermon on the Mount, Jesus does not tell his disciples that they merely *possess* salt and light for the world as an instrument for their mission. Jesus says that his disciples *are themselves* salt, light, and city on a hill (see Matt 5:13–16).[80] Together, they are the community that seeks to love God transparently with all that they are—heart, mind, soul, and strength—and that strives to love their neighbours as themselves. Accordingly, Jesus tells them to let their good deeds shine in the darkness of the unbelieving world. In so doing the church becomes, as Lesslie Newbigin puts it, a "living epistle" and an active and concrete "hermeneutic of the gospel".[81] As such, it becomes an important sign, instrument, and foretaste of the eschatological kingdom of God for its surrounding culture. This notion of the "church for others" as a living "hermeneutic of the gospel" is a fruitful one in the context of contemporary postmodern societies. Since most people in Western culture today possess very little knowledge of the Bible and of basic Christian doctrines, their only experience of genuine Christianity is likely to be their encounters with Christians from local congregations. Thus, a congregation of men and women, who believe, embody, and enact the gospel in their everyday lives, provides culture with the lens though which it can begin to interpret and understand the message of Christ.

---

[78] Dietrich Bonhoeffer, *Letters and Papers from Prison*, ed. Eberhard Bethge (New York: Simon & Schuster, 1997), 381–82.
[79] Bonhoeffer, *Letters and Papers from Prison*, 382–83.
[80] Bonhoeffer, *Discipleship*, 111–13.
[81] Lesslie Newbigin, *The Gospel in a Pluralist Society* (Grand Rapids: Eerdmans, 1989), 227–32; *The Household of God: Lectures on the Nature of the Church* (London: SCM, 1957), 51.

Theology of the cross as a model for cultural critique and the proclamation of justice

The Apostle Paul wrote that in Jesus Christ God reconciled all things to Godself by making peace through Christ's blood, which was shed on the cross (Col 1:19–20). God's own ministry of reconciliation secured our forgiveness and restoration, not by a mere whim but at the tremendous cost of the cross.[82] Miroslav Volf observes that forgiveness involves two essential elements, one negative the other positive.[83] Negatively, forgiveness involves condemnation of a wrong committed. In saying "I forgive you, Johnny, for stealing twenty dollars from my wallet", I am not simply excusing Johnny's actions as insignificant to me, trivial, or morally neutral (even if his stealing is in some sense understandable, for example if he needed the money for food). Rather, I am condemning his actions as morally wrong and naming myself as having been wronged by him. Positively, forgiveness involves releasing the offender from the debt incurred by his wrongful action(s). It means forgoing one's desire for vengeance and one's right to retribution, though it does not rule out reformative discipline and a measure of restitution.[84] Indeed, God disciplines those whom God loves and expects us to make things right with others when we sin. A biblical example is Zacchaeus, who not only acknowledged his sin and received Christ's forgiveness but also vowed to give half of his wealth to the poor and to payback those he had defrauded four times what he had stolen from them (Luke 19:1–10). Just as the act of forgiving involves these two essential elements, the act of receiving forgiveness also involves two parallel essential elements: acknowledging the just condemnation of one's wrongful action(s) and receiving the gift of release from debt from the person whom one has wronged.[85]

The two essential elements of forgiveness mentioned above constitute not only human forgiveness but God's forgiveness as well. In fact, from a Christian perspective, human forgiveness is grounded in, modeled after, and made possible by God's prior work of atonement and forgiveness through the mediation of Christ in the power of the Spirit.[86] In forgiving human beings, God names and condemns sin *and* offers release from the debt of sin on the basis of Christ's atoning work on the cross. The cross represents both God's condemnation and God's forgiveness of human sin; it is both God's *NO* and God's *YES* to sinful

---

[82] Bonhoeffer conveys this point brilliantly in the first chapter of his *Discipleship*.

[83] Miroslav Volf, *Free of Charge: Giving and Forgiving in a Culture Stripped of Grace* (Grand Rapids: Zondervan, 2005), 129–31.

[84] The forgoing of retribution accounts for the fact that restitution alone cannot undo past actions and in many occasions cannot sufficiently compensate for wrongs committed. Indeed, sometimes an infinite gap separates restitution from full compensation, as when the wrong committed is murder.

[85] Volf, *Free of Charge*, 153–54.

[86] See Volf, *Free of Charge*, 131–51.

human beings.[87] By the cross, God condemns all human injustice, oppression, alienation, exploitation, and moral corruption—at the personal, social, and global levels. Yet the cross also embodies God's forgiveness and grounds God's invitation to human beings to receive God's love, acceptance, and transformative grace—and thereby to enter into God's new life in the Spirit. It demonstrates God's initiative in the process of reconciliation and calls human beings to respond in repentance and enter into true freedom.

"When Christ calls a man he bids him 'come and die.'"[88] A theology of the cross equips the church to engage the world by speaking and doing the truth in love.[89] It entails a radical commitment to following Christ whatever the cost. It can thus serve as a helpful model for fruitful cultural critique and transformation (we will also consider incarnation and resurrection as models of cultural engagement in chapters 7 and 8 respectively).[90] Cross-bearing involves means of witness that may not be well received by the dominant culture or its leaders. Examples in Jesus's ministry include: his confrontations with religious and political leaders, which threatened the privileged status quo of the powerful and empowered the lowly; his experience of being rejected by crowds, his home town, religious and political authorities, and even friends; his confrontation of practices that were good for business but oppressive for people (e.g., clearing the temple; see also Paul's confrontation of the selling of idols and superstitious relics); and his exposure of hypocrisy and hard heartedness.

A theology of the cross applied to the church's mission calls the church to seek justice in the world, which involves condemning injustice and immorality *and* actively pursuing peace—thereby fostering forgiveness and reconciliation. The church is called to seek justice in the lives of individual human beings by

---

[87] I am here drawing on the language of Bonhoeffer (who is, in turn, drawing on the language of Barth). Dietrich Bonhoeffer, *Ethics*, ed. Clifford J. Green, trans. Reinhard Krauss, Charles C. West, and Douglas W. Stott, vol. 6, *Dietrich Bonhoeffer Works* (Minneapolis: Fortress, 2005), 252–52, 262, 291,

[88] Dietrich Bonhoeffer, *The Cost of Discipleship* (New York: Simon and Schuster, 1995), 89.

[89] See also Vanhoozer's discussion of cruciform performance in *The Drama of Doctrine: A Canonical-linguistic Approach to Christian Theology* (Louisville: Westminster John Knox, 2005), 428–39.

[90] John W. de Gruchy notes that Bonhoeffer's cultural engagement incorporated reflection on the incarnation, cross, and resurrection. See his essay, "Dietrich Bonhoeffer as Christian Humanist," in *Being Human, Becoming Human: Dietrich Bonhoeffer and Social Thought*, ed. Jens Zimmermann and Brian Gregor (Eugene, OR: Pickwick, 2010), 19. For example, in *Ethics* (157–59), Bonhoeffer rejects a dichotomous choice between radicalism and compromise in his discussion of cultural transformation. Instead, he argues for a threefold approach to cultural engagement pattered after Jesus's incarnation (God's love and affirmation), cross (God's judgement), and resurrection (God's purposes for the new creation). I am taking my initial cue from Bonhoeffer in following this pattern.

calling them to repentance and by sharing the message of God's love and forgiveness. It is called both to condemn the actions of perpetrators and to seek to restore them to relational wholeness and moral integrity before God and fellow human beings. The church is also called to seek social justice and cultural transformation. As Volf writes, "As the Gospel has been preached to many nations, the church has taken root in many cultures, changing them as well as being profoundly shaped by them."[91] The cross symbolizes both God's *YES* and God's *NO* to human culture. Consequently, the cross entails both an affirmation of the goodness in every culture but also "*a judgment against evil in every culture.*"[92] As Volf writes, "There can be no new creation without judgment, without the expulsion of the devil and the beast and the false prophet (Revelation 20:10), without the swallowing up of the night by the light and of death by life (Revelation 21:4; 22:5)."[93]

Christ makes his home in every culture but Christ cannot be domesticated by any. The church must therefore cultivate discernment and the willingness to critique cherished cultural norms, values, expectations, and worldviews that are incompatible with the teachings of Jesus. This includes evaluating and addressing broad social issues, such as nationalism, ethnocentricity, and economic injustice. It also includes evaluating and addressing the influence of culture on the concrete, daily lives of individuals and their choices, including the culture's perspective on moral issues (e.g., concerning money, sex, and power), its notion of success or the good life, its attitude toward the poor, the homeless, the sick, and the oppressed, and its support of religious and personal freedom. Moreover, it will evaluate and address the cultural impact of media on the worldviews and values of people, especially young people who are so easily and pervasively influenced by its content. Finally, the church will condemn institutional, systemic, governmental, and legislative injustice, and advocate instead for the rule of righteousness, justice, love, and peace within these important and potentially life-supporting and culture-forming entities. At the same time, a theology of the cross emphasizes personal engagement and care, sacrifice, graciousness, humble service, and solidarity with those in need. This is in contrast to a theology of glory, which tends to rely on and promote privilege, human charisma, and an approach to leadership and influence characterized by paternalism and triumphalism (e.g., prosperity gospel and many Christendom models).[94] In short, the church will seek to engage the world as Christ did, both

---

[91] Volf, *Exclusion and Embrace*, 51.
[92] Volf, *Exclusion and Embrace*, 52.
[93] Volf, *Exclusion and Embrace*, 52.
[94] Douglas John Hall proposes that only a theology of the cross takes the ambiguities, uncertainties, and sufferings of the world seriously; accordingly, only a theology of the cross offers a hope that is true and profound enough to replace the national philosophies of optimism, which are essentially naive and escapist theologies of glory.

by lovingly condemning evil and by casting a compelling vision of what genuine human life together in the kingdom of God is really like.

Means of engagement

There are many ways in which the church can live out its calling to engage the world as ambassadors of reconciliation for Christ. A congregation's specific missional calling is not something that can be decided in advance by devising abstract objectives or by applying pragmatic methods or formulaic techniques. Genuine worldly engagement depends on theological vision and worldview, combined with spiritual discernment, wisdom, passion, creativity, and a willingness to step out in faith and take risks at God's initiative. Here I will offer just three brief suggestions, and refer the reader to other helpful resources in the footnotes. First, churches can engage the world by considering and discerning what God is doing and then joining in and participating in God's work.[95] One of the ways a church can do this is by finding out what its members are already doing in their daily lives, perhaps identifying patterns and commonalities, and then acting to encourage and support them in it. For example, has someone initiated a Bible study or a book club in their neighbourhood? Does someone coach a sports team or volunteer as a big brother or big sister? Is someone in a position of leadership in a business and so able to influence and mentor others? Does someone have a passion to start a ministry of reaching out to the elderly in a local home, but lacks resources or confidence to do it? The local congregation can ask how it can support its members in each of these situations, if nothing else through prayer and encouragement but potentially also by joining the person in helping them with expressed needs for volunteers, resources, or theological and spiritual guidance and wisdom.

Second, a church can engage the world by sharing in the burdens of its local community.[96] One of the reasons that the early church had such a profound impact on its surrounding culture was that it engaged others in radical acts of hospitality, care, and solidarity. Christine Pohl writes, "Early Christian writers claimed that transcending social and ethnic differences by sharing meals, homes, and worship with persons of different backgrounds was proof of the

---

See John Douglas Hall, "The Changing North American Context of the Church's Ministry," *Currents in Theology and Mission* 22, no. 6D (1995): 409.

[95] This basic idea comes from Henry T. Blackaby and Claude V. King, *Experiencing God: How to Live the Full Adventure of Knowing and Doing the Will of God* (Nashville: Broadman & Holman, 1994).

[96] For some good resources on this theme, see: Robert and Julia Banks, *The Church Comes Home: Regrouping the People of God for Community and Mission* (Peabody: Hendrickson, 1997); Lois Y. Barret, ed., *Treasure in Clay Jars: Patterns in Missional Faithfulness* (Grand Rapids: Eerdmans, 2004); and Michael Frost and Alan Hirsch, *The Shape of Things to Come: Innovation and Ministry for the 21st Century Church* (Peabody: Publishers, 2003).

truth of the Christian faith."[97] She argues that hospitality, as a fundamental *human* practice, always included family, friends, and influential contacts. "What made hospitality distinctly Christian, however, was the emphasis on including the poor and neediest, the ones who could not return the favor."[98] For example, the early church Father John Chrysostom stressed the importance of being proactive in giving hospitality and encouraged his parishioners to make a guest chamber in their house "for Christ" (i.e., the maimed, beggars, and homeless).[99] In addition to active hospitality, Alan Kreider argues that the early church impacted its culture through its "question-posing ways of addressing common problems in society".[100] Examples of this include the early church's novel practice of adopting unwanted babies that were discarded in the garbage dumps of the Roman Empire (many of these babies were girls, which is one of the reasons that the proportion of females in Christian communities was unusually high), its practice of providing free burials for all, including the poor (in a culture in which only the rich typically received the honour of burial), its practice of loving enemies in concrete actions of care, and its response to disease and plague whereby, in contrast to most people who fled in fear, Christians regularly put themselves at risk to care for the sick and diseased.[101] In light of these observations, it would be helpful to ask: what concrete things can local churches do to reach out to their communities in hospitality and in solidarity?

Third, local congregations can engage the world by forming partnerships with others who are seeking justice, reconciliation, and peace. This might include other local church congregations who are open to partnering together to impact the local community. It might include partnering with social justice organizations, perhaps beginning with those that a congregation's own members already support or serve as volunteers. It might include getting to know the local police, school teachers and principals, hospital workers and officials, and municipal government representatives, in order to discern the needs of the community in partnership with those who have a pulse on particular aspects or

---

[97] Pohl, *Making Room*, 5.

[98] Pohl, *Making Room*, 6.

[99] Pohl, *Making Room*, 45, 70.

[100] Alan Kreider, "They Alone Know the Right Way to Live: The Early Church and Evangelism," in *Ancient Faith for the Church's Future*, ed. Mark Husbands and Jeffrey P. Greenman (Downers Grove: InterVarsity Press, 2008), 172. Throughout the article Kreider mines early church literature in order to answer two questions. First, what accounted for the explosive growth of the early church, especially considering the fact that it did not seem to place much emphasis on evangelism in the modern sense (also, because it was persecuted it often had to gather privately and act inconspicuously)? Answer: Its perceived spiritual power, its question-posing behaviour due to Christian convictions and values, and its common life together as resident aliens. Second, what practices formed and sustained the early church to be such a community? Answer: Its distinctive practices of worship and catechesis.

[101] Kreider, "They Alone Know," 172–74.

issues within the community.[102] Finally, in light of the church's global mandate, worldly engagement ought to include some form of partnership with mission organizations and approved non-governmental organizations that are working for justice, peace, and truth across the globe.

Conclusion: Living out of love in an egocentric world

Our contemporary world is full of lonely, alienated, hurting people, who are deeply longing for genuine, life-giving relationships with God and other human beings. The church exists to minister to all such people and to invite them to share in its communal life. As relational communities of the new humanity the church exists to serve the mission of the triune God, who by the Holy Spirit draws alienated human beings into life-giving relationships with God and other human beings by incorporating them into the Body of Christ. Just as God created human beings to be exocentric, other-centred persons, so the Holy Spirit similarly constitutes the church to be an exocentric "church for others" that serves God's mission of reconciliation in the world. The church is inherently missional because it is—first and foremost—inherently relational.

---

[102] For some helpful ideas for engaging political leaders and processes in the Canadian context, see: Brian C. Stiller, *From the Tower of Babel to Parliament Hill: How to be a Christian in Canada Today* (Toronto: HarperCollins, 1997), 185–88, 199–202.

CHAPTER 7

The Church as Rational Communities of Faith

Introduction

In chapter four I described the human being as a rational creature drawn to participate in the intelligible conversation of the Trinity by sharing in the divine *Logos*. This participatory sharing enables human beings to pursue their *telos*, part of which includes knowing God and understanding God's created world. However, human sinfulness creates an impediment to the human's ability to know God, which distorts a genuine understanding of God's creational purposes in and for the world. Sin causes a breakdown in the human being's participation in the intelligible divine conversation and leads to the captivity of the human mind, which I described as a mind turned in upon itself, alienated from and hostile to God. Consequently, human redemption in Christ involves renewal of the mind and restoration to the divine conversation, leading to a life of wisdom characterized by faith and godly living. It is crucial to see, however, that Christians do not cultivate godly wisdom and character on their own; rather, Christians cultivate wisdom and character with the help of their brothers and sisters in Christ in God's family. Moreover, the cultivation of Christian wisdom is not merely a rationalistic endeavour but is pursued by faith within the social context of the church, which is the historical People of God. Thus, the identity, history, traditions, and practices of the church are important for Christian wisdom formation.

This chapter depicts the church as rational communities of faith. As rational communities of faith, church congregations exist to encourage their members toward growth in their knowledge of God and God's purposes, to impart wisdom for understanding God's will for human life and flourishing, and to foster character formation through its community life, ministries, mentoring, discipling, and practices. This aspect of the church guards against mere conformity, groupthink, or manipulation by powerful leaders. As a rational community, the church's goal is not to manipulate or coerce conformity or obedience, but to equip and form people with wisdom to make the right decisions. Moreover, the church exists to serve God's mission of exhorting the broader world toward wise living. It does this by modelling wise living in its own communal life, by advocating for wise and godly social norms, structures and laws, and by affirming, impacting, and directly contributing to the wise functioning of cultural influences and leaders (e.g., in business, politics, health care, education, media, etc.). As such it acts as a social catalyst for wisdom and as leaven for godly social transformation in a posture of humility, graciousness, peacefulness, and sacrificial and redemptive love. It should be noted that this chapter builds upon the relational view of the church articulated in the previous chapter, but to avoid redundancy and to conserve space I will not continually repeat important themes already established there. Thus, for example, in the present chapter I will assume that the church ministers on the basis of its union with Christ in the Spirit and thereby participates in the ministry of God. I will refer to these themes, but not explain them again. I point this out here because discussing the church as a rational community without discussing its union with Christ by the Spirit could lead to a rationalistic ecclesiology, which is something that I am not advocating.

Inner community life of the church

The church as the People of God

In chapter four we observed that Christian wisdom combines rationality with ethical living and that a key ingredient holding rationality and ethical living together is faith.[1] Thus, by faith people live rationally and ethically, in accountability to God as responsible creatures before God; this amounts to wisdom. In parallel to this, the church is a rational-ethical community devoted to the cultivation of wisdom. New members gain access and join the community through faith in Jesus Christ, which means that the church is fundamentally a community of faith. One of the ways that the New Testament portrays the church as a community of faith is by its description of the church as the new People of God. The first letter of Peter relies heavily on terminology associated with the concept of God's people. For example, it describes the community of those "who believe" as "a chosen generation, a royal priesthood, a holy nation, . . . the people of God" (1 Pet 2:7, 9, 10; notice the link between belief, holiness, and being God's people). The epistle never employs the term "church" (*ekklesia*) to refer to God's people but instead uses images such as God's house/temple (2:5), God's flock (5:2) and God's family (4:17). These images carry Old Testament connotations of Israel's privileged position as God's chosen people.[2] Peter deliberately applies these images to his readers, along with

---

[1] As Bonhoeffer and Kierkegaard both stressed, "Faith is not merely a cognitive relation of assent to correct doctrine but is rather a whole-person response to the call of Christ. Faith is inseparable from the obedient response of following after Christ in concrete, everyday existence." Brian Gregor, "Following-After and Becoming Human: A Study of Bonhoeffer and Kierkegaard," in *Being Human, Becoming Human: Dietrich Bonhoeffer and Social Thought*, ed. Jens Zimmermann and Brian Gregor (Eugene, OR: Pickwick, 2010), 153.

[2] I. Howard Marshall, *New Testament Theology: Many Witnesses, One Gospel* (Downers Grove: InterVarsity Press, 2004), 653–54. Other closely related image include "braches of the vine", which is a symbol of Israel that Jesus applied to his disciples in

the title "People of God", so that by faith they would identify themselves with historic Israel.

The phrase "People of God" was a highly significant description of the church for the early Christians and remains important for the present church's historical continuity with the Old Testament covenant community.[3] George Ladd explains that it conveys the idea of standing in a special covenant relationship with God and implies that the church is God's new covenant people.[4] However, in contrast to the Old Testament notion of the People of God, which was built upon the covenant that God made with Abraham and then Israel, the new People of God is based upon *God's covenant with humanity through Jesus Christ* and is radically inclusive. It includes persons from every tribe, language, people, and nation who have been purchased with the blood of Christ (Rev 5:9). Thus, the church as God's new humanity is defined by faith in the Messiah and King, in and through whom it is bound together and toward whom its future is directed.[5] While individuals were often assumed to have entered the Old Testament People of God by virtue of their birth, the New Testament specifies that it includes persons of diverse origins and backgrounds who join the church through *spiritual rebirth*. This is not to deny the existence of pagan saints in the Old Testament who were not ethnic Jews yet had a relationship with God (e.g., Ruth, who joined the covenant people) nor to deny the possibility of ethnic Jews violating the covenant and ceasing to be part of the People of God (e.g., Ahab, Jezebel).[6] True faith had always been crucial for a right standing and relationship with God, though many failed to understand this. As Paul points out, "not all who are descended from Israel are Israel" (Rom 9:6).[7] It is simply to affirm that God made the covenant with Israel in particular, though the covenant had a worldwide salvific goal that would be attained through Christ and completed at the eschatological gathering of all the saints.

It is important for the church as the People of God to remember its continuity with the people of Israel in past, present, and future (Rom 9–11) and to celebrate and treasure its history. As Marshall emphasizes, the church is not merely an existential event or a continual "happening" but is rooted in salvation histo-

---

John's Gospel, and "the saints", which is tied indirectly to the Old Testament notion of a holy remnant of God's elect people. See Marshall, *New Testament Theology*, 523 and Walter Schmithals, *The Theology of the First Christians*, trans. O.C. Dean, Jr. (Louisville: Westminster John Knox, 1997), 154–55.

[3] Schmithals, *Theology of the First Christians*, 153.
[4] George E. Ladd, *A Theology of the New Testament*, ed. Donald A. Hagner (Grand Rapids: Eerdmans, 1993), 582–83.
[5] Marshall, *New Testament Theology*, 123, 338.
[6] It is important to stress that God had always cared about more people than just ethnic Israel (e.g., Ruth, Rahab, Job, Melchizedek, the Ninevites, etc.).
[7] There had always been a faithful remnant, a true and believing people within the larger society who trusted God's promises and acted accordingly (Gal 3). On this point, see Marshall, *New Testament Theology*, 338.

ry.[8] As the historic new People of God, believers enter the church by faith alone and sustain the life of the church (in part) by faithful remembrance and celebration of its place in salvation history, through its engagement with Scripture (Old and New Testaments), its worship and liturgy, and its traditions and practices.[9] This emphasis on the church's history does not imply a preoccupation with the past leading to a stale traditionalism. Rather, the church's rootedness in the past, combined with its eschatological hope for the future, should equip and empower it with the resources, confidence, and ingenuity it needs to pursue its life and mission in the present as it participates with the Spirit who continually draws it toward its fulfillment). Neither nostalgia for the past nor dreaming about the future should characterize the church, but rather faithful improvisation in the present that is inspired by the past, oriented toward the future, and guided by the Word and Spirit of God.

Communities of faith that cultivate wisdom

According to the New Testament, the church is called to teach and exemplify wisdom (Eph 3:10; Jas 13:13–18). Paul says we proclaim Christ, "admonishing and teaching everyone with all wisdom, so that we may present everyone fully

---

[8] Marshall, *New Testament Theology*, 173. This raises the question of the church's relation to ethnic Israel. While this is a broad and complex subject, for my present purposes I will simply state that there is both discontinuity and continuity in the transition from old to new covenant, from Israel to the church (see Marshall, *New Testament Theology*, 123–25, 338, 453–54, 668). On the one hand, the new covenant is in fact new. Jesus's intention was to inaugurate a new era, and his choice of twelve disciples, symbolic of the twelve tribes of Israel, meant that the old era had become obsolete. Not only is this second covenant new, but according to the writer of Hebrews it is also superior to the old covenant both quantitatively and qualitatively. In Christ we are guaranteed a "better covenant" (Heb 7:22), because: (1) Christ is superior to the angels in power, authority, and as one who reveals the glory and being of God (Heb 1:1–4); (2) Christ is superior to Moses, because while the latter was a faithful servant in God's house Christ is the faithful son (Heb 3:1–6); and (3) Christ's priesthood is superior to the Levitical priesthood, because human priests die and are succeeded but Christ lives forever to make incessant intercession for us and because Christ's sacrifice was offered once-for-all and is infinitely efficacious (Heb 7:11–27). On the other hand, there is only one kingdom of God. The church does not simply replace Israel, as if God has forsaken his people or forgotten his promises. Rather, believing Israel finds its true identity and future in the church (Rom 9–11; Gal 3; Eph 2:14–18).

[9] One of the crucial ways that Dietrich Bonhoeffer differed from many of his contemporaries in Germany during the Second World War was his continued engagement with the Jewish Scriptures (i.e. the Old Testament), which the Nazi church discounted and dismissed. For examples of Bonhoeffer's interaction with the Old Testament, see especially *Creation and Fall: A Theological Exposition of Genesis 1–3*, vol. 3 of *Dietrich Bonhoeffer Works*, ed. John W. de Gruchy, trans. Douglas Stephen Bax (Minneapolis: Fortress, 1997) and *Prayerbook of the Bible: An Introduction to the Psalms*, vol. 5 of *Dietrich Bonhoeffer Works*, ed. Geffrey B. Kelly, trans. James H. Burtness (Minneapolis: Fortress, 1996).

mature in Christ" (Col 1:28). Accordingly he instructs the Colossian believers to "teach and admonish one another with all wisdom through psalms, hymns and songs from the Spirit, singing to God with gratitude in your hearts" (Col 3:16).[10] Wisdom enables believers in the church community to know God better (Eph 1:17), understand God's revealed salvation purposes (1 Cor 2:7–16; Eph 1:17; 3:10–11; Rev 13:18; 17:19), and be more effective witnesses for Christ (Luke 21:14–16; Acts 6:9–10). Wisdom is also an important quality for faithful and effective leadership in the church (Acts 6:3; 1 Tim 3:2). In addition, the New Testament's emphasis on instructing and modelling the teachings and character of Christ highlights the importance of wisdom for Christian communities (John 17:17; Rom 15:3–5; 1 Cor 4:16; Phil 2:5–10; Col 3:16; 1 Tim 4:6; 2 Tim 3:14–17).[11] Given the importance of wisdom, it is no wonder that the Apostle James counsels that anyone who lacks wisdom should ask God for it (Jas1:5). But what kind of wisdom does Scripture promote? And what is the character of distinctly *Christian* wisdom? Two biblical emphases attend to these questions: Christian wisdom comes from God and must be distinguished from worldly wisdom.

Wisdom comes from God
As observed in chapter four, the Old Testament teaches that genuine wisdom begins with fear of or reverence for the Lord and becomes manifest in lives that are lived in the light of God's purposes and will. Daniel Treier summarizes that wisdom in the Old Testament involves divine communication (wisdom mediates God's presence in creation through both general and special revelation), which is appropriated in a community for its people to enjoy life, is characterized by their fear for God, and accordingly promotes shalom amongst God's people.[12] As I pointed out in chapter four, while fear of the Lord is the *beginning* of wisdom it is not the *end* (final purpose) of wisdom and does not fully account for its content and character. According to the New Testament the purpose of genuine wisdom, as revealed in the person and ministry of Jesus Christ, is to love God and fellow human beings more deeply and serve God and others more knowledgably and effectively. Consequently, Jesus's love command

---

[10] For a helpful treatment of the importance of song a formative aspect of Christian worship, see James K.A. Smith, *Desiring the Kingdom: Worship, Worldview, and Cultural Formation* (Grand Rapids: Baker Academic, 2009), 170–73.

[11] See also Daniel J. Treier, *Virtue and the Voice of God: Toward Theology as Wisdom* (Grand Rapids: Eerdmans, 2006), 50, 53.

[12] Treier, *Virtue and the Voice of God*, 44–45. Treier points out that the notion of shalom nicely synthesizes the connection between wisdom, the order of creation, and worldly success. He writes, "For Proverbs success means, preeminently, shalom; riches, honor, physical security, family, and the like are derivative. . . . Proverbial 'life' remains ambiguous about the particular shape it will take for a wise person. This means, moreover, acknowledging God's sovereign freedom to grant life rather than assuming an automatic, bluntly casual, domino effect between wisdom and success." (45)

summarizes the entirety of the Torah and the prophets (Matt 22:40; Gal 5:14) and is at the heart of Christian wisdom. As Treier says, Christian practical reasoning (one aspect of wisdom) "has its pattern in Christ and thus its animating principle is love".[13] Such love is not merely a human possibility, but comes from God and indwells us personally by the Spirit (1 John 3:16; 4:7–10, 13, 16–17).

Jesus's own ministry was characterized by profound wisdom, full of love and knowledge (Matt 12:42). Those who encountered him found his wisdom captivating, shocking, refreshing, and liberating—except for the self-promoting religious teachers and authorities.[14] The New Testament declares that all the treasures of wisdom and knowledge are hidden in Jesus Christ (Col 2:3). Since wisdom is closely associated with God's own love and knowledge, which comes to us through Christ by the Spirit, genuine human wisdom is a gift from God (Jas 1:5; 2 Pet 3:15). It is both a natural gift, which all human beings are invited to pursue and develop, and a special gift that the Spirit uniquely gives to particular people in various degrees to edify the church (Rom 12:8; Eph 4:11–13; Col 1:9; 4:16). Wisdom is also given to impart knowledge to the church about God's salvation plan, which in former days was secret but now is revealed through Christ in the Spirit (1 Cor 2:7–16; Eph 1:17). As a gracious gift from God, genuine wisdom is not something that leads to arrogance and boastfulness, but to gratitude and humility along with the intention of serving God and others (1 Cor 1:31; 2 Cor 1:12; Col 2:23).

Worldly wisdom versus godly wisdom
The New Testament contrasts false or distorted wisdom that comes from "the world" with genuine wisdom that comes from God. Before explicating this distinction it is important to clarify what the New Testament does not mean, and therefore does not condemn, when it speaks of wisdom that is "worldly" or "of the world". First, wisdom of the world does not refer to knowledge about the created world.[15] As Treier notes, the wisdom literature of the Bible is closely associated with knowledge about creation and about how the world generally works, which is precisely what grounds its value and relevance for stable and successful living.[16] Second, worldly wisdom does not refer to the knowledge or behaviour of non-Christians simply by virtue of their being non-Christians. Wisdom literature personifies wisdom (e.g. Prov 8) and depicts it as calling out to all who are willing to hear and response to its message. Wisdom mediates God's presence within creation and is both immanent and transcendent, both accessible and inaccessible. As Treier observes, "Wisdom calls (Prov 1–9), but humans must respond (Prov 10–31). In fact, the givenness of Wisdom is what

---

[13] Treier, *Virtue and the Voice of God*, 52.
[14] See: Matt 7:28–29; 13:54; 22:15–22; Mark 6:2; Luke 2:40, 52; 21:14–16; John 1:1–5, 9; 5:36–40; 6:68; 14:6–7.
[15] See also Treier, *Virtue and the Voice of God*, 41.
[16] Treier, *Virtue and the Voice of God*, 33.

invites human seeking that, by fearing YHWH, will find. . . ." Consequently, "This Wisdom clings to YHWH, albeit somehow connected as well with what is cosmically consistent, with what would be successful even for other cultures. . . ."[17] Third, by extension, worldly wisdom does not refer to advanced learning or academic scholarship, such as that conducted at major universities (secular or Christian) in the arts, sciences, social sciences, and humanities. Rather, all truth is God's truth. Such learning, if it represents a genuine pursuit of truth, participates in God's wisdom as it studies what theologians have referred to as God's "book of nature".[18]

What then is the "wisdom of the world" that Scripture condemns? The two New Testament texts that contrast worldly and godly wisdom are 1 Corinthians 1–2 and James 3:13–18. According to these texts, false worldly wisdom seeks after self-glorification as when individual human beings draw attention to their own knowledge, ingenuity, strength, and eloquence. Paul says that worldly knowledge "puffs up" and is opposed to love, which "builds up" or edifies (1 Cor 8:1). Characterized by pride and selfish ambition, its tendency is to breed bitter envy, disorder, and every kind of evil. Accordingly, James calls false wisdom earthly, unspiritual, and demonic. Elsewhere the New Testament associates false wisdom with disobedience (Luke 1:17) and associates it with worldly structures and regulations that disregard God's grace in Christ (Col 2:23). Moreover, worldly wisdom depends on knowledge that is deliberately sought autonomously from God and applied in opposition to God's purposes and plans for human beings and creation.[19]

In contrast, distinctly Christian wisdom is, first of all, cruciform in nature. It is wisdom that corresponds to the message of the cross and points in humility to the power of the cross rather than to human glory and knowledge. As such, it is not condescending or patronizing, seeking to bring others under the sway of its own rhetoric and intelligence; rather it seeks to encourage, edify and build others up according to God's truth and purposes. Thus, Paul says that God called him to proclaim the gospel "not with eloquent wisdom, so that the cross of Christ might not be emptied of its power" (1 Cor 1:17) but to "proclaim Christ crucified" (v. 23) because "God's foolishness is wiser than human wisdom, and God's weakness is stronger than human strength" (v. 25). Accordingly, Paul determined to preach "not with wise and persuasive words, but with a demonstration of the Spirit's power" so that the faith of his hearers "might not rest on human wisdom, but on God's power" (1 Cor 2:4, 5). Second, wisdom from God involves acceptance of God's revelation, especially God's plan to save us in Christ. Paul says that he declares God's wisdom, which is "a mystery that has

---

[17] Treier, *Virtue and the Voice of God*, 35.
[18] See Alister E. McGrath, *A Fine-Tuned Universe: The Quest for God in Science and Theology* (Louisville: Westminster John Knox, 2009), 69–71, 218.
[19] Treier observes that knowledge and morality sought autonomously and in opposition to God is what characterizes the false wisdom that Adam and Eve pursued in the Garden of Eden (Treier, *Virtue and the Voice of God*, 38–40).

been hidden and that God destined for our glory before time began" but now has been revealed by the Holy Spirit (1 Cor 2:7, 10). Third, wisdom from God involves spiritual discernment, which is granted by the Holy Spirit who searches the deep things of God and gives us access to the mind of Christ (1 Cor 2:10–16). Fourth, wisdom that comes from God sometimes seems like foolishness to those who do not know God and who disregard God's purposes and saving plan (1 Cor 1:21–25, 27–29; 1 Cor 2:14). It thus requires trust in God and a pure heart that seeks affirmation primarily from God rather than from other human beings. Fifth, godly wisdom goes beyond the possession of knowledge and skills (though it includes these) and is defined also in relation to appropriate attitudes and results. In terms of attitudes, James tells us that wisdom from above is pure, peace-loving, considerate, submissive, full of mercy and good fruit, impartial, and sincere (Jas 3:17). In terms of its results, genuine wisdom manifests itself through the good deeds that one performs in humble service to God and others (Jas 3:13). Genuine wisdom is therefore a quality that characterizes a person's whole existence. One does not merely *possess* wisdom; rather, one determines to *become a wise person* by cultivating gradually and with discipline the kind of attitudes, patterns of thought, commitments, habits, and virtues that make one wise.[20] In light of these observations, churches should strive to be communities that cultivate in their members' wisdom that is cruciform, knowledgeable of God's Word and saving work, sensitive to the Holy Spirit (spiritually discerning), confident in God's moral truth and priorities, and embodied holistically and pervasively in godly character and holy living.

Ministries of the church that cultivate godly wisdom

Our contemporary culture is in dire need of people characterized by depth and wisdom. Many are seeking a greater sense of profundity and spiritual transcendence in Eastern religions such as Buddhism (or watered down versions of them). They long to find greater meaning than what is offered by a culture wrapped up in materialism and pragmatism. Within Christianity, one of the reasons why many people are drawn to the Emerging Church and other postmodern expressions of church (though some are also migrating to Catholic, Anglican, or Orthodox traditions in order to recover pre-modern roots) is that they have become disenchanted with the intellectual and spiritual superficiality that they observe in modern evangelical churches.[21] They are particularly

---

[20] Joseph J. Kotva, Jr., *The Christian Case for Virtue Ethics* (Washington, D.C.: Georgetown University Press, 1996), 17–37.

[21] Tony Jones, *The New Christians: Dispatches from the Emergent Frontier* (San Francisco: Jossey-Bass, 2008), 109; Dan Kimball, *The Emerging Church: Vintage Christianity for New Generations* (Grand Rapids: Zondervan, 2003, 13–14, 25, 94, 114, 203; Brian McLaren, *More Ready Than You Realize: Evangelism as Dance in the Postmodern Matrix* (Grand Rapids: Zondervan, 2002), 52; Scott Bader-Saye, "Improvising Church: An Introduction to the Emerging Church Conversation," *Interna-*

turned off by seeker sensitive models, which they believe reduce the mysteries of the faith and the complexity of theological and intellectual issues to slick slogans and tips for self improvement. Many Christian scholars have also criticized the tendency toward anti-intellectualism within the evangelical movement.[22] For example, the respected evangelical historian Mark Noll refers to the "scandal of the evangelical mind", which he describes not simply as failure to think but more fundamentally as a failure to integrate Christian faith with advances in human knowledge across the academic disciplines.[23] Similarly, Richard Hughes laments that many Christian academics fail to think *theologically* about the meaning of the Christian faith; though highly educated, they remain "at a Sunday school level of theological literacy".[24] Consequently, they either struggle to relate their faith to their academic life and work or else they maintain a dichotomous separation of faith and learning, which threatens the overall coherence and consistency of their vocation as Christian scholars. Fortunately the situation has been improving dramatically since Noll wrote his book. Evangelicals are making noteworthy contributions in all academic fields and many are increasingly emphasizing an interdisciplinary approach to scholarship and learning.[25] Nevertheless, it is crucial to continue to emphasize the importance

---

tional Journal for the Study of the Christian Church 6, no. 1 (2006): 18–20. See also George Barna, *Revolution* (Carol Streem: Tyndale House, 2005). Barna forecasts a dramatic change in the American religious landscape in coming decades, as increasing numbers of devout Christians pursue and express their faith without attending conventional churches.

[22] Jens Zimmermann doubts that the North American evangelical subculture (including its institutions of learning) is prepared to re-engage the life of the mind creatively and profoundly as it engages contemporary culture. One of the main reasons for this its lack of historical awareness, including a lack of rootedness in its own traditions. He writes, "the recovery of a passionate intellect and a purpose for education requires a grasp of one's history and identity which comes through knowing one's tradition. The sap of a tree comes from its roots. . . . Yet the evangelical subculture reveals its greatest weakness precisely at this crucial point." See his article: "The Passionate Intellect: Christian Humanism and University Education," *Direction* 37 (Spring 2008): para. 20. Online: http://www.directionjournal.org/article/?1505.

[23] Mark A. Noll, *The Scandal of the Evangelical Mind* (Grand Rapids: Eerdmans, 1994).

[24] Richard T. Hughes, *The Vocation of a Christian Scholar: How Christian Faith Can Sustain the Life of the Mind* (Grand Rapids: Eerdmans, 2005), 6.

[25] See for example: Deane E.D. Downey and Stanley E. Porter, eds., *Christian Worldview and the Academic Disciplines: Crossing the Academy* (Eugene, OR: Pickwick, 2009); Kelly Monroe Kullberg, ed., *Finding God at Harvard: Spiritual Journeys of Thinking Christians* (Downers Grove: InterVarsity Press, 1997) and *Finding God beyond Harvard: The Quest for Veritas* (Downers Grove: InterVarsity Press, 2006). See also the American Scientific Affiliation (online: http://www.asa3.org/) and its academic journal *Perspectives on Science and Christian Faith*, the Canadian Scientific and Christian Affiliation (online: http://www.csca.ca/), the C.S. Lewis Foundation (online: http://www.cslewis.org/), the Regent College Marketplace

of the life of the mind within the contemporary evangelical movement. A view of the church as rational communities of the new humanity attends to this. Such communities rationally embody the historic Christian tradition (i.e., MacIntyre's notion of community as an extended argument) and prioritize cultivating people who are characterized by the cumulative and thus historically embedded wisdom offered by that tradition. By participating in such communities believers are equipped to *think Christianly*, to *think theologically* from a Christian perspective, about every aspect of life.

Wisdom cultivation through theological formation
One crucial way of cultivating wisdom is through theological formation. The theological formation of believers in the church has to do primarily with the accumulation of theological knowledge and the development of a coherent Christian worldview.[26] Regarding theological knowledge, congregations have the responsibility to teach their members about the Bible, key doctrines, and important aspects of the congregation's particular theological tradition, as well as important aspects of the historic Christian tradition— for example, the definitive early creeds, knowledge about the Reformation, the Great Awakening and Wesleyan revival, the twentieth century evangelical movement, Vatican II, and other key developments). Evangelicals might find an emphasis on learning about history and tradition odd, but, as writers such as Alasdair MacIntyre, Charles Taylor, and Stanley Hauerwas have convincingly demonstrated, a sense of narrative or historical contextualization is fundamental to the establishment and maintenance of identity—for both individuals and communities.

Knowledge of the Bible, doctrine, and tradition should be taught on at least three levels. The first level concerns facts. This level includes learning basic information, definitions, concepts, and key names and places, for example the prophets and apostles, the cities to which the New Testament epistles are addressed, and major theological figures (e.g., Athanasius, Irenaeus, Tertullian, the Cappadocians, Augustine, Anselm, Hildegard of Bingen, Aquinas, Julian of

---

Institute (online: http://www2.regent-college.edu/marketplace/), and the Veritas Forum (online: http://www.veritas.org/).

[26] Since I am discussing theological knowledge in particular, it is appropriate to use the term "worldview". By using this term, I am not endorsing a rationalistic approach to faith and knowledge. In chapter 8, I emphasize holistic character formation, which includes worldview but goes beyond it to include the role of tradition, narrative, rituals, and practices in the context of community for the cultivation of both intellectual and moral virtues. Combining these two emphases (worldview and the social embodiment of worldview in traditions) leads to an integrative approach that acknowledges the formative role of what Charles Taylor calls "social imaginaries". See Charles Taylor, *Modern Social Imaginaries* (Durham: Duke University Press, 2004). See also James K.A. Smith's discussion of social imaginaries in *Desiring the Kingdom*, 65–71.

Norwich, Luther, Calvin, Wesley, Barth, Bonhoeffer, Catherine Booth, etc.).[27] The second level concerns contexts and the application of facts therein. For example, knowing that God created the heavens and the earth in six days is factual knowledge. Knowing that the creation account was addressed to a specific group operating with a functional ontology in the Ancient Near East is contextual knowledge. Knowing that the writer was encouraging his audience to worship Yahweh alone and to serve as Yahweh's steward-priests is an application of the relevant facts interpreted in context. The third level concerns learning to recognize principles and patterns in Scripture, including analogical comparisons, typological themes, and hermeneutical lenses. Returning to the example just given, a principle might be that our role as steward-priests of Yahweh leads us to think and behave in ways that are different from those who do not follow Yahweh, such as valuing the intrinsic dignity of all people who are created in God's image. An example of a pattern is to notice the significance attributed to the offices of prophet, priest, and king in the Old Testament, leading to their fulfilment in Jesus Christ and finally their reapplication to Christians who share in Christ's ongoing ministry by the Spirit. Doctrines and traditions can similarly be taught in this multileveled way of exploring facts, contexts, principles, and patterns. To employ a literary analogy: factual knowledge is like learning letters and words; contextual knowledge is like realizing that words appear in sentences, paragraphs, chapters, and sections; knowledge of principles is like understanding advanced grammar; and knowledge of patterns is like learning to identify genre, narrative, and plot. The salient point is that accumulating Christian knowledge involves not just memorizing and regurgitating information, but also reflection, analysis, creative engagement, and an ability to integrate what one is learning with concrete situations in one's own life. Churches can provide such teaching in a variety of formats, including preaching (which aims to demonstrate and model such learning), catechism classes (in preparation for baptism), teaching seminars, Sunday school or study classes, small groups led by capable leaders, or through learning opportunities resulting from partnerships with seminaries (e.g., public lectures, colloquiums, conferences, and satellite classes hosted at local churches that members can audit).

The accumulation of knowledge is not an end in itself but aims toward worldview formation and wise living. Worldview formation involves shaping basic convictions in accordance with ultimate reality and the relation of human beings to it. This includes, first, shaping fundamental convictions about the identity and character of the trinitarian God and God's dealings with humanity

---

[27] The stories of godly and influential women in the history of the church are often neglected or ignored, which is something that we should remedy. For a helpful source on the importance and impact of women in the historic Christian tradition, see Ruth A. Tucker and Walter Liefeld, *Daughters of the Church: Women and Ministry from New Testament Times to the Present* (Grand Rapids: Academie/Zondervan, 1987).

(such as are included in the Apostles', Nicene, and Chalcedonian creeds). It includes, secondly, shaping fundamental convictions about human beings as God's creatures, including fundamental convictions about the threefold human *telos* of loving God and other human beings, knowing God and understanding God's created world, and serving God and others as steward-priests of creation. It involves, thirdly, enabling a theological grasp of the salvation narrative that recognizes its four great plot movements: (1) God created the world and human beings to be good; (2) human sin distorts the created goodness of human beings and the natural world; (3) in and through Jesus Christ all things are reconciled, redeemed, and restored; human participation in this involves a faith response; and (4) the Holy Spirit is drawing all things that are reconciled in Christ toward eschatological fulfillment and final perfection in glory.[28] Fourth, it involves shaping fundamental convictions about what constitutes a genuine and satisfying human life.[29] Finally, it involves shaping fundamental convictions about where one finds trustworthy and authoritative teaching concerning what constitutes a genuine and satisfying human life.[30] For Christians, such teaching is found primarily in Scripture, interpreted with the aid of tradition, reason, and the direct illumination and guidance of the Holy Spirit.

In addition to gaining theological knowledge and developing a Christian worldview grounded in vital basic theological convictions, believers also need the church to equip them to *think theologically*. Many people in the contemporary church who hear the word "theology" react negatively. They immediately picture anxious and uptight people engaged in highly abstract and theoretical debate over obscure issues and minor details. Others simply equate theology with doctrine and assume that theological study concerns memorizing and re-

---

[28] For the overall structure of the biblical salvation narrative, see also: Brian J. Walsh and J. Richard Middleton, *The Transforming Vision: Shaping a Christian World View* (Grand Rapids: InterVarsity Press, 1984), part 2 (chapters 3–5); Cornelius Plantinga, Jr., *Engaging God's World: A Christian Vision of Faith, Learning, and Living* (Grand Rapids: Eerdmans, 2002), chapters 2–4; and Michael W. Goheen and Craig G. Bartholomew, *Living at the Crossroads: An Introduction to Christian Worldview* (Grand Rapids: Baker Academic, 2008), chapters 3–4.

[29] See Dallas Willard, *Knowing Christ Today: Why We Can Trust Spiritual Knowledge* (New York: HarperOne, 2005), 51–3.

[30] Walsh and Middleton suggest a slightly different approach, based on the following four questions (*The Transforming Vision*, 35): (1) Who am I? Or, what is the nature, task and purpose of human beings?; (2) Where am I? Or, what is the nature of the world and universe in which I live?; (3) What's wrong? Or, what is the basic problem or obstacle that keeps me from attaining fulfillment?; (4) What is the remedy? Or, how is it possible to overcome this hindrance to my fulfillment? Dallas Willard suggests the following four worldview questions, each of which Jesus answers (*Knowing Christ Today*, 50–55): (1) What is reality? (God and God's kingdom); (2) Who is truly well-off or blessed? (Anyone who is alive in the kingdom of God); (3) Who is a really good person? (Anyone who is pervaded with love); and (4) How do you become a really good person? (You place your confidence in Jesus Christ and become his student or apprentice in kingdom living).

gurgitating doctrinal statements and positions. Sometimes such views about theology are justified. Too often there is a disconnection between the church and the world of academic theology, a problem that goes in two directions. On the one hand, theologians sometimes forget that their calling is to serve the church. Instead, they focus on their academic careers and dedicate their energies to making specialized contributions to their professional field without drawing out the relevance of their work for the church or the lives of Christian believers. Consequently, theology becomes an abstract academic discipline to which regular church-going people cannot relate. On the other hand, sometimes the problem lies with churches. Sometimes churches forget that their mission and ministries are theological in nature. Such churches end up operating with unexamined cultural assumptions and values, such as pragmatism, consumerism, and worldly notions of success. Consequently, they begin to resemble secular organizations or corporations and lose their prophetic voice and Christian distinctiveness. Young pastors entering these churches after seminary find that their theological and pastoral training is regarded as less valuable than their ability to run programs efficiently and lead the church successfully (success is often equated with numerical growth). So they become absorbed in church business and lose interest in maintaining current theological competence and knowledge. Their own theology becomes rote and outdated, which has detrimental effects on their teaching. Some simply neglect theology altogether, which results in unreflective teaching that ends up reinforcing cultural values and assumptions rather than addressing them critically.[31] Some occasionally address theological topics, but then fail to integrate theology with everyday life and the pressing issues that contemporary people are facing. Such teaching confuses the regurgitation of doctrine with thoughtful and contextual theological engagement; hence it fails to facilitate the cultivation of wisdom and intensifies the sense that theology is stuffy, boring, and irrelevant.

The overall effect of the academic–pragmatic theological dichotomy is that a distinctly Christian worldview becomes stifled and exerts less and less influence on the daily thinking and living of Christians. In contrast to this dichotomy, the church needs to exhort and equip *all Christians* to think theologically. Thinking theologically involves the accumulation of theological knowledge and the development of Christian worldview as discussed above, but it also involves a conscious effort to reflect in a disciplined way about *all of life* in light of Christian truth. The goal of theology is to enable Christians to know God more deeply and coherently, to help them develop characteristically Christian patterns of thought and evaluation, to guide them in living lives that correspond

---

[31] Stanley Hauerwas cautions that "when a sermon is thought to be no more than a speech by the minister to provide advice to help us negotiate life, the content of sermons usually are exemplifications of the superficial and sentimental pieties of a liberal culture." See *A Cross-Shattered Church: Reclaiming the Theological Heart of Preaching* (Grand Rapids: Brazos, 2009), 19.

to God's character and purposes, and to equip them to share their knowledge of God with others accurately, effectively, and humbly as they seek to edify others in the church and share the gospel with those outside the church. In this sense, *every Christian should be a theologian.*

Pastors are charged with the special task of equipping Christians in their congregations to think theologically.[32] This requires that pastors themselves continually seek to grow in their theological knowledge and competence through ongoing theological study and awareness of contemporary theological developments. Staying up-to-date is important, not in order to be theologically trendy but because theology is inherently a dynamic enterprise that develops and shifts as it attempts to relate the knowledge of God to developments in human learning and experience. Sometimes theology can seem irrelevant because pastors rely on outdated theological knowledge and training to address complex contemporary issues, hence they address them inadequately (e.g., the origins of human life debate). Or sometimes reliance on outdated theology makes pastors ignorant of contemporary developments in human knowledge, which leads to the dismissal or avoidance of pressing contemporary issues and concerns facing congregants (e.g., current issues in bioethics, such as reproductive or genetic interventions). In contrast, pastors should strive always to grow in theological wisdom, which involves continual growth of their knowledge of God and their knowledge of the world. Perhaps an apt and helpful analogy for the *pastor as wise theologian* is the role of a physician or medical doctor. Medicine is a practice that involves a mixture of daily, down-to-earth involvement with everyday people (bedside manner), practical skills in diagnosing and treating medical problems, mastery of theoretical knowledge about human anatomy and biology, and ongoing education with respect to new discoveries and developments in the medical field. The best physicians relate well to people, have mastered medical knowledge and key skills, and stay up-to-date with contemporary medical advances. In a similar way, the pastoral role as a *theological call* involves practical involvement in the lives of real people, the ability to use acquired skills effectively (e.g., skills required for effective pastoral care and counselling,

---

[32] Kevin J. Vanhoozer, *The Drama of Doctrine: A Canonical-linguistic Approach to Christian Theology* (Louisville: Westminster John Knox, 2005), 447–48. In Vanhoozer's dramatic analogy, pastors and elders are charged with the task of "directing the company" of actors. The church needs discipline and direction in order to perform the Scriptures faithfully. Doctrine provides such direction, but doctrine must be instructed. Such instruction takes place primarily through the sermon. Pastors and elders serve as assistant directors (to the Holy Spirit) to help people understand the play (the theo-drama) and grow into their parts. This involves helping people see their identity as being in Christ, learning the script (the Bible) and understanding how to perform it faithfully in the contemporary context. "What the pastor/director really needs to do is take the congregation's imagination captive to the Scriptures so that the theo-drama becomes the governing framework of the community's speech and action (2 Cor 10:5). The pastor/director needs to instil confidence in a congregation that *this* script is the way to truth and abundant life." (448)

preaching, mentoring, etc.), the mastery of biblical and theological knowledge, and continuing education leading to an awareness of advances in the study of theology and its related disciplines such as pastoral and spiritual theology, apologetics, ethics, and missiology.

While we should regard all Christians as theologians in some sense, and pastors even more so, there remains a crucial need in the church for people with a special call and recognized giftedness to study and teach theology, in other words theologians proper. Advanced theological study and practical involvement in concrete ecclesial life are mutually enriching. As Daniel Treier writes,

> The call for every-believer theologizing does not trivialize the word 'theology,' but heightens responsibility. Nor does that call deny the special gift or office of teaching the church, in which the intensity of discernment—and usually of engagement with scholarship—is heightened. However, the difference concerns degree, not kind.[33]

The unique task of professional theologians is to study at an advanced level the sources of Christian theology—Scripture, tradition (including doctrine and history), reason (rational and empirical knowledge), and religious experience (of the Spirit of God)—and to make the fruit of their study relevant to and fruitful for the church. Such advanced study is most likely to be relevant and fruitful when theologians care deeply about the church and are aware of its pressing needs, are committed members of a local congregation, and are involved in ministry at some level (anything from helping ministries to hospitality to teaching). Theologians impact the church positively when they share the fruit of their study with others, for example by teaching pastors at seminaries, by speaking at conferences and seminars for pastors and lay people, by writing books that help people grow in theological competence, and by contributing to the theological formation and education of their congregations.

Wisdom cultivation through constitutive and formative practices that shape the mind

Within the church Christians also cultivate wisdom as they participate in the church's constitutive and formative practices. First, they cultivate wisdom by participating in the church's constitutive practices of the Word and the sacramental ordinances. Through the ministry of the preached Word, believers receive theological and practical instruction in the Christian faith. Preachers should aim not simply to disseminate theological information or, at the other end of the spectrum, to offer theology-light practical self-help tips for successful living. Rather, preachers should aim to increase their congregants' knowledge and understanding of God and God's purposes, shape their basic convictions and worldview accordingly, and help them narrate their lives in

---

[33] Treier, *Virtue and the Voice of God*, 90.

light of Scripture.[34] The latter involves helping people to see their own place in God's overarching story, which addresses them personally and reorients their lives, so that they can improvise upon it faithfully and wisely under the guidance of the indwelling Holy Spirit.[35] In addition to hearing and being shaped by the preached Word, individual Christians cultivate wisdom as they study Scripture together—by reading and analyzing it, meditating and reflecting upon it, and engaging with it practically by sharing how it addresses them personally, applies to their lives, and challenges them to grow.

Through the practice of the sacramental ordinances, Christians develop wisdom as they remember and symbolically re-enact the ministry and saving work of Jesus Christ. Such acts of remembrance continually ground the church's life in the life of Christ and guide its ongoing life and ministry.[36] For example, to encourage his readers toward faithful Christian living, the apostle Paul reminded them of their baptism and exhorted them to live in accordance with their new resurrection life in Christ (Rom 6:3–6; Col 2:12). At the Last Supper, Jesus shared bread and wine with his disciples as symbols of his body and blood, which he would soon sacrifice for the sake of sinners. He told them "Do this in remembrance of me" (Luke 22:19) and thus initiated the meal of remembrance that the church celebrates as the Lord's Supper. In addition to grounding the life and ministry of Christians in Christ, the sacramental ordinances also unite them to the historic Christian church, which has practiced both baptism and the Lord's Supper since its inception and throughout its history (though the formal sacramental ritual developed over time).[37] Paul's instructions to the Corinthians concerning proper celebration of the Lord's Supper revealed that he was passing on to them the tradition that he himself had received, a tradition that went back to Christ (1 Cor 11:23). He discussed not just proper order for the Supper, but also the implications it entailed for genuine Christian life and community (1 Cor 11:27–34). In summary, the sacramental ordinances remind Christians of

---

[34] On the theme of narrating our lives by the story of Scripture, see Stanley Hauerwas, *A Community of Character: Toward a Constructive Christian Social Ethic* (Notre Dame: University of Notre Dame Press, 1981), 9–12, 50–52, *Christian Existence Today: Essays on Church, World, and Living in Between* (Grand Rapids: Brazos, 2001), 47–61; 101–103, and *The Peaceable Kingdom: A Primer in Christian Ethics* (Notre Dame: University of Notre Dame Press, 1983), 99–100.

[35] Treier argues that Scripture does not "provide a complicated and comprehensive calculus for scientific, topical application to every judgment. Rather, Scripture and its derivative healthy teaching are to form us wisely as Christian persons and communities, enabled by the Spirit (within certain commanded boundaries) to discern how the 'logic' of the gospel fits particular circumstances." Treier, *Virtue and the Voice of God*, 54.

[36] Stanley Hauerwas, *In Good Company: The Church as Polis* (Notre Dame: University of Notre Dame Press, 1995), 160. See also Vanhoozer, *The Drama of Doctrine*, 410.

[37] Miroslav Volf, *After Our Likeness: The Church as the Image of the Trinity* (Grand Rapids: Eerdmans, 1998), 152–53.

Christ's saving work and encourage them to live out the implications of their salvation in their thinking, ministry, and shared life together.

The church also helps Christians to cultivate wisdom through its corporate worship practices. As mentioned in the previous chapter, worship is a broad topic encompassing all of Christian life; as James K.A. Smith argues, "worship is at the heart of being human".[38] One of the aspects of worship that is often neglected in contemporary churches is its formative function in shaping Christian thought and life. Yet a fundamental component of worship in the Bible concerns its role in shaping the beliefs and actions of God's people as they rehearse God's Word (e.g., God's Law and promises) and celebrate God's mighty acts in salvation history (especially the Exodus in the Old Testament and the Christ event in the New Testament).[39] There are many examples of rehearsing God's Word and celebrating God's saving deeds in the Psalms. The New Testament similarly includes hymns and worship scenes, which rehearse and celebrate God's character and saving activity in Christ and encourage believers toward specific beliefs, attitudes, and actions in the present (e.g., Phil 2:5–11; Rev 4–5). The Bible indicates that there is a deep connection between whom or what one worships and the kind of person one is becoming. Biblical worship aligns people to God and conforms their character and actions to God's own. As Smith puts it, "Worship is the ordering and reordering of our material being to the end for which it was meant."[40] Unfortunately, worship as an alignment mechanism can work in the opposite direction as well: false or distorted worship shapes people in negative ways, often quite subtly.[41] As N.T. Wright puts it,

> *You become what you worship.* When you gaze in awe, admiration, and wonder at something or someone, you begin to take on something of the character of the object of your worship. Those who worship money become, eventually, human calculating machines. Those who worship sex become obsessed with their own attractiveness or prowess. Those who worship power become more and more ruthless.[42]

One of the reasons why idolatry is so disastrous is that it aligns and conforms people to what is distorted or evil. For instance, Psalm 115:4–8 suggests that those who make idols become like them (i.e., without sense, lifeless) and Jeremiah criticizes the Israelites who "worshiped worthless idols, only to become worthless themselves" (Jer 2:5). While contemporary Westerners are unlikely

---

[38] Smith, *Desiring the Kingdom*, 166.
[39] See, for example, Robert E. Webber, *Worship Old & New* (Grand Rapids: Zondervan, 1994).
[40] Smith, *Desiring the Kingdom*, 143.
[41] Smith, *Desiring the Kingdom*, 23, 85–88, 93–101, 103–18, 121–26.
[42] N.T. Wright, *Surprised by Hope: Rethinking Heaven, the Resurrection, and the Mission of the Church* (New York: HarperOne, 2008), 147–49.

to worship idols in the form of literal statues or images, they are constantly invited to give themselves over to forms of idolatry that are subtler yet equally insidious (perhaps even more so), such as consumerism, nationalism, or political correctness.[43] True worship aligns people with the truth; false worship aligns them with illusion and distortion and amounts to idolatry.[44] Genuine Christian worship is crucial to the development of true wisdom in believers, as a practice of formation in the way of Jesus and as a practice of counter-formation against the ways of the world. As Alan Kreider reminds us concerning the early church,

> The churches' worship services were not designed to be evangelistic. Nor were their services designed to move the hearts of the worshipers. The churches' acts of worship rather were designed to glorify God and to form the worshipers into attractive, intriguing disciples of Jesus Christ and their congregations into communities that embodied the way of Jesus.[45]

Churches would do well to reflect carefully about how they are shaping people in worship. For example, worship that caters to consumer tastes will reinforce consumerist patterns of thought and behaviour. Whatever style and form worship takes, churches need to be intentional and diligent about what its worship practices are communicating, teaching, and embodying.[46] Worship is a wonderful experience, something people often enjoy; it is a great opportunity to teach and shape people with solid theological content, whether through song, poetry, prayer, responsive readings from Scripture and the creeds, or meaningful and intentionally crafted artistic expressions and symbolic acts.

---

[43] James K.A. Smith provides an intriguing discussion of how several contemporary secular institutions and practices actively seek to form and shape peoples' desires and allegiances, often operating under the facade of neutrality or pragmatism. He seeks to expose the way in which such institutions and practices operate as subtle (often operating at sub-conscious or pre-cognitive level) yet deeply formative liturgies, which strategically train people to think and feel in certain distinct ways (e.g., inferiority for lacking some product) and thus direct their love and energy toward certain ends (e.g., purchasing the product to address the lack). Smith argues that these liturgies lead people into false worship or idolatry, which Christian worship must correct through counter-formation. Examples of such secular liturgies include "the mall", "the military entertainment complex" (professional sports), and the university as a "cathedral of learning". See Smith, *Desiring the Kingdom*, 89–129.

[44] For an extended treatment of this theme, see G.K. Beale, *We Become What We Worship: A Biblical Theology of Idolatry* (Downers Grove: InterVarsity Press, 2008).

[45] Alan Kreider, "They Alone Know the Right Way to Live: The Early Church and Evangelism," In *Ancient Faith for the Church's Future*, ed. Mark Husbands and Jeffrey P. Greenman (Downers Grove: InterVarsity Press, 2008), 185–86.

[46] Kevin Vanhoozer writes, "Worship is ritualized theology; theology is reflective worship" (*The Drama of Doctrine*, 410). Thus, the quality of a congregation's worship reflects the quality of its theology.

The Church as Rational Communities of Faith

A third way that the church is called to help congregants cultivate wisdom is by encouraging them to participate in spiritual disciplines that form healthy habits of thought and action. In order for spiritual disciplines to be effective in cultivating wisdom, churches need to instruct their members on the purpose of such disciplines (e.g., Matt 6).[47] It needs to be clear that spiritual disciplines are not meritorious actions that automatically earn God's favour, although practicing them properly can generate awareness of God's presence and providence. Accordingly, Jesus told his disciples not to babble on like the pagans when they prayed. God is not impressed with fancy words chanted repeatedly; God already knows one's needs and wants to be addressed with simplicity and sincerity (Matt 6:7–8). Moreover, the spiritual disciplines do not of themselves make Christians holier or more righteous. They are not necessarily morally valuable in and of themselves, though they are often closely tied to moral goals. For example, the discipline of simplicity can help people attend to what is most important in their lives and lead to better stewardship of time, money, and resources. The discipline of fasting can help people become aware of their dependency on God and increase their gratitude to God. In addition, practicing a spiritual discipline should not draw the attention of others to oneself, but rather increase the intensity of the practitioner's attention to God (Matt 6:5–6, 16–18).

Some examples of spiritual disciples that help Christians cultivate wisdom include meditation, study, and receiving guidance from other Christians.[48] In addition, the discipline of prayer helps Christians to be attentive to God and thus grow in wisdom. Thus in his prayer for the Ephesians, Paul prays that God would give his readers spiritual wisdom and understanding to know God better and to discern God's purposes for their lives (Eph 1:16–23). Meditative prayer and contemplative prayer are particularly important in this regard, as is persistent prayer for God's specific guidance in one's life.[49] Prayer also leads to wisdom by helping believers grow in faith and trust in God (recall the connection between faith and wisdom). As they bring their lives before God in prayer, believers come to God in a spirit of humility and surrender, bringing their needs and concerns to God and waiting expectantly for God's provision and guidance in their daily lives.

---

[47] For an excellent introduction and analysis, see Dallas Willard, *The Spirit of the Disciplines: Understanding How God Changes Lives* (San Francisco: Harper & Row, 1988).

[48] For a helpful discussion of these spiritual disciplines, see Richard J. Foster, *The Celebration of Discipline: The Path to Spiritual Growth* (New York: Harper and Row, 1978). See also the helpful discussion of "listening prayer" in Glen H. Stassen and David P. Gushee, *Kingdom Ethics: Following Jesus in Contemporary Context* (Downers Grove: InterVarsity Press, 2003), 459–64.

[49] See Richard J. Foster, *Prayer: Finding the Heart's True Home* (New York: HarperSanFrancisco, 1992).

Wisdom cultivation through wise leadership
The scope of this chapter precludes a full discussion of leadership structures in the church, but I do want to comment briefly on the kind of leadership that is implied by the notion of the church as a rational community of faith. Regardless of the specific ecclesial leadership structures churches have in place, all should emphasize the importance of wisdom, maturity of character, and a desire and commitment to lead by serving and equipping others.[50] Leadership is not about promoting mere conformity to authority or rule-following; it is about raising others up into maturity of faith and wisdom and preparing them for ministry in the church and mission in the world. Even Paul, despite his being an apostle instilled with great authority, was inclined to persuade and exhort the congregations rather than giving outright commands (consider the care and effort he takes in crafting his letters to help readers anticipate the ethical implications of the gospel). In terms of essential leadership qualities, the New Testament places an immense emphasis on wisdom: leaders should be characterized by wisdom and godly character and seek to cultivate the same qualities in others. Leaders should therefore be humble, morally upright and trustworthy, knowledgeable of Scripture and theology (able to teach), self-disciplined in their own affairs with their priorities properly aligned, mature in the faith, and have a good reputation in the church and broader community (1 Tim 3:1–12).

The church engaging the world

Participating in Christ's prophetic ministry

As witnesses and servants of the truth
As rational communities of the new humanity, the church is called not only to cultivate wisdom among its members but also to influence the world toward wise living. Of course, the two are intimately connected: as the church cultivates wisdom in its members it is thereby preparing them to influence the world. Consequently, everything in the previous section about cultivating wisdom in the church is relevant to the church's engagement with the world. Wisdom enables Christians to prioritize what is truly valuable, to make the best of their time, money, and resources, to develop healthy and satisfying friendships, to enjoy their marriages and experience God's blessing and guidance as they

---

[50] Authority in the early church was exercised by leaders who led by example and through service. Their leadership was not authoritarian in nature, but was always a derivative of Christ's ultimate authority, hence church leaders acted as stewards of Christ's authority. They were called and gifted for their task by the Holy Spirit. There seems to have been flexibility and diversity in the leadership structures of the church, however those who were called to be apostles, prophets, teachers, elders, and shepherds had primary leadership responsibilities (but we must be careful not to import anachronistic notions of leadership back into the New Testament). See Schmithals, *Theology of the First Christians*, 170, and Guthrie, *New Testament Theology*, 760–62.

raise children. None of this comes automatically. Wisdom calls, but people must listen and respond with diligence. Moreover, the pursuit of wisdom is not a lonely venture, but one that places people in a community that is dedicated to pursuing wisdom together and accordingly offers teaching, encouragement, guidance, and accountability. When duly cultivated and confidently lived out, such wise living is attractive to the surrounding world and thus strengthens the Christian community's witness and maximizes its impact in influencing the world. Accordingly, Jesus instructs the community of his disciples to let their light shine brightly, so that everyone will see the quality of their God-infused life and give praise and glory to God (Matt 5:16).

As the church lives out the life of wisdom in the midst of the world, it participates in Christ's prophetic ministry as witnesses and servants of the truth. Of the many things that prophets do in Scripture, two things stand out for the purposes of the present discussion: prophets *proclaim* and *demonstrate* God's truth to the world, often in compelling and even provocative ways. Similarly, the church is called to proclaim and demonstrate God's truth to the world. It is important to emphasize that the church does not accomplish this merely by its own intelligence, ingenuity, and strength, but is called to pursue its mission actively and confidently as it participates by the Spirit in Christ's own prophetic ministry in the world. We will briefly consider what it means to proclaim the gospel in the present section and subsequently consider what it means to demonstrate the truth of the gospel in the next section.

Proclaiming the gospel means publically declaring the explicit content of the Christian good news that Jesus Christ is Lord and King, that the kingdom of God is at hand and is coming in fullness and permanence, and that Christ invites us to enter a new way of life in his eternal kingdom. In his Great Commission, Jesus instructed his disciples to "go and *make disciples* of all the nations, *baptizing* them in the name of the Father and the Son and the Holy Spirit and *teaching them to obey all the commands I have given you*" and then he assured them "surely I am with you always, even to the end of the age" (Matt 28:19–20; emphasis added). Three insights from this passage are instructive concerning the church's mission of proclamation. First, proclaiming God's truth involves making and baptizing disciples of Jesus Christ. The church's ministry of proclaiming the truth in the world includes not just teaching the world how to live better, or how to be more successful, or how to achieve personal self-fulfillment and prosperity. Ultimately, the church's ministry of proclamation aims for worldview transformation or what Scripture calls "conversion".[51] As a religion, Christianity is unique in that it does not just offer answers and solu-

---

[51] I think this is what Stanley Hauerwas is getting at when he says that the church's primary task is not to make the world "just" but to make the world "the world". In other words the church, as an alternate community or *polis* in allegiance to a different Lord, calls the world to make a fundamental choice about Jesus. See, for example, Hauerwas, *In Good Company*, 19–21, 251, and *Christian Existence Today*, 101–103.

tions to life problems that come from a great teacher; rather, Christianity's great teacher and Lord *is himself the answer*. The teachings of Jesus are unique not because they are novel and totally different from the wisdom offered by other religions and philosophies (there are both close similarities and vast differences between the teachings of Christianity and other world religions and philosophies). The teachings of Jesus are unique because of who Jesus is. Jesus himself claimed: "I am the way and the truth and the life. No one comes to the Father except through me" (John 14:6). As the incarnation of the *Logos* of God, Jesus Christ uniquely and authoritatively embodies the presence, mind, and character of God (John 1:1, 14, 18; Col 1:15). This claim is consistent with orthodox Christology, which maintains that Christ's person and Christ's work are intimately and indissolubly linked together.[52] Christian wisdom claims knowledge of the truth and boldly proclaims the way to life only because Jesus Christ is himself the truth and the way to eternal life. As Peter responded after hearing some of Christ's difficult teachings and being asked if he, like the others, would desert Jesus, "Lord, to whom would we go? You alone have the words that give eternal life. We believe them, and we know you are the Holy One of God" (John 6:68–69). Christian wisdom coincides with natural knowledge derived from creation, but it makes comprehensive sense only when one sees and acknowledges that Jesus Christ is Lord. Consequently, the church's call to proclaim the truth involves evangelism.

    Second, while proclaiming the truth aims at conversion it also involves more than evangelism. It includes training disciples and teaching them all that Christ instructed. It is significant that the Great Commission appears at the end of Matthew's gospel rather than at the beginning. The commission presupposes everything that precedes it in the gospel, including all of Jesus's teaching, the intimate time Jesus spent with his disciples in mentoring them, the on-the-job missionary training the disciples received as they followed Jesus and joined him in ministry, and the difficulties they encountered along the way such as confrontations with religious and political leaders. The majority consensus of New Testament scholarship is that the central theme of Jesus's proclamation in the synoptic gospels is the kingdom of God.[53] In light of this, the full meaning of Jesus's Great Commission in context is to go and make *kingdom disciples or apprentices*. Consequently, Christian proclamation aims not merely to win new converts but to enlist, instruct, mentor, and train apprentices of Christ's kingdom life, so that they too become servants of the kingdom and agents of the new creation. Moreover the instruction to baptize new believers in the name of the Father, the Son, and the Holy Spirit indicates that proclaiming the gospel involves introducing people to a whole new kind of life. Baptism indicates death to one life and rebirth into another (Rom 6). It also involves joining in

---

[52] Alister E. McGrath, *Christian Theology: An Introduction* (Cambridge: Blackwell, 2007), chapters 11 and 13.

[53] See Stassen and Gushee, *Kingdom Ethics*, 19.

community with others who are pursuing and living out the new kingdom life in a comprehensive and holistic way.

Third, Christ promises to be with the church as it pursues its ministry of proclaiming the truth. Christ's presence imbues the church with Christ's own prophetic authority and power to teach and demonstrate the truth. As Jesus makes clear, "All authority on heaven and earth has been given to me. *Therefore*, go and make disciples . . . ." (Matt 28:18–19a; emphasis added). The church is not itself the ultimate authority of truth; the church's authority is a derivative authority that is contingent upon its faithfulness to Christ and Christ's teachings. In addition, Christ does not simply leave the church alone to fulfill its mission, but promises to be present and involved as the church actively seeks first the kingdom of God. Christ's promise in the Great Commission assures the church that when it pursues its mission it does so not merely by its own strength and wisdom, but in the power and presence of its active and living Lord, Jesus Christ.

Incarnation as a model for demonstrating truth in the church's engagement with the world

Jesus not only proclaimed the kingdom; he also demonstrated its presence and power by his character and actions. Jesus not only preached the gospel; his whole life embodied it. When John the Baptist sent Jesus a message asking him if he was the Messiah, Jesus responded: "Go back to John and tell him about what you have heard and seen—the blind see, the lame walk, the lepers are cured, the deaf hear, the dead are raised to life, and the Good News is being preached to the poor" (Matt 11:4). By responding in this way, Jesus was not evading John's question but was essentially saying "Yes! And here's the proof. . . so be confident!" Jesus responded not just with words and arguments, but by pointing to his own actions as a compelling demonstration of the dawning of the kingdom and *thus* to his status as Messiah and King. However, Jesus's ability to demonstrate the gospel and the kingdom was dependent upon a prior and more fundamental event, namely the incarnation. In order to reach out to the world and to demonstrate the kingdom of God, Jesus first came into the world to dwell among us. God did not merely send yet another messenger to give a new law. God the Son became human and entered into our existence in order to relate to us intimately and show us *in person* what kingdom life is really like. "The Word became human and lived here on earth among us. He was full of unfailing love and faithfulness. And we have seen his glory, the glory of the only Son of the Father" (John 1:14). Since God became incarnate in order to demonstrate to us in person the good news of the kingdom, the incarnation can serve as a model for the church as it engages its culture and world to demonstrate God's truth.

The incarnation as a model of cultural and worldly engagement emphasizes three principles. First, an incarnational model requires the church to go out into the world, rather than always expecting the world to come to the church. This reflects the sending model of God's own redemptive mission to save humanity: "But [Jesus] said to them, 'I must proclaim the good news of the kingdom of God to the other cities also; for I was sent for this purpose'" (Luke 4:43; cf. Luke 9:1–2). Accordingly, Jesus became incarnate and went forth into the world to proclaim and demonstrate the good news. Jesus repeated the pattern with his own disciples. When Jesus called them to follow him, he told them that he would "send" them out to "fish for people" (Mark 1:17). Later, as he apprenticed his disciples, Jesus sent them out in pairs into the mission field for training (Mark 6:7). He instructed them to pray that God would send more workers into the harvest field (the world) to reach people with the gospel (Matt 9:38; Luke 10:2). In his Great Commission, the Risen Jesus reiterated the sending model by commanding his disciples to *go out* and make disciples of *all nations* (Matt 28:19). The Gospel of John similarly records the Risen Jesus telling his disciples, "As the Father has sent me, so I am sending you" (John 20:21). And again, in Acts 1:8, the Risen Christ reaffirms the church's mandate to go out into the world, saying: "You will be my witnesses in Jerusalem, throughout Judea, in Samaria, and to the ends of the earth."

Engaging the world relevantly does not mean endorsing a seeker model of church. Rather, it means being a church that equips believers *to be sensitive seekers* as they go out into the world to seek and reach others with the love and truth of Christ.[54] It does not entail being an attractional church, which devises worship services and programs to satisfy the needs of religious consumers who (hopefully) come through its doors.[55] Rather, an incarnational model involves forming believers *to lead attractional lives* that are characterized by the wisdom of God and model a way of living according to God's purposes and priorities in their whole existence in the world. As Marva Dawn nicely puts it,

> We gather together in worship to speak our language, to read our narratives of God at work, to sing authentic hymns of the faith in all kinds of styles, to chant and pour out our prayers until we know the truth so well that we can go out to the world around us and invite that world to share this truth with us. In our worship, we are formed by biblical narratives that tell a different story from that of the surrounding culture.[56]

Second, an incarnational model involves reaching people by forming relationships. It especially supports approaches to evangelism and witness that are personal and relationship-building rather than mechanistic or impersonal. Throughout his ministry Jesus took time to relate to people, to care for them as

---

[54] Kreider, "They Alone Know," 185–86.
[55] Michael Frost and Alan Hirsch, *The Shape of Things to Come: Innovation and Ministry for the 21st Century Church* (Peabody: Hendrickson, 2003), 17–59, 157–58.
[56] Marva J. Dawn, "Worship to Form a Missional Community," *Direction* 28 (Fall 1999): 141.

individuals, and to minister to them in intimately personal ways. He pronounced the forgiveness of their sins (e.g., Mark 2:5), he gave specific spiritual advice or counselling (e.g., Nicodemus in John 3). He delivered many individuals from sickness, disease, blindness, paralysis, and demonic oppression. Granted, Jesus also addressed large crowds, so we should not dismiss large scale evangelistic efforts out of hand; evangelism needs to take place at multiple levels and contexts. Nevertheless, Jesus prioritized investing time and effort to reach and train a small group of disciples (especially the twelve) so that they could, in turn, do the same and achieve growth that is exponential, deeply transformative and sustainable in the long run (see also Paul's encouragement to Timothy in 2 Tim 2:2). In addition, an incarnational model patterned after Jesus commits churches to reaching not only people who fit a homogenous target demographic but also people who are quite different, especially those who are marginalized or looked down upon by the world. Examples of this in Jesus's ministry include his ministry to the Samaritan woman and her community (John 4), his practice of eating with sinners and tax collectors (e.g., at the homes of Levi and Zacchaeus), his deliverance of those caught in adultery or prostitution, and his outreach to lepers and other untouchables (i.e., those deemed unclean by the religious authorities). Like Jesus, a church with an incarnational approach to worldly engagement will deliberately form its members to invest themselves in the lives of people with whom they come into contact, regardless of their social background or status, to share and enact the gospel.

Third, an incarnational model encourages the church to recognize and form bridges of mutual understanding and agreement wherever possible, in order to enter into further dialogue in the pursuit of truth. There are several ways that Christians can build bridges with others, but for now let us consider just three. Christians can find common ground with the beliefs of others in order to articulate the uniqueness of Christ in a relevant, gracious, and humble way. Examples of this in the New Testament include the Gospel of Matthew's portrayal of Jesus as the fulfillment of Jewish prophecy (see also the book of Hebrews) and Paul's speech at Athens to those who worshipped an unknown god (17:16–34). Sometimes writers who dislike rationalistic apologetics point out that Paul's speech at Athens was not very successful. My purpose here, however, is not to endorse rationalistic apologetics but to endorse incarnational apologetics. Whether or not Paul's speech instantly led others to conversion is beside the point. What is most instructive is that Paul took the opportunity to build bridges by finding common ground with others in order to preach the gospel of Jesus Christ. This approach reflects Paul's overall apologetic strategy of becoming "all things to all people so that by all possible means I might save some" (1 Cor 9:22). Christians can also find common ground with others by affirming and contributing to whatever is good, true, and beautiful in the world. In his closing admonition to the Philippians Paul exhorts his readers to fix their thoughts on "*whatever* is true, *whatever* is noble, *whatever* is right, *whatever* is pure, *whatever* is lovely, *whatever* is admirable—if *anything* is excellent or praiseworthy"

(Phil 4:8; emphasis added).[57] Paul can offer such advice because, ultimately, everything that is genuinely good, true, and beautiful has its origin in God and accordingly reflects God's character and glory to some degree (sometimes clearly, often ambiguously). Consequently, Christians can join with others in discovering and celebrating the wonders of creation in order to point them beyond creation to the Creator. Finally, Christians can find common ground with others by joining with people who are legitimately pursuing the cause of justice in the world, regardless of their culture or religion. As Jesus said about a man who was ministering in his name even though he was not among the twelve disciples, "Do not stop him . . . for whoever is not against us is for us" (Mark 9:39a, 40). Likewise, the church should rejoice when others contribute to the cause of Christ, whether or not they do so knowingly. Another important text supporting this point is Matthew 25, in which Jesus says that anyone who feeds the hungry, shows hospitality to the stranger, clothes the naked, cares for the sick, or visits the prisoner is doing kingdom business and serving the King himself (whether they are conscious of it or not): "And the King will tell them, 'I assure you, when you did it to one of the least of my brothers and sisters, you were doing it to me!'" (Matt 25:40).[58] Such joint action with people of other cultures and/or religions does not imply agreeing with them on all matters. As discussed in chapter six, an incarnational model of cultural engagement needs to be balanced with a theology of the cross that recognizes both God's *YES* and God's *NO* to the world. However, it does mean acknowledging and affirming whatever principles and efforts we share in common in our joint pursuit of social and global justice for all of humanity.

Incarnational means of engagement

As a general guideline for incarnational means of engaging the world, let me return briefly to the idea of finding common ground with others by affirming and contributing to whatever is good, true, and beautiful in the world. C.S. Lewis once insightfully observed that the most effective way for Christian scholars to influence the world is not for them to write books about Christianity but to make excellent contributions to every field of scholarship with their Christian presuppositions and values implicitly infused rather than explicitly stated or argued. Lewis's words are worth quoting at length:

---

[57] In context, Paul offers this instruction primarily as advice concerning Christian sanctification to help believers conform their thoughts and attitudes to Christ's. However, a few verses earlier Paul says, "Let everyone see that you are considerate in all you do" (v. 5). In light of this, the passage is primarily about the formation of Christian believers, but such formation has apologetic implications.

[58] See also Mark 9:36–37: "[Jesus] took a little child whom he placed among them. Taking the child in his arms, he said to [the disciples], "Whoever welcomes one of these little children in my name welcomes me; and whoever welcomes me does not welcome me but the one who sent me."

> What we want is not more little books about Christianity, but more little books by Christians on other subjects—with their Christianity latent. You can see this most easily if you look at it the other way round. Our Faith is not very likely to be shaken by any book on Hinduism. But if whenever we read an elementary book on Geology, Botany, Politics, or Astronomy, we found that its implications were Hindu, that would shake us. It is not the books written in direct defense of Materialism that make the modern man a materialist; it is the materialistic assumptions in all the other books. In the same way, it is not books on Christianity that will really trouble him. But he would be troubled if, whenever he wanted a cheap popular introduction to some science, the best work on the market was always by a Christian. The first step to the re-conversion of this country is a series, produced by Christians, which can beat *Penguin* and the *Thinkers Library* on their own ground. Its Christianity would have to be latent, not explicit: and *of course* its science perfectly honest. Science *twisted* in the interest of apologetics would be sin and folly.[59]

Lewis is not saying that books about Christianity are unnecessary or insignificant (he himself wrote several such books!). What he is arguing is that books about Christianity are not sufficient to impact society in a pervasive and comprehensive way. For one thing, the market for Christian books is simply not large enough to have that kind of influence. Moreover, although a narrow apologetic attempting to prove Christianity directly and explicitly is helpful for certain purposes (perhaps chiefly to affirm Christian believers in their faith), it has difficulty overcoming the power of pervasive assumptions and presuppositions that people hold implicitly and subconsciously. Hence, a subtle, implicit approach—what Kierkegaard referred to as ironic or indirect communication—can often be more effective. More importantly though, Christianity is most compelling when people get a sense of its comprehensive coherence, its ability not only to defend its own claims but to cohere with and shed light on all matters of truth and all experiences of reality. To cite Lewis again, "I believe in Christianity as I believe that the Sun has risen, not only because I see it, but because by it I see everything else."[60] Christianity in all its breadth and depth provides us with a "more inclusive rationality", to cite Lesslie Newbigin.[61]

What Lewis says about Christian scholarship can also be applied to other forms of Christian witness, whether in community life, vocation, or service in the world. For example, it is helpful when Christian theologians construct and articulate Christian perspectives on business, politics, science, or music. How-

---

[59] C.S. Lewis, "Christian Apologetics," in *God in the Dock: Essays on Theology and Ethics*. Quoted in Harry Lee Poe, *Christianity in the Academy: Teaching at the Intersection of Faith and Learning* (Grand Rapids: Baker Academic, 2004), 51.

[60] C.S. Lewis, "Is Theology Poetry?", in *The Weight of Glory and Other Addresses* (New York: HarperCollins, 2001), 140.

[61] Lesslie Newbigin, *Foolishness to the Greeks: The Gospel and Western Culture* (Grand Rapids: Eerdmans, 1986), 52–53.

ever, to have maximum impact on our culture we also need wise, theologically informed Christian business leaders, politicians, scientists, and musicians who achieve excellence in their vocations and consequently exert great influence on their peers and perhaps the larger culture.[62] Similarly, we need wise, theologically informed educators, counsellors, lawyers, physicians, journalists, and film and media experts. We need wise and theologically informed parents, school teachers, guidance counsellors, police officers, and local business owners. And we need wise and theologically formed athletes, actors, construction workers, trades people, and others who serve God faithfully and contribute to the world joyfully in their unique spheres of influence. In sum, the most compelling witness to the truth of the gospel in the world is the combined wisdom of the universal church, as it is displayed in the lives of myriad individual believers who, in faithfulness to God and in participation with God's Spirit, bless and influence the world by serving and contributing to the best of their ability wherever God places them. In their life together, in their various tasks and activities, and in their contributions to the world, Christians are called to bear witness to and embody the manifest wisdom of Christ and thereby to make Christian belief and life coherent and compelling to an unbelieving world.

Conclusion: Living by faith in a world of distrust and scepticism

"They alone know the right way to live". Such was the impression of many in response to the communal life and witness of the early Christian church.[63] This is because genuine Christian life leads to a new way to be human, a way that yields deep satisfaction, joy, fulfilment, and practical wisdom for navigating life meaningfully and fruitfully, though of course not without problems or hardships. Unfortunately, very few people today have this impression of the contemporary western church. Cultural forces such as secularism, materialism, and relativism have contributed to the church's waning influence in society. At the same time many Christians live in ways that are virtually indistinguishable from others in society; indeed, it often seems like contemporary culture is shaping the church more than the church is influencing contemporary culture. To make things even worse, scandals within the church and disunity between churches send the message that Christians today do not know "the right way to live" (or at least, no more than anyone else). As a result, many have become cynical about the church's integrity in moral leadership. In such times as these,

---

[62] It is important here distinguish between a superficial and an integrated synthesis of theology and pursuits like politics and business. See, for example, Oliver O'Donovan's helpful discussion of "theological politics" versus "political theology", based on Kant's distinction between the "moral politician" and the "political moralist", in *The Desire of the Nations: Rediscovering the Roots of Political Theology* (Cambridge, NY: Cambridge University Press, 1996), 6–12.

[63] Kreider, "They alone know," 169–76.

it is absolutely critical to the life and witness of the church for Christians to regain an emphasis on being a people characterized by wisdom.

This chapter depicted the church as rational communities of the new humanity, which are part of God's redemptive plan to draw human beings back into the divine intelligible conversation. Such communities exist by faith before God and strive to live according to God's purposes and plans. They are dedicated to cultivating wisdom in their members through theological formation, constitutive and formative practices, and wise leadership and discipleship. They also seek to influence the broader culture by participating in Christ's prophetic ministry as witnesses and servants of the truth. They do so by engaging the world incarnationally, in order to demonstrate the attractiveness and coherence of the Christian faith in every aspect of life as the fulfilment of all that is good, true, and beautiful.

CHAPTER 8

The Church as Eschatological Communities of Hope

Introduction

Eschatology is influential for all dimensions of ecclesiology. The church is by nature a forward-looking entity that finds its identity in the Risen Christ and lives by the Spirit in the *already-not yet* dimension of the new creation. There is, at present, a distinction to be made between the "believed church" and the "experienced church".[1] The believed church is what Christians affirm about the church by faith concerning its *not yet* fulfilled aspects, specifically that it is one, holy, catholic, and apostolic. The "experienced church" is the concrete reality that Christians experience in the church's present or *already* existence. Luther captures this experience with his famous notion that believers are *simul justus et peccator* (justified and sinful at the same time) and with his depiction of the church as a community of justified sinners.[2] The eschatological concept of anticipation resolves the difference between the two. The present church is one (or unified) through its faith in Jesus Christ and by the presence of the Spirit who is drawing it toward its anticipated eschatological unity. It is holy as a community elected and justified by faith in Christ, which the Spirit is sanctifying and drawing toward its anticipated eschatological holiness. The present church is catholic as a world-wide community of faith in Christ into which the Spirit is drawing people from every tribe, language, people, and nation (Rev

---

[1] For this distinction, see Fernando Enns, "Believers Church Ecclesiology: A Vital Alternative within the Ecumenical Family," in *New Perspectives in Believers Church Ecclesiology*, ed. Abe Dueck, Helmut Harder, and Karl Koop (Winnipeg: CMU, 2010), 108–13. For a discussion of eschatological anticipation as a way to resolve the tension between the present and the future church, see Miroslav Volf, *After Our Likeness: The Church as the Image of the Trinity* (Grand Rapids: Eerdmans, 1998), 140.

[2] For a summary of Luther's conception of the church as just and sinful, see Veli-Matti Kärkkäinen, *An Introduction to Ecclesiology: Ecumenical, Historical and Global Perspectives* (Downers Grove: InterVarsity Press, 2002), 39–49. Recall also Bonhoeffer's argument that the church is not an ideal, but a divine reality in Christ which believers experience by faith. Dietrich Bonhoeffer, *Life Together*, vol. 5 of *Dietrich Bonhoeffer Works*, ed. Geffrey B. Kelly, trans. Daniel W. Bloesch and James H. Burtness (Minneapolis: Fortress, 1996), 35–38.

The Church as Eschatological Communities of Hope

5:9–10) in anticipation of the final gathering of the whole people of God.³ Finally, the church is apostolic by virtue of its faith in Jesus Christ, as witnessed and attested to by the apostles and the prophets and as the Spirit draws it to its anticipated destiny as a cloud of witnesses stretching back in time and gathering up all of salvation history.⁴ Accordingly, Volf summarizes the eschatological nature of church as follows:

> Every congregation that assembles around the one Jesus Christ as Savior and Lord in order to profess faith in him publicly in pluriform fashion, including through baptism and the Lord's Supper, and which is open to all churches of God and to all human beings, is a church in the full sense of the word, since Christ promised to be present in it through his Spirit as the first fruits of the gathering of the whole people of God in the eschatological reign of God. Such a congregation is a holy, catholic, and apostolic church.⁵

In this chapter, we will explore the notion of the church as eschatological communities of the new humanity. Specifically, we will observe the ways in which an eschatological framework impacts our understanding of the church's inner community and ministries and its outward mission within and to the world. I will begin with a discussion of the church as a Temple of the Holy Spirit, since it is the Spirit who sanctifies the church and draws it toward eschatological fulfilment. Next, I will describe the church as a kingdom community that forms kingdom disciples to become representatives and witnesses of God's present and coming reign. Finally, I will explore some implications for the church's mission as it engages the world by sharing in Christ's reign.

Inner community life of the church

The church as the Temple of the Holy Spirit

The Christian church is fundamentally a pneumatological community.⁶ The Holy Spirit plays a crucial role in constituting and forming the church and in

---

³ Volf writes, "The local church is not a concrete realization of the existing universal church, but rather the real anticipation or proleptic realization of the eschatological gathering of the entire people of God." Volf, *After Our Likeness*, 140.
⁴ Volf writes, "Wherever the Spirit of Christ, which as the eschatological gift anticipates God's new creation in history (see Rom 8:23; 2 Cor 1:22; Eph 1:14), is present in its *ecclesially constitutive* activity, there is the church. The Spirit unites the gathered congregation with the triune God and integrates it into a history extending from Christ, indeed, from the Old Testament saints, to the eschatological new creation." Volf, *After Our Likeness*, 129.
⁵ Volf, *After Our Likeness*, 158 (original italics removed).
⁶ Marshall stresses that "fellowship in the Holy Spirit" in 2 Corinthians is not simply companionship provided by the Spirit but is actually the fruit of joint participation in the Holy Spirit. I. Howard Marshall, *New Testament Theology: Many Witnesses, One Gospel* (Downers Grove: InterVarsity Press, 2004), 290.

sustaining, empowering, and guiding its life and mission.[7] Consider the following passages that describe the Spirit's relationship to the church: the Spirit gave birth to the church at Pentecost (Acts 2);[8] the Spirit binds the church together in unity (1 Cor 12; Eph 4); the Spirit speaks to and teaches the church (Rev 2:7, 11, 17, 29, 3:6, 13, 22); the Spirit strengthens and encourages the church (Acts 9:31); the Spirit appoints the church's leaders (Acts 20:28); and the Spirit gives charismatic gifts to the church (1 Cor 12). In chapters six and seven we briefly explored the New Testament's depiction of the church as the Body of Christ and the People of God. A third basic way that the New Testament depicts the church is as the Temple of the Holy Spirit. In his first letter to the Corinthians Paul writes, "Do you not realize that all of you together are the temple of God and that the Spirit of God lives in you?" (1 Cor 3:16). In his second letter he writes, "For we are the temple of the living God. As God has said: 'I will live with them and walk among them, and I will be their God, and they will be my people'" (2 Cor 6:16). In Ephesians, Paul says that believers are being built up "to become a holy temple in the Lord" and "a dwelling in which God lives by his Spirit" (Eph 2:19–22).[9] Similarly, the first letter of Peter records that "God is building you, as living stones, into his spiritual temple" characterized by belief in Jesus Christ, obedience to God's Word, holiness, goodness, and honour, having been called out of darkness into God's wonderful light (1 Pet 2:5–12).

These passages describing the church as the Temple of the Holy Spirit reveal at least five essential characteristics about the nature of the church. First, as a *temple*, the church is the community that God's Spirit uniquely fills and indwells. Of course, God's Spirit is not confined to the church but is omnipresent and active in creation wherever life exists and flourishes.[10] However, Scripture teaches that the Holy Spirit fills and indwells the church in a unique and special way. The Spirit's presence in the church is unique because here the Spirit draws people into the manifest presence of God and points them simultaneously to the concrete revelation of God in Jesus Christ. Outside the church, the Spirit of God fills and animates all of creation, pointing people to the Creator by means of general revelation (Ps 19). Inside the church, the Spirit of God is experienced specifically as *the Spirit of Jesus Christ* who brings people to explicit and concrete knowledge of Christ by means of special revelation. The presence of

---

[7] Of course all three members are involved in the creation, formation, and transformation of the church, but each in each is involved in these in a particular way. As a summary, we might say that the church's constitution is "of God", "in Christ", and "by the Holy Spirit".

[8] See George E. Ladd, *A Theology of the New Testament*, ed. Donald A. Hagner (Grand Rapids: Eerdmans, 1993), 384.

[9] See also: Matt 21:13; 1 Cor 3:16–17; and Heb 10:19–15.

[10] Jürgen Moltmann, *The Spirit of Life: A Universal Affirmation*, trans. Margaret Kohl (Minneapolis: Fortress, 2001).

Christ in the church is vital to the church's existence and expansion.[11] In the Great Commission, Jesus promised his disciples that he would be with them always, even to the end of the age (Matt 28:20). The way in which Christ remains present with his disciples is by the Holy Spirit. Consequently, after his resurrection Jesus tells his disciples that he will send the Spirit to them shortly and instructs them not to leave Jerusalem until the Spirit comes and fills them with power from heaven (Luke 24:49; Acts 1:4–5). Moreover, the entire book of Acts demonstrates that the presence of Christ by the Spirit is crucial to the church's ongoing community life and its effectiveness in mission.

Second, as the Temple of the Holy Spirit the church is a community of the covenant and thus a community of God's salvation. In 2 Corinthians, after describing the church as a temple of the living God, Paul applies Old Testament covenant language to the church: "As God has said, I will be their God and they will be my people" and "I will be your Father, and you will be my sons and daughters, says the Lord Almighty" (2 Cor 6:16, 18). These statements repeat the covenant blessings of the Old Testament and imply that the church is now God's people, God's sons and daughters. This is the community that God has redeemed and made God's own. It is the community that has experienced God's mighty act of deliverance in Jesus Christ. As such, it is the community of salvation, which knows God's saving grace and lives its renewed life according to God's purposes and plan.

Third, as the Temple of the Holy Spirit the church is characterized by God's peace. In Ephesians, directly before he describes the church as a temple of the Spirit, Paul argues that God has brought peace between Jews and Gentiles and joined them together in Christ. He writes, "For Christ himself has made peace between us Jews and you Gentiles by making us all one people. He has broken down the wall of hostility that used to separate us" (Eph 2:14). Paul goes on to say, "Now all of us . . . may come to the Father through the same Holy Spirit because of what Christ has done for us" (Eph 2:18). Finally, Paul says that Jews and Gentiles together form a "holy temple in the Lord" because through Christ "Gentiles are also joined together as part of this dwelling where God lives by his Spirit" (Eph 2:22). The implication is that the church is a community in which God's peace reigns supreme, putting an end to hostility, animosity, and ethnocentricity and bringing forgiveness and reconciliation between alienated groups and enemies as they find peace together in Christ by the Spirit.

Fourth, as the Temple of the Holy Spirit the church is a community of spiritual and moral transformation characterized by "righteousness, peace, and joy in the Holy Spirit" (Rom 14:17). The church is the community that the Spirit of Love and Holiness uniquely sets apart, sanctifies, and sends into the world as a holy royal priesthood to reflect God's presence, bear witness to the gospel, and

---

[11] This is a strong theme in Karl Barth's, "The Church: The Living Congregation of the Living Lord Jesus Christ," in *God Here and Now*, ed. Paul van Buren (New York: Harper and Row, 1964), 61–85.

pursue God's missional purposes (1 Cor 3:17; 2 Cor 6:17; 1 Pet 2:9–10). The early Christian creeds, such as the Apostles' and Nicene creeds, spoke of the church in reference to the Holy Spirit (in the third article after discussing the Father and the Son) and identified holiness as a defining characteristic or mark of the church. Accordingly, many traditional systematic theologies follow the basic layout of the early creeds and discuss the church in close relation to the Holy Spirit and the doctrine of sanctification.[12] While all of the persons of the Trinity are always united in action and thus involved in every aspect of Christian existence, the creeds associate each trinitarian person in a special way with particular roles and activities: God the Father with creation, God the Son with redemption, and God the Holy Spirit with sanctification or transformation. The church is identified especially with the Holy Spirit because its task is most *directly* associated with spiritual and moral transformation (rather than creation or redemption) toward the new creation. The church does not redeem or save people, because Christ accomplished salvation on our behalf once and for all by his death and resurrection, though as a community of salvation the church does *embody* salvation and *participate* by the Spirit in reconciliation, witness, evangelism, acts of justice, and so forth. The church *is* actively and directly involved in transforming people as it participates in the Spirit's ministry of sanctification. As a Temple of the Holy Spirit, the church is called to form its members deliberately in love and holiness. It does this by helping them to cultivate the fruit of the Spirit, by immersing them in the worshipping life of the community, by instructing them in the Word of God and in theological education, by placing them with others in relationships of spiritual edification and accountability, and by apprenticing them in the spiritual practices and disciplines that help foster love and holiness.

Fifth, as the Temple of the Holy Spirit the church is the community in which God's reign is acknowledged, obeyed, and continually sought. In chapter five we observed that the early chapters of Genesis (in collaboration with several other OT passages) depict creation as God's palace-temple, which God fills and reigns and in which God places human beings to serve as steward-priests. Similarly, the image of the church as God's temple indicates that God is manifestly present and reigning amongst God's people, who are God's "royal priesthood". As a royal priesthood, this new covenant community is dedicated to seeking and serving God's reign. As the church seeks and serves God's reign, the Holy Spirit makes God's eschatological kingdom a present, experienced reality for God's people in the church.[13] Moreover, the Spirit continually calls the church

---

[12] These two affirmations are expressed by the doctrine of the unity of operations and the doctrine of appropriation.

[13] Interestingly, the church as the temple of the Holy Spirit possesses several characteristic that identify it with God's kingdom reign. In their discussion of the impact of God's reign, as demonstrated in the gospels read in light of the book of Isaiah, Stassen and Gushee identify seven characteristic marks of the kingdom. These include the following (notice the parallels to the present discussion of the church as the Spir-

into its future, shaping and transforming it in light of its ultimate destiny when it will enter into the kingdom of God in fullness. Thus, filled and guided by the Spirit, the church is called to seek first God's kingdom (Matt 6:33) and to embody the reality of God's presence and reign in its life and mission by existing as a sign, instrument, and foretaste of the eschatological kingdom.[14] In the following section, we will explore what it means for the church to be a kingdom community.

The church as a kingdom community

Called to a task and a destiny

In chapter five we observed that as eschatological creatures, human beings were created for a God-given task and destiny. God gave human beings the task of ruling over the created world as steward-priests of creation by faithfully sustaining, restoring, and improving it. Moreover, God did not create human beings as fully mature to remain in a static state, but in a seed-like state of infancy to change, develop, and advance over time. Their ultimate destiny is to mature into the image of Jesus Christ and to serve as his steward-priests in the new creation. As eschatological communities of the new humanity, the church is similarly called to a task and a destiny. Its task is to form and equip Christian believers to be people who bear witness to the reality and reign of God by seeking first Christ's kingdom, by embodying its values and priorities, and by participating in its expansion in the world.[15] As Grenz puts it, "Believers enter into covenant with God and each other so that they might be an eschatological community, the fellowship that pioneers in the present the principles that characterize the reign of God."[16] The church's destiny is ultimately to be transformed, along with all things being redeeming in Christ, into the eschatological kingdom of God. This destiny fills the church with Spirit-inspired hope for the future, which guides and empowers its life together and mission in the present. Accordingly, Bonhoeffer says that "the church of Jesus Christ is the place—that is, the space—in the world where the reign of Jesus Christ over the whole

---

it's temple, marked in italics): (1) *deliverance/salvation*; (2) *righteousness/justice*; (3) *peace*; (4) *joy*; (5) *God's presence as Spirit or light*; (6) healing; and (7) return from exile (perhaps we could include this last characteristic as well, since there is no temple in exilic existence). Glen H. Stassen and David P. Gushee, *Kingdom Ethics: Following Jesus in Contemporary Context* (Downers Grove: InterVarsity Press, 2003), 25.

[14] Lesslie Newbigin, *The Gospel in a Pluralist Society* (Grand Rapids: Eerdmans, 1989), 229; Darrell L. Guder, ed., *Missional Church: A Vision for the Sending of the Church in North America* (Grand Rapids: Eerdmans, 1998), 101, 104, 106.

[15] Stanley J. Grenz, *Theology for the Community of God* (Grand Rapids: Eerdmans, 1994), 475–79.

[16] Grenz, *Theology*, 479.

world is to be demonstrated and proclaimed."[17] Presently, however, while the church is intimately related to the kingdom of God the two should not be equated. In order for the church to seek the kingdom appropriately, it is important to be aware of the continuities and discontinuities between the church and the kingdom.

The church and the kingdom
George Ladd points out that the kingdom of God is not simply equivalent to its subjects. Rather, the subjects of God's kingdom enter it, live under it, and are governed by it.[18] To explain further the distinction between church and kingdom, Ladd offers five clarifying points.[19] First, the church is not the kingdom

---

[17] Dietrich Bonhoeffer, *Ethics*, vol. 6 of *Dietrich Bonhoeffer Works*, ed. Clifford J. Green, trans. Reinhard Krauss, Charles C. West, and Douglas W. Stott (Minneapolis: Fortress, 2005), 63.

[18] Scot McKnight has recently challenged Ladd's distinction between the church and the kingdom in his book *Kingdom Conspiracy: Returning to the Radical Mission of the Local Church* (Grand Rapids: Brazos, 2014). His concern is that many contemporary Christians have pushed this distinction into a dichotomy, which first separates church from kingdom and then prioritizes the latter over the former. The result is that people claim to be pursuing the kingdom and doing "kingdom work" but understand this to be something that happens beyond the local, gathered church. Thus, for some (e.g., so-called progressive evangelicals), "Kingdom means good deeds done by good people (Christian or not) in the public sector for the common good" (4). For others, the kingdom refers God's rule or reign, "a *redemptive rule dynamic*", not to a specific people *per se* (4). In contrast, McKnight argues that in the Bible the word kingdom refers to "a people governed by a king" (chapter 5). Moreover, the kingdom is intrinsically and necessarily connected to the church. "*The church, then, is what is present and peopled in the realization of the kingdom now*"; or, more strongly, "there is no kingdom now outside the church" (87; Note that McKnight insists that we must compare the present church with the present kingdom, not the present church with the future kingdom). Thus, "*kingdom mission is church mission, church mission is kingdom mission, and there is no kingdom mission that is not church mission*" (96). McKnight's insistence upon the intrinsic connection between church and kingdom is important and valid. However, I do not see the words as completely synonymous. I appeal to Ladd's distinction not to affirm good works in the world to the exclusion of kingdom work in and on behalf of the church. Rather, I understand Ladd's point to be that the kingdom ought to ground and orient the visible or institutional church in the sense that the kingdom is its purpose and goal. I take McKnight's broader point, but still insist that one can build the present institutional church without necessarily expanding the present kingdom. McKnight later seems to acknowledge this when he writes, "sometimes churches fail to embody the kingdom, and this means at times that perception of kingdom mission turns against the realities of church life. In other words, the kingdom sometimes protests the inadequacies and failures of the church" (122). Precisely! This, it seems to me, is Ladd's point. In any case, it captures what I intend by referring to Ladd's distinction.

[19] See also Grenz, *Theology*, 478–79. Grenz similarly argues that the kingdom is broader than the church, that the church is dependent on the kingdom (a product of the

but is oriented to it. "The kingdom is the rule of God; the church is a society of men and women."[20] The church may properly be called a community of the kingdom, one dedicated to living out God's rule, but it cannot simply be equated with the kingdom. The genuine church always points beyond itself to God's glory and rule. Second, the kingdom creates the church. In one of Jesus's parables the kingdom is like a net that is drawn through the sea, catching both good and bad fish. When it is brought to shore the fish are sorted: the good fish are kept, while the bad ones are thrown away (Matt 13:47–50). The first batch, which includes both good and bad fish, represents the church. Significantly, the sorting between the two does not take place until the end of time.[21] This implies that the church is not an ideal society of perfect people, but a mixed and often messy human community. The kingdom of God does not create a pure fellowship in the present era, but a mixed fellowship of both genuine and false members (and even genuine members are, as Luther says, justified and sinful at the same time). Not everyone in the church is genuine, but we are called nonetheless to love and serve every member, to refrain from prejudging their hearts (only God can discern hearts), and to encourage one another lovingly and truthfully toward holiness and obedience. That the kingdom creates the church also means that while kingdom growth leads necessarily to church growth, church growth does not necessarily lead to kingdom growth. Accordingly, in our efforts to grow churches we need to be very careful not to compromise the values, priorities, practices, and worldview of the kingdom. This point is particularly important in light of our culture's warped understanding of success and power and its commitment to materialism and consumerism. As Gareth Brandt cautions,

> When churches are something we shop for based on personal need, when salvation becomes a product that is marketed and sold, there is a theological problem. The is not so much with particular programs and all the good that they may have accomplished for individuals and churches involved, but with the underlying individualistic theology and the ecclesiology of consumerism.[22]

In contrast, Jesus commands us to prioritize the kingdom above all else and to align our concerns, agendas, and plans accordingly (Matt 6:33).

---

kingdom), that the church derives its purpose from God's activity in the world, and that the church is determined by its future destiny.

[20] Ladd, *Theology of the New Testament*, 110.

[21] Ladd, *Theology of the New Testament*, 111. See also Jesus's parable of the wheat and the weeds (Matt 13:24–30).

[22] Gareth Brandt, "How Anabaptist Theology and the Emergent Church Address the Problem of Individualism in the Believers Church," in *New Perspectives in Believers Church Ecclesiology*, ed. Abe Dueck, Helmut Harder, and Karl Koop (Winnipeg: CMU, 2010), 273.

Third, the church bears witness to the kingdom. Ladd argues that the church does not build, create, or grow the kingdom (God does this), but *bears witness* to the rule of God in its speaking and acting. It is called to live provocatively as a sign and foretaste of God's kingdom—not to build it.[23] Ladd's cautionary point is well-taken: kingdom building is first and foremost God's work and the church must resist a triumphalist, semi-Pelagian mindset that equates its own efforts, growth, and success with the gracious work of God and the expansion of God's reign. Indeed, Jesus teaches that the kingdom grows mysteriously, secretly, and with power and impact that far exceeds human efforts and initiatives and is beyond human control (e.g., Jesus's parables of the farmer scattering seed and the mustard seed in Matt 13 and the story of the farmer who planted seed that grew without the farmer's help in Mark 4:26–29). However, Ladd's insight should not be overstressed to the point that it downplays the importance of active human involvement in the expansion of the kingdom (an exclusive emphasis on witness seems to do this). After all, Jesus told his disciples to *seek* the kingdom actively and to let their *good deeds* shine before others. He called them to be *workers* in the harvest field and implied that they would be involved in kingdom work at various levels and stages (planting seed, watering, harvesting, etc.). Thus, God's initiative, grace and power in building and advancing the kingdom should be emphasized together with human responsibility, service, and strategic and disciplined effort in faithfulness to God's call. Consequently, I suggest that the best way to account for both of these emphases is by invoking the concept of participation. In union with Christ by the Spirit, believers *actively participate* in *God's work* of extending the kingdom by God's grace, presence, and power.

Fourth, the church is the instrument of the kingdom.[24] It is the servant of the kingdom and of the God who is sovereign over it. Just as Abraham's election and calling involved being a blessing to all of the peoples on earth (Gen 12:3), so the church is elected and called to be salt, light, a city set on a hill, and a blessing to the nations (Matt 5:13–16; Acts 1:6–8; 10:34–35, 44–48). Consequently, a kingdom community is not insular and inward-focused, but serves God's broader social and global kingdom purposes in and for the world. Finally, the church is the custodian of the kingdom. To the church Jesus gave the keys of the kingdom, which Ladd interprets as spiritual insight to lead others through the door of revelation.[25] In other words, the church is *apostolic*, standing not on its own authority but on the Word of God and the foundation laid by the apostles and prophets who bore original witness to that Word.

---

[23] Ladd writes, "If Jesus' disciples are those who have received the life and fellowship of the kingdom, and if this life is in fact an anticipation of the eschatological kingdom, then it follows that one of the main tasks of the church is to display in the present age the life and fellowship of the Age to come" (*Theology of the New Testament*, 113).

[24] Ladd, *Theology of the New Testament*, 114.

[25] Ladd, *Theology of the New Testament*, 114–17.

Communities of kingdom character formation

N.T. Wright argues that according to the New Testament, Christian character formation is part of becoming more genuinely human. Consequently, the transformation of character takes on central significance in the lives of believers after they come to faith in Christ.[26] Joseph J. Kotva, Jr. argues persuasively that Christianity views the moral life as a journey toward becoming a certain kind of person within a certain kind of community, one that cultivates Christian virtues.[27] Stanley Hauerwas portrays the church as a "school of virtue" and asserts that "the most important social task of Christians is to be nothing less than a community capable of forming people with virtues sufficient to witness to God's truth in the world."[28] I agree with these authors and would specify further that God calls church congregations to exist as communities of kingdom character formation that experience the blessings of the kingdom in their inner community lives and exhibit the presence and characteristics of the kingdom in their mission to the world. In their discussion of Christian character ethics, Stassen and Gushee list four crucial components of character formation, including: (1) worldview immersion in a larger drama (Scripture); (2) the cultivation of virtues; (3) through specific character forming practices, and (4) within the context of a community of disciples.[29] They summarize as follows:

> In *biblical character* ethics, the good we serve is the *reign of God*, and the reign of God is oriented toward *community* with God (God's presence and salvation) and community with our fellow human beings (peace and justice). The biblical *virtues* are keys to community well-being: peacemaking, hungering for justice, doing mercy, integrity, humility and caring for the poor and the mourning. And they are the way of *participation* in community with God.[30]

We will discuss the role of Scripture and formative practices below and this whole chapter is about the role of community in shaping and equipping king-

---

[26] N.T. Wright, *After You Believe: Why Christian Character Matters* (New York: HarperOne, 2010), 26, 29.

[27] Joseph J. Kotva, Jr., *The Christian Case for Virtue Ethics* (Washington, D.C.: Georgetown University Press, 1996).

[28] Stanley Hauerwas, *A Community of Character: Toward a Constructive Christian Social Ethic* (London: University of Notre Dame Press, 1981), 3, 83–86.

[29] Stassen and Gushee, *Kingdom Ethics*, 56–57.

[30] Stassen and Gushee, *Kingdom Ethics*, 53 (emphasis added to highlight key components). N.T. Wright states the key points slightly differently: (1) the goal is the new heaven and new earth, with human beings raised from the dead to be the renewed world's rulers and priests; (2) this goal is achieved through the kingdom-establishing work of Jesus and the Spirit, which we grasp by faith, participate in by baptism, and live out in love; (3) Christian living in the present consists of anticipating this ultimate reality though the Spirit-led, habit-forming, truly human practice of faith, hope, and love, sustaining Christians in their calling to worship God and reflect his glory in the world. N.T. Wright, *After You Believe*, 67.

dom disciples and representatives. At present, let us briefly consider the role of virtues in kingdom community formation. A virtue is a disposition or quality, usually cultivated through practice, which predisposes a person to think and act consistently or characteristically in morally fitting ways that are oriented toward a conception of the good (*telos*) and framed within a comprehensive vision of reality.[31] Christian virtues are qualities that enable believers to pursue and attain their *telos* as relational, rational, and eschatological creatures that love God and other human beings, know God and understand God's created world, and serve God and others as steward-priests infused with new creation hope and vision.

One of the debates among virtue or character ethicists concerns the question of which virtues should be prioritized and pursued. Christian virtue ethicists generally agree that Scripture does not provide a single comprehensive and definitive list of virtues, but most argue that certain virtues have greater prominence than others. I suggest that three orienting questions can help us specify which virtues to prioritize. The first question concerns being human: Which virtues relate most fundamentally to the human *telos* and thus aid the ongoing transformation of redeemed persons into new human beings in the new creation? In response to this question, I suggest that while there are many Christian virtues, the three most basic to our transformation into the new humanity are love, faith, and hope (and among these love is prominent according to 1 Cor 13). These three are most basic to human transformation for two reasons. First, they are basic because they most fundamentally and broadly serve the human *telos*.[32] Love enables human beings to purse a right relationship with God and other human beings, faith enables humans to pursue genuine knowledge of God and seek understanding about the created world (together amounting to wisdom), and hope enables humans to pursue their task and destiny as steward-priests of the new creation. Second, these three virtues are basic because they orient and infuse the other virtues in distinctly Christian ways. For example, in his discussion of Christian virtues Augustine reinterpreted and modified the classic Platonic virtues of courage, temperance, wisdom, and justice to reflect the centrality of love in Christian ethics.[33] While I do not wish to follow Augustine's retention of the priority of the Platonic virtues (even when reinterpreted), his insight that Christian love infuses the other virtues is helpful. Every Christian virtue requires love because love is the essence of God's character and the basis of all God's laws and commands (as Jesus and Paul attest, love for God and others summarizes the law and the prophets). The same holds for faith and

---

[31] For other helpful discussions of Christian virtues, see: Hauerwas, *Community of Character*, 121–23; Kotva, *The Christian Case*, 17–26; Stassen and Gushee, *Kingdom Ethics*, 32–54; and Wright, *After You Believe*, 181–218.

[32] As Kotva argues, the virtues are both means to and constituent elements of the human *telos* (*The Christian Case*, 20–22).

[33] Hauerwas, *Community of Character*, 122. See also Stassen and Gushee, *Kingdom Ethics*, 51–53.

hope. Faith is a necessary ingredient to every virtue because Christian virtues are not abstract principles drawn from a general metaphysics but particular qualities oriented to the person, character, and concrete teachings of Jesus Christ. Jesus does not just point the way toward authentic humanness—he *is* the authentic human being; he *is the way* to authentic humanness (John 14:6). His followers pursue the virtues that characterize Jesus's own life and teaching. In addition, hope infuses every virtue because Christian virtues are not just future-seeking but, more specifically, eschatologically oriented, which means that they are envisioned, guided, empowered, and perfected by the presence and power of the Holy Spirit. As such, hope is crucial to the effectiveness of Christian formative practices interpreted as transforming initiatives (see below). Viewed as mere rules, acts such as turning the other cheek or going the extra mile seem hopeless and idealistic. However, as transforming initiatives they reflect the Christian eschatological hope for a better future in God's kingdom and provide concrete ways of breaking present vicious cycles of sin in light of God's in-breaking reign in the presence and power of the eschatological Spirit—a point to which we will return later.

The second orienting question concerns being in community: What are the purpose and key characteristics of Christian community and which virtues enable Christians to become healthy and contributing members that promote the community's well-being? As virtue ethicists point out, virtues are partially defined in relation to a conception of human sociality and how individual members relate to one another and jointly contribute to its life and purpose.[34] Different conceptions of society prioritize different kinds of virtues. For example, in ancient Greek societies people understood their identity and responsibilities in terms of their social roles and relations to others as contributing to the well-being of society in the context of the Homeric world. That society was believed to reflect the structure of the *cosmos*, in which human beings were subject to the gods and to their earthy representative (kings). Virtues were defined according to social roles, as qualities that enabled people to fulfill their function in society, the most important of which was the role of the warrior-king who epitomized the heroic virtues (e.g., courage).[35] In contrast, in classical Athens the philosophers challenged the older worldview and gave prominence to reason, which in the Platonic cosmology structurally reflected the eternal Mind as mediated by *Logos*. In light of this conception Plato proposed that the supreme virtue is justice, which aligns both the functioning of society (the *polis*) and the roles of individuals within it according to reason.[36] He understood social and personal virtues in correspondence with the *telos* of the Greek *polis*; hence, the philosopher king now replaced the warrior king. Throughout this book, I have

---

[34] Stassen and Gushee, *Kingdom Ethics*, 53.
[35] Alasdair MacIntyre, *Whose Justice? Which Rationality?* (Notre Dame: University of Notre Dame Press, 1988), 14–16.
[36] MacIntyre, *Whose Justice? Which Rationality?*, 74.

described Christian sociality in terms of the church as relational, rational, and eschatological communities in which human beings are being formed, personally and socially, to reflect the image of Jesus Christ. Christian virtues, consequently, enable Christians to become healthy and contributing members who promote the well-being of such communities. This involves cultivating both relational virtues (infused with love) and rational virtues (infused with faith to foster wisdom), both of which are oriented (in hope) toward the future of God's already-not yet eschatological kingdom reign. Stassen and Gushee propose that the virtues promoting kingdom life and effectiveness include: peacemaking, hungering for justice, doing mercy, integrity, humility, and caring for the poor and the mourning. These virtues serve the well-being of the church community and reflect the seven marks of God's reign, which are: deliverance/salvation, righteousness/justice, peace, joy, God's presence as Spirit or light, healing, and restoration from exile.[37] They also permeate Jesus's discussion of kingdom living in Matthew 5:21–48, as qualities that equip disciples to respond in characteristically kingdom ways to concrete problems threatening community life, such as anger, divorce, lust, deception, vengeance, and hatred. Additionally, they pervade Jesus's discussion of kingdom spiritual formation in Matthew 6–7 as qualities that equip disciples to approach spirituality in characteristically kingdom ways as they pray, fast, and practice simplicity and charity toward others while avoiding the traps of false spirituality—hypocrisy, vainglory, greed, anxiety, and self-righteousness. In sum, the point is not simply to compile a list of virtues, but to reflect on what characteristic qualities and behaviours best foster kingdom community life and equip disciples to resist harmful social temptations and vices.

The third orienting question concerns Christian witness or mission: What context-specific virtues will enable Christians to impact the world missionally, both as members of a local congregation and in their personal vocation or calling? In his Sermon on the Mount, Jesus clearly intends his teaching to have an impact not just *within* Christian communities, but also *through* them in order to transform the world (Matt 5:13–16; 7:24–29). Consider also Paul's discussion of the fruit of the Spirit in Galatians 5, which in many ways parallels Jesus's teaching in purpose and content. When Paul lists the fruit of the Spirit, he is not intending a comprehensive catalogue of virtues but providing concrete examples of what the transformative presence of the Holy Spirit looks like in the life of believers. Moreover, Paul is not creating a general or abstract list but one that addresses a particular cultural context (his letters were always occasioned by the concrete contexts and issues of the congregations). Preceding his discussion of the fruit of the Spirit is a list of cultural vices (5:19–21a) that were threatening the Galatians' ability to be kingdom people: "anyone living that sort of life will not inherit the kingdom of God" (5:21b). In this context, the fruit of the Spirit names virtues that identify and characterize people of the kingdom

---

[37] Stassen and Gushee, *Kingdom Ethics*, 37–48, 53.

over against those living according to the vices of the sinful nature. Paul's discussion has missional implications because Christian mission has to do with the redemption and transformation of individuals and society, from the corrupt nature of the old creation to the Spirit-filled nature of the new creation. The fruit flowing from the Spirit's presence in the lives of Christians includes qualities that must be cultivated to help them resist and conquer the vices and idols of their culture—an important aspect of their mission of social transformation.[38]

To summarize the implications of the present discussion, contemporary churches should employ three guidelines when considering which virtues they should prioritize as they seek to form their members. First, they should ensure that Christian formation always aims to foster love, faith, and hope, which are crucial to the transformation of believers into the new humanity. Second, they should consider the inner life of their congregations and seek to cultivate virtues that promote genuine kingdom relationships and guard against cultural influences that threaten to destroy the integrity and distinctiveness of the kingdom community. Finally, they should ponder which qualities are especially relevant to the community's concrete missional context (see below).

Ministries of kingdom orientation and training

In the previous two chapters I discussed church practices that help to promote relational formation and wisdom cultivation in Christian communities. Here I will discuss church practices that promote the eschatological formation of Christian believers by immersing them in kingdom life and forming them to be kingdom people. Stassen and Gushee state that *"according to Jesus, there is no authentic Christianity, discipleship or Christian ethics apart from doing the deeds he taught his followers to do."*[39] Jesus intended such deeds not to be moralistic works of self-righteousness that earn God's favour, but concrete acts of faithful obedience that gradually form people to exemplify the character of Jesus and the reality of God's reign.[40] Given that my purpose here is to focus on

---

[38] The fruit of the Spirit refers not primarily to a set of imperative commands or laws but to the Spirit-formed character of believers demonstrating the fulfilment of the law in the Spirit-filled life. As N.T. Wright nicely puts it, Paul "is *not* saying, 'Once the Spirit has taken up residence in a person or community, these are the things which will happen automatically,' as though thereby to reinforce the romantic or existentialist approach to behavior against some kind of legalism. Nor is he saying, 'Now that you've got the Spirit, isn't it great that you can get rid of that silly old Law with all its moral restrictions?' Rather, he is saying, 'This, after all, is the behavior which the Spirit produces; can't you see that you don't need to impose the Mosaic Law on converts in order to generate people like that?'" Wright, *After You Believe*, 194–95 (emphasis original).

[39] Stassen and Gushee, *Kingdom Ethics*, 486 (emphasis original).

[40] Stassen and Gushee include several examples (not intended to be an exhaustive list), including biblical study and reflection, peacemaking, protecting human life, sexual purity, gender equality, marriage fidelity and commitment, acts of mercy and love toward the those who are underprivileged, suffering or oppressed, honesty and integrity, work for just racial and economic relations, creation care, spiritual disciplines

ecclesiology in light of theological anthropology, rather than to develop a full-blown Christian ethics, I will restrict my present focus to practices that are especially relevant for forming the church as a kingdom community.

Word and sacramental ordinances

The ministry of preaching helps people to see themselves as characters in God's ongoing drama of creation, redemption, and eschatological transformation. Interpreted specifically as a kingdom forming practice, preaching helps people to envision and anticipate God's kingdom reign and live accordingly. This provides at least four guidelines for Christian preaching. First, as a kingdom practice preaching is a pneumatological activity. Helping people to envision and anticipate the kingdom is not equivalent to organizational vision casting or mission strategizing. It is revelatory work and involves actively seeking to participate in the Spirit's ministry of opening eyes to see, ears to hear, and minds to understand. Consequently, the preacher's own spiritual life is of the utmost importance. Preachers should know God's presence and voice. They should immerse themselves in the Scriptures and take adequate time to engage the Bible in depth—analytically *and* imaginatively, reflectively *and* prayerfully. To increase their imaginative depth and spiritual vitality in preaching, preachers could benefit from practicing not just exegetical methods but also spiritual exercises such as *lectio divina*, gospel contemplation, and the daily examen.[41] Second, preachers should put creative energy into articulating the wonder and attractiveness of life in the kingdom. Just as Jesus made the kingdom of God come alive for people through parables, stories, and personally relevant interaction, so Christian preachers should strive to render kingdom life compelling to believers and thus help them envisage the glorious scope and magnitude of God's purposes and plan. Third, kingdom preaching strives always to integrate biblical exegesis and theological reflection with contextual implications for ethical living. Kingdom preaching means drawing from deep theological wells in order to elicit profound life transformation. It aims to renovate values, realign priorities, and redirect energies in accordance with God's reign. Fourth, kingdom preaching involves concrete and practical application to the lives of hearers. Concreteness and practicality stipulate that preachers promotes neither lofty, even unattainable ideals nor burdensome and legalistic rules but practical steps that people can take, by God's grace and power, as they

---

such as prayer, fasting, and almsgiving, and retaining distinctiveness as kingdom people even while engaging the world in mission. Stassen and Gushee, *Kingdom Ethics*, 487–88.

[41] For examples of books introducing such exercises, see: M. Basil Pennington, *Lectio Divina: Renewing the Ancient Practice of Praying the Scriptures* (Chestnut Ridge: Crossroad, 1998); Richard J. Foster, *Life With God: Reading The Bible For Spiritual Transformation* (New York: HarperCollins, 2008); Jeannette A. Bakke, *Holy Invitations: Exploring Spiritual Direction* (Grand Rapids: Baker, 2000); and Alice Fryling, *Seeking God Together: An Introduction to Group Spiritual Direction* (Downers Grove: InterVarsity Press, 2009).

begin the process of transformation and increasingly exhibit kingdom living. Such preaching puts forth what Stassen and Gushee call "transforming initiatives" or what N.T. Wright calls "initial guidelines", which are specific, practical steps of obedient action that simultaneously set people walking on the path of kingdom transformation. Wright explains the concept this way:

> There is an old saying: Give someone a fish and you feed them for a day; teach someone to fish and you feed them for life. Paul's normal practice, in teaching his converts, is the latter. His version of the saying seems to be: Give people a command for a particular situation, and you help them live appropriately for a day; teach them to think Christianly about behavior, and they will be able to navigate by themselves into areas where you hadn't given any specific instructions. But what Paul does, again and again, is to give *initial guidelines*, especially in areas where the outworking of Christian virtue will lead people into behavior patterns that will look surprising to them, and perhaps shocking to their neighbours.[42]

Like the ministry of the Word, the sacramental ordinances are also designed to nurture believers in kingdom life and worldview by immersing them in God's grand salvation drama. As special practices that Jesus himself inaugurated, they are constitutive for the life of the church and formative for its identity and destiny. As Stanley Hauerwas asserts, "The church is where the stories of Israel and Jesus are told, enacted, and heard, and it is our conviction that as a Christian people there is literally nothing more important we can do."[43] Baptism as an eschatological practice signifies new birth (or new creation) to a new life in the Spirit. It also signifies a transfer of loyalties, from serving primarily personal, cultural, national, and demonic agendas and kingdoms to serving Christ as King of kings and Lord of lords and dedicating oneself to praying for and pursuing Christ's kingdom.[44] The Lord's Supper is also an eschatological practice. It looks not only backward in time to remember Christ's sacrifice, but also forward in time to the great banquet or feast at the final gathering of the People of God when Christ's kingdom is fully established (Matt 22:1–14; Luke 14:15–24). Earlier, we observed that as a relational practice the Lord's Supper is a Holy Communion, which brings people together in the presence of Christ and fosters love for God and one another (chapter 6). As a rational practice, the Lord's Supper is a meal of remembrance and thanksgiving (Eucharist), which recalls Christ's last supper with his disciples and binds present believers to Christ's life and ministry by faith (chapter 7). As an eschatological practice, the Supper looks forward with hope and joy to the wedding feast of the Lamb (Rev 19:6–9) and brings motivation and encouragement to persist in following Christ

---

[42] Wright, *After You Believe*, 199 (emphasis original).
[43] Stanley Hauerwas, *The Peaceable Kingdom: A Primer in Christian Ethics* (Notre Dame: University of Notre Dame Press, 1983), 99.
[44] Grenz, *Theology*, 522.

in the present. Together, baptism and the Lord's Supper as eschatological practices help believers look forward in hope to the fulfillment of God's saving work and the full establishment of God's kingdom. They emphasize new life in the Spirit, loyalty to Christ, and hope in God's grand salvation plan, not only for individual believers but also in anticipation of the whole of God's new creation.

Formative practices

Worship is an important formative practice for the church as an eschatological community, continually renewing the church in its identity, mission, and destiny. Several characteristics of Christian worship highlight its eschatological significance. First, worship is about seeking God's manifest presence with the expectation of encountering God's Spirit. God's Spirit makes God's future reign a present reality for believers and makes the church community into a sign and foretaste of God's kingdom. Second, worship is about celebrating and anticipating God's future reign with hope and expectancy. For example, the christological hymn recorded in Philippians 2:5–11 ends with the eschatological declaration that "at the name of Jesus, every knee will bow, in heaven and on earth and under the earth, and every tongue will confess that Jesus Christ is Lord, to the glory of God the Father" (vv.10–11). The structure of many traditional hymns also demonstrates such eschatological anticipation, often beginning with rehearsing and praising God's works in creation and redemption and then typically leading to a final verse that anticipates the glory of the eschaton—thus involving past, present, and future.[45] Third, worship is about reorienting our thoughts, attitudes, and worldview according to kingdom teachings, loyalty to Jesus Christ as Lord, and the reality of God's reign. Fourth, worship realigns our affections and desires, forming us to love God and neighbour.[46] Fifth, worship is about renewing our dedication to the Great Commission and to the task of seeking first the kingdom of God in our own lives as well as through our influence in the world. Sixth, worship is about receiving refreshment, encouragement, insight, strength, and power from God's Spirit to participate in God's mission of eschatological transformation and new creation.

Another key formative eschatological practice is prayer, particularly prayer that is patterned after the Lord's Prayer. Given its place in the Sermon on the Mount, the Lord's Prayer is an example of how kingdom people characteristi-

---

[45] Think for example of hymns such as: *Amazing Grace*: "When we've been there ten thousand years . . ."; *Holy, Holy, Holy*: "All thy works shall praise thy name in earth and sky and sea . . ." (in fact, the whole song derives image-ry from Rev 4–5); *My Jesus I Love Thee*: "In mansions of glory and endless delight . . ."; and *All Hail the Power of Jesus' Name*: "We'll join the everlasting song and crown him Lord of all".

[46] For an extensive treatment of worship as a fundamental practice that realigns our desires and loves, see James K.A. Smith, *Desiring the Kingdom: Worship, Worldview, and Cultural Formation* (Grand Rapids: Baker Academic, 2009).

cally pray. Space precludes an in-depth analysis here, but let us consider briefly some key features of the Lord's Prayer as a kingdom prayer. The prayer begins by glorifying God and specifically pleading for the coming of God's kingdom into the lives of believers and the world: "Our Father, hallowed be your name. Your kingdom come. Your will be done, on earth as it is in heaven." It then requests God's sustenance for daily needs: "Give us today our daily bread." In its kingdom-oriented context, this requests refers not only to biological nourishment but also, and perhaps especially, to everything that is necessary for enjoying and pursuing kingdom life to its fullest. In praying, "Forgive us our sins, as we forgive those who have sinned against us", the prayer reflects the nature of the church as a community of kingdom reconciliation in which grace, forgiveness, and mercy are defining marks. Finally, the prayer emphasises loyalty to God and God's kingdom purposes, which means renouncing the influence of Satan and the kingdom of darkness: "Lead us not into temptation, and deliver us from the evil one." The Lord's Prayer is a continual reminder that the church's allegiance lies not with the world and its agendas, but with Christ and his kingdom.[47]

A third major way that Christians are formed for kingdom life is by practicing what Stassen and Gushee call "transforming initiatives".[48] Transforming initiatives are deliberate, specific, concrete, and achievable actions that initiate kingdom transformation by breaking vicious cycles or patterns of sin. For example, one breaks the vicious cycle of lust by doing concrete things to remove temptations (e.g., avoiding watching videos with sexual content). Such transforming initiatives are performed in a posture of humility, grace, and truth, and receive strength and motivation from the fundamental Christian virtues of love, faith, and hope. Their aim is not simply to solve problems in the present (vicious cycles rarely have instant solutions) but to initiate incremental yet provocative change and to cultivate consistent virtue on the basis of a hope-filled

---

[47] In addition to these specific observations of the Lord's Prayer, the practice of prayer strengthens believers to prioritize and pursue the kingdom in many other ways. In their insightful discussion of the relevance of prayer for Christian life and ethics, Stassen and Gushee argue that prayer deepens our commitment to the narrative of the kingdom of God, binds us more thoroughly to God in Jesus Christ, connects us more closely with fellow brothers and sisters who are also giving their lives to the reign of God, aligns our will with God's will and the contours of God's reign, allows us to participate in the advancement of the kingdom by petitioning for its coming, alerts us to the wiles of the devil and strengthens us to resist, deepens our trust in God and strengthens our willingness to take risks, purifies us of mixed allegiances, trains our hearts to seek heavenly rather than earthly rewards, keeps us from the idolatrous pursuit of worldly security, helps us to be critical of unjust worldly powers and systems, and aids our moral and decision making processes.Stassen and Gushee, *Kingdom Ethics*, 449–66.

[48] See Stassen and Gushee, *Kingdom Ethics*, 125–45.

vision of the future.[49] Performed in and by the liberating presence and power of God's eschatological Spirit, transforming initiatives thus invade the myopic and self-enclosed strongholds of sin in the present with the hope and vision of God's future. While it is possible to suggest numerous transforming initiatives on the basis of the Bible's teachings, Stassen and Gushee derive fourteen directly from the teachings of Jesus in the Sermon on the Mount. They notice that the Sermon presents fourteen triads each consisting of a traditional ethical command, a vicious cycle caused by a root problem that the popular misapplication of the command reinforced, and a transforming initiative to break the vicious cycle. These fourteen cases provide a good overall example of how transforming initiatives function. They are depicted in the following chart, which I have borrowed from Stassen and Gushee and modified with the inclusion of a virtues column in order to demonstrate the relationship between transforming initiatives and virtues in the development of Christian character.[50]

The 14 Triads of the Sermon on the Mount and Corresponding Virtues

Traditional Righteousness	Vicious Cycle	Transforming Initiative	Relevant Virtues
1. You shall not kill	Anger, saying "you fool"	Go, be reconciled	Peacemaking, humility, gentleness
2. You shall not commit adultery	Lust as committing adultery in one's heart	Remove the cause of temptation	Self-control, goodness, sorrow over sin.
3. Whoever divorces, give a certificate	Divorcing involves you in adultery	(Be reconciled: 1 Cor. 7:11)	Righteousness/justice, peacemaking
4. You shall not swear falsely	Swearing by anything involves dishonesty	Let your yes be yes, and your no be no	Honesty, faithfulness, purity of heart

---

[49] Transforming initiatives link together being and becoming in a holistic and integrated way, thus overcoming the limitations inherent to the proposals of both Idealists (who emphasize *being* as true identity) and Existentialists (who emphasize *becoming through choice and action* as true identity). As Kotva argues, being precedes doing but doing also shapes being. Who we have become, including our states of character, precedes and informs our choices and actions. However, our choices and actions also shape who we are and thus also what we will choose and do in the future. Kotva, *The Christian Case*, 30.

[50] For the original table, see Stassen and Gushee, *Kingdom Ethics*, 142.

The Church as Eschatological Communities of Hope

Traditional Righteousness	Vicious Cycle	Transforming Initiative	Relevant Virtues
5. Eye for eye, tooth for tooth	Vengeance or retaliation by evil means	Turn the other cheek, go the second mile, etc.	Humility, peacemaking, self control, kindness
6. Love neighbour and hate enemy	Hating enemies is the same vicious cycle you see in the Gentiles and tax collectors	Love enemies, pray for persecutors; be all-inclusive as God is	Goodness (like God), peacemaking, humility, kindness, merciful, forbearing
7. When you give alms	Righteousness for show	Give in secret	Purity of heart, hunger for righteousness
8. When you pray	Righteousness for show	Pray in secret	Purity of heart, hunger for righteousness
9. When you pray	Vain repetition	Pray like this (Lord's Prayer)	Purity of heart, honesty, righteousness, faithfulness
10. When you fast	Righteousness for show	Dress with joy	Purity of heart, hunger for righteousness
11. Do not pile up treasures on earth	Moth and rust destroy, thieves enter and steal	Pile up treasures in heaven	Righteousness, purity of heart, faithfulness, patience.
12. No one can serve two masters	Serving God & wealth, anxiety over food & clothes	Seek God's kingdom and righteousness	Righteousness/justice, purity of heart, faithfulness
13. Do not judge, lest you be judged	Judging others means you'll be judged by the same measure	First take the log out of your own eye	Humility, sorrow over sin, merciful, patience, kindness, gentleness

Traditional Righteousness	Vicious Cycle	Transforming Initiative	Relevant Virtues
14. Do not give holy things to dogs . . .	They will trample them and tear you to pieces	Give your truth to God in prayer	Purity of heart, faithfulness, forbearance, patience

The church engaging the world

Participating in Christ's reign

As heralds and representatives of the kingdom

I have argued in this chapter that an eschatological ecclesiology implies that being the church includes both a task and a destiny, which is to pursue the kingdom of God and to demonstrate its reality as a sign and foretaste. In investing its time and energy in forming kingdom disciples, the church does not thereby become inward-focused or separate itself from the problems and concerns of the world. Recall that the eschatological kingdom of God is broader than the present church and as such always aims to impact the world with God's transformative grace, righteousness, justice, and peace. Sometimes people erect false dichotomies between discipleship and evangelism, spiritual formation and social justice, or personal piety and social ethics. However, training kingdom disciples transcends such dichotomies, because the kingdom of God is both redemptive and transformative. It redeems and transforms believers in the church community, equipping them to influence the world as heralds and representatives of a new way to be human under the reign of God.

As heralds of the kingdom, Christians proclaim the good news that Jesus Christ is Lord and that that through him a new kind of life is available, one that is abundant, deeply satisfying, full of wisdom and purpose, and characterized by love, joy, peace, patience, kindness, goodness, gentleness, faithfulness, and self-control. Moreover, this new life places one in life-giving relationships with others in a community of love, faith, and hope, within which one finds acceptance and belonging, encouragement and edification, teaching and instruction, renewal and refreshment, and equipping and commissioning to make a difference in the lives of others and in the world. As representatives of the kingdom, Christian communities embody what they proclaim and proclaim what they embody. As "salt" and "light", they exist in the world in a distinctive and provocative way as counter-cultural communities, which exude the character of Jesus Christ, reach out to others with his love and grace, and live out his teachings in joyful obedience (Matt 5:13–16).[51] Though they are humble and often outnumbered in society, genuine kingdom representatives have a pro-

---

[51] Stassen and Gushee, *Kingdom Ethics*, 468–73.

found influence on their world. They are like yeast that a baker adds to a bread mixture: just a small amount permeates all of the dough and has a transformative effect on what is finally produced (Matt 13:33; Luke 13:20–21).

As a missional church
One influential concept in contemporary ecclesiology that theologians employ to speak of the church simultaneously in terms of task and destiny, function and identity, is the missional church. I will have some constructively critical things to say about the missional church concept in the final chapter. Presently, however, I suggest that it is fruitful way of thinking about the church's engagement with the world, particularly in the context of contemporary postmodern culture.

Theologians use the term "missional" to make several interrelated claims about the church. First, the term reflects the understanding that mission is not simply a sub-category of ecclesiology, but belongs to the essence of what it means to be the church. According to missional church advocates, the church does not merely *do* mission; rather, the church *is* mission.[52] Second, the missional concept is based on the missional or sending nature of God (i.e., the *missio Dei*). As Arnold Neufeldt-Fast puts it, "God the Father sends the Son into the world in the power of the Holy Spirit to bring salvation in all its dimensions, that is, God's reign in its fullness."[53] Moreover, "The self-understanding of the church is grounded in the work of God's Spirit who brings the church into existence as a gathered community, equips and prepares it, and then sends it into the world to participate fully in God's mission (*missio Dei*)."[54] Third, the missional church concept is based on the missional narrative of the Bible, which in broad summary includes: (1) God's covenant with Abraham, in which God promises to bless all nations of the earth through him (Gen 18:18; 22:17–18); (2) the biblical portrayal of the joint mission of the Father, Son, and Holy Spirit (e.g., John 14:26; 15:26–27; 20:21–22); (3) biblical statements concerning God's love for the world (John 3:16; 1 John 4:8); (4) the Great Commission (Matt 28:18–20) and the Great Commandments to love God and neighbour (e.g., Mark 12:29–31). Fourth, the missional church concept is based on reflection about how the church can faithfully engage contemporary postmodern, post-Christendom culture with a genuine gospel witness that is not compromised by unexamined Western cultural assumptions.[55] Fifth, missional ecclesi-

---

[52] Darrell L. Guder, "Missional Theology for a Missionary Church," *Journal for Preachers* 22, no. 1 (1998): 5.
[53] Arnold Neufeldt-Fast, "Examining the Believers Church within a Trinitarian-Missional Framework," in *New Perspectives in Believers Church Ecclesiology*, ed. Abe Dueck, Helmut Harder, and Karl Koop (Winnipeg: CMU, 2010), 203.
[54] Neufeldt-Fast, "Examining the Believers Church," 204.
[55] The concept of the missional church has its roots in the work of Lesslie Newbigin, particularly his observations of modern Western culture and his proposal that the Western church become a "missionary church" existing as the living "hermeneutic of the gospel" before God in the midst of the world (Newbigin, *The Gospel in a Pluralist Society*, 227–32). In part, this view of the church has arisen out of a renewed em-

ology promotes an incarnational, kingdom-oriented, and communal approach to church over-against attractional, consumerist, and individualistic church models.[56] In a missional view, local congregations do not exist merely for themselves (i.e., their own wellbeing, growth, and happiness), but are called to serve the broader reign of God in the world as a kingdom-people sent on a mission. This requires a commitment to go out into the world to reach people for Christ just as missionaries do, rather than expecting the world to come to them. It also means directing time and resources outside the church into the surrounding community and world, rather than pouring time, money, and energy exclusively into its own buildings, programs, and promotional strategies in order to attract people to venture through its doors on Sunday mornings. In short, a missional church dedicates its time and resources to kingdom growth, not merely to institutional church growth. Sixth, some of the dominant images or metaphors used by advocates to depict the missional church include: representing the reign or kingdom of God; the church as the people of God in exile; the church as resident aliens (borrowing from Hauerwas and Willimon); the church as an alternate community; and the church as a local congregation existing as a contextual hermeneutic of the gospel with a missionary presence in its community.[57]

---

phasis upon the need for the gospel to confront and convert Western culture and to alert the church to the ways in which it has uncritically or unwittingly assimilated Western cultural assumptions into its theology and life. One such assumption, which is challenged by the missional view of the church, is the belief in a Christianized Western culture. This view is often described as the Christendom model and is usually traced back to the Constantinian era, when the church first became a major political and religious force with a secure leadership role in society. In contrast, there is a renewed focus on the need for mission to occur within and convert Western culture itself, as opposed to the traditional understanding that depicts mission as something Western Christianized nations accomplish in foreign countries. The missional church concept is expanded in the works of the Gospel and Our Culture Network, a group of scholars which has developed and applied Newbigin's ideas with the North American context in view. They have published their research and reflection as a collaborative series, entitled *The Gospel and Our Culture Series*. See for example: Guder, *Missional Church* and *The Continuing Conversion of the Church* (Grand Rapids: Eerdmans, 2000); George R. Hunsberger and Craig Van Gelder, eds., *The Church Between Gospel and Culture: The Emerging Mission in North America* (Grand Rapids: Eerdmans, 1996); and Craig Van Gelder, ed., *Confident Witness—Changing World: Rediscovering the Gospel in North America* (Grand Rapids: Eerdmans, 1999).

[56] For more on the distinction between incarnational and attractional, see Michael Frost and Alan Hirsch, *The Shape of Things to Come: Innovation and Ministry for the 21st Century Church* (Peabody: Hendrickson, 2003), 17–59, 157–58. For concrete examples of churches that are attempting to reach out in incarnational ways, see Lois Y. Barret, ed., *Treasure in Clay Jars: Patterns in Missional Faithfulness* (Grand Rapids: Eerdmans, 2004).

[57] In addition to the books cited in footnote 53, see: Michael Frost, *Exiles: Living Intentionally In A Post-Christian Culture* (Peabody: Hendrickson, 2006); Stanley Hauerwas and William H. Willimon, *Resident Aliens: Life in the Christian Colony*

Resurrection as a model for moving in God's power into new possibilities

In chapter six I proposed that a theology of the cross can serve as a model of cultural engagement emphasizing the church's role in engaging culture critically; the cross represents God's judgment of human sinfulness, which leads to inauthentic and destructive ways of being human. In chapter seven I proposed an incarnational model of cultural engagement that emphasizes affirming and contributing to whatever is good, true, and beautiful in human culture. Presently, I propose that the resurrection can serve as a model of cultural engagement to emphasize living with eschatological hope and imagination to inspire the world with new possibilities for existence. Thinking about cultural engagement through the lens of the resurrection reminds the church that it does not pursue its mission solely on the basis of its own strengths and resources, but by God's resurrection power. As Lesslie Newbigin argues, when the Christian church engages in mission it is not merely obeying a command (though mission is an imperative) or following a mission strategy (though mission is often strategic). Such a narrow view of mission "tends to make mission a burden rather than a joy, to make it part of the law rather than part of the gospel."[58] Primarily, mission results from an explosion of joy in the church community, which overflows into the world.[59] It is the manifestation of the church's experience of the presence and power of the Holy Spirit. When the church has been granted a taste of God's presence, God's power, God's grace, and God's reconciliatory and unifying love, it is transformed into a living testimony to the gospel. When it exhibits the selfless and sacrificial love of Christ, living not for itself but for the sake of its neighbours, it lives provocatively as a sign and foretaste of the kingdom of God.[60]

The resurrection as a model of cultural engagement entails at least three specific implications. First, it means being inspired by God's vision for new *possibilities*. Problems often seem insurmountable to those presently encountering them. People need to be inspired with dreams and visions that transcend their present circumstances and lift them into God's greater purposes and plans (Isa 55:8–9). Just as the Old Testament prophets cast a vision of hope and redemption for the people of Israel (e.g., Ezekiel's vision of dead bones coming to life) and as John the seer cast a hopeful vision of the future victory and reign of

---

(Nashville: Abingdon, 1993); and Craig Van Gelder, *The Essence of the Church: A Community Created by the Spirit* (Grand Rapids: Baker, 2000).

[58] Newbigin, *The Gospel in a Pluralist Society*, 116.

[59] Newbigin, *The Gospel in a Pluralist Society*, 116.

[60] Newbigin, *The Gospel in a Pluralist Society*, 229. Elsewhere Newbigin writes, "The life of the Church is a real participation in the life of the Triune God, wherein all life and all glory consist in self-giving, a *koinonia* wherein no one will ever say that aught of the things which he possesses is his own. The ultimate mystery of the Church's being is the mystery of love, and love 'seeketh not its own.'" Lesslie Newbigin, *The Household of God: Lectures on the Nature of the Church* (London: SCM, 1957), 129.

Christ in the book of Revelation, so God continues to motivate and inspire the church with visions of new possibilities for world transformation. Second, a resurrection model implies moving in God's *power* to accomplish what otherwise would be impossible. Jesus told his disciples that if they only had faith as small as a mustard seed they could move mountains, because nothing that God wills for them is impossible to accomplish (Matt 17:20). According to Paul, the same Spirit that empowered Jesus's ministry and raised Christ from the dead also indwells believers and empowers them for mission (Rom 8:11). Thus, by God's power the church can move in faith and hope to address problems and pursue goals that seem insolvable or unreachable from a finite point of view. Third, a resurrection model implies being refreshed and encouraged in God's *presence*. As Isaiah prophesied long ago, "Is anyone thirsty? Come and drink—even if you have no money! Come, take your choice of wine or milk—it's all free! Why spend your money on food that does not give you strength?" A few verses later, Isaiah continues, "I will give you all the mercies and unfailing love that I promised to David. *He displayed my power by being my witness and a leader among the nations*" (Isa 55:1–2b, 3b–4; emphasis added). In these verses, Isaiah associates faithful and effective cultural influence with resting in God's presence and depending on God's spiritual nourishment. Similarly, Jesus told his disciples, "*Come to me*, all of you who are weary and carry heavy burdens, and *I will give you rest*. Take my yoke upon you. Let me teach you, because I am humble and gentle, and you will find rest for your souls" (Matt 11:28–29; emphasis added). Jesus promised the church not only that it would minister in his authority and power, but also that it would minister in and through his presence (Matt 28:20). Doing Christ's will and pursuing Christ's mission requires being continually immersed and refreshed in his presence by the Spirit. As Newbigin argued, "It is impossible to stress too strongly that the beginning of mission is not an action of ours, but the presence of a new reality, the presence of the Spirit of God in power."[61]

Means of engaging the world with eschatological hope and resurrection power
The church is called to engage culture eschatologically through its being, proclaiming, and doing. Much of this chapter has sought to demonstrate that as a community of kingdom formation the church is called to *be* and increasing *become* a people that practices Jesus's teachings and is thereby characterized by kingdom values, priorities, commitments, relationships, and worldview. In this sense, "the first social ethical task of the church is *to be the church*", as Stanley Hauerwas often asserts.[62] The task of the church is *to be* both a foretaste and an instrument of the coming kingdom—a living, breathing, walking demonstration of a new way of being human in the midst of the present, fallen world. To bring genuine transformation to the world, the church itself must undergo continual

---

[61] Newbigin, *The Gospel in a Pluralist Society*, 119.
[62] Hauerwas, *The Peaceable Kingdom*, 99 (emphasis added).

transformation. It must be, as the Protestant Reformers taught, simultaneously *reformed and always reforming.*[63]

The church is called to engage culture by proclaiming kingdom values and pursuing kingdom justice. This includes advocacy for the "little ones" for whom Jesus cared so much—the poor, the hopeless, the underprivileged, the naked, the sick, the lonely, and the countless women, men, and children in the world who so often suffer at the hands of those who are violent and greedy. In essence, it means advocating for human dignity and protecting human rights in all spheres of life and in all parts of the world. As Moltmann so eloquently puts it,

> In the name of the creation of the human being in the image of God, in the name of the incarnation of God for the reconciliation of the world, and in the name of the coming kingdom of God for the fulfillment of history, the church is charged with responsibility for the humanity of persons as well as for their rights and duties in time. We see the theological contribution of the Christian church in the grounding of the fundamental human rights upon God's right to human beings. The Christian faith has over and above the different rights and duties of humanity to esteem the one indivisible dignity of the human being in his or her life with God—without, in so doing, excluding other religious or humanistic conceptions of human rights.[64]

The church can play in important role in advocating for human dignity and human rights by raising awareness of social issues and problems, for starters by teaching their own congregants that *justice matters and is essential to the church's mission*. It can deliberately seek to educate and equip Christians to be positive agents of change for God's new creation in whatever spheres of influence in which they operate. It can encourage people to take an interest in politics and to implore government (by voting, petitioning, or even direct participation by holding office) to create just laws and policies and to operate with moral integrity.

In his book, *From the Tower of Babel to Parliament Hill: How to be a Christian in Canada Today*, Brian Stiller offers practical and concrete advice in this regard to Canadian Christians living in a deeply secular cultural and political landscape. Stiller challenges them to make a political difference by proclaiming and living out the gospel in ways that are unabashedly Christian yet peculiarly contextual (i.e., Canadian). He argues that Christian Canadians have a fivefold responsibility, which includes: (1) to remind the nation that it is under God; (2) to remind the nation that it is not eternal or ultimate; (3) to remind

---

[63] On the relevance of this theme for the missional church, see Guder, *The Continuing Conversion of the Church*.

[64] Jürgen Moltmann, *On Human Dignity: Political Theology and Ethics* (Minneapolis: Fortress, 1984), 15.

Canada that it is part of something larger (globally, cosmologically); (4) to remind its people that political service is a high calling; and (5) to remind the nation that there are consequences for its policies and actions.[65] Stiller also provides several practical tips for engaging culture effectively with the gospel. For example, believers need to get their facts straight and demonstrate an understanding of and sensitivity toward the relevant issues. They should meet the major political players and learn how their own political system works (i.e., Canadians should not assume that their political system is the same as the American system). They should build coalitions and networks in order to draw on vast resources and create a united front. And they should learn the appropriate place of compromise, recognizing that all relationships require time, effort, and reciprocity.[66] Stiller's suggestions provide a helpful start for churches seeking to reflect deeply about how they can teach and train their members to bear witness and make a difference in a secular culture.

The church is called to engage culture in its actions. In so doing, the church must carefully guard itself against being drawn into mere social activism. A regression into mere activism sometimes occurs because churches begin to compromise the uniqueness of Jesus Christ, the importance of correct doctrine, and/or the authority of concrete ethical teachings of the Bible (for example, the Social Gospel Movement or the Unitarian Church). Such churches are in danger of becoming absorbed by the values and causes of contemporary culture and hence compromising the distinctiveness of Christian worldview and moral teaching in favour of political correctness and popular moral trendiness. As Hauerwas helpfully reminds us, the church is not simply another agency that does good, but a people called to bear witness to God's presence in the world.[67] Regression into mere activism can also result when churches that are faithful to Christ and sensitive to hurting and underprivileged people become overwhelmed by the depth and pervasiveness of the world's needs. The needs seem so vast and the urgency of mission so pronounced that other important aspects of Christian life—such as community, worship, discipleship, and biblical and theological education—can seem impractical and of lesser importance. Gradually, this can lead to a kind of activism that breeds exhaustion, burnout, and despair. Moreover, it can lead to resentment and judgment of others in the Christian community who have passions and callings that differ from one's own cause. In essence, this approach ends up trying to save the world by its own works, efforts, and plans.

In contrast to such activist approaches, I suggest that a more fitting mode of engagement is an eschatological, grace-based, Spirit-filled, participatory ap-

---

[65] Brian C. Stiller, *From the Tower of Babel to Parliament Hill: How to be a Christian in Canada Today* (Toronto: HarperCollins, 1997), 185–88.

[66] Stiller, *From the Tower of Babel to Parliament Hill*, 199–202.

[67] Stanley Hauerwas, *Christian Existence Today: Essays on Church, World, and Living in Between* (Grand Rapids: Brazos, 2001), 121.

proach. In this approach, believers participate (with resurrection vision, power, and refreshment) in the Spirit's redemptive and transformative ministry in concrete and practical ways by "planting mustard seeds of deliverance".[68] Such seed-acts serve as transforming kingdom initiatives within the surrounding community and broader society. As mustard seed planting, this approach emphasizes taking the initiative to act promptly and work diligently while releasing the mountainous magnitude of need to God's responsibility and leaving the results of one's dedicated labour in God's hands. Such an approach promotes neither idealism nor naive optimism, but genuine eschatological *hope* based on God's purposes, promises, power, and in-breaking, liberating presence by the Holy Spirit. As transforming *missional* initiatives, such efforts do not aim to solve present societal problems *per se*, but to initiate a process of transformation by involving people in concrete acts of missional (trans)formation that aim to break vicious cycles of social sin or systemic injustice. Sometimes people look at social problems and respond with despair because the need seems too great; one's efforts seem unlikely to make much of a difference. But if the focus is on acts of service as transforming missional initiatives, then every contribution holds greater significance—both as formation of the person/community engaged in the act and as a prophetic or eschatological form of concrete witness to the recipient(s) of the act. Serving in a soup kitchen may not, in and of itself, solve the problem of social poverty and hunger overnight, but as a transformative initiative and act of missional formation such service can effect real change and have a long-range positive impact on society. By practicing such transforming missional initiatives, churches gradually become the kinds of communities that embody the justice, hospitality, peace, and charity that the gospel proclaims and promises.

Conclusion: Living with hope in a world of fear and despair

Stanley Hauerwas argues that "the Hebrew-Christian tradition helps us sustain the virtue of hope in a world which rarely provides evidence that such hope is justified."[69] The church is called to bear witness to a new way of being human together in the world, one which is framed by the story of God's dealings with humanity in Jesus Christ, directed by God's purposes, priorities, and plans, and oriented toward the glorious new creation by the power and guidance of the Holy Spirit. Such witness is eschatological in nature. This means that it is inspired by a vision of the future that is grasped by faith and pursued in hope, as churches live according to the reality of the new creation in the present in anticipation of its eschatological fulfilment in glory. Such hope-filled witness does not just happen automatically, but must be cultivated through disciplined character formation empowered by God's Spirit. Consequently, the church must

---

[68] Stassen and Gushee, *Kingdom Ethics*, 53.
[69] Hauerwas, *Community of Character*, 166.

commit to being a community of kingdom formation that teaches and trains disciples of Jesus Christ to be representatives and witnesses of God's reign. Only a church that is immersed in the grace and transformative presence of God, built upon and shaped according to the teachings of Jesus, and guided and empowered by the Holy Spirit can exist as a hope-filled sign, foretaste, and instrument God's kingdom in a world full of fear and despair.

Conclusion

Church for the Twenty-First Century

Introduction

In this book I have explored the significance of theological anthropology for ecclesiology with a view to clarifying the nature and purpose of the church's inner community life and its outward engagement with the world in mission.

Part I outlined the challenge to be addressed. Chapter one identified common problems afflicting attempts to define the human person in contemporary culture and the unfortunate consequences that follow from our culture's anthropological agnosticism, including the dissolution of human community, the dichotomization and disintegration of personal and social ethics, and the collapse of social and global justice. Chapter two argued that different models of community depend on different conceptions of what it means to be human. It identified and analyzed six models of community operative in contemporary culture based (implicitly or explicitly) on differing conceptions of the human person and suggested ways in which these models are impacting the church. It concluded that none are fully satisfying theologically.

Part II consisted of three chapters outlining a theological anthropology in trinitarian perspective, each of which addressed one dimension of being human and its corresponding teleological emphasis. Chapter three depicted the human person as a relational creature whose *telos* is to love God and other human beings and to care for God's world. Chapter four depicted the human person as a rational creature whose *telos* is to know God and understand God's created world. Chapter five depicted the human being as an eschatological creature whose *telos* is to serve God and others as steward-priests of the new creation.

Part III consisted of three chapters paralleling those in section II, thus depicting the church as relational, rational, and eschatological communities of the new humanity. An overriding theme in Parts II and III was to connect ethics with both personhood and community/ecclesiology in an integrated way, in order to resolve dualisms and false dichotomies that continually plague the church's inner social life (e.g., individualism vs. collectivism) and its outer engagement with the world in mission (e.g., spiritual vs. humanitarian goals and advocacy).

In this final chapter I will draw out and summarize some key conclusions and implications of my argument for the integration of the church's inner life and outward mission. I will then briefly suggest some preliminary implications that follow from viewing the church as God's new humanity called to promote and embody the welfare and flourishing of all human beings.

Inner community life of the church as the new humanity

A community in union with Christ in the Spirit

The ground of Christian community is the union of believers with Christ and one another in the Spirit. Union with Christ is neither something that Christians achieve nor an ideal toward which they strive, but a reality that God establishes which Christians receive by faith and in which they participate by the Spirit. This corrects two common misunderstandings of the social nature of the church. At one extreme end of the spectrum is a conception of the church as a purely voluntary association, in which becoming a member is like joining a club. One joins together with others who possess like beliefs, preferences, and/or interests, which in the present socio-historical context often reflect the egocentric values of contemporary western consumer culture. The church is thus conceived not as being intrinsically related to Christian life and salvation but as a secondary support system that enriches the private spiritual lives of individual Christians. At the other end of the spectrum is a conception of the church that lacks an appropriate place for personal choice. This view stresses that church commitment is more stable than choosing an association on the basis of one's personal or family preferences. Conversely, one enters the church by birth or simply attends whatever congregation is closest to one's home (i.e., one's parish) regardless of differences of belief, doctrine, or one's sense of personal calling to a congregation.

In contrast to both of these extremes, I wish to stress the importance of balancing both choice and commitment. In place of personal voluntary choice I would stress making a responsible decision with wisdom and discernment. Such wise discernment does take one's personal and family needs into account, but places them within a larger frame of discerning one's calling to serve God's people as part of God's missional and transformative purposes for the world. Accordingly, while a personal decision is involved, the emphasis is not on the congregation that *I am choosing* but on wisely discerning the congregation that *God is choosing for me* to enjoy, serve, and partner with others in God's missional kingdom community. In place of unconditioned commitment to the church of one's birth, geographical location, or denominational affiliation, I would emphasize the importance of entering by faith into the covenant community.[1] As Stanley Grenz points out, the biblical notion of covenant is grounded in important beliefs and core convictions but also provides a deeper bond of

---

[1] One's calling might be to a particular denomination or association of churches (especially pastors ordained by a particular group), though the calling to a denomination is relative to basic faith commitments, not absolute in itself.

sociality than purely voluntary, associative, or institutional notions.² Grenz writes, "The covenant enhances the community dimension of the church. Indeed, the presence of the covenant is what transforms a loosely related group of people into a community."³ The covenant binds people to God and to one another in faith and implies sharing the benefits of the community as well as the responsibility of contributing to and serving the community and its mission.⁴ This involves a deep spiritual bond of fellowship in the Holy Spirit (not merely vague or sentimental feelings of togetherness), who indwells every believer and draws each into union with others "in Christ" who is in turn "in the Father" (John 17:20–23). What I am essentially endorsing is a modified form of congregationalism. This retains the voluntary aspect of the church as a community *of faith* but also places a strong emphasis on the social and spiritual bond between believers, in order to counter the powerful influence of consumerism, individualism, and pluralism in contemporary Western societies—to which free churches are particularly vulnerable.⁵

Another way of describing the deep spiritual bond of believers in the church is by recognizing the social nature of Christian life, wherein God draws believers to participate together in the life of the Trinity (see chapters 3 and 6). Recall that an important purpose of the church is to serve God's redemptive and transformative plan to heal and restore human relationships by reconciling believers to God and to one another through Christ in the Spirit. Since human sinfulness has destructive social ramifications (*cor curvum in se*, alienation, oppression, etc.), redemption and eschatological transformation must also have an intrinsically social dimension. As Lesslie Newbigin asserts, drawing also on the eschatological orientation of the church,

---

² Stanley J. Grenz, *Theology for the Community of God* (Grand Rapids: Eerdmans, 2000), 465.
³ Grenz, *Theology*, 480.
⁴ Grenz writes, "By establishing the eschatological community of love, the covenant people, God brings into being a new humankind, a people who mirror for all creation the divine character and essence" (*Theology*, 489).
⁵ See Stanley Hauerwas, *In Good Company: The Church as Polis* (Notre Dame: University of Notre Dame Press, 1995), 75. Grenz similarly argues in favour of what he calls "balanced congregationalism", in which the essence of the church lies with its people who join voluntarily but not simply as an aggregate collection of individuals (Grenz, *Theology*, 471–72). Miroslav Volf, in his own free church proposal, helpfully distinguishes between organic and associative church structures. Organic structures refer to "communities of being", which are groups into which one is born (e.g., family, tribe, ethnicity, etc.), while associative structures are alliances created for achieving specific ends and goals. He argues that the church cannot be neatly classified into either category but transcends both. One *joins* the church by *spiritual birth*. Consequently, Volf suggests the term "sibling friends" to describe the social bond between believers. See Miroslav Volf, *After Our Likeness: The Church as the Image of the Trinity* (Grand Rapids: Eerdmans, 1998), 179–81.

> In the final consummation of God's loving purpose we and all creation will be caught up into the perfect rapture of that mutual love which is the life of God Himself. What is given to us now can only be a foretaste, for none of us can be made whole till we are made whole together.[6]

In this sense, the church is not just a community of spiritual benefit or growth; it is actually a community of salvation. Moreover, it is not just an instrumental means or an external aid to salvation, but is itself a dimension of the salvific experience.[7] To clarify, as stated in chapter six, this is not because the church is an institutional dispenser of salvation (e.g., Luther's target: the medieval church system) but because it is the community in which reconciliation is embodied and transformation takes place. It is the social context in which redeemed human persons practice and live out intentionally, concretely, and holistically their restored relationships with God and others. To account fully for the importance of the church in Christian soteriology, one needs to grasp the comprehensive, life-integrating, and eschatological character and orientation of Christian redemption.

An emphasis on union with Christ and participation in the life of the Trinity is a helpful corrective to the rival models of human community explored in chapter two. All but one of those models are grounded in individualism, self interest, or self preservation. They consequently lack a sufficiently other-oriented motivation for community and relational grounds for human sociality. The model of community implied by the ethics of care (i.e., concentric circles of care) provides a better relational starting point, but it lacks a theological or otherwise transcendent grounding for the primacy of relationships. In the final analysis, its selection of caring as the ultimate criterion for ethics is arbitrary. All of the models explored in chapter two thus lack a sufficiently relational ontology of personhood and community. Union with Christ and participation in the life of the Trinity also provides a helpful corrective to many forms of evangelical ecclesiology. Many theological critics have observed that the purpose and significance of the church are ambiguous in the evangelical tradition. On the one hand, church seems to be a matter of peripheral importance to many evangelicals, subordinate to the personal spiritual growth and well being of individuals. Church has secondary importance as a means to this end, but it is often not valued as an end in itself. Many tend to see the church as a kind of spiritual gymnasium, an aid to personal spiritual fitness and growth but not intrinsic to salvation. On the other hand, many of the most vibrant and growing churches in North America in recent history have been evangelical churches. Accordingly, John Stackhouse suggests that while evangelicals have often not

---

[6] Lesslie Newbigin, *The Household of God: Lectures on the Nature of the Church* (London: SCM, 1957), 130.

[7] Volf, *After Our Likeness*, 174.

articulated their ecclesiology explicitly, they do nevertheless live one out implicitly by their actions and life together.[8]

In any case, the charge of many theologians (both within and outside the evangelical movement) that Evangelicalism lacks a coherent ecclesiology has merit.[9] Theologians and historians have attributed the ecclesiological ambivalence of evangelicals to deep-seated roots in the historical origins and development of the movement. For example, Stanley Grenz points to the parachurch ethos of historic evangelicalism, in which a desire to be inclusive led to an emphasis on general commonalities rather than ecclesiological precision.[10] Others have pointed to various additional factors, some of which include: widespread disillusionment with established church structures following the religious wars of the sixteenth and seventeenth centuries; the influence of pietism and the religious awakenings, which promoted individual religious experience, experimentation, and an anti-institutional and anti-ecclesial bias; the critique of established churches by radical reformation and free church traditions leading to an ad-hoc approach to ecclesiology (and ironically in some cases to a tradition of denying traditions), the impact of democracy and the importance of individual choice, and the American spirit of entrepreneurship and the influence of market values.[11] In light of such observations, Van Dyk suggests that the "ecclesiologi-

---

[8] John G. Stackhouse, Jr., "Preface," in *Evangelical Ecclesiology: Reality or Illusion?*, ed. John G. Stackhouse, Jr. (Grand Rapids: Baker Academic, 2003), 9. Commenting on David Bebbington's now classic description of evangelicalism which identifies its four key characteristics as crucicentrism, biblicism, conversionism, and activism, Leanne Van Dyk observes, "Noticeably absent in these common lists of evangelical characteristics are references to the church, including liturgy, worship, tradition, sacraments, ordination, or church government." Leanne Van Dyk, "The Church in Evangelical Theology and Practice," in *The Cambridge Companion to Evangelical Theology*, ed. Timothy Larsen and Daniel J. Treier (Cambridge: Cambridge University Press, 2007), 128. Van Dyk notes that these characteristics were identified by the 1996 Angus Reid Survey given to three thousand Americans and are similar to other lists of distinctive evangelical markers. While her point is interesting and perhaps indicates that evangelicals lack a *distinctive* ecclesiology, it does not prove that evangelicals have no ecclesiology. Ecclesiological details do not appear on Bebbington's list because they are not of themselves distinctive of the movement (e.g., Bebbington does not refer to the Trinity, even though mainstream evangelicals clearly affirm it).

[9] For examples (and responses), see the various essays in John G. Stackhouse, Jr., *Evangelical Ecclesiology: Reality or Illusion?* (Grand Rapids: Baker Academic, 2003).

[10] See Stanley J. Grenz, *Renewing the Center: Evangelical Theology in a Post-Theological Era* (Grand Rapids: Baker Academic, 2000).

[11] For a helpful survey of these historical roots and developments, see Van Dyk, "The Church in Evangelical Theology and Practice," 125–28. See also: Grenz, *Renewing the Center*; D.G. Hart, "The Church in Evangelical Theologies, Past and Future," in *The Community of the Word: Toward an Evangelical Ecclesiology*, ed. Mark Husbands and Daniel J. Treier (Downers Grove: InterVarsity Press, 2005), 23–40, and *Deconstructing Evangelicalism: Conservative Protestantism in the Age of Billy Gra-*

cal imagination among evangelicals must expand, deepen, and grow more textured. But this ecclesiological deficit can only be overcome if the theological exploration is thorough and integrative."[12] It is my hope that the view of the church as the new humanity united together through Christ in the Spirit, as cast in this dissertation, will assist in expanding, deepening, and enriching such ecclesiological imagination.

An ethical community

As a transformative community the church is also intrinsically an ethical community, a place of personal and social ethical orientation and formation. I have discussed the ethical nature of the church in three dimensions, in order to draw out the intrinsically and holistically ethical character of the church as the new humanity. Specifically, the church is a relational community of love, a rational community of faith, and an eschatological community of hope. Each of these dimensions implies that Christian life impacts not just personal ethics, but also social, cultural, and global ethics. First, as a relational community of love, the church is a community of reconciliation. It embodies the reconciliatory message of the gospel as believers commit to living together in love and peace, as brothers and sisters reconciled by the atoning death of Jesus Christ. This life together includes other ethically significant commitments, including edifying others, bearing the burdens of others, and forming counter cultural relationships as cruciform disciples of Jesus. Second, as a rational community of faith the church seeks to impart wisdom to its members, which equips them to flourish and live meaningful and impactful lives. Such wisdom combines genuine knowledge of and faith in God with accurate and practical knowledge about the world in order to live according to God's purposes. Third, as an eschatological community of hope, the church has both a task and a destiny with respect to the present-yet-coming kingdom of God. Its task is to participate with God in serving and expanding the kingdom in its community life and actions. As a kingdom community, the church is composed of people who are committed to the values and priorities of God's kingdom and who live out those values and priorities in how they think, relate, treat others (especially those who are different or are marginalized), make decisions, spend their money, and use their time and other resources. In addition to being the church's task and calling, the kingdom of God is also the church's destiny. While in the present era there is a distinction between the institutional church and the eschatological kingdom, one day

---

ham (Grand Rapids: Baker Academic, 2004); Bruce Hindmarsh, "Is Evangelical Ecclesiology an Oxymoron?" in *Evangelical Ecclesiology: Reality or Illusion?*, ed. John G. Stackhouse, Jr. (Grand Rapids: Baker Academic, 2003), 15–38; Mark A. Noll, *American Evangelical Christianity: An Introduction* (Oxford: Blackwell, 2001); and George M. Marsden, *Understanding Fundamentalism and Evangelicalism* (Grand Rapids: Eerdmans, 1991).

[12] Van Dyk, "The Church in Evangelical Theology and Practice," 132.

the church will enter fully into the kingdom of God. Presently, it is called to be an instrument, sign, and foretaste of the coming kingdom.

The ethical dimension of the church as the new humanity offers a helpful corrective to the rival models of community analyzed in chapter two. Love defines the church's relational-ethical dimension (chapters 3 and 6) and overcomes the deficiencies of mechanistic, individualistic, and/or self-preserving conceptions of community (e.g., rationalism, existentialism, sociobiology). Faith defines the church's rational-ethical dimension (chapters 4 and 7) and overcomes the deficiencies of communities based upon abstract ethical systems or generalizations, which lack thick descriptive frameworks combining traditions, narratives, and basic convictions in the context of formative communities. Hope defines the church's eschatological-ethical dimension (chapters 5 and 8) and overcomes the deficiencies of communities that lack a valid teleological orientation (i.e., an adequate understanding of the purpose and destiny of human beings) and/or separate being from becoming. All of the rival models surveyed offer reductionist explanations of the human *telos*. For example, existentialist models separate being from becoming and focus on the latter to the exclusion of the former; the future desires and present choices of individuals trump the significance of tradition, history, and community well being. With respect to the evangelical church context, conceiving the church as ethical communities of the new humanity helps to overcome false dualisms and dichotomies that have often plagued the tradition, such as personal versus social ethics, justification versus sanctification, body versus soul, spirituality versus social justice, evangelism versus humanitarian work, and holiness and purity versus incarnational affirmation and the enjoyment of creation and culture. Envisioning the church as the new humanity helps us to see that these are not dualistically opposed but dialogically enriching. It is perilous to separate them and/or to emphasize one over the other. Neglecting one's body by failing to get enough rest makes it difficult to fast and pray;[13] likewise, inattention to moral and spiritual values can lead to physical harm (e.g., casual sex leading to emotional instability and possibly sexually transmitted diseases). Neglecting justice leads to false spirituality; ignoring spiritual reality prevents us from pursing and establishing holistic justice. Neglecting the need for humanitarian work harms the church's evangelistic witness; failure to evangelize (leading to worldview transformation) undermines the very values that ground humanitarian work (e.g., Christian love/charity, human dignity and intrinsic worth). Denying the goodness of creation and the affirmation of bodily life degenerates holiness and purity into sectarian legalism; neglecting an appropriate emphasis on holiness and purity leads us to abuse the good things (and people) that God has created and entrusted to us.

---

[13] James C. Peterson makes a similar point in *Changing Human Nature: Ecology, Ethics, Genes, and God* (Grand Rapids: Eerdmans, 2010), 76.

A formative community of kingdom disciples oriented to the new creation
As a deeply relational and intrinsically ethical human community that is oriented to God's presence and purposes, the church is inherently a formative community. In chapter six we observed that the church is a community of relational formation. It is a community called together by the gospel of reconciliation and devoted to the Great Commandments of loving God and others. Moreover, it is a community of persons who speak God's Word to each other in order to teach, edify, encourage, correct, and sometimes even rebuke each another in love. The constitutive practices of baptism and the Lord's Supper have definitive implications for Christian relationships. The former ratifies the new life together in Christ while the latter brings us into regular communion with Christ and others and reminds us that Christian life together involves mutual care, support, interdependence, and the sharing of resources. Moreover, the formative practices of solitude and confession help maintain the integrity and authenticity of the Christian community.

In chapter seven we observed that the church is a community of rational formation; more specifically, it is a community dedicated to cultivating wisdom. It cultivates wisdom through theological formation, by which members grow in knowledge that equips them for wise living and shapes their worldview in light of Christian truth and basic convictions. The church also cultivates wisdom in its members through the ministry of the preached Word, which provides theological and practical instruction for Christian faith and life. Moreover, by practicing the sacramental ordinances of baptism and the Lord's Supper, Christians remember, rehearse, and celebrate the ministry and saving work of Jesus Christ. These constitutive church practices are deeply formational for the minds of Christian disciples, uniting them to the life of Christ and the tradition of the historic Christian church. In addition, Christian worship is deeply formative for Christian thinking and living. In worship, believers join with others to celebrate God's character, creativity, providence, and saving deeds. Such worship reminds Christians of God's faithfulness in the past and promises for the future, thus reinforcing the worldview and framework that equips them to think theologically and make wise life decisions. Similarly, participation in spiritual disciplines such as meditation, study, receiving guidance from others, and prayer (meditative, contemplative, supplication) can help Christians grow in knowledge, faith, and thus wisdom. Finally, the church fosters wisdom cultivation by calling wise leaders to serve as models, teachers, mentors, and guides to instruct and equip the whole church to discern God's voice and to grow in obedience, maturity, witness, and service in its communal life and mission.

Chapter eight described the church as a community of kingdom character formation that immerses believers in the drama of Scripture and Christian worldview and helps them to cultivate the Christian virtues. Such virtues are cultivated within the context of a community of disciples dedicated to following the concrete ethical teachings of Jesus. They include: (1) love, faith, and hope as the foundational virtues of the new humanity; (2) virtues related to the health of the kingdom community; and (3) virtues related to a congregation's contextual missional calling. The chapter highlighted several ecclesial practices that foster kingdom character formation. First, the ministry of the preached Word as a kingdom practice creatively and imaginatively helps people to indwell the Scriptures and to see themselves as characters in God's ongoing drama of creation, redemption, and eschatological transformation. Such preaching aims to help people envision God's reign and exhorts them to live accordingly. Second, as eschatological practices, the sacramental ordinances immerse believers dramatically, symbolically, and corporeally in God's salvation story and direct them toward its grand finale. Baptism emphasizes new spiritual birth (or new creation) into a Spirit-filled life, which anticipates the believer's final transformation in glory. The Lord's Supper looks forward to the wedding feast of the Lamb and the great banquet in the consummated kingdom of God and fills believers with hope, inspiration, and power to live as kingdom people in the present. Third, worship as an eschatological practice continually renews the church in its kingdom identity, mission, and destiny. Fourth, prayer patterned after the Lord's Prayer characterizes those who earnestly seek first the kingdom of God. Finally, the church as an eschatological community of kingdom character formation initiates disciples of Jesus into practicing transforming initiatives, which are concrete actions that break vicious cycles of sin by demonstrating and nurturing characteristic patterns of kingdom thinking and living.

The church engaging the world as the new humanity

The threefold ethical dimension of the church as the new humanity forms the basis of its engagement with the world. The church lives out of its ethical dimension and engages the world not merely by its own strength, vision, and resources, but by participating by the Spirit in Christ's ministry and mission in the world. Thus, it engages the world relationally by participating in Christ's *priestly* ministry as ambassadors of reconciliation. It engages the world rationally (in wisdom) by participating in Christ's *prophetic* ministry as witnesses and servant of the truth. It engages the world eschatologically by participating in Christ's *reign* as heralds and representatives of the kingdom of God.

Participating by the Spirit in Christ's mission

I proposed a participatory model of engaging the world in mission that emphasizes participating by the Spirit in the *missio Dei*. The church participates in Christ's *priestly* ministry as ambassadors of reconciliation. In so doing it proclaims and enacts the good news of peace and reconciliation leading to restored relationships with God and other human beings. Both *speaking* the message and *being* the message, as God's other-centred, exocentric community of love, are crucial. The church participates in Christ's *prophetic* ministry as witnesses and servants of the truth by seeking to influence the world toward wise living. This involves proclaiming and demonstrating the truth of Christian faith in compelling, winsome ways. It means declaring the explicit truth content of the gospel through baptizing and making disciples, training and teaching them all that Christ instructed, and relying on Christ's authoritative and revelatory presence while bearing witness. The church participates in Christ's *reign* as heralds and representatives of the kingdom of God. The kingdom of God orients the identity of the church toward its task and destiny, which is to be and increasingly become a kingdom community of the new creation. Moreover, conceiving the church in terms of both task and destiny leads to a missional understanding of the church, in which mission is a defining or constitutive element of what it means to be the church.

Social-ecclesial ethics of love, faith, and hope

The ecclesiology I have articulated in this book promotes a threefold model of cultural engagement, which I described as the social-ecclesial ethics of love, faith, and hope. The social-ecclesial ethics of love reflects the exocentric, ecstatic nature of the church as a relational community filled with the overflowing Love (Spirit) of God (chapter 6). God's love is evident in both God's *YES* to humanity as God intends it to be and God's *NO* to sinful and destructive distortions of God's purposes for human beings. Accordingly, I suggested that a theology of the cross provides us with a helpful model of cultural engagement emphasizing both (negatively) God's judgment and (positively) God's redemptive activity by the death of Christ. Such a model exhorts the church to be critical of culture (all human cultures), to expose oppression and injustice, and to advocate for shalom in all human relationships and social structures. While the church's specific mission must be discerned concretely in the context of local congregations, I proposed that three principles provide helpful guidelines. These include discerning what God is doing and joining in to participate in God's work, sharing the burdens of a congregation's local community, and partnering with others who are pursuing social justice, reconciliation, and peace. Such means of engagement follow the church's call to live-out-love in the midst of an egocentric world.

The social-ecclesial ethics of faith reflects the nature of the church as a rational community of wisdom formation and propagation (chapter 7). I proposed that the incarnation provides the church with a model of cultural engagement emphasizing going out into the world (rather than expecting the world to come to the church), reaching people by forming relationships and investing in others, and recognizing and actively forming bridges of mutual understanding and agreement wherever they can be found. As an overarching guideline for engaging the world wisely, I proposed the general theme of pursuing and contributing to whatever is good, true, and beautiful, thereby infusing the world with implicit Christian values and principles and demonstrating the comprehensive coherence of the Christian faith. Through such means, Christians demonstrate what it means to live by faith in a world that is full of distrust and scepticism.

The social-ecclesial ethics of hope reflects the nature of the church as an eschatological community of the new creation (chapter 8). I proposed that the resurrection offers a hope-filled model of cultural engagement and transformation. In particular, a resurrection model implies that the church's missional engagement with culture receives inspiration from God's vision for new *possibilities*, moves in God's *power* to persevere and accomplish what otherwise would not be possible, and is refreshed and encouraged by God's ongoing *presence* with the church as it pursues its mission. The means of engaging culture in eschatological hope involve the church's being, proclaiming, and doing. As a community of kingdom formation the church is committed to being and becoming increasingly a people characterized by Jesus's teachings, values, priorities, commitments, worldview and relationships. In its ministry of proclamation, the church promotes kingdom values within society and advocates for kingdom justice as it continually prays to the Father in Jesus's name: "May your kingdom come; May your will be done on earth as it is in heaven." Moreover, the church engages culture by performing deeds and actions that are characteristic of the kingdom. Such activity is not mere activism, but involves participating with the Spirit of God in mustard seed planting by practicing transforming missional initiatives that break vicious cycles of social sin and structural evil by gradually forming both practitioners and society in the ways of the kingdom. Through such being, proclaiming, and acting Christians demonstrate the hope of the gospel in the midst of a world characterized by fear and despair.

Christ and Culture: Which posture best suits the church as the new humanity?
In his classic book *Christ and Culture*, H. Richard Niebuhr proposes a five-fold typology as a heuristic devise for analyzing and organizing characteristic ways that various church traditions have understood and practiced the relation of church to culture.[14] The first type, Christ *against* culture, generally has a negative view of human culture and consequently emphasizes rejecting culture out of loyalty to Jesus Christ. It posits a clear line of separation between the church and the world and envisions the church as a separate community or society. Examples Niebuhr provides of this approach include Tertullian, Tolstoy, and the Anabaptists. The second type, Christ *of* culture, sees Christianity as the fulfilment of the human cultural impulse to overcome the limitations of nature. It envisions harmony between church and society and depicts the church as a progressive religious association. Representatives of this type include Abélard, Kant, Locke, Jefferson, the early Schleiermacher, Ritschl, and cultural Protestantism generally. The third type, Christ *above* culture, involves a synthesis of church and culture in which the church directs people to their supernatural end, assists in the ordering of social-temporal life, and is the custodian of divine law. In contemporary ecclesiological terms this type epitomizes a Christendom model of church.[15] Representatives of the synthetic type include Justin Martyr,

---

[14] H. Richard Niebuhr, *Christ and Culture* (New York: HarperSanFrancisco, 2001).

[15] Craig Carter criticizes Niebuhr's typology with being thoroughly compromised by Christendom assumptions and values. He writes, "By calling *Christ and Culture* a product of and apology for Christendom, I mean that it takes Christendom for granted

Clement of Alexandria, and especially Thomas Aquinas. The fourth type, Christ and culture *in paradox*, envisions church and culture in a paradoxical yet dialogical relationship, in which the tension between church and culture helps to preserve the legitimacy of both. Representatives of this type include Luther and Kierkegaard. The fifth and final type, Christ the *transformer* of culture, contends against both the cultural pessimism of type one and the accommodation to culture evident in type two. Niebuhr argues that this type characterizes mainstream Christianity (as represented by Augustine and Calvin) and that it most resembles type four but demonstrates a more optimistic attitude toward culture. It stresses the biblical-theological themes of creation, fall, redemption (in history), and eschatology (God's power to transform present circumstances).

Of these options, the posture most befitting the church as the new humanity is Niebuhr's transformative type, though with certain qualifications. The theological anthropology and corresponding ecclesiology that I have been developing requires a more nuanced view of the church's role in transforming culture. First, it requires that we speak not primarily about the church transforming culture or even of Christ transforming culture but rather of the church as *participating* by the Spirit in the transformative ministry and mission of the Son to the glory and honour of the Father. Second, it posits that this socially transformative mission has a threefold ethical dimension. In love, the church participates in Christ's priestly ministry of relational transformation and engages culture in a cruciform pattern modelled after the theology of the cross (i.e., putting others

---

as its starting point and assumes that Christendom is real, permanent, and on the whole a good thing. Although there is no state church in the United States, there is a strong sense of America being a Christian nation and of the church having a key role to play in maintaining public morality, inspiring patriotism in the citizenry, and giving religious legitimacy to the government." See Craig A. Carter, *Rethinking Christ & Culture: A Post-Christendom Perspective* (Grand Rapids: Brazos, 2006), 56. While I appreciate some aspects of Carter's critique of Niebuhr (granted, Niebuhr does not account for the complexity and historical variants of Anabaptism), I do not finally find his argument convincing. I personally do not find Niebuhr arguing that Christendom is "real, permanent, and on the whole a good thing." Actually, in some ways Niebuhr distances himself from Christendom thinking, for instance he criticizes the synthetic type (the only type that in my view corresponds closely to the Christendom model) for having an over-realized eschatology (*Christ and Culture*, 147). I also do not see where Niebuhr talks about "inspiring patriotism" or "granting religious legitimacy to the government" (whatever that means?). Carter also charges Niebuhr with failing to recognize that an "against culture" stance can be a way of impacting a society. However, Niebuhr explicitly acknowledges this: his position is that the "Christ against culture" type is both a necessary and an inadequate response (see *Christ and Culture*, 65–81). Carter's underlying presupposition is his commitment to pacifism. He accordingly categorizes as "Christendom" any theology of culture that rejects pacifism. See the chart which depicts Carter's six proposed types, dividing them evenly into two broad categories—Christendom/non-pacifist and non-Christendom/pacifist (*Rethinking Christ & Culture*, 113). This seems to me to be overly simplistic.

first, serving, breaking through socio-economic or cultural walls that typically divide people). By faith and knowledge leading to wisdom, the church participates in Christ's prophetic ministry of rational transformation with the incarnation as its model of cultural engagement. And in hope, the church participates in Christ's kingly ministry (or reign) of eschatological transformation guided by a resurrection model of cultural engagement. Third, it is important to stress that all three of these dimensions are important and that neglecting or focusing exclusively on one leads to a distortion of Christian mission.[16] For example, an exclusive focus on the cruciform model leads to a sectarian stance and/or a martyr complex. An exclusive focus on the incarnational model leads to antinomianism, rationalism, and epistemological naivety. And an exclusive focus on the resurrection model leads to triumphalism, false optimism, or utopian idealism. The church must balance all three modes of witness and discern which mode to emphasize according to its missional context and the opportunities and challenges that its particular context presents to the proclamation of the gospel and the extension of the kingdom.[17]

A Trinitarian revision of missional ecclesiology

In chapter eight I argued in favour of a missional understanding of the church. Here I want to offer a word of constructive criticism of at least some versions of missional theo-logic in light of a trinitarian-participatory ecclesiology. Missional church advocates criticize the tendency of traditional approaches to ecclesiology to derive the church directly from Christology and consequently neglect to include mission as a constitutive element of ecclesiology. Instead, they propose that ecclesiology must be derived from missiology. Unfortunately however, this sometimes leads missional church thinkers into a tendency to depict Christian life and community in overly instrumental or functional terms

---

[16] John Stackhouse similarly argues that various mission contexts call for different responses. He sees a place for each of Niebuhr's types, but favours as normative a combination of types four and five. See John G. Stackhouse, Jr., *Making the Best of It: Following Christ in the Real World* (New York: Oxford University Press, 2008). My position is somewhat similar to his, but instead of proposing a hybrid I am embracing a more nuanced version of the transformative view (with due attention to missional context and the three dimensions of transformation—relational, rational, and eschatological).

[17] For example, the Confessing Church's context in Nazi Germany at the height of Hitler's power called primarily for a cruciform approach to cultural engagement, though even then the resurrection and incarnation models were necessary to sustain hope and affirm the value of all human life (e.g., Bonhoeffer argued incarnationally that Christ was present especially in the oppressed Jewish brother). Bonhoeffer himself affirmed all three models at different times, the theology of the cross in the early to mid 1930s (evident in *Creation and Fall*, the "Lectures on Christology," and *Discipleship*), the incarnation from the mid 1930s to the early 1940s (evident in *Life Together* and *Ethics*), and resurrection near the end of his life while in prison (in the prison letters Bonhoeffer's reflections on the future are filled with hope and faith in new possibilities for a post-Nazi Germany).

whereby church becomes merely a means to an end (this is probably not the intent of such writers, but I would argue that it is the logical conclusion of their position). For instance, one popular missional thinker argues that *cause creates community*. He insists, "We build community incidentally, when our imaginations and energies are captured by a higher, even nobler cause . . . Christian community results from the greater cause of Christian mission."[18] The intention behind this statement is helpful, namely to caution the church against becoming inwardly fixated and viewing its communal life as an end in itself. However, I suggest that the author overstates his case; he maintains the end-means dichotomy and simply reverses the trend by reducing the church to a means instead of an end. Moreover, out of a desire to emphasize mission, advocates of the missional church sometimes downplay the personal and relational aspects of ecclesiology in favour of functional or task-oriented ones. For example, consider the following claims of Darrell Guder:

> The biblical record places *no emphasis* on the special significance of conversion stories.
>
> *One does not find a concern* for 'the establishment of their personal well-being in their relationship with God' in the stories of the call of Abraham, Moses, the prophets, the disciples or Paul. The issue in these encounters is not 'the saving of their souls' or 'their experience of grace and salvation.'
>
> [T]he experience of the benefits [of salvation] is *always subordinated* to the call and its purpose.[19]

Guder accordingly argues for the "preeminence of witness as *the fundamental definition* of the church", for "witness" as the "*all-encompassing definition*" of Christian existence", and subordinates other important functions of the church to witness including proclamation, community, and service/ministry.[20] This position, along with similar views expressed in the missional church literature, leads to a functional or task-oriented understanding not only of the church and human relationships, but also of God and the Scriptures (mission becomes a controlling theological metanarrative).[21]

---

[18] Michael Frost, *Exiles: Living Intentionally In A Post-Christian Culture* (Peabody: Hendrickson, 2006), 108. For similar statements by other authors in the missional church discussion, see Darrell L. Guder, ed., *Missional Church: A Vision for the Sending of the Church in North America* (Grand Rapids: Eerdmans, 1998), 4–6, 8, 19, 227; and Darrell L. Guder, *Be My Witnesses: The Church's Mission, Message, and Messengers* (Grand Rapids: Eerdmans, 1985), 44.

[19] Darrell L. Guder, *The Continuing Conversion of the Church* (Grand Rapids: Eerdmans, 2000), 129 (emphasis added).

[20] Guder, *Be My Witnesses*, 109, 233, 49 (emphasis added).

[21] See Darrell L. Guder , "Missional Theology for a Missionary Church," *Journal for Preachers* 22, no. 1 (1998), 7, and *The Continuing Conversion of the Church*, 129.

Conclusion: Church for the Twenty-First Century

In contrast to the functionalism implied by some accounts of missional ecclesiology, it is important to ground the church's mission in the love and ecstatic character of God. While it is true that God sends the church on a mission to the world, it is crucial to recognize that before God sends the church God must create, reconcile, renew, edify, and empower it. God's people can be authentic witnesses in the world only if they know God intimately and experience the transformative presence of God's Spirit. As Newbigin reminds us, mission results from an explosion of joy in the church community, which overflows into the world.[22] Consequently, the missional church movement is correct in placing mission within the essence of the church, but only if it defines the missional nature of the church in primarily relational terms rather than functional ones (though not to the exclusion of functions). The problem is not that missional church advocates understand mission as being part of the essence of the church, but that some emphasize doing over being, corporate and objective aspects of salvation over personal and subjective aspects, and existing-for-others over existing-in-community.

Dietrich Bonhoeffer's missional ecclesiology provides a helpful corrective to this line of thinking.[23] Following the logic of the creation-fall-redemption narrative, Bonhoeffer demonstrates that the church must exist simultaneously for the sake of its own community and for the sake of others. To illustrate his point, Bonhoeffer distinguishes the church community from two other types of social gathering. First, he distinguishes it from "society".[24] Society is "an association of rational action", for which people accept responsibility only out of their own self-interest in pursuing a common goal. Christian community, by contrast, is part of the social structure of life and, as such, is an end willed by God. Moreover, while personal bonds in society are expressed in looseness or indifference, in community they are expressed in closeness or intimacy. In addition, while society is joined voluntarily and secured contractually, Christian community is

---

See also Allan Janssen, review of *Missional Church: A Vision for the Sending of the Church in North America*, by Darrell L. Guder, ed. *Perspectives* 14 (April 1999): 21; Andreas J. Köstenberger, review of *Confident Witness, Changing World: Rediscovering the Gospel in North America*, by Craig Van Gelder, ed., *Evangelical Missions Quarterly* 36 (January 2000): 114.

[22] Lesslie Newbigin, *The Gospel in a Pluralist Society* (Grand Rapids: Eerdmans, 1989), 116.

[23] See my article, "Bonhoeffer's Missional Ecclesiology," *McMaster Journal of Theology and Ministry* 9 (2007–2008): 96–128.

[24] Bonhoeffer draws on Ferdinand Tönnies's distinction between community (*Gemeindschaft*) and society (*Gesellschaft*). See Dietrich Bonhoeffer, *Sanctorum Communio: A Theological Study of the Sociology of the Church*, vol. 1 *Dietrich Bonhoeffer Works*, ed. Clifford C. Green, trans. Reinhard Krauss and Nancy Lukens (Minneapolis: Fortress Press, 1998), 89–91. I recognize that Tönnies's sociological model is obsolete, but I find Bonhoeffer's conceptual use of Tönnies helpful for constructive and heuristic purposes.

created and preserved by God.[25] Secondly, community should not be confused with the concept of the "mass", by which Bonhoeffer means a group of people drawn together by a common stimulus.[26] In such a group, people come together to share a common experience (a theatre audience, a rock concert, a literary circle, etc.) and their community is the by-product of that common experience. Bonhoeffer argues that while the mass represents the simplest form and most powerful feeling of unity, and thus can be deceptively idealistic, it is not built upon the separateness of persons and cannot last beyond the common experience. For Bonhoeffer, Christian community is never a human ideal or utopian dream, but a divine reality established by Christ in the Spirit. Bonhoeffer shows that the Christian church community exists *both* as an end in itself *and* as a means to a greater end in the eschatological reality of already and not-yet. It exists for the sake of itself because God's missional intention is to establish a new creation, a community of love and new life in which people live in restored communion with God and one another. Yet, the church also exists for others because its Lord, Jesus Christ, the "man for others", is conforming it to his own image (the *imago Dei*), which means being-free-for others. To employ an Augustinian trinitarian analogy, divine community within the Godhead does not derive from some impersonal, instrumental cause, law, or mechanism, but from God's ecstatic nature as Love. Augustine thus uses the image of Lover, Beloved, and Love to depict the Trinity.[27] Divine community is primarily a perichoretic union of love, not an instrumental association of common purpose (though the latter does flow from the former). In this relational sense, everything the church does is indeed mission. The church exists to experience and share the reconciliation and intimate communion with God and others that the gospel of Christ makes possible; everything it does embodies and bears witness to this. Thus, Bonhoeffer locates mission within the essence of the church without thereby reducing the latter to instrumental or functional categories. Accordingly, his missional ecclesiology is able to provide theological grounding for understanding the church both as a community of love and worship *and* as an agent of social justice that stands in solidarity with those who suffer and those who are in need.[28]

Being missional means being a church that exists for others, not merely in the sense of being outward-focused or outreach-driven, but more foundationally in the sense of being *essentially* a relational, ecstatic entity. The church is a part

---

[25] See also James B. Torrance, "The Covenant Concept in Scottish Theology and Politics and its Legacy," *Scottish Journal of Theology* 34, no. 3 (1981): 225–43.

[26] Bonhoeffer, *Sanctorum Communio*, 94.

[27] Augustine, *The Trinity* V/5.14, vol. 5 *The Works of St. Augustine: A Translation for the 21st Century*, ed. John E. Rotelle, trans. Edmund Hill (New York: New City, 1991), 255.

[28] For an exploration of Bonhoeffer's christological critique of oppression and injustice, see my article "Bonhoeffer's Anti-Logos and its Challenge to Oppression," *Crux* 41, no. 2 (2005): 2–9.

of God's plan to deliver human beings from the destructive social consequences of human sin. Originally created in God's image to be free-for-God-and-others, human beings became corrupted by sin and are ensnared in idolatry and self-centredness. Originally created with a heart oriented toward God and others, fallen human beings now possess a heart turned in upon itself. Redemption from sin, consequently, includes redemption from self-captivity, self-isolation, and the self's attempt to have absolute dominion over others (including God). The church is the place where God turns people inside-out, bringing them together into union with Christ in one Spirit, thus reversing their self-orientation and freeing them to love and serve God and others. To be sure, as the eschatological emphasis of chapter eight emphasized, the church is not the final consummation of God's plan or the full realization of God's kingdom. Nevertheless, God intends the church to be a sign and foretaste of what is to come, a sacrament and catalyst of the eschatological kingdom.

The church in the service of human flourishing: some preliminary implications

Many Protestant Christians in the West are accustomed to thinking about church in consumerist and individualistic terms. They begin with "me and my or my family's needs", subsequently seek out a church that caters to those needs, then possibly consider getting involved in the ministry of the church, and perhaps finally express interest in the church's kingdom mandate and its broader mission to the world. In contrast, the view of the church that I have presented encourages us to think in the reverse order. Conceiving the church as the new humanity helps us understand that the church is essential to God's global project of redeeming and transforming all human beings and all human societies and cultures. We must therefore begin our thinking about the church with the loving, ecstatic nature and character of the triune God, which undergirds God's own mission of redeeming and transforming the whole world. Ecclesiology is first and foremost theocentric. As the Body of Christ, the People of God, and the Temple of the Holy Spirit, the church is oriented and dedicated to the presence and purposes of the Trinity. Its primary focus should be to participate with God in pursuing and expanding God's kingdom in response to the Great Commandments (e.g., Mark 12:29–31) and the Great Commission (Matt 28:18–20). The establishment of God's kingdom and the mission it entails for the church implies that the church must be a community of kingdom character formation, which trains Christian disciples in the way of Jesus Christ. When looking to join a congregation, Christians should seek out those that excel not in satisfying the needs of religious consumers but in training and equipping believers for ministry in the church and for mission in the world (i.e., see the formative practices and means of engagement discussed in chapters 6–8). Involvement in such churches will align their thinking, desires, and priorities; lesser needs and desires can still be addressed, but in due order (Matt 6:33).

Believers will find that God meets many of their deepest needs through their involvement in such communities.

In terms of the big picture for ecclesiology, the church as the new humanity serves human flourishing as an assigned mandate from God. The contours of what it means for human beings to flourish are set within the framework of a distinctly Christian worldview. Let me briefly mention five ways in which the church is called to advocate for and pursue the flourishing of all human beings. It should be emphasized that these suggestions are preliminary and require a fuller treatment than can be offered at present. They identify topics that deserve future treatment in light of the conclusions of this book.

First, the church must be concerned about the personal ethics of its individual members. The church is called to be a community of kingdom character formation with a threefold emphasis: relational formation, wisdom formation, and missional formation in light of God's kingdom and the new creation. Second, the church must be concerned about social ethics. Loving God includes loving one's neighbour, not just the neighbours in one's own church community but also the fellow human beings in one's broader network of relationships and society. As Kathryn Tanner argues, the church is not properly a separate society (sociologically), but a formative voluntary—and I would add *covenantal*—community within a wider human society that lives out a different way of life. The church exists to impact society by active engagement and involvement, not just by trying to bring people into its fold.[29] Third, the church must be concerned with politics because the gospel has socio-political implications for large-scale human relationships and institutions.[30] The church and the state have different roles to play in promoting God's justice, yet both have the mandate of fostering human flourishing and, in this respect, they are united in purpose (though not always in agreement concerning the best means of achieving that purpose).[31] Christians begin to think politically whenever they ask the

---

[29] Kathryn Tanner, *Theories of Culture: A New Agenda for Theology* (Minneapolis: Fortress, 1997), 97–103.

[30] John Howard Yoder helps us see the thoroughly political nature of Jesus's ministry and mission. We might not agree with Yoder on all of the exegetical questions and their implications, but we are indebted to Yoder for alerting us to the political relevance of Jesus in a particularly clear and compelling way. See *The Politics of Jesus: Vicit Agnus Noster* (Grand Rapids: Eerdmans, 1994) and *Body Politics: Five Practices of the Christian Community Before the Watching World* (Scottdale, PA: Herald, 2001).

[31] Having said this, it is important also to emphasize that the church has a God-given mandate over-against the state, which is to call it to account and sometimes even to engage in active resistance when the state oversteps its authority by violating or neglecting its God-given mandate to serve human flourishing. When the state does this, it ceases truly to be the state (as God intended, as a steward of God's own justice) and has become a usurper and imposter. See Bonhoeffer, *Ethics*, 388–94. Elsewhere, Bonhoeffer argues that the power of government is a "gift from above", not something existing merely for its own sake in autonomy from God. See his discussion of

question: how do we serve our neighbours and influence our society strategically and effectively (i.e., in an organized way)? This is a question that the church simply must not neglect and much more work needs to be done to answer it, not just in general terms but from within particular contexts—countries, states/provinces, regions, cities, municipalities, and local institutions. For example, with respect to my own Canadian context, there are likely to be insights from how Christians think and act in the United States or England, but such cannot be automatically implemented across national or other cultural borders. Neither the United States nor England can provide settled models for the work of the church in Canada. Different contexts call for different forms of response.[32] Fourth, the church must be concerned about global justice, in faithful response to the question: who is my neighbour *in a globalized context*? Answer: whoever falls within my sphere of influence and power to help, thus making an ethical claim on me as a responsible steward-priest of the new creation (in a global age this sphere is large, though more defuse than it used to be, particularly for many Christians in the global North and West). Christians must always remember that God's redemptive plan concerns reaching the whole world with the whole gospel.[33] Pursuing God's global missional call depends upon the universality (or catholicity) and unity of the world-wide church, because no single congregation, denomination, parachurch organization, or theo-

---

the divine character of government and the relationship between government and church in Dietrich Bonhoeffer, *Conspiracy and Imprisonment: 1940–1945*, vol. 16 Dietrich Bonhoeffer Works, ed. Mark S. Brocker, trans. Lisa E. Dahill (Minneapolis: Fortress, 2006), 513–28. Note that Bonhoeffer distinguishes between "state" as an ancient pagan concept and "government" as the New Testament describes it. He writes, "State means an ordered commonwealth; government is the power that creates and upholds the order" (503). And, "Government is the power set in place by God to exercise worldly rule with divine authority. Government is the vicarious representative action of God on earth. It can only be understood from above" (504). Moreover, Bonhoeffer limits the authority of the government both in terms of the cross (taking account of sin) and eschatologically (only the future city of God, the new Jerusalem, will God exhibit God's perfect justice). In addition, Bonhoeffer argues that both church and state find their legitimacy and true vocation only in and through Christ the Mediator (511–12).

[32] See for example: John Douglas Hall, "The Changing North American Context of the Church's Ministry," "A Theological Proposal for the Church's Response to Its Context," and "The Church and Its Ministry: Responding to the Changing Context in Worship, Preaching, Education, Outreach," *Currents in Theology and Mission* 22, no. 6D (1995): 402–50; Seymour Martin Lipset, *Continental Divide: The Values and Institutions of the United States and Canada* (New York: Routledge, 1990); Mark A. Noll, *A History of Christianity in the United States and Canada* (Grand Rapids: Eerdmans, 1992), and "What Happened to Christian Canada?," *Church History* 75 (June 2006): 245–73; and Brian C. Stiller, *From the Tower of Babel to Parliament Hill: How to be a Christian in Canada Today* (Toronto: HarperCollins, 1997).

[33] John Stott, ed., *Making Christ Known: Historic Mission Documents from the Lausanne Movement 1974–1989* (Grand Rapids: Eerdmans, 1996).

logical tradition can fulfill the global call to mission on its own. Seeking the establishment of the kingdom of God in the whole world requires partnership. I do not believe that this requires institutional uniformity, but it does require of all Christians an openness to other churches and Christian traditions and a commitment to partnering together to pursue the cause of justice and righteousness for the nations. Finally, pursuing human flourishing requires active dialogue and relationship building with the world's major religions and their representatives. Different worldviews undergird and exhort different conceptions of ethics and justice.[34] At the same time, common ground can be found and a degree of ethical consensus can be reached, as evidenced by the Universal Declaration of Human Rights voted unanimously by the member nations of the United Nations, despite the differences in the interpretation and implementation of the declarations by various member countries and cultures.[35] Such dialogue and relationship building will require much grace, charity, goodwill, humility, patience, diligence, and hope-filled endurance, while simultaneously guarding the uniqueness of Christian theological convictions. It involves a contest of conflicting worldviews, which is threatening for all parties involved. Yet, as Christians we can enter such relations with confidence because we believe that Jesus Christ is the hope of humanity, the desire of the nations, the ultimate answer to all of our deepest questions and longings. As H. Richard Niebuhr insightfully writes,

> [T]he fact that Christians have found kinship between Christ and the prophets of the Hebrews, the moral philosophers of Greece, the Roman Stoics, Spinoza, and Kant, humanitarian reformers and Eastern mystics, may be less indicative of Christian instability than of a certain stability in human wisdom. Though apart from Christ it is difficult to find unity in what is sometimes called the great tradition of culture, with his aid such a unity can be discerned.[36]

May the church of Jesus Christ never lose its confidence in this great truth!

---

[34] Alasdair MacIntyre, *Whose Justice? Which Rationality?* (Notre Dame: University of Notre Dame Press), 1988.

[35] See the "Universal Declaration of Human Rights," in *Human Rights Documents: Compilation of Documents Pertaining to Human Rights*, 63–68. Washington: Committee on Foreign Affairs, 1983.

[36] Niebuhr, *Christ and Culture*, 107–108.

ANTHROPOLOGY AND ECCLESIOLOGY: *A TYPOLOGY*

Type	Anthropology	Social bond	Contemporary Expressions
Contractual	Enlightenment; Being human as rational capacity. Representatives: Descartes, Hobbes, Locke	Social contract; Arrangement to pursue mutual benefits	'Attractional': many seeker and independent churches
Moral	Enlightenment; Being human as rational capacity. Representative: Kant	Association of duty; Common commitment to the moral law	'Attractional': churches devoted to traditional values and lifestyles
Erotic	Nihilist; Being human as power-seeking and submission. Representative: Nietzsche	Will to power; Power struggle and conformity	Cult groups groups under a 'cult' leader/ personality
Phileic	Existentialist; Being human as authentic self-creation and self-expression. Representatives: Sartre, de Beauvoir	Shared interests, experiences, and expressions	Emerging Church
Instrumental	Sociobiology; Being human as self-preserving animal. Representative: E.O. Wilson	Biological (instinctual); Exists for self-preservation and replication	Church Growth Movement, Prosperity churches
Caring	Ethics of care; Being human as *caring for others*. Representative: Nel Noddings	Relational 'ontology'; Concentric circles of care	'Community churches' Mainline Liberal Emerging Church

Bibliography

Adam, A.K.M., Stephen E. Fowl, Kevin J. Vanhoozer, and Francis Watson. *Reading Scripture with the Church: Toward a Hermeneutic for Theological Interpretation*. Grand Rapids: Baker Academic, 2006.

Anderson, Ray S. *On Being Human: Essays in Theological Anthropology*. Pasadena: Fuller Seminary Press, 1982.

Anselm. *Proslogium; Monologium; An Appendix in Behalf of the Fool by Gaunilon; and Cur Deus Homo*. Translated by Sidney Norton Deane. Chicago: Open Court, 1926.

Athanasius. *On the Incarnation of the Word*. In *Athanasius: Select Works and Letters*. Volume 2–04 of *Nicene and Post-Nicene Fathers*. Edited by Philip Schaff and Henry Wace. Edinburgh: T & T Clark, 1891.

Augustine. *The Confessions of St. Augustine*. Translated by John K. Ryan. New York: Doubleday, 1960.

— *The Literal Meaning of Genesis*. Volume 13 of *The Works of St. Augustine: A Translation for the 21st Century*. Translated by Edmund Hill. Edited by John E. Rotelle. New York: New City, 2002.

— *The Trinity*. Volume 5 of *The Works of St. Augustine: A Translation for the 21st Century*. Translated by Edmund Hill. Edited by John E. Rotelle. New York: New City, 1991.

— "Sermon 52." *Sermons III: On the New Testament*. Volume 3 of *The Works of Saint Augustine: A Translation for the Twenty First Century*. Translated by Edmund Hill. Edited by John E Rotelle. New York: New City, 1991.

Avise, John C. *The Genetic Gods: Evolution and Belief in Human Affairs*. Cambridge, MA: Harvard University Press, 1998.

Ayres, Lewis. *Nicaea and Its Legacy: An Approach to Fourth-Century Trinitarian Theology*. New York: Oxford University Press, 2004.

— "On Not Three People: The fundamental Themes of Gregory of Nyssa's Trinitarian Theology as Seen in To Ablabius: On Not Three Gods." *Modern Theology* 18 (Oct. 2002): 445–74.

Bader-Saye, Scott. "The Emergent Matrix." *Christian Century* 121, no. 24 (2004): 20–25.

Bibliography

— "Improvising Church: An Introduction to the Emerging Church Conversation." *International Journal for the Study of the Christian Church* 6, no. 1 (2006): 12–23.

Bailey, Kenneth D. *Typologies and Taxonomies: An Introduction to Classification Techniques.* Thousand Oaks: Sage, 1994.

Bakke, Jeanette A. *Holy Invitations: Exploring Spiritual Direction.* Grand Rapids: Baker, 2000.

Balthasar, Hans Urs von. *Theo-drama: Theological Dramatic Theory.* Volumes 1–4. San Francisco: Ignatius, 1998–94.

Banks, Robert, and Julia Banks. *The Church Comes Home: Regrouping the People of God for Community and Mission.* Peabody: Hendrickson, 1997.

Barna, George. *Revolution.* Carol Stream: Barna Books; Tyndale House, 2005.

Barret, Lois Y., ed. *Treasure in Clay Jars: Patterns in Missional Faithfulness.* Grand Rapids: Eerdmans, 2004.

Barth, Karl. "The Church: The Living Congregation of the Living Lord Jesus Christ." In *God Here and Now*, 61–85. Edited by Paul van Buren. New York: Harper and Row, 1964.

— *The Doctrine of Creation: Church Dogmatics III/1.* London: T & T Clark, 2009.

— *Evangelical Theology: An Introduction.* Grand Rapids, MI: Eerdmans, 1963.

Bartholomew, Craig, Mary Healy, Karl Möller, and Robin Parry, eds. *Out of Egypt: Biblical Theology and Biblical Interpretation.* Grand Rapids: Zondervan, 2004.

Bayer, Oswald. *Martin Luther's Theology: A Contemporary Interpretation.* Translated by Thomas H. Trapp. Grand Rapids: Eerdmans, 2008.

Beale, G.K. *We Become What We Worship: A Biblical Theology of Idolatry.* Downers Grove: InterVarsity Press, 2008.

Beauchamp, Tom L. and James F. Childress. *Principles of Biomedical Ethics.* New York: Oxford University Press, 2001.

Bebbington, David W. *Evangelicalism in Modern Britain: A History from the 1730s to the 1980s.* London: Routledge, 2005.

Bellah, Robert N., ed. *Habits of the Heart: Individualism and Commitment in American Life.* New York: Harper and Row, 1986.

Benner, David G. *The Gift of Being Yourself: The Sacred Call to Self-Discovery.* Downers Grove: InterVarsity Press, 2004.

— Benner, David G. *Spirituality and the Awakening Self: The Sacred Journey of Transformation.* Grand Rapids: Brazos, 2012.

Bethell, Tom. "Against Sociobiology." *First Things* (January 2001): 18–24.

Bilder, Richard B. "Human Rights and U.S. Foreign Policy: Short-Term Prospects." *Virginia Journal of International Law* 14, no. 4 (1974): 597.

Blackaby, Henry T. and Claude V. King. *Experiencing God: How to Live the Full Adventure of Knowing and Doing the Will of God.* Nashville: Broadman and Holman, 1994.

Bloesch, Donald. *The Church: Sacraments, Worship, Ministry, Mission.* Downers Grove: InterVarsity Press, 2002.

Boda, Mark J. and Gordon T. Smith, eds. *Repentance in Christian Theology.* Collegeville, MN: Liturgical, 2006.

Boff, Leonardo. *Ecclesiogenesis: The Base Communities Reinvent the Church.* Translated by Robert R. Barr. Maryknoll: Orbis, 1986.

— *Trinity and Society.* Translated by Paul Burns. Maryknoll: Orbis, 1988.

Bonhoeffer, Dietrich. *Act and Being: Transcendental Philosophy and Ontology in Systematic Theology.* Volume 2 of *Dietrich Bonhoeffer Works.* Edited by Wayne Whitson Floyd, Jr. Translated by H. Martin Rumscheidt. Minneapolis: Fortress, 1996.

— *Berlin: 1921–33.* Volume 12 of *Dietrich Bonhoeffer Works.* Edited by Larry L. Rasmussen. Translated by Isabel Best and David Higgins. Minneapolis: Fortress, 2009.

— *Conspiracy and Imprisonment: 1940–1945.* Volume 16 of *Dietrich Bonhoeffer Works.* Edited by Mark S. Brocker. Translated by Lisa E. Dahill. Minneapolis: Fortress, 2006.

— *The Cost of Discipleship.* New York: Simon and Schuster, 1995.

— *Creation and Fall: A Theological Exposition of Genesis 1–3.* Volume 3 of *Dietrich Bonhoeffer Works.* Edited by John W. de Gruchy. Translated by Douglas Stephen Bax. Minneapolis: Fortress, 1997.

— *Discipleship.* Volume 4 of *Dietrich Bonhoeffer Works.* Edited by Geffrey B. Kelly and John D. Godsey. Translated by Barbara Green and Reinhard Krauss. Minneapolis: Fortress, 2001.

— *Ethics.* Volume 6 of *Dietrich Bonhoeffer Works.* Edited by Clifford J. Green. Translated by Reinhard Krauss, Charles C. West, and Douglas W. Stott. Minneapolis: Fortress, 2005.

— *Ethics.* New York: Simon & Schuster, 1995.

— *Letters and Papers from Prison.* New Greatly Enlarged Edition. Edited by Eberhard Bethge. New York: Simon & Schuster (Touchstone), 1997.

— *Life Together.* Volume 5 of *Dietrich Bonhoeffer Works.* Edited by Geffrey B. Kelly. Translated by Daniel W. Bloesch and James H. Burtness. Minneapolis: Fortress, 1996.

— *Prayerbook of the Bible: An Introduction to the Psalms.* Volume 5 of *Dietrich Bonhoeffer Works.* Edited by Geffrey B. Kelly. Translated by James H. Burtness. Minneapolis: Fortress, 1996.

— *No Rusty Swords: Letters, Lectures and Notes 1928–1936.* Edited by Edwin H. Robertson. Translated by John Bowden and Eberhard Bethge. London: Collins, 1965.

— *Sanctorum Communio: A Theological Study of the Sociology of the Church.* Volume 1 of *Dietrich Bonhoeffer Works.* Edited by Clifford J. Green. Translated by Reinhard Krauss and Nancy Lukens. Minneapolis: Fortress, 1998.

— *Temptation*. Edited by Eberhard Bethge. Translated by Kathleen Downham. London: SCM, 1955.

— *Voices in the Night: The Prison Poems of Dietrich Bonhoeffer*. Edited and Translated by Edwin Robertson. Grand Rapids: Zondervan, 1999.

— *The Way to Freedom: Letter, Lectures and Notes 1935–1939*. Edited by Edwin H. Robertson. Translated by Edwin H. Robertson and John Bowden. New York: Harper and Row, 1966.

Bowman, Curtis. "Johann Gottlieb Fichte (1762–1814)." *Internet Encyclopedia of Philosophy*. No pages. Online: http://www.iep.utm.edu/fichtejg/

Brandt, Gareth. "How Anabaptist Theology and the Emergent Church Address the Problem of Individualism in the Believers Church." In *New Perspectives in Believers Church Ecclesiology*, 272–89. Edited by Abe Dueck, Helmut Harder, and Karl Koop. Winnipeg: CMU, 2010.

Braaten, Carl E. "The Finnish Breakthrough in Luther Research." *Pro Ecclesia*, 5 (Spring 1996): 141–43.

Bruce, F. F. *The Epistle of Paul to the Romans: An Introduction and Commentary*. Grand Rapids: Eerdmans, 1963.

Brunner, Emil. *The Christian Doctrine of Creation and Redemption*. Translated by Oliver Wyon. Philadelphia: Westminster, 1953.

— *Man in Revolt: A Christian Anthropology*. Translated by Oliver Wyon. London: Lutterworth, 1939.

— *The Misunderstanding of the Church*. London: Lutterworth, 1954.

Bultmann, Rudolf. *Theology of the New Testament*. Two Volumes. Translated by Kendrick Grobel. New York: Charles Scribner's Sons, 1955.

Burridge, Richard A. *Imitating Jesus: An Inclusive Approach to New Testament Ethics*. Grand Rapids: Eerdmans, 2007.

Calvin, John. *Institutes of the Christian Religion*. Translated by Henry Beveridge. Grand Rapids: Eerdmans, 1989.

Campbell, Cynthia. "Imago Trinitatis: the Being of God as a Model for Inclusion." *Austin Seminary Bulletin* 102 (1987): 5–15.

— "The Triune God: A Model for Inclusion." *Austin Seminary Bulletin* 97 (1981): 13–20.

Canlis, Julie. "Being Made Human: the Significance of Creation for Irenaeus' Doctrine of Participation." *Scottish Journal of Theology* 58, no. 4 (2005): 434–54.

Carr, Anne. *Transforming Grace: Christian Tradition and Women's Experience*. San Francisco: Harper and Row, 1988.

Carson, D. A. "Systematic and Biblical Theology." In *New Dictionary of Biblical Theology*, 102. Edited by T.D. Alexander and B.S. Rosner. Downers Grove: InterVarsity Press, 2000.

Carter, Craig A. *Rethinking Christ and Culture: A Post-Christendom Perspective*. Grand Rapids: Brazos, 2006.

Charles, J. Daryl, ed. *Reading Genesis 1–2: An Evangelical Conversation*. Peabody, MA: Hendrickson, 2013.

Clement of Alexandria. *The Instructor*. In *Fathers of the Second Century: Hermas, Tatian, Athenagoras, Theophilus, and Clement of Alexandria (Entire)*. Volume 2 of *Ante-Nicene Fathers*. Edited by Philip Schaff. Grand Rapids: CCEL, 2004.

Coffey, David. *Deus Trinitas: The Doctrine of the Triune God*. New York: Oxford University Press, 1999.

Collins, Francis S. *The Language of God: A Scientist Presents Evidence for Belief*. New York: Free Press/Simon & Schuster, 2006.

Cortez, Marc. *Theological Anthropology: A Guide for the Perplexed*. New York: T & T Clark, 2010.

Crouch, Andy. "The Emergent Mystique." *Christianity Today* 48, no. 11 (2004): 36–41.

Cunningham, Agnes, Donald Miller, and James E. Will. "Toward an Ecumenical Theology for Grounding Human Rights." *Soundings* 67 (Summer 1984): 209–39.

Cyprian. *The Epistles of Cypria*. Translated by Ernest Wallis. In *ANF05: Fathers of the Third Century: Hippolytus, Cyprian, Caius, Novatian, Appendix*. Edited by Philip Schaff. Grand Rapids: Christian Classics Ethereal Library (Public Domain).

Daigle, Christine, ed. *Existentialist Thinkers and Ethics*. Montreal; Kingston: McGill-Queens University Press, 2006.

Davion, Victoria. "Autonomy, Integrity, and Care," *Social Theory and Practice* 19, no. 2 (1993): 161–82.

Dawn, Marva J. "Worship to Form a Missional Community." *Direction* 28 (Fall 1999): 139–52.

De Beauvoir, Simone. *The Ethics of Ambiguity*. Translated by Bernard Frechtman. New York: Citidel; Kensington, 1948.

De Gruchy, John W. "Dietrich Bonhoeffer as Christian Humanist." In *Being Human, Becoming Human: Dietrich Bonhoeffer and Social Thought*, 3–24. Edited by Jens Zimmermann and Brian Gregor. Eugene, OR: Pickwick, 2010.

De Gruchy, John W., ed. *The Cambridge Companion to Dietrich Bonhoeffer*. Cambridge: Cambridge University Press, 1999.

De Lubac, Henri. *Catholicism, Christ and the Common Destiny of Man*. Translated by Lancelot Sheppard. San Francisco: Ignatius, 1988.

De Nys, Martin J. *Hegel and Theology*. New York: T & T Clark, 2009.

Downey, Deane E.D. and Stanley E. Porter, eds. *Christian Worldview and the Academic Disciplines: Crossing the Academy*. Eugene: Pickwick, 2009.

Dramm, Sabine. *Dietrich Bonhoeffer: An Introduction to His Thought*. Translated by Thomas Rice. Peabody, MA: Hendrickson, 2007.

Dreyer, F. "Faith and Experience in the Thought of John Wesley." *American Historical Review* 88 (1983): 12–30.

Dulles, Avery. *Models of the Church*. New York: Doubleday, 1987.

Bibliography

Elshtain, Jean Bethke. "The Dignity of the Human Person and the Idea of Human Rights: Four Inquiries." *Journal of Law and Religion* 14, no. 1 (1999–2000): 53–65.

— *Sovereignty: God, State, and Self.* New York: Basic, 2008.

Enns, Fernando. "Believers Church Ecclesiology: A Vital Alternative within the Ecumenical Family." In *New Perspectives in Believers Church Ecclesiology*, 107–24. Edited by Abe Dueck, Helmut Harder, and Karl Koop. Winnipeg: CMU, 2010.

Fee, Gordon D. *Revelation*. Eugene, OR: Cascade, 2010.

Feuerbach, Ludwig. *The Essence of Christianity*. Translated by George Eliot. Amherst: Prometheus, 1989.

Finger, Thomas N. *A Contemporary Anabaptist Theology: Biblical, Historical, Constructive*. Downers Grove: InterVarsity Press, 2004.

Flett, Eric G. "Priests of Creation, Mediators of Order: the Human Person as a Cultural Being in Thomas F. Torrance's Theological Anthropology." *Scottish Journal of Theology* 58, no. 2 (2005): 161–83.

Foster, Richard J. *The Celebration of Discipline: The Path to Spiritual Growth*. New York: Harper and Row, 1978.

— *Life With God: Reading The Bible For Spiritual Transformation*. New York: HarperCollins, 2008.

— *Prayer: Finding the Heart's True Home*. New York: HarperSanFrancisco, 1992.

Fowl, Stephen E. *Engaging Scripture: A Model for Theological Interpretation*. Oxford: Blackwell, 1998.

Fowl, Stephen E. and Gregory Jones. *Reading in Communion: Scripture and Ethics in Christian Life*. Grand Rapids: Eerdmans, 1991.

Franklin, Patrick. "Bonhoeffer's Anti-Logos and its Challenge to Oppression." *Crux* 41, no. 2 (2005): 2–9.

— "Bonhoeffer's Missional Ecclesiology." *McMaster Journal of Theology and Ministry* 9 (2007–2008): 96–128.

— "John Wesley in Conversation with the Emerging Church." *Asbury Theological Journal* 63 (Spring 2008): 75–93.

— *Rewired: Exploring Religious Conversion* by Paul Markham. Review in *Perspectives on Science and Christian Faith* 60 (December 2008): 274–75.

— "Teaching, Scholarship, and Christian Worldview: A Review of Recent Literature." *McMaster Journal of Theology and Ministry* 11 (2009–2010): 28–61.

— "The Human Person in Contemporary Science and Theology." *Perspectives on Science and Christian Faith* 64, no. 2 (June 2012): 120–29.

— "Women Sharing in the Ministry of God: A Trinitarian Framework for the Priority of Spirit Gifting as a Solution to the Gender Debate." *Priscilla Papers* 22 (Autumn 2008): 14–20.

— "Understanding the Beginning in Light of the End: Eschatological Reflections on Making Theological Sense of Evolution." *Perspectives on Science and Christian Faith* 66, no. 3 (September 2014): 154–70.

Frost, Michael. *Exiles: Living Intentionally In A Post-Christian Culture.* Peabody: Hendrickson, 2006.

Frost, Michael and Alan Hirsch. *The Shape of Things to Come: Innovation and Ministry for the Twenty First Century Church.* Peabody: Hendrickson, 2003.

Fryling, Alice. *Seeking God Together: An Introduction to Group Spiritual Direction.* Downers Grove: InterVarsity Press, 2009.

Gabler, Johann P. "An Oration on the Proper Distinction Between Biblical and Dogmatic Theology and the Specific Objectives of Each." In *Old Testament Theology: Flowering and Future*, 499–506. Edited by Ben C. Ollenburger. Winona Lake, IN: Eisenbrauns, 2004.

Geertz, Clifford. *The Interpretation of Cultures.* New York: Basic, 1973.

Gibbs, Eddie and Ryan K. Bolger. *Emerging Churches: Creating Christian Community in Postmodern Cultures.* Grand Rapids: Baker, 2005.

Goheen, Michael W. and Craig G. Bartholomew. *Living at the Crossroads: An Introduction to Christian Worldview.* Grand Rapids: Baker Academic, 2008.

Green, Clifford J. *Bonhoeffer: A Theology of Sociality.* Grand Rapids: Eerdmans, 1999.

— "Sociality, Discipleship, and Worldly Theology in Bonhoeffer's Christian Humanism." In *Being Human, Becoming Human: Dietrich Bonhoeffer and Social Thought*, 71–90. Edited by Jens Zimmermann and Brian Gregor. Eugene, OR: Pickwick, 2010.

Green, Joel B. *Body, Soul, and Human Life: The Nature of Humanity in the Bible.* Grand Rapids: Baker Academic, 2008.

Gregersen, Niels Henrik. "God's Public Traffic: Holist Versus Physicalist Supervenience." In *The Human Person in Science and Theology*, 153–88. Grand Rapids: Eerdmans, 2000.

— "Varieties of Personhood: Mapping the Issues." In *The Human Person in Science and Theology*, 1–17. Grand Rapids: Eerdmans, 2000.

Gregor, Brian. "Following-After and Becoming Human: A Study of Bonhoeffer and Kierkegaard." In *Being Human, Becoming Human: Dietrich Bonhoeffer and Social Thought*, 152–75. Edited by Jens Zimmermann and Brian Gregor. Eugene, OR: Pickwick, 2010.

Grenz, Stanley J. *The Baptist Congregation: A Guide to Baptist Belief and Practice.* Vancouver: Regent College, 1996.

— "Die Begrenzte Gemeinschaft ('The Bounded People') and the Character of Evangelical Theology." *Journal of the Evangelical Theological Society* 45 (June 2002): 301–16.

— "Jesus as the *Imago Dei*: Image of God Christology and the Non-Linear Linearity of Theology." *Journal of the Evangelical Theological Society* 47 (Dec. 2004): 617–28.

Bibliography

———. *The Moral Quest: Foundation of Christian Ethics.* Downers Grove: InterVarsity Press, 2000.
———. *A Primer on Postmodernism.* Grand Rapids: Eerdmans, 1996.
———. *Reason for Hope: The Systematic Theology of Wolfhart Pannenberg.* Oxford: Oxford University Press, 1990.
———. *Rediscovering the Triune God: The Trinity in Contemporary Theology.* Minneapolis: Fortress, 2004.
———. *Renewing the Center: Evangelical Theology in a Post-Theological Era.* Grand Rapids: Baker Academic, 2000.
———. *The Social God and the Relational Self: A Trinitarian Theology of the Imago Dei.* Louisville: Westminster John Knox, 2001.
———. "The Social God and the Relational Self: Toward a Theology of the Imago Dei in the Postmodern Context." *Horizons in Biblical Theology* 24, no. 1 (2002): 33–57.
———. *Theology for the Community of God.* Grand Rapids: Eerdmans, 1994.
Grenz, Stanley J. and John R. Franke. *Beyond Foundationalism: Shaping Theology in a Postmodern Context.* Louisville: Westminster John Knox, 2000.
Gresham, Jr., John L. "The Social Model of the Trinity and its Critics." *Scottish Journal of Theology* 46, no. 3 (1993): 325–43.
Guder, Darrell L. *The Continuing Conversion of the Church.* Grand Rapids: Eerdmans, 2000.
———. "Missional Theology for a Missionary Church." *Journal for Preachers* 22, no. 1 (1998): 3–11.
Guder, Darrell L., ed. *Missional Church: A Vision for the Sending of the Church in North America.* Grand Rapids: Eerdmans, 1998.
Gunton, Colin E. *The Christian Faith: An Introduction to Christian Doctrine.* Malden, MA: Blackwell, 2002.
———. *The One, the Three, and the Many: God, Creation, and the Culture of Modernity.* New York: Cambridge University Press, 1993.
———. *The Promise of Trinitarian Theology.* Edinburgh: T & T Clark, 1991.
Gunton, Colin E. and Christoph Schwöbel, eds. *Persons, Divine and Human: King's College Essays in Theological Anthropology.* Edinburgh: T & T Clark, 1991.
Gushee, David P. *The Sacredness of Human Life: Why an Ancient Biblical Vision Is Key to the World's Future.* Grand Rapids: Eerdmans, 2013.
Gutiérrez, Gustavo. *A Theology of Liberation: History, Politics, and Salvation.* Edited and translated by Sister Caridad Inda and John Eagleson. Maryknoll, NY: Orbis, 1973.
Hall, John Douglas. "The Changing North American Context of the Church's Ministry." *Currents in Theology and Mission* 22, no. 6D (1995): 402–50.
Halwani, Raja. "Care Ethics and Virtue Ethics." *Hypatia* 18 (Fall 2003): 161–92.

Hamilton, Brian. "The Ground of Perfection: Sattler on the 'Body of Christ.'" In *New Perspectives in Believers Church Ecclesiology*, 143–60. Edited by Abe Dueck, Helmut Herder, and Karl Koop. Winnipeg: CMU, 2010.

Harrold, Philip. "Deconversion in the Emerging Church." *International Journal for the Study of the Christian Church* 6, no. 1 (2006): 79–90.

Hart, D. G. "The Church in Evangelical Theologies, Past and Future." In *The Community of the Word: Toward an Evangelical Ecclesiology*, 23–40. Edited by Mark Husbands and Daniel J. Treier. Downers Grove: InterVarsity Press, 2005.

— *Deconstructing Evangelicalism: Conservative Protestantism in the Age of Billy Graham*. Grand Rapids: Baker Academic, 2004.

Hart, Trevor. "Systematic – In What Sense?" In *Out of Egypt: Biblical Theology and Biblical Interpretation*. Edited by Craig Bartholomew, Mary Healy, Karl Möller, Robin Parry. Grand Rapids: Zondervan, 2004.

Hasel, Gerhard F. "The Relationship Between Biblical Theology and Systematic Theology." *Trinity Journal* 5 NS (1984): 113–27.

Hauerwas, Stanley. *A Community of Character: Toward a Constructive Christian Social Ethic*. Notre Dame: University of Notre Dame Press, 1981.

— *A Cross-Shattered Church: Reclaiming the Theological Heart of Preaching*. Grand Rapids: Brazos, 2009.

— *Character and the Christian Life: A Study in Theological Ethics*. San Antonio: Trinity University Press, 1975.

— *Christian Existence Today: Essays on Church, World, and Living in Between*. Grand Rapids: Brazos, 2001.

— *In Good Company: The Church as Polis*. Notre Dame: University of Notre Dame Press, 1995.

— *The Peaceable Kingdom: A Primer in Christian Ethics*. Notre Dame: University of Notre Dame Press, 1983.

Hauerwas, Stanley, and William H. Willimon. *Resident Aliens: Life in the Christian Colony*. Nashville: Abingdon, 1993.

Hays, Richard B. *The Moral Vision of the New Testament: Community, Cross, New Creation: A Contemporary Introduction to New Testament Ethics*. San Francisco: HarperSanFrancisco, 1996.

Hefner, Philip. "Imago Dei: The Possibility and Necessity of the Human Person." In *The Human Person in Science and Theology*, 73–94. Grand Rapids: Eerdmans, 2000.

Hegel, Georg Wilhelm Friedrich. *The Philosophy of History*. Translated by J. Sibree. New York: Dover; Toronto: General, 1956.

Hempton, David. "John Wesley (1703–1791)." In *The Pietist Theologians*, 256–71. Edited by Carter Lindberg. Malden, MA: Blackwell, 2005.

Highfield, Ron. *Great is the Lord: Theology for the Praise of God*. Grand Rapids: Eerdmans, 2008.

Hindmarsh, Bruce. "Is Evangelical Ecclesiology an Oxymoron?" In *Evangelical Ecclesiology: Reality or Illusion?* 15–38. Edited by John G. Stackhouse, Jr. Grand Rapids: Baker Academic, 2003.

Hobbes, Thomas. *Leviathan.* Edited by A. P. Martinich. Peterborough, ON: Broadview, 2005.

Hodgson, Leonard. *The Doctrine of the Trinity.* New York: Charles Scribner's Sons, 1944.

Hughes, Richard T. *The Vocation of a Christian Scholar: How Christian Faith Can Sustain the Life of the Mind.* Grand Rapids: Eerdmans, 2005.

Hunsberger, George R. and Craig Van Gelder, eds. *The Church Between Gospel and Culture: The Emerging Mission in North America.* Grand Rapids: Eerdmans, 1996.

Hütter, Reinhard. *Bound to be Free: Evangelical Catholic Engagements in Ecclesiology, Ethics, and Ecumenism.* Grand Rapids: Eerdmans, 2004.

International Covenant on Civil and Political Rights. In *Human Rights Documents: Compilation of Documents Pertaining to Human Rights*, 79–95. Washington: Committee on Foreign Affairs, 1983.

International Covenant on Economic, Social, and Cultural Rights. In *Human Rights Documents: Compilation of Documents Pertaining to Human Rights*, 69–78. Washington: United States. Congress. House. Committee on Foreign Affairs, 1983.

Irenaeus. *Against Heresies.* In *The Apostolic Fathers with Justin Martyr and Irenaeus*, 309–567. Edited by Philip Schaff. Grand Rapids: Eerdmans, 2001.

Janssen, Allan. Review of *Missional Church: A Vision for the Sending of the Church in North America*, by Darrell L. Guder, ed. *Perspectives* 14 (April 1999): 20–22.

Jensen, Peter. "The Teacher as Theologian in Theological Education." *Reformed Theological Review* 50 (September–December, 1991): 81–90.

Jenson, Matt. *Christ Present in Faith: Luther's View of Justification* by Tuomo Mannermaa. Review in the *International Journal of Systematic Theology* 7 (Oct. 2005): 482–85.

Jenson, Robert W. *Systematic Theology. Volume 2: The Works of God.* New York: Oxford University Press, 1999.

Jones, D. Gareth. "Peering into People's Brains: Neuroscience's Intrusion into Our Inner Sanctum." *Perspectives on Science and Christian Faith* 62 (June 2010): 122–32.

Jones, Tony. *The New Christians: Dispatches from the Emergent Frontier.* San Francisco: Jossey-Bass, 2008.

Joyce, Richard. *The Evolution of Morality.* Cambridge, MA: MIT Press, 2006.

Julian of Norwich. *Showings.* Translated by Edmund Colledge and James Walsh. New York: Paulist, 1978.

Kant, Immanuel. *Critique of Practical Reason.* Translated by Werner S. Pluhar. Indianapolis: Hackett, 2002.

— *Religion Within the Limits of Reason Alone*. Translated by Theodore M. Greene and Hoyt H. Hudson. New York: Harper and Row, 1960.

Kapic, Kelly M. *A Little Book for New Theologians: Why and How to Study Theology*. Downers Grove: IVP Academic, 2012.

Kärkkäinen, Veli-Matti. *An Introduction to Ecclesiology: Ecumenical, Historical and Global Perspectives*. Dowers Grove: InterVarsity Press, 2002.

Kaveny, M. Cathleen. "Between Example and Doctrine: Contract Law and Common Morality." *Journal of Religious Ethics* 44, no. 4 (2005): 669–95.

Keener, Craig S. *A Commentary on the Gospel of Matthew*. Grand Rapids: Eerdmans, 1999.

Kelly, Anthony. *The Trinity of Love: A Theology of the Christian God*. New Theology Series 4. Edited by Peter C. Phan. Wilmington: Michael Glazier, 1989.

Kelsey, David H. *Eccentric Existence: A Theological Anthropology*. 2 Volumes. Louisville: Westminster John Knox, 2009.

Keuss, Jeff. "The Emergent Church and Neo-correlational Theology after Tillich, Schleiermacher and Browning." *Scottish Journal of Theology* 61, no. 4 (2008): 450–61.

Kierkegaard, Søren. *Concluding Unscientific Postscript to Philosophical Fragments*. 2 Volumes. Edited by Howard V. Hong and Edna H. Hong. Princeton: Princeton University Press, 1992.

— *Fear and Trembling*. Translated by Alastair Hannay. London: Penguin, 1985.

— *The Sickness Unto Death: A Christian Psychological Exposition for Edification and Awakening*. Translated by Alastair Hannay. London: Penguin, 1989.

Kimball, Dan. *The Emerging Church: Vintage Christianity for New Generations*. Grand Rapids: Zondervan, 2003.

Klassen, Norman and Jens Zimmermann. *The Passionate Intellect: Incarnational Humanism and the Future of University Education*. Grand Rapids: Baker Academic, 2008.

Köstenberger, Andreas J. Review of *Confident Witness, Changing World: Rediscovering the Gospel in North America*, ed. Craig Van Gelder, *Evangelical Missions Quarterly* 36 (January 2000): 114–16.

Kotva, Jr., Joseph. H. *The Christian Case for Virtue Ethics*. Washington, D.C.: Georgetown University Press, 1996.

Kreider, Alan. "They Alone Know the Right Way to Live: The Early Church and Evangelism." In *Ancient Faith for the Church's Future*, 169–86. Edited by Mark Husbands and Jeffrey P. Greenman. Downers Grove: InterVarsity Press, 2008.

Kullberg, Kelly Monroe, ed. *Finding God at Harvard: Spiritual Journeys of Thinking Christians*. Downers Grove: InterVarsity Press, 1997.

— *Finding God beyond Harvard: The Quest for Veritas*. Downers Grove: InterVarsity Press, 2006.
LaCugna, Catherine Mowry. *God For Us: The Trinity and Christian Life*. New York: HarperSanFrancisco, 1993.
Ladd, George E. *A Theology of the New Testament*. Edited by Donald A. Hagner. Grand Rapids: Eerdmans, 1993.
Lamoureux, Denis O. *Evolutionary Creation: A Christian Approach to Evolution*. Eugene: Wipf and Stock, 2008.
— *I Love Jesus and I Accept Evolution*. Eugene, OR: Wipf and Stock: 2009.
Langiulli, Nino. "Two Cheers for Existentialism." *Logos: A Journal of Catholic Thought and Culture* 7, no. 4 (2004): 92–108.
Larsen, Timothy. "Defining and Locating Evangelicalism." The Cambridge Companion to Evangelical Theology, 1–14. Edited by Timothy Larsen and Daniel J. Treier. Cambridge: Cambridge University Press, 2007.
Lewis, C.S. "Is Theology Poetry?" In *The Weight of Glory and Other Addresses*, 116–40. New York: HarperCollins, 2001.
— *Surprised by Joy*. New York: HarperCollins, 1998.
— *The Weight of Glory*. Grand Rapids: Eerdmans, 1949.
Lindberg, Carter, ed. *The Pietist Theologians*. Malden, MA: Blackwell, 2005
Lints, Richard, Michael S. Horton, and Mark R. Talbot, eds. *Personal Identity in Theological Perspective*. Grand Rapids: Eerdmans, 2006.
Lipset, Seymour Martin. *Continental Divide: The Values and Institutions of the United States and Canada*. New York: Routledge, 1990.
Locke, John. *Two Treatises of Government*. In *Philosophical Works and Selected Correspondence of John Locke*, 139–427. Edited by Mark C. Rooks. Charlottesville: InteLex, 1995.
Logan, James. "Liberalism, Race, and Stanley Hauerwas." *Cross Currents* 55 (Winter 2006): 522–33.
Lumsden, Charles and Edward O. Wilson. *Genes, Mind, and Culture: The Co-evolutionary Process*. Singapore; Hackensack: World Scientific, 2005.
Luther, Martin. *On Christian Liberty*. Translated by W.A. Lambert and Harold J. Grimm. Minneapolis: Fortress, 2003.
— *Luther's Works*. Volume 52: *Sermons II*. Edited by Hans J. Hillerbrand and Helmut T. Lehmann. Philadelphia: Concordia/Fortress, 1974.
Lyotard, Jean-François. *The Postmodern Condition: A Report on Knowledge*. Translated by Geoff Bennington and Brian Massumi. Minneapolis: University of Minnesota Press, 1984.
MacIntyre, Alasdair. *A Short History of Ethics: A History of Moral Philosophy from the Homeric Age to the Twentieth Century*. Notre Dame: University of Notre Dame Press, 1998.
— *After Virtue: A Study in Moral Theology*. Notre Dame: University of Notre Dame Press, 1984.
— *Dependent Rational Animals: Why Human Beings Need the Virtues*. Chicago: Open Court, 1999.

— *Whose Justice? Which Rationality?* Notre Dame: University of Notre Dame Press, 1988.
MacKay, Donald M. *Human Science and Human Dignity*. Downers Grove: InterVarsity Press, 1979.
Macmurray, John. *Persons in Relation*. Atlantic Highlands: Humanities, 1991.
Mannermaa, Tuomo. *Christ Present in Faith: Luther's View of Justification*. Edited by Kirsi Stjerna. Minneapolis: Fortress, 2005.
Markham, Paul N. *Rewired: Exploring Religious Conversion*. Eugene: Pickwick, 2007.
Marsden, George M. *The Outrageous Idea of Christian Scholarship*. New York: Oxford University Press, 1997.
— *Understanding Fundamentalism and Evangelicalism*. Grand Rapids: Eerdmans, 1991.
Marshall, Bruce D. *Trinity and Truth*. Cambridge Studies in Christian Doctrine 3. Edited by Colin Gunton and Daniel W. Hardy. Cambridge: Cambridge University Press, 1999.
Marshall, I. Howard. *Beyond the Bible: Moving from Scripture to Theology*. Grand Rapids: Baker, 2004.
— *New Testament Theology: Many Witnesses, One Gospel*. Downers Grove: InterVarsity Press, 2004.
Maslow, Abraham. *Motivation and Personality*. New York: Harper and Row, 1954.
McFadyen, Alistair I. *The Call to Personhood: A Christian Theory of the Individual in Social Relationships*. Cambridge: Cambridge University Press, 1990.
McGrath, Alister E. *A Fine-Tuned Universe: The Quest for God in Science and Theology*. Louisville: Westminster John Knox, 2009.
— *Christian Theology: An Introduction*. Fourth Edition. Cambridge: Blackwell, 2007.
McKnight, Scot. *A Community Called Atonement*. Nashville: Abingdon, 2007.
— *Kingdom Conspiracy: Returning to the Radical Mission of the Local Church*. Grand Rapids: Brazos, 2014.
McLaren, Brian D. *A Generous Orthodoxy: Why I am a missional + evangelical + post/protestant + liberal/conservative + mystical/poetic + biblical + charismatic/contemplative + fundamentalist/calvinist + green + incarnational + depressed-yet-hopeful + emergent + unfinished Christian*. Grand Rapids: Zondervan, 2004.
— *Everything Must Change: Jesus, Global Crises, and a Revolution of Hope*. Nashville: Thomas Nelson, 2008.
— *The Secret Message of Jesus: Uncovering the Truth that Could Change Everything*. Nashville: W. Publishing Group, 2006.
— *More Ready Than You Realize: Evangelism as Dance in the Postmodern Matrix*. Grand Rapids: Zondervan, 2002.

Middleton, J. Richard. "A New Heaven and a New Earth: The Case for a Holistic Reading of the Biblical Story of Redemption." *Journal for Christian Theological Research* 11 (2006): 73–97.

— *The Liberating Image: The Imago Dei in Genesis 1*. Grand Rapids: Brazos, 2005.

Mill, John Stuart. *Utilitarianism*. Edited by George Sher. Indianapolis: Hackett, 2001.

Mitchell, Beverly E. "Human Dignity as a Theo-Political Reality." *American Baptist Quarterly* 27 (Summer 2008): 101–16.

Moes, Paul. "Minding Emotions: The Embodied Nature of Emotional Self-Regulation." *Perspectives on Science and Christian Faith* 62 (June 2010): 75–87.

Moltmann, Jürgen. *The Church in the Power of the Spirit: A Contribution to Messianic Ecclesiology*. Minneapolis: Fortress, 1993.

— *The Crucified God: The Cross of Christ as the Foundation and Criticism of Christian Theology*. Translated by R.A. Wilson and John Bowden. New York: Harper & Row, 1974.

— *On Human Dignity: Political Theology and Ethics*. Minneapolis: Fortress, 1984.

— *The Spirit of Life: A Universal Affirmation*. Translated by Margaret Kohl. Minneapolis: Fortress, 2001.

— *Trinity and the Kingdom: The Doctrine of God*. Translated by Margaret Kohl. San Francisco: Harper and Row, 1981.

Mouw, Richard. *He Shines in All That's Fair: Culture and Common Grace*. Grand Rapids: Eerdmans, 2001.

Nagel, Thomas. *Mind and Cosmos: Why the Materialist Neo-Darwinian Conception of Nature Is Almost Certainly False*. New York: Oxford University Press, 2012.

Neufeldt-Fast, Arnold. "Examining the Believers Church within a Trinitarian-Missional Framework." In *New Perspectives in Believers Church Ecclesiology*, 199–220. Edited by Abe Dueck, Helmut Harder, and Karl Koop. Winnipeg: CMU, 2010.

Newbigin, Lesslie. "Context and Conversion." *International Review of Mission* 68 (July 1979): 301–12.

— *Foolishness to the Greeks: The Gospel and Western Culture*. Grand Rapids: Eerdmans, 1986.

— *The Gospel in a Pluralist Society*. Grand Rapids: Eerdmans, 1989.

— *The Household of God: Lectures on the Nature of the Church*. London: SCM, 1957.

— *The Open Secret: An Introduction to the Theology of Mission*. Grand Rapids: Eerdmans, 1995.

— *Proper Confidence: Faith, Doubt and Certainty in Christian Discipleship*. Grand Rapids: Eerdmans, 1995.

— *Truth to Tell: The Gospel as Public Truth*. London: SPCK, 1991.

Ngien, Dennis. *The Suffering of God According to Martin Luther's Theologia Crucis*. Eugene, OR: Wipf and Stock, 1995.
Niebuhr, H. Richard. *Christ and Culture*. New York: HarperSanFrancisco, 2001.
Nietzsche, Friedrich. *Beyond Good and Evil: Prelude to a Philosophy of the Future*. Mineolo: Dover, 1997.
— *Human, All too Human*. Translated by Gary Handwerk. Stanford: Stanford University Press, 1997.
— *On the Genealogy of Morals*. Cambridge: Cambridge University Press, 1994.
Noddings, Nel. *Caring: A Feminine Approach to Ethics and Moral Education*. Los Angeles: University of California Press, 1984.
— *Educating for Intelligent Belief or Unbelief*. New York: Teachers College Press, 1993.
— *Educating Moral People: A Caring Alternative to Character Education*. New York, Teachers College Press, 2002.
Noll, Mark A. *A History of Christianity in the United States and Canada*. Grand Rapids: Eerdmans, 1992.
— *American Evangelical Christianity: An Introduction*. Oxford: Blackwell, 2001.
— *The Scandal of the Evangelical Mind*. Grand Rapids: Eerdmans, 1994.
— "What Happened to Christian Canada?" *Church History* 75 (June 2006): 245–73.
Nouwen, Henri J.M. *In the Name of Jesus: Reflections on Christian Leadership*. New York: Crossroad, 1989.
Novak, David. "Human Dignity and the Social Contract." In *Recognizing Religion in a Secular Society: Essays in Pluralism, Religion, and Public Policy*, 51–68. Edited by Douglas Farrow. Montreal; Ithaca: McGill-Queens University Press, 2004.
Novak, Michael. "The Judeo-Christian Foundation of Human Dignity, Personal Liberty, and the Concept of the Person." *Journal of Markets and Morality* 1 (Oct. 1998): 107–21.
— *The Spirit of Democratic Capitalism*. New York: Simon and Schuster, 1982.
Nozick, Robert. *Anarchy, State, and Utopia*. New York: Basic, 1974.
O'Donovan, Oliver. *The Desire of the Nations: Rediscovering the Roots of Political Theology*. New York: Cambridge University Press, 1996.
O'Donovan, Oliver and Joan Lockwood O'Donovan. *Bonds of Imperfection: Christian Politics, Past and Present*. Grand Rapids: Eerdmans, 2004.
Ollenburger, B.C. "Biblical Theology: Situating the Discipline." In *Understanding the Word: Essays in Honour of Bernard W. Andersen*, 37–62. Sheffield: JSOT, 1985.
Oppenheimer, Mark. "Miroslav Volf Spans Conflicting Worlds." *The Christian Century* (January 11, 2003): 18–23.

Osborn, Eric. *Irenaeus of Lyons*. Cambridge: Cambridge University Press, 2001.
Packer, James I. *Fundamentalism and the Word of God*. Grand Rapids, MI: Eerdmans, 1958.
Pannenberg, Wolfhart. *Anthropology in Theological Perspective*. Translated by Matthew J. O'Connell. Edinburgh: T & T Clark, 1999.
— *The Church*. Translated by Keith Crim. Philadelphia: Westminster, 1983.
— *Systematic Theology*. 3 Volumes. Translated by Geoffrey W. Bromiley. Grand Rapids: Eerdmans, 1991–98.
Pennington, M. Basil. *Lectio Divina: Renewing the Ancient Practice of Praying the Scriptures*. Chestnut Ridge: Crossroad, 1998.
Perry, John. "John Locke's America: The Character of Liberal Democracy and Jeffrey Stout's Debate with the Christian Traditionalists." *Journal of the Society of Christian Ethics* 27, no. 2 (2007): 227–52.
Perry, Michael J. *The Idea of Human Rights*. New York: Oxford University Press, 1998.
Peters, Ted. *Anticipating Omega: Science, Faith, and Our Ultimate Future*. Göttingen: Vandenhoeck & Ruprecht, 2006.
Peterson, James C. *Changing Human Nature: Ecology, Ethics, Genes, and God*. Grand Rapids: Eerdmans, 2010.
— *Genetic Turning Points: The Ethics of Human Genetic Intervention*. Grand Rapids, Eerdmans, 2001.
— "*Homo Sapiens* as *Homo Dei*: Paleoanthropology, Human Uniqueness, and the Image of God." *Toronto Journal of Theology* 27, no. 1 (2011): 17–26.
— "The Religion of Genetics in Epistemology and Ethics," *Theology and Science* 9, no. 2 (2011): 213–21.
Peters, Ted. *God as Trinity: Relationality and Temporality in Divine Life*. Louisville: Westminster John Knox, 1991.
Pierce, Ronald W. and Rebecca Merrill Groothuis, eds. *Discovering Biblical Equality: Complementarity Without Hierarchy*. Downers Grove: InterVarsity Press, 2005.
Pinnock, Clark H. *Flame of Love: A Theology of the Holy Spirit*. Downers Grove: InterVarsity Press, 1996.
— *Most Moved Mover: A Theology of God's Openness*. Grand Rapids: Baker, 2001.
Plantinga, Jr., Cornelius. *Engaging God's World: A Christian Vision of Faith, Learning, and Living*. Grand Rapids: Eerdmans, 2002.
Poe, Harry Lee. *Christianity in the Academy: Teaching at the Intersection of Faith and Learning*. Grand Rapids: Baker Academic, 2004.
Pohl, Christine D. *Making Room: Recovering Hospitality as a Christian Tradition*. Grand Rapids: Eerdmans, 1999.
Polkinghorne, John C. *Science and the Trinity: The Christian Encounter with Reality*. New Haven, CT: Yale University Press, 2004.

Poon, Michael Nai-Chiu. "Show me the Worth of a Human Person: An East Asian Perspective." *Transformation* (January 1998): 13–15.

Pope, Stephen J. "Engaging E.O. Wilson: Twenty-Five Years of Sociobiology. E.O. Wilson as a Moralist." *Zygon* 36 (June 2001): 233–53.

Porter, Stanley E. "The Future of Theology and Religious Studies from a Confessional Standpoint." *McMaster Journal of Theology and Ministry* 11 (2009–10): 121–38.

Rack, Henry D. *Reasonable Enthusiast: John Wesley and the Rise of Methodism*. Third Edition. London: Epworth, 2002.

Rahner, Karl. *The Shape of the Church to Come*. London: SPCK, 1976.

— *The Trinity*. New York: Continuum, 2001.

Ramsey, Paul. *Christian Ethics and the Sit-In*. New York: Association, 1961.

Rawls, John. *A Theory of Justice*. Cambridge, MA: Belknap of Harvard University Press, 1999.

Reno, R.R. "Series Preface." In Stanley Hauerwas, *Brazos Theological Commentary on the Bible: Matthew*, 12–14. Edited by R. R. Reno. Grand Rapids: Brazos, 2006.

Richard of St. Victor. *Book Three of The Trinity*. In *Richard of St. Victor: The Twelve Patriarchs, The Mystical Ark, and Book Three of the Trinity*. Translated by Grover A. Zinn. Toronto: Paulist, 2002.

Ringma, Charles. *Catch the Wind: The Shape of the Church to Come—And Our Place in It*. Vancouver: Regent College, 1994.

Ruse, Michael. *Taking Darwin Seriously: A Naturalistic Approach to Philosophy*. Oxford: Blackwell, 1986.

Rushton, J. Philippe. "Altruism and Society: A Social Learning Perspective." *Ethics* 92 (April 1982): 425–46.

Sartre, Jean-Paul. *Existentialism and Human Emotions*. New York: The Philosophical Library, 1957.

Schaff, Philip. *The History of the Christian Church*. Volume 5: *The Middle Ages: From Gregory VII., 1049, to Boniface VIII., 1294*. Grand Rapids: Christian Classics Ethereal Library; Public Domain.

Schleiermacher, Friedrich. *On Religion: Speeches to Its Cultured Despisers*. Translated by John Oman. Westminster: John Knox, 1994.

Schliesser, Christine. *Everyone Who Acts Responsibly Becomes Guilty: Bonhoeffer's Concept of Accepting Guilt*. Louisville: Westminster John Knox, 2008.

Schmithals, Walter. *The Theology of the First Christians*. Translated by O.C. Dean, Jr. Louisville: Westminster John Knox, 1997.

Segundo, Juan. *Our Idea of God*. Maryknoll: Orbis, 1974.

Shults, F. LeRon. *The Postfoundationalist Task of Theology: Wolfhart Pannenberg and the New Theological Rationality*. Grand Rapids: Eerdmans, 1999.

— *Reforming Theological Anthropology: After the Philosophical Turn to Relationality*. Grand Rapids: Eerdmans, 2003.

Bibliography

Smith, Christian. *What is a Person? Rethinking Humanity, Social Life, and the Moral Good from the Person Up*. Chicago: University of Chicago Press, 2010.

Smith, James K.A. *Desiring the Kingdom: Worship, Worldview, and Cultural Formation*. Grand Rapids: Baker Academic, 2009.

Smith, Louis M. "B.F. Skinner." *Prospects* XXIV, no. 3/4 (1994): 519–32. Accessed online: http://www.ibe.unesco.org/publications/ThinkersPdf/skinnere.PDF

Snyder, Howard A. *The Community of the King*. Downers Grove: InterVarsity Press, 2004.

Solomon, Robert C. *Existentialism*. Second Edition. New York: Oxford University Press, 2005.

Stackhouse, Jr., John G. *Making the Best of It: Following Christ in the Real World*. New York: Oxford University Press, 2008.

Stackhouse, Jr., John G., ed. *Evangelical Ecclesiology: Reality or Illusion?* Grand Rapids: Baker Academic, 2003.

Stackhouse, Max L. "Human Rights and Public Theology: The Basic Vindication of Human Rights." In *Religion and Human Rights: Competing Claims?*, 12–30. Edited by Carrie Gustafson and Peter Juviler. Armonk, NY: M.E. Sharpe, 1999.

Stark, Rodney. *For the Glory of God: How Monotheism Led to Reformations, Science, Witch-hunts, and the End of Slavery*. Princeton: Princeton University Press, 2003.

— *The Victory of Reason: How Christianity Led to Freedom, Capitalism, and Western Success*. New York: Random House, 2005.

Stassen, Glen H. and David P. Gushee. *Kingdom Ethics: Following Jesus in Contemporary Context*. Downers Grove: InterVarsity Press, 2003.

Steenberg, Matthew C. *Irenaeus on Creation: The Cosmic Christ and the Saga of Redemption*. Boston: Brill, 2008.

Stein, K. James. "Philipp Jakob Spener (1635–1705)." In *The Pietist Theologians*, 84–99. Edited by Carter Lindberg. Malden, MA: Blackwell, 2005.

Stevens, R. Paul. *The Other Six Days: Vocation, Work, and Ministry in Biblical Perspective*. Grand Rapids: Eerdmans, 2000.

Stiller, Brian C. *From the Tower of Babel to Parliament Hill: How to be a Christian in Canada Today*. Toronto: HarperCollins, 1997.

Stott, John, ed. *Making Christ Known: Historic Mission Documents from the Lausanne Movement 1974–1989*. Grand Rapids: Eerdmans, 1996.

— *The Message of Romans: God's Good News for the World*. Downers Grove: InterVarsity Press, 1994.

Stout, Jeffrey. *Democracy and Tradition*. Princeton: Princeton University Press, 2004.

Studebaker, Steven M. "Jonathan Edwards's Social *Augustinian* Trinitarianism: An Alternative to a Recent Trend." *Scottish Journal of Theology* 56, no. 3 (2003): 268–85.

— *Jonathan Edwards' Social Augustinian Trinitarianism in Historical and Contemporary Perspectives*. Piscataway, NJ: Gorgias, 2008.

Seybold, Kevin S. "Biology of Spirituality." *Perspectives on Science and Christian Faith* 62 (June 2010): 89–98.

Tanner, Kathryn. *Theories of Culture: A New Agenda for Theology*. Minneapolis: Fortress, 1997.

Taylor, Charles. *A Secular Age*. Cambridge, MA: Harvard University Press, 2007.

— *Modern Social Imaginaries*. Durham: Duke University Press, 2004.

— *Sources of the Self: The Making of the Modern Identity*. Cambridge, MA: Harvard University Press, 1989.

Tertullian, *The Prescription Against the Heretics* XXXII. In *ANF03: Latin Christianity: Its Founder, Tertullian*. Edited by Philip Schaff and Allan Menzies. Translated by Peter Holmes. Grand Rapids: Christian Classics Ethereal Library. Public domain.

Thiselton, Anthony C. *The Hermeneutics of Doctrine*. Grand Rapids: Eerdmans, 2007.

Torrance, Alan J. *Persons in Communion: An Essay on Trinitarian Description and Human Participation*. Edinburgh: T & T Clark, 1996.

Torrance, James B. "The Covenant Concept in Scottish Theology and Politics and its Legacy." *Scottish Journal of Theology* 34, no. 3 (1981): 225–43.

— *Worship, Community and the Triune God of Grace*. Downers Grove: InterVarsity Press, 1996.

Torrance, Thomas F. *Calvin's Doctrine of Man*. London: Lutterworth, 1949.

— *The Christian Doctrine of God: One Being Three Persons*. New York: T & T Clark, 1996.

— *Divine Meaning: Studies in Patristic Hermeneutics*. Edinburgh: T & T Clark, 1995.

— *The Mediation of Christ*. Colorado Springs: Helmers and Howard, 1992.

Treier, Daniel J. "Scripture and Hermeneutics." In *The Cambridge Companion to Evangelical Theology*, 35–49. Edited by Timothy Larsen and Daniel J. Treier. Cambridge: Cambridge University Press, 2007.

— *Virtue and the Voice of God: Toward Theology as Wisdom*. Grand Rapids: Eerdmans, 2006.

Tucker, Ruth A. and Walter Liefeld. *Daughters of the Church: Women and Ministry from New Testament Times to the Present*. Grand Rapids: Academie/Zondervan, 1987.

United Nations. *Universal Declaration of Human Rights*. In *Human Rights Documents: Compilation of Documents Pertaining to Human Rights*, 63–68. Washington: Committee on Foreign Affairs, 1983.

Bibliography

Van Dyk, Leanne. "The Church in Evangelical Theology and Practice." In *The Cambridge Companion to Evangelical Theology*, 125–41. Edited by Timothy Larsen and Daniel J. Treier. Cambridge: Cambridge University Press, 2007.

Van Gelder, Craig. *The Essence of the Church: A Community Created by the Spirit*. Grand Rapids: Baker, 2000.

Van Gelder, Craig, ed. *Confident Witness—Changing World: Rediscovering the Gospel in North America*. Grand Rapids: Eerdmans, 1999.

Vanhoozer, Kevin J. "Into the Great Beyond: A Theologian's Response to the Marshall Plan." In *Beyond the Bible: Moving from Scripture to Theology*, 87–88. Grand Rapids: Baker, 2004.

— *The Drama of Doctrine: A Canonical-linguistic Approach to Christian Theology*. Louisville: Westminster John Knox, 2005.

— "Exegesis and Hermeneutics." In *New Dictionary of Biblical Theology*, 52–64. Edited by T. Desmond Alexander, Brian S. Rosner, D.A. Carson, and Graeme Goldsworthy. Downers Grove: InterVarsity Press, 2000.

Vanhoozer, Kevin J., Craig G. Bartholomew, Daniel J. Treier, and N.T. Wright, eds. *Dictionary for Theological Interpretation of the Bible*. Grand Rapids: Baker Academic, 2005.

Volf, Miroslav. *After Our Likeness: The Church as the Image of the Trinity*. Grand Rapids: Eerdmans, 1998.

— "Being as God Is: Trinity and Generosity," in *God's Life in Trinity*, 3–12. Minneapolis: Fortress, 2006.

— *The End of Memory: Remembering Rightly in a Violent World*. Grand Rapids: Eerdmans, 2006.

— *Exclusion and Embrace: A Theological Explanation of Identity, Otherness, and Reconciliation*. Nashville: Abingdon, 1996.

— *Free of Charge: Giving and Forgiving in a Culture Stripped of Grace*. Grand Rapids: Zondervan, 2005.

— "'The Trinity as our Social Program': The Doctrine of the Trinity and the Shape of Social Engagement." *Modern Theology* 14 (July 1998): 403–23.

— *Work in the Spirit: Toward a Theology of Work*. Eugene, OR: Wipf and Stock, 2001.

Volf, Miroslav and Dorothy C. Bass, eds. *Practicing Theology: Beliefs and Practices in Christian Life*. Grand Rapids: Eerdmans, 2002.

Walls, Andrew F. *The Missionary Movement in Christian History: Studies in the Transmission of Faith*. Maryknoll: Orbis Books, 1996.

Walsh, Brian J. and J. Richard Middleton. *The Transforming Vision: Shaping a Christian World View*. Grand Rapids: InterVarsity Press, 1984.

Walton, John H. *Genesis 1 As Ancient Cosmology*. Winona Lake: Eisenbrauns, 2011.

— *The Lost World of Genesis One: Ancient Cosmology and the Origins Debate*. Downers Grove: InterVarsity Press, 2009.

Watson, Francis. *Text, Church and World: Biblical Interpretation in Theological Perspective*. Grand Rapids: Eerdmans, 1994.
— *Text and Truth: Redefining Biblical Theology*. Grand Rapids: Eerdmans, 1997.
Watts, Rikki E. "Making Sense of Genesis 1." No pages. Online article: American Scientific Affiliation: http://www.asa3.org/ASA/topics/Bible-Science/6-02Watts.html. Also published as "On the Edge of the Millennium: Making Sense of Genesis 1." In *Living in the LambLight: Christianity and Contemporary Challenges to the Gospel*, 129–51. Edited by Hans Boersma. Vancouver: Regent College Publishing, 2001.
— "The New Exodus/New Creational Restoration of the Image of God: A Biblical-Theological Perspective on Salvation," in *What Does it Mean to be Saved? Broadening Evangelical Horizons of Salvation*, 15–41. Edited by John G. Stackhouse, Jr. Grand Rapids: Baker Academic, 2002.
Webber, Robert E. *Worship Old and New*. Grand Rapids: Zondervan, 1994.
Webster, John. *Barth's Moral Theology: Human Action in Barth's Thought*. Grand Rapids: Eerdmans, 1998.
— "Biblical Theology and the Clarity of Scripture." In *Out of Egypt: Biblical Theology and Biblical Interpretation*. Edited by Craig Bartholomew, Mary Healy, Karl Möller, and Robin Parry. Grand Rapids: Zondervan, 2004.
Wells, Samuel. *Improvisation: The Drama of Christian Ethics*. Grand Rapids: Brazos, 2004.
Wesley, John. *The Works of John Wesley*. Volume 1. Grand Rapids: Zondervan, 1958.
Whitmore, Todd. "Beyond Liberalism and Communitarianism in Christian Ethics: A Critique of Stanley Hauerwas." *Annual of the Society of Christian Ethics* (1989): 207–25.
Willard, Dallas. *The Divine Conspiracy: Rediscovering Our Hidden Life in God*. New York: HarperSanFrancisco, 1998.
— *Knowing Christ Today: Why We Can Trust Spiritual Knowledge*. New York: HarperCollins, 2009.
— *Renovation of the Heart*. Colorado Springs: NavPress, 2002.
— *The Spirit of the Disciplines: Understanding How God Changes Lives*. San Francisco: Harper & Row, 1988.
Wilson, Edward O. *On Human Nature*. Cambridge, MA: Harvard University Press, 2004.
Wolterstorff, Nicholas. "Can Human Rights Survive Secularization? Part I." *Perspectives* 23 (March 2008): 10–14.
— "Can Human Rights Survive Secularization? Part II." *Perspectives* 23 (April 2008): 12–17.
— "Jeffrey Stout on Democracy and its Contemporary Critics." *Journal of Religious Ethics* 33, no. 4 (2005): 633–47.
— *Justice: Rights and Wrongs*. Princeton, NJ: Princeton University Press, 2008.

Bibliography

Wondra, Ellen K. "Participating Persons: Reciprocity and Asymmetry." *Anglican Theological Review* 86 (Winter 2004): 57–73.

Woodhead, Linda. "Theology and the Fragmentation of the Self." *International Journal of Systematic Theology* 1 (March 1999): 53–72.

Wright, N.T. *After You Believe: Why Christian Character Matters*. New York: HarperOne, 2010.

— "The Letter to the Galatians: Exegesis and Theology." In *Between Two Horizons: Spanning New Testament Studies and Systematic Theology*, 205–36. Edited by Joel B. Green and Max Turner. Grand Rapids: Eerdmans, 2000.

— *The Resurrection of the Son of God*. Minneapolis: Fortress, 2003.

— *Surprised by Hope: Rethinking Heaven, the Resurrection, and the Mission of the Church*. New York: HarperOne, 2008.

Wüstenberg, Ralf K. *A Theology of Life: Dietrich Bonhoeffer's Religionless Christianity*. Grand Rapids: Eerdmans, 1998.

Yoder, John Howard. *Body Politics: Five Practices of the Christian Community Before the Watching World*. Scottdale, PA: Herald, 2001.

— *The Politics of Jesus: Vicit Agnus Noster*. Grand Rapids: Eerdmans, 1994.

— *The Royal Priesthood: Essays Ecclesiastical and Ecumenical*. Edited by Michael G. Cartwright. Waterloo, ON: Herald, 1998.

Zimmermann, Jens. "Being Human, Becoming Human: Dietrich Bonhoeffer's Christological Humanism," in *Being Human, Becoming Human: Dietrich Bonhoeffer and Social Thought*, 25–48. Edited by Jens Zimmermann and Brian Gregor. Eugene, OR: Pickwick, 2010.

— *Incarnational Humanism A Philosophy of Culture for the Church in the World*. Downers Grove, IL: IVP Academic, 2012

— *Recovering Theological Hermeneutics: An Incarnational-Trinitarian Theory of Interpretation*. Grand Rapids, Mich: Baker Academic, 2004.

— "The Passionate Intellect: Christian Humanism and University Education." *Direction* 37 (Spring 2008): 19–37.

Zizioulas, John D. *Being as Communion: Studies in Personhood and the Church*. Crestwood, NY: St. Vladimir's Seminary Press, 2002.

— "The Church as Communion." *St. Vladimir's Theological Quarterly* 38, no. 1 (1994): 3–16.

— "Communion and Otherness." *St. Vladimir's Theological Quarterly* 38, no. 4 (1994): 347–61.

— "Human Capacity and Human Incapacity: A Theological Exploration of Personhood." *Scottish Journal of Theology* 28, no. 5 (1975): 401–448.

— *Communion and Otherness*. Edited by Paul McPartlan. London: T & T Clark, 2006.

Author Index

Abélard, Peter, 275
Anderson, Ray S., 94f, 95f, 99f
Anselm, 13, 84f, 90, 90f, 114, 123f, 127f, 216
Aquinas, Thomas, 13, 114, 216, 276
Aristotle, 5, 18, 88
Athanasius, 13, 21f, 84f, 87f, 90, 113, 120f, 145, 158, 158f, 216
Augustine, 10, 10f, 13, 16, 16f, 17, 18, 22, 84f, 86, 86f, 87, 87f, 90, 99f, 112, 112f, 113, 113f, 114, 127f, 145, 145f, 216, 246, 276, 280, 280f
Ayres, Lewis, 86f, 98f

Bader-Saye, Scott, 80f, 214f
Bailey, Kenneth D., 9f, 51f
Balthasar, Hans Urs von, 141f
Banks, Julia, 204f
Banks, Robert, 204f
Barna, George, 215f
Barr, James, 142
Barr, Robert R, 6f
Barth, Karl, 10, 10f, 11f, 66, 93f, 126, 126f, 129, 129f, 130, 133f, 138f, 182, 202f, 217, 239f
Bartholomew, Craig G., 126f, 128f, 218f
Bayer, Oswald, 91f, 111f
Beale, G.K., 224f
Beauchamp, Tom L., 39f
Bebbington, David W., 11f, 269f
Benner, David G., 2f, 99f
Bethell, Tom, 72f
Bilder, Richard B., 48
Blackaby, Henry T., 204f
Bloesch, Donald, 55f, 100f, 179f, 194f, 236f
Boda, Mark J., 127f
Boff, Leonardo, 6, 6f, 10f
Bolger, Ryan K. Bolger, 79f
Bonhoeffer, Dietrich, 10, 10f, 12, 13, 14, 16f, 17f, 18f, 48f, 49f, 55f, 59f, 60f, 66, 66f, 67, 68f, 71f, 93, 93f, 94, 94f, 95, 95f, 96, 96f, 99f, 100, 100f, 101, 101f, 102, 102f, 103, 103f, 104f, 106f, 107f, 109f, 110f, 115f, 116, 116f, 117, 117f, 119, 119f, 154, 154f, 155, 155f, 156, 156f, 157, 157f, 160, 160f, 165f, 171, 171f, 178f, 179, 179f, 180, 180f, 181, 181f, 182, 183f, 185, 185f, 186f, 188f, 189, 189f, 190, 190f, 191f, 192f, 193, 193f, 195, 195f, 196, 196f, 197, 199, 199f, 200, 200f, 201f, 202f, 208f, 210f, 217, 236f, 241, 242f, 277f, 279, 279f, 280, 280f, 282f, 283f
Booth, Catherine, 217
Bowman, Curtis, 23, 23f
Braaten, Carl E., 91f
Brandt, Gareth, 243, 243f
Bruce, F. F., 168, 168f
Brunner, Emil, 5, 5f, 10, 10f
Burridge, Richard A., 60f, 109f, 128f, 135f, 136, 136f, 138f

Calvin, John, 12, 13, 17, 17f, 85f, 90, 91, 92, 92f, 96, 99f, 112, 114, 127f, 192f, 217, 276
Campbell, Cynthia, 6, 6f
Canlis, Julie, 145f
Cappadocians, the, 13, 87, 88, 216
Carr, Anne, 6
Carson, D. A., 127, 127f
Carter, Craig A., 275f, 276f
Charles, J. Daryl, 151f
Childress, James F., 39f
Clement of Alexandria, 84f, 99f, 113, 127f, 159f, 276
Coffey, David, 75f, 86f
Collins, Francis S., 34f, 147f, 148f
Cortez, Marc, 15f, 41f
Crouch, Andy, 80f
Cunningham, Agnes, 34f, 35f
Cyril of Alexandria, 120f

Author Index

Cyril of Jerusalem, 113

Daigle, Christine, 28f, 60f, 65f
Davion, Victoria, 77f
Dawn, Marva J., 230, 230f
De Beauvoir, Simone, 28f, 34, 37f, 60f, 64, 64f, 65f, 68, 285
De Gruchy, John W., 10f, 17f, 93f, 94f, 154f, 202f, 210f
De Lubac, Henri, 105, 105f
De Nys, Martin J., 37f
Descartes, René, 18, 52, 285
Dramm, Sabine, 107f
Dreyer, F., 19f
Dulles, Avery, 5f, 8, 8f, 9f, 82f
Dworkin, Ronald, 47

Edwards, Jonathan, 10, 10f, 13, 86f, 164f
Edwards, Paul, 60f
Elshtain, Jean Bethke, 15f, 34f, 44f
Enns, Fernando, 236f

Fee, Gordon D., 67f
Feuerbach, Ludwig, 36, 37, 37f, 86
Fichte, Johann Gottlieb, 23, 23f
Finger, Thomas N., 194f, 195f
Flett, Eric G., 118, 118f, 159, 159f
Foster, Richard J., 196f, 225f, 250f
Foucault, Michel, 16f, 24
Fowl, Stephen E., 7f, 11f, 60f, 128f, 135f, 136f, 139f, 140, 140f, 141, 141f
Franke, John R., 14f
Franklin, Patrick S., 33f, 79f, 116f, 121f, 145f, 146f, 147f, 188f, 199f, 279f, 280f
Frost, Michael, 78f, 204f, 230f, 258f, 278f
Fryling, Alice, 250f

Gabler, Johann P., 31f
Geertz, Clifford, 27f
Gibbs, Eddie, 79f
Goheen, Michael W., 218f
Green, Joel B., 15f, 33f

Gregersen, Niels Henrik, 15f, 18f, 19f, 33f, 147f
Gregor, Brian, 49f, 93f, 119f, 199f, 202f, 208f
Gregory of Nazianzus, 87, 87f, 120f
Gregory of Nyssa, 97f, 98f, 131
Grenz, Stanley J., 5, 5f, 8, 8f, 10, 10f, 11, 11f, 12, 13, 14, 14f, 16, 16f, 17, 17f, 18f, 19, 19f, 20, 20f, 21, 21f, 22, 22f, 23f, 24, 24f, 30f, 52f, 75f, 85f, 86f, 87f, 89, 89f, 90f, 91f, 94, 94f, 95f, 96, 96f, 97, 97f, 98f, 104f, 105f, 106f, 108, 108f, 112f, 113f, 114f, 124, 124f, 145f, 148f, 150, 150f, 157f, 158f, 160, 160f, 182, 182f, 183f, 184f, 185, 185f, 187, 187f, 188f, 192f, 193f, 194f, 241, 241f, 242f, 251f, 266, 267, 267f, 269, 269f
Gresham Jr., John L., 6f, 98f
Grimm, Harold J., 91f, 136f, 185f
Groothuis, Rebecca Merrill, 188f
Guder, Darrell L., 6, 6f, 9f, 81f, 88f, 241f, 257f, 258f, 260, 278, 278f, 279f
Gunton, Colin E., 5, 5f, 10, 10f
Gushee, David P., 34f, 109f, 129f, 136, 137, 137f, 143f, 225f, 228f, 240f, 241f, 245, 245f, 246f, 247f, 248, 248f, 249, 249f, 250, 253, 253f, 254, 254f, 256f, 263f

Hall, John Douglas, 203f, 204f, 283f
Hamilton, Brian, 183f
Harrold, Philip, 80f
Hart, D. G., 269f
Hart, Trevor, 138, 138f
Hasel, Gerhard F., 31f
Hauerwas, Stanley, 8, 8f, 27f, 29, 30, 30f, 38f, 39, 39f, 40, 40f, 60f, 77, 77f, 81f, 100f, 135f, 159f, 192f, 194f, 216, 219f, 222f, 227f, 245, 245f, 246f, 251, 251f, 258,

258f, 260, 260f, 262, 262f, 263, 263f, 267f
Hays, Richard B., 109f, 135f
Healy, Karl Möller, 126f
Hefner, Philip, 33f, 147f
Hegel, Georg Wilhelm Friedrich, 28, 36, 37, 37f
Hempton, David, 20f
Henry, Carl F., 129
Highfield, Ron, 132
Hildegard of Bingen, 216
Hindmarsh, Bruce, 270f
Hirsch, Alan, 78f, 204f, 230f, 258f
Hobbes, Thomas, 38, 47, 52, 52f, 53, 53f, 54, 55f, 56, 65, 67, 285
Hodge, Charles, 129, 142
Hodgson, Leonard, 6f
Hughes, Richard T., 120, 120f, 121, 121f, 215, 215f
Hunsberger, George R., 258f
Hütter, Reinhard, 60f

Irenaeus, 13, 113, 145, 145f, 146, 146f, 147, 158, 158f, 159f, 166f, 216

Jefferson, Thomas, 275
Jensen, Peter, 126f
Jenson, Matt, 91f
Jenson, Robert, 192f
Jones, D. Gareth, 33, 33f
Jones, Gregory, 60f, 128f
Jones, Tony, 79f, 80f, 214f
Joyce, Richard, 30f
Julian of Norwich, 120f, 216
Justin Martyr, 113, 145f, 159f, 275

Kant, Immanuel, 18, 18f, 19, 19f, 23, 36, 36f, 38, 46, 52, 56, 56f, 57, 57f, 58, 59, 59f, 60, 61, 67, 78, 103, 114, 115, 135, 234f, 275, 284, 285
Kapic, Kelly M., 131f
Kärkkäinen, Veli-Matti, 9f, 236f
Kaveny, M. Cathleen, 40f
Kelsey, David H., 11

Keuss, Jeff, 79f
Kierkegaard, Søren, 60f, 66, 66f, 84, 84f, 98, 98f, 103, 103f, 115f, 208f, 233, 276
Kimball, Dan, 79f, 214f
King, Claude V., 204f
Klassen, Norman, 30f, 120, 120f
Köstenberger, Andreas J., 279f
Kotva Jr., Joseph. H., 135f, 214f, 245, 245f, 246f, 253f, 254f
Kreider, Alan, 205, 205f, 224, 224f, 230f, 234f
Kullberg, Kelly Monroe, 215f

LaCugna, Catherine Mowry, 5, 5f, 10, 10f, 75f, 87, 87f
Ladd, George E., 81f, 186, 186f, 209, 209f, 238f, 242, 242f, 243, 243f, 244, 244f
Lamoureux, Denis O., 34f, 147f, 170f
Larsen, Timothy, 11f, 20f, 269f
Lewis, C.S., 76f, 215f, 232, 233, 233f
Liefeld, Walter, 217f
Lindberg, Carter, 19f, 20f, 21f
Lipset, Seymour Martin, 283f
Locke, John, 18, 18f, 20f, 52, 52f, 53, 53f, 56, 67, 275, 285
Logan, James, 30f, 40f
Luther, Martin, 3f, 12, 13, 85, 85f, 90, 91, 91f, 92, 96, 102, 106, 106f, 109, 109f, 111f, 112, 116, 136f, 185, 185f, 190, 197, 217, 236, 236f, 243, 268, 276
Lyotard, Jean-François, 29f

MacIntyre, Alasdair, 8, 8f, 27, 27f, 28f, 30f, 38f, 39f, 40, 40f, 41, 41f, 42, 42f, 47f, 48f, 55f, 58f, 60f, 62f, 67f, 122, 122f, 136f, 138, 139, 139f, 140, 140f, 216, 247f, 284f
MacKay, Donald M., 32, 32f
Macmurray, John, 5, 5f, 10f
Mannermaa, Tuomo, 91f

Author Index

Markham, Paul N., 33f, 34f, 147f
Marsden, George M., 31f, 270f
Marshall, I. Howard, 127f, 128f, 182f, 186f, 189f, 208f, 209, 209f, 210f, 237f
Marx, Karl, 36, 37, 62, 156f
Maslow, Abraham, 21, 21f
McFadyen, Alistair I., 5, 5f, 10f, 94f, 99f, 100, 100f
McFague, Sally, 142
McGrath, Alister E., 213f, 228f
McKnight, Scot, 2f, 120f, 242f
McLaren, Brian D., 79, 79f, 80f, 214f
Middleton, J. Richard, 146, 146f, 148, 148f, 149, 151, 151f, 161f, 165f, 168, 168f, 169f, 172f, 218f
Miller, Donald, 34f
Moes, Paul, 33f
Moltmann, Jürgen, 6f, 34f, 92f, 105f, 131f, 238f, 261, 261f
Mouw, Richard, 59f

Nagel, Thomas, 69f
Neufeldt-Fast, Arnold, 257, 257f
Niebuhr, H. Richard, 8, 8f, 9, 9f, 275, 275f, 276, 276f, 277f, 284, 284f
Nietzsche, Friedrich, 23, 23f, 24, 24f, 28f, 38, 42, 42f, 43f, 60, 60f, 61, 61f, 62, 62f, 63, 63f, 67f, 68, 69f, 80, 117f, 121f, 156f, 285
Noddings, Nel, 38, 73f, 73, 74, 74f, 75, 75f, 76, 76f, 77, 285
Noll, Mark A., 35f, 215, 215f, 270f, 283f
Nouwen, Henri J.M., 103f
Novak, David, 52f
Novak, Michael, 35f, 44f, 54f
Nozick, Robert, 54f

O'Donovan, Joan Lockwood, 54f
O'Donovan, Oliver, 54f, 234f
Ollenburger, B.C., 31f
Oppenheimer, Mark, 14f
Osborn, Eric, 145, 145f, 158f, 159f

Packer, James I., 129, 129f
Pannenberg, Wolfhart, 10, 11f, 14, 14f, 86f, 94f, 98, 98f, 102f, 118f, 133f, 147, 147f, 154
Parry, Robin, 126f
Pennington, M. Basil, 250f
Perry, John, 52f
Perry, Michael J., 15f, 44f, 46, 46f, 47, 47f, 48f
Peters, Ted, 75f, 172, 172f
Peterson, Eugene, 177f
Peterson, James C., 3f, 15f, 27f, 32, 32f, 33f, 34, 34f, 39f, 47f, 72f, 84f, 145f, 147f, 163, 167f, 172f, 173, 173f, 174f, 271f
Pierce, Ronald W., 188f
Pinnock, Clark H., 86f, 92f, 128, 128f, 130f, 194f
Plantinga, Alvin, 133f
Plantinga Jr., Cornelius, 218f
Plato, 28, 61, 247
Poe, Harry Lee, 120f, 233f
Pohl, Christine D., 60f, 76f, 191f, 204, 205f
Polkinghorne, John C., 134f
Poon, Michael Nai-Chiu, 44f
Pope, Stephen J., 69f, 72f
Porter, Stanley E., 31f, 120f, 215f

Rack, Henry D., 19f
Rahner, Karl, 75f, 89f
Ramsey, Paul, 46f
Rawls, John, 39f, 52f
Reno, R.R., 31f, 32f, 140, 140f
Richard of St. Victor, 10, 10f, 13
Ringma, Charles, 12f
Ritschl, Albrecht, 275
Rorty, Richard, 8, 35, 45, 45f
Ruse, Michael, 31, 31f
Rushton, J. Philippe, 70f

Sartre, Jean-Paul, 28, 28f, 29f, 34, 38, 43f, 60, 60f, 61f, 63, 63f, 64, 64f, 67f, 68, 285
Saussure, Ferdinand, 24

Schaff, Philip, 21f, 84f, 127f, 131f, 145f, 158f
Schleiermacher, Friedrich, 22, 22f, 36, 36f, 52f, 79f, 129, 275
Schmithals, Walter, 209f, 226f
Schopenhauer, Arthur, 23, 23f
Shults, F. LeRon, 8, 8f, 17f, 28f, 33f, 35f, 94f, 98, 99f, 118f, 145f, 159f
Skinner, B.F., 30, 30f
Smith, Christian, 27f, 28f
Smith, Gordon T., 127f
Smith, James K.A., 211f, 216f, 223, 223f, 224f, 252f
Smith, Louis M., 30f
Solomon, Robert C., 24f, 60f
Stackhouse Jr., John G., 149f, 268, 269f, 270f, 277f
Stackhouse, Max L., 45, 45f, 46, 49f
Stark, Rodney, 35f
Stassen, Glen H., 109f, 129f, 136, 137, 137f, 143f, 225f, 228f, 240f, 241f, 245, 245f, 246f, 247f, 248, 248f, 249, 249f, 250, 253, 253f, 254, 254f, 256f, 263f
Stein, K. James, 20f
Stevens, R. Paul, 175f
Stiller, Brian C., 206f, 261, 262, 262f, 283f
Stott, John, 71f, 283f
Stout, Jeffrey, 40f, 52f
Studebaker, Steven M., 10f, 86f, 106f

Tanner, Kathryn, 40f, 282, 282f
Taylor, Charles, 1f, 8, 8f, 16f, 17f, 18, 18f, 19f, 23f, 24f, 25, 25f, 26, 26f, 30f, 32f, 39f, 42f, 52f, 216, 216f
Tertullian, 131, 131f, 159f, 216, 275
Thiselton, Anthony C., 128f
Torrance, Alan J., 105, 105f
Torrance, James B., 75f, 107f, 182, 183f, 195, 195f, 280f

Torrance, Thomas F., 10, 35f, 75f, 85f, 86f, 87f, 88, 88f, 89f, 92f, 110f, 118f, 120f, 128f, 129f, 159f, 182f
Treier, Daniel J., 11f, 128f, 135f, 211, 211f, 212, 212f, 213f, 221, 221f, 222f, 269f
Tucker, Ruth A., 217f

United Nations, 15f, 44, 48, 284

Van Dyk, Leanne, 269, 269f, 270f
Van Gelder, Craig, 258f, 279f
Vanhoozer, Kevin J., 32f, 81f, 118, 118f, 124, 125f, 127, 128f, 129, 129f, 130, 132, 132f, 133f, 135f, 140f, 141, 141f, 142, 142f, 202f, 220f, 222f, 224f
Volf, Miroslav, 5, 5f, 6f, 10, 10f, 12, 13, 14, 14f, 51f, 55f, 71f, 85, 85f, 97, 97f, 98f, 99, 99f, 102, 102f, 103, 103f, 104f, 105, 105f, 106, 107, 117f, 119f, 162, 163, 163f, 164, 164f, 165, 165f, 166, 166f, 167, 167f, 168, 169, 169f, 170, 170f, 171f, 181, 181f, 182f, 183, 183f, 184, 184f, 185, 185f, 186f, 187, 187f, 188f, 193f, 194f, 201, 201f, 203, 203f, 222f, 236f, 237, 237f, 267f, 268f

Walls, Andrew F., 132f
Walsh, Brian J., 218f
Walton, John H., 149f, 150f, 151, 151f, 152, 152f, 153, 153f, 157, 157f, 169
Watson, Francis, 128f, 140f
Watts, Rikki E., 149, 149f, 150, 150f, 151, 151f, 161f
Wells, Samuel, 141f
Wesley, John, 13, 19f, 20f, 79f, 164f, 192f, 217
Whitmore, Todd, 40f
Will, James E., 34f
Willard, Dallas, 60f, 109f, 148f, 172, 172f, 218f, 225f

Author Index

Willimon, William H., 192f, 258, 258f
Wilson, Edward O., 68, 68f, 69, 69f, 70, 70f, 71, 71f, 72f, 285
Wolterstorff, Nicholas, 15f, 34f, 35f, 40f, 44f, 45, 45f, 46, 46f, 47f, 48f, 49, 49f, 52f, 76f
Wondra, Ellen K., 41, 41f
Woodhead, Linda, 1f, 17f
Wright, N.T., 31f, 34f, 35f, 60f, 128f, 131f, 165f, 223, 223f, 244, 245f, 246f, 249f, 250, 251, 251f
Wüstenberg, Ralf K., 156f

Yoder, John Howard, 118f, 282f

Zimmermann, Jens, 30f, 48f, 49f, 93f, 111f, 114, 114f, 119f, 120, 120f, 199f, 202f, 208f, 215f
Zizioulas, John D., 5, 5f, 10, 10f, 14, 35f, 86f, 88f

Scripture Index

Genesis
1	148, 149f, 150, 151, 151f, 153, 173
1:1	151
1:1, 3	111
1:11	172f
1:20	172f
1:24	172f
1:26	148
1:26-27	90f, 94, 96
2	94, 146, 150, 152f, 154
2:2	153f
2:5	169
2:15	148
2:17	101
2:23	95
2:24	95
3	101, 104, 154
3-11	155
3:4	101
3:7-8	101
3:12-13	102
3:19	173
3:21	102
3:23-24	102
4-11	102
4:7	158
6-8	157
6:6	157
6:11-22	157
8:22	152
12:3	244
18:18	257
22:17-18	257

Exodus
20:11	153f
23	76f
25-39	153f
35-40	153f
35:2-3	163
40	153f
40:34	149f

Judges
3:10	163

1 Samuel
23:2	163
16:13	163

1 Kings
6:20	161f
8:28	149f

1 Chronicles
28:11-12	163

2 Chronicles
3:8	161f

Psalms
8:3-8	148
19	238
19:1-4	115
111:10	123
115:4-8	223
132	153f

Proverbs
1-9	212
1:7	123
3:5-6	123
3:11-12	123
3:19-20	123
3:33-35	124
8	212
9:10	123
10-31	212
16:10	163

Isaiah
1:12-17	195
6:3	115, 149
11:6-10	168
55	260
55:8-9	259
65:17-25	169
66:1	149

Jeremiah
2:5	223

Ezekiel
42:16-20	161f
45:2-3	161f

Amos
5	195

Micah
6:8	195

Matthew
1:18-25	162
3:2	165f
3:16-17	162
3:22	162
4:1	162
4:8, 20	195
4:17	165f
5-7	58f, 192
5:1-12	192
5:5	165
5:8	160
5:10-12	189, 192
5:13-16	192, 200, 244, 248, 256
5:13-20	166f
5:16	227
5:17-20	129f
5:21-48	248
5:23-24	195
5:42	189, 191
6	225
6-7	248

Scripture Index

6:1-4	191	22:40	212	4:43-54	192
6:1-18	192	24:37-41	169f	6:43-45	109, 136
6:5-6	225	25	76f, 170,	7:1-10	192
6:7-8	225		174f, 232	7:26-27	134
6:9-13	165	25:14-30	170	7:36-50	192
6:14	190	25:31-46	191	9:1-2	230
16-18	225	25:40	232	9:27	165f
6:19-21	192	28:18-19a	229	9:46-48	192
6:21	160	28:18-20	257, 281	10:2	230
6:22-23	140f, 160	28:19	192f, 230	10:9, 11	165f
6:33	82, 160,	28:19-20	227	10:21-22	126
	170, 241,	28:20	166f, 239,	11:20	165f
	243, 281		260	11:28	134
7:24-27	166f			11:34-36	140f
7:24-29	248	**Mark**		12:13-34	192
7:28-29	212f	1:10-11	162	13:12	66f
8:11-12	97	1:12	162	13:29	166f
9:38	230	1:15	165f	13:20-21	257
10:7	165f	1:17	230	14:15	166f
10:38	189	2:5	231	14:15-24	97, 194f
11:4	229	4:26-29	244	17	169f
11:12	165f	5:34	66f	17:21	165f
11:28-29	260	6:2	212f	18:18-30	192
12:28	165	6:7	230	19:1-10	201
12:29-31	257	7:1-23	192	19:11	164f
12:42	212	9:1	165f	21:14-16	211, 212f
13	244	9:33-37	71, 192	21:31	165f
13:24-30	243f	9:36-37	232f	22:16, 18	165f
13:33	257	9:39a, 40	232	22:19	192f, 222
13:47-50	243	10:35-45	192	23:34	105
13:54	212f	10:44	65f	24:30-31	194f
14:15-24	251	12:29-31	109, 118,	24:44	129f
16:17	126		281	24: 45	194f
16:17-19	2	12:38-40	156	24:49	239
16:24	189	14:25	165f		
17:16-34	231			**John**	
17:20	260	**Luke**		1:1	126, 228
17:24	71	1:17	213	1:1, 3	111
18:15	190	1:35	162	1:1-5, 9	212f
18:15-20	191	2:40, 52	212f	1:14	126, 228,
19:16-30	59f	2:52	146		229
20:28	65f	4:1	162	1:17	124
21:13	238f	4:8	66f	1:18	124, 126,
22:1-14	97, 194f,	4:16-20	162		228
	251	4:18-21	129f	1:33	162
22:15-22	212f	4:43	230	3	231

315

3:5-8	121	4:8, 13	122	8:2	65f, 122
3:16	174, 257	4: 29	122	8:4-6, 14	162
3:34	162	4:32-37	191	8:5	122
4	231	5:32	122	8:9	162
4:21-24	110	6:1-4	191	8:10	189
5:36-40	212f	6:3	211	8:11	162, 260
6:11	194f	6:9-10	211	8:15-17	162
6:68	212f	6:10	122	8:16	121
6:68-69	228	9:10	122	8:19-22	104
8:31-32	166f	9:31	238	8:20-24	167f
8:32	66f	10:3, 7	122f	8:21	168
8:34	158	10:10-16	122f	8:22	168
8:36	66f	10:34-35	244	8:23	169, 237f
12:37-41	126	10: 44-48	244	8:26-27	122
14:1-3	169f	13:9	122	8:29	96, 160, 177
14:6	228, 247	16:9-10	122f		
14:6-7	212f	18:25	122	9-11	209, 210f
14:15	135	20:28	238	9:6	209
14:15-16	122	22:17-18	122f	12	58f, 163, 187, 189
14:16-17	121				
14:16-20	106f	**Romans**		12-14	195
14:23-24	166f	1	117	12:1	195
14:26	121, 126, 257	1, 7	115	12:1-2	118, 127, 192
		1:18	127f		
15:18-27	192	1:18-32	102f, 158	12:2	158
15:26-27	257	2:15	115	12:3-8	186, 187
16:7	121	3:21	168	12:4-5	97
17:17	211	5	177	12:5	177
17:20-23	267	5:1	104, 179f	12:8	212
17:21	104, 106f, 183	5:5	86f	12:9	191
		5:12-14	158	14	191
17:26	86f	5:12-21	177	14:17	162, 239
19:26-27	105	5:17	177	15:3-5	211
20:20-28	192	6	135, 177, 189, 198, 228		
20:21	230			**1 Corinthians**	
20:21-22	257			1-2	213
		6:3-6	222	1:17	213
Acts		6:7, 18	65f	1:18-2:5	189
1:4-5	239	6: 22	65f	1:18-31	192
1:6-8	164f, 244	6:23	158	1:21-25	214
1:8	126, 164f, 230	7	121	1:27-29	214
		7:5	158	1:23	213
1:10-12	164f	7:24	121	1:25	213
2	238	8	125, 169, 177	1:31	212
2:42	194f			2	118
2:43-47	191	8:1ff	162	2:4, 5	213

Scripture Index

2:6-12	120	**2 Corinthians**		5:22	86f, 162
2:7, 10	121, 214	1:12	212	5:22-23	122, 140f
2:7-16	211, 212	1:22	162, 237f	5:24	163
2:10, 11	111	3:14-17	122f	5:25	162, 163
2:10-12	122	3:17	65f	6:1-2	191
2:10-16	214	3:18	96, 162, 177	6:2	189
2:11, 12	121			6:7-10	100
2:14	214	4:4	96, 117, 159, 177	6:8	158
2:16	120	5:1-10	169f	**Ephesians**	
3:16	238	5:4	162	1	181
3:16-17	238f	5:16-17	190	1:9-10	168
3:17	240	5:16-21	77f	1:13-14	162
4:16	136, 211	5:17	107, 168	1:14	237f
6:9-11	162	5:18-21	179f, 198	1:16-23	225
6:9-20	195	5:21	146, 198	1:17	211, 212
7:11	254	6:16	238	2:8-10	135
7:31	166f	6:16, 18	239	2:11-18	77f
8	65f	6:17	240	2:14	239
8:1	213	8:1-15	189, 191	2:14-15	177
9:22	231	9:1-15	189, 191	2:14-18	210f
10:1	177	10:5	220f	2:14, 16	179f
10:16	194f	11:16-33	189	2:18	239
11:17-22	194f	13:5	189	2:19	179f
11:17-24	194f	13:13	179f	2:19-22	238
11:17-34	194			2:22	239
11:23	222	**Galatians**		3:10	210
11:24	194f	2:19-20	105	3:10-11	211
11:27-30	194f	2:20	189, 198	3:12	65f
11:27-34	222	3	209f, 210f	3:16-19	86f
12:12-13	97	3:13	65f	4	163, 238
12	163, 238	3:26-28	76, 190	4:1-16	186
12-13	187	3:27-28	177	4:3-4	122, 179f
12:3	121	3:28	105	4:4-6	97
12:4, 7	188f	4:4	65f	4:11	187
12:8-11	122f	4:6	162	4:11-13	122, 212
12:11b	188f	4:6-7	162	4:12	191
12:12-31	186	5	248	4:13	125
12:27-31	187	5:1, 13	163	4:17-32	58f, 100
13	246	5:13	65f	4:24	96, 177
15:14	131	5:14	124, 212	4:28	189, 191
15:45-49	177	5:16ff	162	5-6	195
15:49	96, 160f, 177	5:16, 18	162	5:15-20	100
16:1-4	189, 191	5:16-21	163	6:12	105
		5:19-21a	248		
		5:21b	248	**Philippians**	

1:6	108	4:16-17	191	2:1-9	190
1:19	162			3	118
2:1	179f	**1 Thessalonians**		3:13	214
2:1, 5-11	122	4:13-18	108, 169f	3:13-18	192, 213, 210
2:5-10	136, 211				
2:5-11	71, 135, 189, 192, 223, 252	**2 Thessalonians** 1:1-18 2:1	189 108	3:17 5:19-20	122, 214 190
2:10-11	252, 189			**1 Peter**	
2:13	107, 161f	**1 Timothy**		1:11-12	122
3:12-14	107, 135	2:6	65f	1:18	65f
3:12-16	100	3:1-12	226	2:5	188, 208
3:17-21	58f, 192	3:2	211	2:5, 9, 10	185
4:5	232	3:16	130	2:5-12	238
4:8	232	3:16-17	130	2:7, 9, 10	208
		4:1-16	191	2:9	161, 188, 240
Colossians		4:6	211	2:9-10	
1-2	189			2:9-12	58f
1:9	212	**2 Timothy**		2:10	179f
1:15	96, 126, 159, 177, 228	1:7 2:2 3:14-17	86f 231 211	2:16 3:9 3:13-22	65f 173 189
1:15ff	186	3:16-17	134	4:12-19	189, 192
1:15, 18	160			4:17	208
1:16-17	111	**Titus**		5:2	208
1:19-20	168, 201	1:15	117		
1:19-22	179f	2:13	65f	**2 Peter**	
1:20	104, 108, 110	3:5	121	1:20-21 1:57	122 122
1:21	117	**Hebrews**		3:9	108
1:22	65f	1:1-4	210f	3:13	169
1:28	211	1:3	96, 177	3:15	212
2:3	212	2:15	65f		
2:6b-7	189f	2:17-18	146	**1 John**	
2:9-10	105f	3:1-6	210f	1:7	100
2:12	222	7:11-27	210f	1:8-10	100
2:15	67f, 105	7:22	210f	2-3	58f
2:23	212, 213	9:15	65f	2:3-6	100
3-4	195	10:15-19	238f	3:2	96, 177
3:9-10	96	12:14-17	191	3:16	212
3:10	177			3:16	86f
3:12	100			3:18	191
3:16	211	**James**		4:7-10, 13, 16-17	212
4:12-13	190	1:5	211, 212	4:7-21	77f
4:15	190	1:13-15	158	4:8	85, 257
4:16	212	1:22-25	134	4:9	89

4:9-10	100
4:9-12	179f
4:10-12	86f
4:11-12	191
4:15	189
4:16	87, 113f
4:16-17	108
4:18	123, 124

Revelation

1:5	65f
1:6	188
2:7, 11	238
2:17, 29	238
3:6, 22	238
4-5	223, 252f
5:9	209
5:9-10	161, 173, 236
5:10	188
6:9	97
11:15	149
13:18	211
17:19	211
19:6-9	97, 194f, 251
20:6	188
21	169
21-22	108, 146
21:2	97
21:4	203
21:5	108, 168, 203
21:9ff	97
22:17	97
21:22	161f
21:22-27	97

Subject Index

Alienation, 101-104, 115-117, 178, 202, 267
Anthropological Agnosticism, 15-16, 16f, 40, 44, 49-50, 265

Change/ Development/ Evolution, 18, 27f, 31, 34, 34f, 68-70, 70f, 72-73, 145-147, 146f, 147f, 148f, 170-171, 170f
Christology, 96, 116, 116f, 125, 135f, 159, 188-189f, 194f, 228, 252, 277, 280f
Church and kingdom, 242-244, 242-244f
Church, as missional, 4-7, 9, 9f, 83, 88-89, 142, 197, 199f, 204, 204f, 206, 239, 248, 249, 250f, 257-258, 257f, 258f, 260f, 263, 266, 273- 275, 277-281, 277f, 278f, 282, 283; Critique of, 4, 6, 7, 88-89, 277-281
Church, as new humanity, 3, 4, 7, 13, 83, 108, 159f, 175, 176-177, 178, 185f, 187f, 193, 206, 209, 216, 226, 235, 237, 241, 246, 249, 265-266, 270-276, 281, 282
Church, as the Body of Christ, 12, 77, 97, 110, 162, 177, 181, 183f, 185, 185f, 186-190, 191, 193, 194f, 196, 197f, 198, 206, 238, 281
Church, as the People of God, 81f, 97, 133, 141, 146, 161, 161f, 174, 185, 186f, 187, 198, 207, 208-210, 208f, 209f, 210f, 211, 223, 235, 237-240, 237f, 242f, 251, 258, 262, 266-267, 267f, 275, 279, 281
Church, as the Temple of the Holy Spirit, 185, 208, 237-241, 240f, 241f, 281
Community, 1-5, 3f, 7, 8, 9, 13, 13, 16, 35, 38-40, 39f, 51-83, 92, 98, 100, 105, 108, 109, 123, 125, 131, 136,138f, 142, 163, 178-182, 179f, 183-189, 183f, 184f, 185f, 187f, 188f, 189f, 190-198, 190f, 193f, 196f, 198f, 200, 204, 205f, 207-209, 211, 216, 216f, 222, 227,227f, 229, 236-245, 247-250, 249f, 252-253, 256-260, 262-263, 265-268, 267f, 270-275, 277-282, 279f
Corruption, 115-116, 133f, 144, 154, 155, 202
Covenant/ al, 12, 68, 85f, 89, 93, 175, 183-184, 192f, 193, 193f, 209, 210f, 239-241, 257, 266-267, 267f, 282
Creation, 34f, 35, 41, 71, 85f, 94-96, 98, 98f, 100f, 106f, 111-112, 115, 133f, 135f, 144-147, 146f, 148-154, 149f, 153f, 157-158, 165f, 166-168, 166f, 167f, 169, 171-175, 172f, 181, 192f, 211-212, 211f, 217, 228, 232, 238, 240, 250, 261, 271, 273, 276, 279
Creatureliness, 94, 94f, 96, 99, 101-102, 155f
Cross/ Cruciform/ Theology of the Cross, 7, 67f, 71, 104-106, 106f, 118, 118f, 167f, 181, 188f, 189, 189f, 192, 194f, 199, 201-204, 202f, 203f, 213-214, 232, 258, 259, 270, 274, 276-277, 277f, 283f
Cultural Engagement, 4, 7, 167f, 202, 202f, 203-205, 229-234, 257-263, 274-277, 277f

Enlightenment, 18-22, 20f, 21f, 27, 29, 39f, 42, 42f, 51, 52-60, 61, 67f, 164
Eschatology/ Eschatological, 3, 4, 4f, 7, 11, 14, 20-21, 20f, 35, 81, 89, 97, 98f, 108, 140f, 144-175,

Subject Index

176, 178, 181, 183f, 185, 186f, 187, 193, 194f, 200, 209-210, 218, 236-264, 265, 267-268, 267f, 270-271, 273-277, 276f, 277f, 280, 281, 283f
Ethics, 3-4, 4b, 5-7, 36, 39f, 41-50, 42f, 43f, 56-60, 61, 63-65, 69-77, 85, 100-110, 101f, 107f, 110f, 112-115, 119f, 124-125, 134-138, 137f, 138f, 142-143, 170-175, 183f, 185, 244-249, 249f, 250-256, 253f, 260-264, 268, 270-271, 274-275, 281-284
Evangelical/ Evangelicalism, 11-12, 11f, 19-20, 80, 80f, 214-216, 215f, 242f, 268-270, 269f, 271
Existentialism, 43f, 60-68, 60-65f, 67f, 78-80
Exocentricity, 7, 98, 100-103, 147, 147f, 154, 184, 187, 197, 197f, 199, 206, 273-274

Faith, 7, 57f, 91-92, 91f, 92f, 97, 100, 100f, 103, 105, 112-114, 123-125,123f, 130-131, 134, 139f, 142, 156, 165-166, 190f, 191-192, 199, 207-235, 208f, 216f, 236, 236f, 245f, 246, 248, 251, 259-260, 263, 266-267, 271, 274-275, 277, 277f
Formation/ Transformation/ Discipleship, 124-125, 128, 134-136, 135-136f, 138-140, 138f, 146, 160-164, 168-169, 184, 186, 189, 191-192, 195-197, 214, 216-217, 216f, 221-225, 222f, 232, 232f, 235, 239, 245-255, 245f, 263-264, 270, 272-273, 281-282
Free Church, 12, 14, 183-184, 266-267, 267f, 269
Freedom, 13, 28f, 29f, 36, 40f, 44, 48f, 52, 53, 55f, 56-68, 56-57f, 60f, 65f, 79-80, 83, 89, 91, 93, 93f, 95, 100, 102-103, 105-107, 112, 119f, 163, 168, 171, 174, 202, 203, 211f, 280, 281
Functional Ontology, 151-154, 151-154f, 157-158, 169, 217

Holy Spirit/ Pneumatology, 11, 13, 20f, 39, 55f, 59, 65f, 68, 71, 75f, 77-78, 85-89, 86-87f, 89f, 92f, 93, 96-98, 98f, 105-108, 106f, 111-112, 119, 119f, 121-122, 121f, 124-131, 129-130f, 132f, 138, 140f, 141, 141f, 143-144, 148, 150, 157, 159, 159f, 160-164, 165f, 167, 169-172, 170-171f, 175, 177-179, 178-179f, 181-191, 182f, 186f, 188f, 193, 194f, 195, 197-199, 201-202, 206, 210-214, 217-218, 220f, 221-222, 222f, 226f, 227-227, 234, 236-241, 237-238f, 240-241f, 244, 245f, 247-252, 249f, 254, 257, 259-260, 262-264, 266-270, 273-276, 279, 280-281; see also Spirit
Hope, 3, 7, 14, 136, 139f, 144, 161, 164-175, 164-165f, 203f, 210, 241, 245f, 246-249, 251-254, 256, 259, 260-264, 270-277, 277f, 284
Human Flourishing, 4, 4f, 170, 172, 207, 266, 281-284, 282f
Human Rights/ Dignity/ Equality, 2, 6, 15, 26, 29f, 34f, 35, 41, 44-50, 44-49f, 53, 53f, 54, 56-58, 62-63, 104-105, 107, 119, 150, 158, 187, 217, 249, 261, 271, 284

Identity, 1f, 13, 16, 16f, 24, 26-28, 38, 43, 49, 55, 66, 84-85, 89, 98-99, 101-102, 107, 139, 147, 154-156, 181, 185f, 193-194f, 196, 207, 210f, 215f, 216, 220f, 236, 247, 251-252, 253f, 257, 273, 274

Idolatry, 116, 131, 155, 195, 202, 223-224, 224f, 249, 253f, 281

Image of God/ Christ/ Trinity, 3, 4, 34, 71, 84f, 87, 89-98, 90f, 92f, 94f, 103-104, 105, 109, 112-113, 113f, 124, 138, 144-146, 148-153, 150f, 155, 158-160, 160f, 162, 175, 177, 180, 183, 184, 217, 241, 248, 261, 280, 281; Relational view, 89-100; Rational view, 112-115; Eschatological view, 144-155, 158-160, 162

Incarnation[al], 7, 22f, 34, 37, 59, 59f, 75, 86, 96, 106-107, 106f, 118-121, 118-120f, 146, 159, 159f, 165f, 167f, 171f, 181, 188, 188f, 199, 202, 202f, 228, 229-235, 258, 258f, 259, 261, 271, 274, 277, 277f

Judgment, 66f, 105, 118, 154, 157, 167, 167f, 194f, 202f, 203, 259, 274

Kingdom of God, 2, 2f, 4, 12, 63, 78, 79, 81-82, 97, 118, 120, 144, 160-162, 164-166, 164-166f, 169-170, 172, 174-175, 188, 192, 200, 204, 210f, 218f, 227-230, 232, 237, 240-242, 240f, 242-243f, 244, 245, 245f, 247-255, 249f, 253f, 256, 258-261, 263-264, 266, 270-275, 281-282, 284

Kingdom of Ends, 38, 57, 58

Love, 3, 4, 7, 10, 21, 42f, 56, 67-68, 71, 71f, 75-77, 80f, 85-89, 87f, 88-95, 92f, 94f, 97, 100, 104-114, 106f, 112-113f, 118, 121f, 122-125, 131, 133, 139-140f, 142-143, 162, 166, 174-175, 178, 179f, 181-185, 182f, 187, 190-191, 193, 195, 197, 200, 202-203, 202f, 206, 208, 211-213, 218f, 224f, 230, 239-240, 243, 245f, 246, 248-249, 249f, 251-254, 252f, 256-257, 259, 259f, 265, 267f, 268, 270-274, 276, 279, 280-281

Metanarrative/ Grand Narrative: 29, 29f, 40f, 278

Missio Dei/ Mission of God, 4, 88, 257, 273

Mission, 1-2, 4-7, 9, 9f, 12, 36f, 39, 51, 79-83, 88-89, 92f, 132, 142, 144, 148, 169f, 176, 178, 180, 192, 197, 200, 202, 204-207, 210, 219, 226-230, 237-239, 241, 242f, 245, 248-249, 249f, 252, 257-263, 257-260f, 265-267, 272-284, 277f, 282f

Missional formation, 226, 230f, 245, 249-250, 252, 259, 260, 262-263, 272, 273, 274, 275, 277-281, 277f, 278f, 280, 282, 283

Modern/ Premodern/ Postmodern, 1, 8, 12, 14, 16-20, 17f, 22, 22f, 24, 26, 29, 29f, 35, 36f, 38-44, 38f, 40f, 43f, 48-49f, 51, 51f, 55, 55f, 67-68, 78-79, 82, 88, 93, 117f, 147, 151, 156, 200, 214, 257, 257f

Narrative, 8, 25f, 26-27, 27f, 29, 32, 34-37, 39, 77, 80, 86, 132, 137, 150, 152, 216-218, 216f, 218f, 230, 253, 257, 271, 279

New Creation, 4, 34-35f, 83, 106-108, 119-120, 144, 149f, 154, 160-162, 161f, 164-175, 167-168f, 170-171f, 178, 190, 194f, 202f, 203, 228, 236, 237f, 240-241, 246, 248, 251-252, 261, 263, 265, 272-274, 280, 282-283

New Humanity, 3-4, 7, 13, 83, 108, 159f, 175-178, 185f, 187f, 193, 206, 209, 216, 226, 235,

Subject Index

237, 241, 246, 249, 265-266, 270-277, 281-282
Participation, 4, 7, 55, 91, 97, 100, 101f, 107, 107f, 111, 114, 117, 119, 120, 125, 129f, 141-142, 144, 159f, 160, 160f, 163, 170, 171f, 172, 172f, 176, 178, 178f, 182-186, 183f, 185f, 191-192, 192f, 194f, 195, 198-199, 204, 207, 208, 210, 213, 216, 218, 226-227, 234-235, 237f, 240-241, 244, 250, 252, 256-257, 259f, 262, 266-268, 270, 272-277, 281
Pentecost, 75f, 86, 118, 121-122, 238
Perichoresis, 87-89, 87f, 125, 182, 182f, 184, 280
Pietism, 19-20, 19-20f, 269
Pneumatological Community, 237-241, 237f, 240f, 250
Preaching, 20f, 82, 122, 168, 192-193, 203, 213, 217, 219f, 220f, 221-222, 229, 231, 240, 250-251, 272, 273
Priestly, 4, 161, 174, 183f, 192, 198-204, 198f, 245f, 273, 276
Proleptic, 4, 164-165, 178, 187, 236, 273f, 280
Prophetic, 4, 122, 142, 219, 226-232, 235, 263, 273, 277
Puritanism, 19-20

Rationality, 10f, 18, 21, 39, 46, 47f, 58, 89-90, 112-118, 123, 125, 208, 233
Reality, 13, 19, 22-23, 26-27, 32-34, 42-43, 49f, 61-62, 73, 75, 77, 101f, 107f, 114-115, 119, 128, 130, 133, 138f, 156f, 160, 160f, 165-166, 165f, 168, 171-172, 171f, 181, 217, 218f, 233, 240-241, 245f, 246, 249, 252, 256, 260, 263, 271, 280

Reason, 4f, 11-13, 18-19, 22, 25-26, 25f, 29, 33, 36, 39, 40f, 42f, 52, 55-59, 57f, 59f, 62f, 69, 72-73, 78, 84f, 86f, 90-91, 90f, 109, 112-114, 116-118, 125, 129, 130f, 132, 133-138, 135f, 140, 142-143, 212, 218, 221, 247
Recapitulation, 146, 158-159, 159f
Reconciliation, 3-4, 11, 39, 59, 89, 101-110, 110f, 160, 162, 168-169, 176-179, 186, 190, 193, 194f, 195, 197-206, 218, 239, 240, 253-254, 261, 267-268, 270, 272-274, 279-280
Redemption, 65, 71, 97, 100f, 104, 106, 106f, 118, 120-121, 127f, 141, 145-146, 160, 168-169, 171, 171f, 177-178, 181, 185, 207, 240, 248, 250, 252, 259, 267-268, 273, 276, 279, 281
Reign/ Sovereignty of God, 4, 67f, 81, 123, 144, 148f, 151, 161, 171-172, 186f, 237, 240-241, 240f, 242f, 244-245, 247-250, 252, 253f, 256-263, 273-274, 277
Relational/ Relationships, 3-7, 3-4f, 10-11, 10f, 13, 24, 33f, 34-35, 55, 59, 73-77, 73f, 80f, 82-83, 84-110, 112, 112-113f, 114, 116, 140, 147, 176-206, 230, 246-249, 251, 256, 265, 267-268, 270-274, 276, 277f, 278-280, 282, 284
Resurrection, 7, 34, 34-35f, 75f, 86, 106, 106f, 107, 119, 120-121, 136, 140-141, 158-159, 165f, 167f, 169, 171f, 177, 181, 189, 198-199, 202f, 222, 239-240, 258-263, 275, 277, 277f
Romanticism, 22, 23, 25f, 36, 249f

Sacramental Ecclesiology, 9, 9f, 54f
Sacramental Ordinance, 192-194, 192-195f, 221-223, 237, 250-252, 272-273

Salvation/ Soteriology, 3, 20, 20f, 41, 59f, 65, 66-67f, 98, 120f, 125, 127-128, 165f, 168, 169f, 183-184f, 185-186, 185f, 197, 212, 218, 218f, 223, 239-240, 240f, 243, 245, 248, 257, 266, 268, 278, 279; relational, 104-108; of mind, 118-123; of purpose/ destiny, 158-164

Scientific Reductionism, 16, 25f, 28, 30-34, 30f, 49, 68-73, 71-72f, 82

Scripture, 11-12, 59, 77-78, 96, 125, 128-134, 129-130f, 132f, 134-135, 140f, 142-143, 210, 210f, 217-218, 220f, 221-222, 222f, 224, 226, 245, 250, 272-273; interpretation of, 11, 11f, 12-13, 31, 32f, 86, 86f, 90, 96-98, 124-125, 129-142, 130f, 135-136f, 139-140f, 151-154, 151-152f, 177, 200, 217-218, 220f, 221-222, 222f

Secular, 22, 22f, 118-119f, 224f

Self, 1f, 2, 16-25, 17-18f, 21f, 23f, 25f, 26, 28, 38f, 49, 60, 96, 98-100, 99-100f, 102-105, 107, 114, 116-117, 127, 147f, 156-157, 173, 178, 180-181, 185f, 193, 196, 198, 281

Sin, 20f, 65f, 89, 92, 100-104, 102f, 115-117, 117f, 121, 121f, 127, 144, 146, 154-158, 155f, 157f, 163, 166f, 178-179, 190-191, 190f, 193-194f, 196, 196f, 198, 201, 207, 218, 236, 236f, 248, 253-255, 263, 267, 273-275, 281

Sociobiology, 30-31, 38, 51, 68-72, 69-72f, 80, 271

Spirit, as bond of love, 87f, 92f, 106; effecting communion, 85-89, 96-98, 181-190, 266-270; empowering transformation, 124-125, 160-164, 169-170, 247-252, as liberating presence; 105-108, 184; as revealer, 121, 125-131, 130f, 132f, 212, 214; as source of wisdom/ guidance/ illumination, 11-12, 111-112, 143, 162, 193, 218, 222, 225, 263

Spirit, Fruit of, 122, 140f, 162-163, 240, 248-249, 249f, 256

Spirit, Gifts of, 122, 133, 163, 187-188, 188f, 212, 238

Spiritual Disciplines, 60, 60f, 195-196, 196f, 225, 225f, 240, 249-250f, 272

Spiritual Formation/ Spirituality, 2, 2f, 7, 13, 20f, 59, 60, 62f, 66, 67, 71, 75, 76, 78, 79, 81, 83, 90, 91, 99f, 107, 112, 140, 147, 163, 225, 225f, 239-240, 248, 249-250f, 250, 256, 268, 271, 272

Steward[ship]/ Steward-Priest, 4, 90, 90f, 95-96, 104, 110, 144, 146f, 148-158, 161-162, 172-175, 217-218, 225, 226f, 240-241, 246, 265, 283

Telos / Teleology, 1-2, 8, 16, 21, 25-30, 27, 27f, 28f, 29, 35, 38, 42-43, 43f, 48f, 49, 123-124, 135f, 139, 141, 140f, 146, 154, 170-172, 170f, 175, 207, 218, 246-247, 246f, 265, 271

Theological Formation/ Education/ Study, 20f, 100, 109, 116, 118, 120-121, 125, 126, 126f, 128-142, 128f, 131f, 135f, 138f, 142f, 211f, 215-216, 216-221, 215f, 216f, 224f, 225, 226, 233f, 234, 234f, 235, 240, 249f, 250f, 262, 272

Theosis, 21, 21f

Tradition, 11-13, 25f, 29, 31, 38f, 39, 39-40f, 52, 59, 59f, 78-79, 84f, 86, 86-87f, 114, 125, 128-129, 131-133, 132f, 139-140, 142-143, 207, 210, 216, 215-

Subject Index

217f, 218, 221-222, 269, 269f, 272-272
Trinitarian Anthropology, 3-5, 10-11, 10-11f, chapters 3-5, 265
Trinitarian Ecclesiology, 4, 9-10, 183-184f, 184-185, 259f, 267, 279, 281
Trinity, 5-7, 10-11, 11f, 14, 34-35, 59f, 75, 75f, 85-98, 86-87f, 89f, 97-98f, 106, 108, 111-113, 113f, 120, 124-125, 144, 178, 182-186, 184f, 207, 240, 267-268, 269f, 277-281; mutual love model, 10, 86-87, 87f, 106, 106f, 113f, 182; social trinitarianism, 7, 7f, 10, 96-98, 97-98f, 182-186, 184f
Typology, 7-9, 51-82, 275-277, 275-276f, 285

Ultimate & Penultimate, 171, 171-172f, 261
Union/ Union with Christ/ Spiritual Union, 55, 60, 71, 78, 84-85, 91f, 96-97, 105f, 106-108, 106f, 111, 158, 159f, 160-161, 178-186, 183f, 193, 193f, 194f, 195, 208, 244, 266-270, 280, 281

Vatican II, 9, 9f, 216
Vocation/ Work, 14, 33f, 35, 90, 90f, 112, 119, 144, 148-158, 159f, 163, 166-168, 215, 219, 233-234, 248, 283f

Wesleyan, 19-20, 19-20f, 182, 216
Will, 23, 23f, 56, 56f, 89, 117, 121
Will to Power, 23, 23-24f, 42f, 61-63, 62-63f, 117, 117f, 121f, 180
Wisdom, 3-4, 11, 112, 30f, 58, 66, 90, 97, 109, 111-112, 118, 120-128, 132, 134-135, 140-142, 161, 163, 204, 207-208, 210-230, 211f, 213f, 227, 234-235, 246, 248-249, 256, 266, 270, 272, 274, 277, 282

World, 118-119, 118-119f, 156f, 165-166, 165-166f, 211-214, 226
Worldview/ Framework/ Social Imaginary, 25-30, 25f, 32, 32f, 39f, 41, 54-55, 100, 109, 117-118, 121f, 127, 137, 139, 143, 152, 168, 203-204, 216-219, 216f, 218f, 221, 227, 243, 245, 251-252, 252f, 260, 262, 271-272, 275, 282, 284
Worship, 2, 46, 60, 71, 76, 78, 80f, 93, 106, 125, 150f, 155, 189f, 191, 195, 196, 204, 205f, 210-211, 211f, 223-224, 224f, 230, 240, 245f, 252, 252f, 262, 269f, 272-273, 280